NEPAL

THE ROUGH GUIDE

THE ROUGH GUIDES

OTHER AVAILABLE ROUGH GUIDES

FRANCE • PARIS • PROVENCE • BRITTANY & NORMANDY
ITALY • VENICE • SICILY • SPAIN • PORTUGAL • IRELAND
HOLLAND, BELGIUM & LUXEMBOURG • AMSTERDAM
WEST GERMANY • BERLIN • SCANDINAVIA • GREECE
CRETE • YUGOSLAVIA • HUNGARY • EASTERN EUROPE
MOROCCO • TUNISIA • KENYA • ZIMBABWE & BOTSWANA
ISRAEL • CHINA • MEXICO • BRAZIL • GUATEMALA & BELIZE
PERU • NEW YORK • CALIFORNIA & WEST COAST USA
PYRENEES • WOMEN TRAVEL • MEDITERRANEAN WILDLIFE

FORTHCOMING
WEST AFRICA • TURKEY • EGYPT • HONG KONG

ROUGH GUIDE CREDITS

Series Editor: Mark Ellingham
Editorial: Martin Dunford, John Fisher, Jack Holland, Jonathan Buckley, Greg Ward
Production: Susanne Hillen, Kate Berens
Typesetting: Andy Hilliard, Gail Jammy
Series Design: Andrew Oliver

Special thanks to Lesley Delacourt-Smith of VSO for unflagging support and hospitality; and to Hikmat Bisht, Ramesh Raj Kunwar, Bagh Bir Mukhiya, Dadi Ram Sapkota and Earl Thompson for inspiration and insights. Thanks also to: Dave and Barbara Ackroyd for notes on Jiri, Rajendra Adhikari, Tony Bondurant, Deepak Chaudhary, Lisa Choegyal of Tiger Mountain, Eric Cruikshank, Jon Darrah, Bob Davis, Richard de Soldenoff for a wonderful Burns Night, Dharma Gautam, Ken Genskow for maps, Mog Greenwood for surviving without haggis, Jane Gronow, Deepak Gyawali, Liz Hawley, Annie Holte, Frances Higgins of Himalayan Mountain Bikes, Jackie Howell and Chris Vickery, Kim Hudson for help with the far west, Walter Jansen, Krysia Carter-Giez for encouragement and advice, Bijaya Kattel, R. C. Khatiwada, Tom Laird, Robin Marston, John Meyer of Exodus, Hemanta Mishra, Jock Montgomery, Charles Parrish, Alan Perrin, Carole Presern, Prem R. Rai, Ratan Kumar Rai, Charles Ramble, Karna Sakya, Mingma Norbu Sherpa, Padma Shrestha, Rod Stickland, Saila Tamang and Greg Vann for mountain-biking notes.

Thanks too to all who helped produce this book, especially Jack Holland and Dan Richardson, who edited it; Susanne Hillen and Kate Berens for patiently handling the production; Andy Hilliard and Gail Jammy for typesetting; and Jules Brown for proofing.

The publishers and authors have done their best to ensure the accuracy and currency of all the information in **Nepal: The Rough Guide**; however, they can accept no responsibility for any loss, injury, or inconvenience sustained by any traveller as a result of information or advice contained in the guide.

Published by Harrap Columbus, Chelsea House, 26 Market Square, Bromley, Kent BR1 1NA

Typeset in Linotron Univers and Century Old Style
Printed by Cox & Wyman, Reading, Berks

Illustrations in the Guide by Hal Aqua; Incidental illustrations in Part One and Part Three by Ed Briant. Basics Illustration by Tommy Yamaha. Contexts Illustration by Sally Davies.

352 pp
includes index

British Library Cataloguing in Publication Data
    Reed, David
    Nepal: the rough guide. – (The Rough Guides)
    1. Nepal. – Visitors guides
    I. Title II. Series
    915.496

    ISBN 0-7471-0256-2

NEPAL

THE ROUGH GUIDE

Written and researched by

DAVID REED

with additional contributions by
Andy Balestracci, Charles Leech, Anna Robinson
and Kesang Tseten

Edited by
JACK HOLLAND
with Dan Richardson

HARRAP-COLUMBUS ■ LONDON

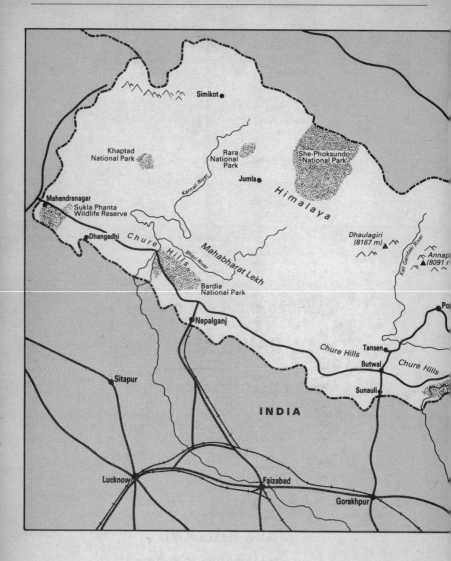

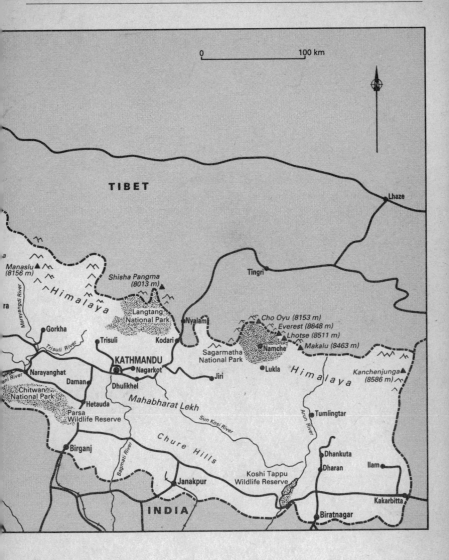

0   100 km

N

TIBET

Lhaze

Manaslu ▲
(8156 m)

Shisha Pangma
(8013 m) ▲

Tingri

Marsyangdi River

Himalaya

Langtang
National Park

Nyalam

Cho Oyu (8153 m)
Everest (8848 m)
Lhotse (8511 m)
Makalu (8463 m)

Gorkha

Trisuli

Kodari

Trisuli River

KATHMANDU

Nagarkot

Sagarmatha
National Park

Namche

Himalaya

Kanchenjunga ▲
(8586 m)

Lukla

Jiri

Narayanghat

Daman

Dhulikhel

ani River

Chitwan
National Park

Hetauda

Mahabharat Lekh

Parsa
Wildlife Reserve

Sun Kosi River

Arun River

Tumlingtar

Chure Hills

Birganj

Bagmati River

Dhankuta

Dharan

Ilam

Janakpur

Koshi Tappu
Wildlife Reserve

Kakarbitta

INDIA

Biratnagar

CONTENTS

INTRODUCTION

Nepal forms the very watershed of Asia. Landlocked between India and Tibet, it spans terrain from subtropical jungle to the icy Himalaya, and contains eight of the world's ten highest mountains. Its cultural landscape is every bit as diverse: a dozen major **ethnic groups**, speaking as many as fifty dialects, coexist in this narrow, jumbled buffer state, while two of the world's great **religions**, Hinduism and Buddhism, overlap and mingle with older tribal traditions – yet it's a testimony to the Nepalis' tolerance and good humour that there has never been an instance of ethnic or religious strife. Unlike India, Nepal was never colonised, a fact which comes through in fierce national pride and other, more idiosyncratic ways. Founded on trans-Himalayan trade, its dense, medieval **cities** display a unique pagoda-style architecture, not to mention an astounding flair for festivals and pageantry. But above all, Nepal is a nation of unaffected **villages** and terraced hillsides – more than ninety percent of the population lives off the land – and whether you're trekking, biking or bouncing around in packed buses, sampling this simple lifestyle is perhaps the greatest pleasure of all.

It would be misleading to portray Nepal as a fabled Shangri-la. One of the world's poorest countries (if you go by per capita income), it suffers from many of the pangs and uncertainties of the Third World, including overpopulation and deforestation; **development** is coming in fits and starts, and not all of it is being shared equitably. Heavily reliant on its big-brother neighbours, Nepal was, until recently, run by one of the last remaining absolute monarchies, a regime that combined China's repressiveness and India's bureaucracy in equal measure. Inspired by the changes in Eastern Europe, the **democracy movement** in early 1990 plunged the country into temporary crisis and unnerved many tourists; but while aftershocks can be expected for some time yet, the political concessions won promise to make Nepal a better place in the long run.

All this means that travel in Nepal isn't a straightforward or predictable activity. **Getting around** is tough and time-consuming, and facilities in most places are rudimentary – Nepalis are well used to shrugging off inconvenience with the all-purpose phrase, *ke garne?* ("what to do?"). Nepal is also a more fragile country than most – culturally as well as environmentally – so it's necessary to be especially sensitive as a traveller; tips for minimising your impact are given later in *Basics*.

Topography is obviously a key consideration when travelling in Nepal; generally speaking, the country divides into three altitude zones running from west to east. The northernmost of these is, of course, the **Himalayan chain**, broken into a series of *himals* (massifs) and inhabited, at least part of the year, as high as 5000m. The largest part of the country consists of a wide belt of middle-elevation **foothills and valleys**, Nepal's traditional heartland; two ranges, the Mahabharat Lekh and the lower, southernmost Chure (or Siwalik) Hills, stand out. Finally, the **Tarai**, a thin strip of flat, lowland jungle and farmland along the southern border, has more in common with India than with the rest of Nepal.

Where to go

Given the country's primitive transport network, most travellers stick to a well-worn circuit, with the result that certain sights and trekking routes have become rather commercialised. Don't be put off: the beaten track is remarkably thin and easy to escape in Nepal – and this book is intended, first and foremost, to give you the confidence to do just that.

Everyone spends at least some time in **Kathmandu**, which for all its exotic bustle remains, at heart, an endearingly small-time capital. Hindu temples, Buddhist stupas, rolling countryside and huddled brick villages provide incentives for day-trips in the prosperous **Kathmandu Valley**, as do the historically independent city-states of **Patan** and **Bhaktapur**. The surrounding **central hills** are surprisingly undeveloped, apart from a couple of mountain view points, yet a few lesser routes, such as the intriguing road to the **Tibet border** (which is, if anything, falling into disuse) and especially **the Rajpath**, make for adventurous travel – and even better mountain-biking.

The views get more dramatic, or at least more accessible, in the **western hills**. **Pokhara**, set beside a lake under a looming wall of peaks, is the closest thing you'll find to a resort in Nepal; other hill towns – notably **Gorkha** and its impressive fortress – offer scenery with history to boot.

It's in the teeming jungle and ethnic villages of **the Tarai** that Nepal's diversity really becomes apparent. Most travellers venture no farther than **Chitwan National Park**, where endangered Asian one-horned rhinos are easily viewable, but three other parks and wildlife reserves are out there for the more adventurous. **Lumbini**, Buddha's birthplace in the western Tarai, is stunningly peaceful and unwesternised, as is **Janakpur**, a Hindu holy city in the east. Rolling tea plantations, weekly markets and a rich cultural mix figure prominently in the spectacular and little-visited **eastern hills**, most easily reached from the Tarai.

The Himalaya are covered separately in the last chapter of the *Guide*, along with all hill areas that fall within the government's prescribed **trekking regions**. Special rules apply in this roadless half of Nepal: distances are reckoned in days of walking, and trailside inns provide only basic shelter. The terrain can vary from infernal valley bottoms and cultivated foothills to lush rhododendron forests and glacial deserts. You'll encounter people everywhere you walk, and the cultural interactions are often, in retrospect, the most rewarding part of a trek.

When to go

Nepal's climate is governed by the **monsoon**, a seasonal wind that draws moisture up from the Indian Ocean from approximately mid-June (somewhat earlier in the eastern part of the country) till early October, and blows dry air down from central Asia for most of the rest of the year. The summer monsoon brings heavy rain (or snow) everywhere except north of the main Himalayan chain; late January usually brings a few days of rain as well. Rainfall varies considerably, however – places at the foot of south-facing slopes tend to be the wettest.

In general, five **seasons** prevail: **autumn** (dry and mild) through October and November; **winter** (mostly dry and cold) from December to mid-February; **spring** (dry and mild) from mid-February to mid-April; the **pre-monsoon** (dry, often squally, and hot) from mid-April to mid-June; and the **monsoon** (wet and warm) from mid-June to the end of September. **Temperatures**, of course, depend on elevation.

October and November are considered the **best months** to visit Nepal: with clear skies and the air washed clean by the rains, the mountains are at their most visible, while temperatures aren't too cold in the high country nor too hot in the Tarai; but bear in mind that autumn is also the busiest season. In winter the snow line descends to 2000–3000m, and while it never snows in Kathmandu, the "mists of Indra" make the capital feel cold and clammy. Mid-February to mid-April is good for watching game in the Tarai, and in the hills the rhododendrons are in bloom, but the air can be disappointingly hazy for mountain-viewing; the pre-monsoon is stifling at lower elevations. Nepal certainly isn't at its best during the monsoon – watch out for leeches if you're trekking – although it would make an improvement over northern India.

	AVERAGE TEMPERATURE AND RAINFALL																
	FEB			APR			JUN			AUG			OCT			DEC	
	°C Min	Max	Rain cm	°C Min	Max	Rain cm	°C Min	Max	Rain cm	°C Min	Max	Rain cm	°C Min	Max	Rain cm	°C Min	Max	Rain cm
Ilam (1200m)	10	18	0	16	25	6	18	25	32	19	25	28	16	25	8	8	18	0
Janakpur (70m)	9	24	1	16	35	4	24	36	23	25	34	24	20	29	5	10	24	0
Jumla (2420m)	-3	13	4	3	22	3	13	24	7	15	24	17	6	24	4	-5	15	0
Kathmandu (1300m)	4	20	3	11	27	6	19	29	29	20	28	36	13	26	6	2	20	0
Namche (3450m)	-6	6	2	1	12	3	6	15	14	8	16	24	2	12	8	-6	7	4
Pokhara (800m)	8	21	3	15	30	9	20	29	57	21	29	71	17	26	22	7	20	0
Sunauli (90m)	10	26	1	18	37	6	24	38	28	26	35	41	21	30	8	10	25	0

PART ONE

THE

BASICS

THE RISING NEPAL

GETTING THERE

BY PLANE

If Nepal is your only destination, **flying direct to Kathmandu** is the logical option. However, only a few airlines serve this route: flights in the spring and (especially) autumn high seasons get booked up months ahead, while during slack times carriers sometimes refuse to confirm reservations until they've decided whether it's worth their while to fly.

FROM LONDON
The cheapest flights **from London** hover between £450 and £570 return, depending on the season. The fastest flights, stopping off in Frankfurt and Dubai, take around 16 hours. *Royal Nepal Airlines Corporation* (*RNAC*) and *Biman Bangladesh*, which discount their own fares through "consolidating" agents, tend to offer the best deals; handily, *Biman*'s low-season fares apply during part of Nepal's high season, although you have to stop over in Dhaka. Bucket shops – or, more reliably, specialist agents like *STA Travel* or *Trailfinders* (addresses given below) – will be able to give comparative quotes; you could also try checking out the travel sections in the Sunday papers or London's *Time Out* magazine.

You're unlikely to save money by flying **via Delhi**, but the seat availability might be better, especially during the high season. About a dozen airlines fly this route, typically charging £420–500 return – a specialist agent can recommend

the cheapest current deals – with connecting flights to Kathmandu adding £75-90 each way.

FROM EIRE
Easiest option is to get to London and make your bookings from there, though independent travel experts *USIT* (7 Angelsea St., Dublin 2; ☎0001/798833) offer youth and student fares across a variety of routes.

FROM ASIA AND AUSTRALIA
Standard one-way fares **from Asian cities** to Kathmandu (all in US dollars) include: Bangkok ($190), Calcutta ($96), Delhi ($142), Dhaka ($77), Hong Kong ($275), Karachi ($150), Singapore ($275) and Varanasi ($71). *Indian Airlines*, which flies the Calcutta, Delhi and Varanasi routes, gives 25 percent off to under-30s.

From Sydney or **Auckland**, one-way fares to Kathmandu go for about A$875/NZ$1150, but chances are you'll be stopping elsewhere en route: *Thai, Qantas, Garuda* and others fly from Sydney to Bangkok for around A$600 each way, or from Perth for A$550; fares to Delhi are about the same as to Kathmandu. Check out *STA Travel*, 1a Lee St, Railway Square, Sydney 2000 (☎2/212 1255) or *STS Travel*, 10 High St, PO Box 4156, Auckland (☎9/399723) for the best fare deals.

AIRLINES AND AGENTS

Biman Bangladesh, c/o *United Air Travel*, 5–6 Coventry St, London W1V 7FL (☎071/734 6668).

Royal Nepal Airlines, 114 Tottenham Court Rd, London W1P 9HL (☎071/387 1541).

STA Travel, 74–86 Old Brompton Rd, London SW7 3LQ (☎071/937 9962).

Trailfinders, 42–48 Earls Court Rd, London W8 6EJ (☎071/938 3366).

PACKAGES
Package trips exist only in a specialised sense in Nepal, being based around trekking, rafting, cycling or wildlife-viewing itineraries. These cost as much as ten times what you'd spend by doing things independently (around £30–60 per day, not taking into account the cost of the flight), but are worth considering if you're on a tight schedule.

OVERLAND AND SPECIALIST OPERATORS

Art of Travel, 268 Lavender Hill, London SW11 1LJ (☎071/738 2038). Trekking, rafting, wildlife.

Classic Nepal, 33 Metro Avenue, Newton, Derbyshire DE55 5UF (☎0773/873497). Trekking, rafting, wildlife.

Encounter Overland, 267 Old Brompton Rd, London SW5 9JA (☎071/370 6951). Overland, trekking, rafting, wildlife.

Exodus Expeditions, 9 Weir Rd, London SW12 0LT (☎081/675 5550). Overland, trekking, rafting, wildlife.

Explore Worldwide, 1 Frederick St, Aldershot, Hants GU11 1LQ (☎0252/319448). Trekking, rafting, wildlife.

ExplorAsia, 13 Chapter Street, London SW1P 4NY (☎071/630 7102). Trekking, rafting, wildlife.

Hann Overland, 201–203 Vauxhall Bridge Rd, London SW1V 1ER (☎071/834 7337). Overland, trekking, rafting, wildlife.

Himalayan Kingdoms, 20 The Mall, Clifton, Bristol BS8 4DR (☎0272/237163). Trekking, rafting, wildlife.

Himalayan Quest, 30 Hamilton Terrace, Leamington Spa, Warwickshire CV32 4LY (☎0926/450835). Trekking, rafting, cycling, wildlife.

Sherpa Expeditions, 131a Heston Road, Hounslow, Middlesex TW5 0RD (☎081/577 2717). Trekking, rafting, wildlife.

Top Deck Travel, 131 Earls Court Rd, London SW5 9RH (☎071/370 4555). Overland.

OVERLAND ROUTES

The classic **Asia overland** trip is still alive and kicking, despite periodic political reroutings. Leaving Europe behind at Istanbul, the usual route traverses Turkey, angles down through Iran, crosses Pakistan and enters India at Amritsar; Iran is off-limits to UK and US passport holders, however, who have to fly from Istanbul to Karachi. Several **overland expedition operators** (see above) run 6- to 18-week trips in specially designed vehicles all the way through to Kathmandu. Expect to pay between £700 and £1500 for the one-way trip, depending on the level of luxury.

If you're already touring the subcontinent, connections between **India** and Nepal are well-developed, with travel agents in Delhi, Darjeeling and other major rail junctions in the north selling **bus** packages to Kathmandu. However, it's an easy matter to ride to the border and make your own way from there. Three border crossings are open to foreigners: Sunauli, the most developed entry point, reachable from Delhi, Varanasi and most of north India (via Gorakhpur); Birganj, accessible from Bodh Gaya and Calcutta (via Patna); and Kakarbitta, serving Darjeeling and Calcutta (via Siliguri). These crossings are described fully in the relevant sections of Chapters Five and Six.

To bring a **motorcycle** or any other vehicle into Nepal, you'll have to enter at Birganj and wade through predictably sluggish customs procedures. A *carnet de passage*, available from the *AA* or similar motoring organisation in your home country, is required to import a **car** or any other four-wheeled vehicle. Entering by **bicycle** involves no special paperwork.

The border crossing from **Tibet** to Nepal at Kodari is still nominally open to travellers, although at the time of writing it was only possible to visit Tibet as part of a tour group. If China starts allowing individuals back into Tibet, charter tourist buses between Lhasa and the border will no doubt resume, making possible overland routes from Hong Kong, Pakistan and even Europe by way of the Trans-Siberian Railway.

LEAVING NEPAL – A NOTE

If you're flying out of Nepal, remember there's a Rs300 **airport tax**. For clues on getting to India and other Asian destinations, see the "On from Kathmandu" section in Chapter One.

RED TAPE AND VISAS

All foreign nationals (except Indians) need a visa to enter Nepal. "Transit" visas are issued on arrival with a minimum of fuss at Kathmandu airport and at all three entry points along the Indian border. A visa costs $10 (see "Costs" overleaf) and no photo is necessary; it's only valid for 15 days, but Central Immigration in Kathmandu and Pokhara (see Chapters One and Four for addresses) will convert it into a 30-day tourist visa at no extra charge.

Nepalese embassies and consulates in most foreign capitals issue thirty-day tourist visas. The cost, again, should be $10 or equivalent, but the London embassy charges £10.

Tourist visas can be **extended**, up to one month at a time, for a maximum of three months. Extensions are granted only at the Kathmandu or Pokhara Central Immigration offices – a simple procedure, although high-season queues can run to two hours or more, especially just before and after the week-long festival of *Dasain* in October. The cost is Rs75 per week for extensions in the second month, Rs150 per week in the third. You must show official receipts proving that you have changed **$10 a day** for an identical period of time to that which you wish to extend your stay. Thus, if you wanted to stay for a further ten days, you would need receipts showing that you had exchanged a minimum of $100. Note that exchange receipts are issued not only by banks but also by all hotels, trekking/rafting companies and travel agencies that require payment in foreign currency.

Visa regulations have been getting steadily tighter in recent years. Central Immigration's current position is that they'll allow tourists a **maximum** of four months in Nepal in any 12-month period, and no more than three months at a time. If you stay a full three months, you'll have to leave the country for a month before being allowed to re-enter. Given extenuating circumstances, Central Immigration may grant a fourth consecutive month. The fine for overstaying is double the amount that you would have paid had you properly extended your visa.

NEPALESE EMBASSIES AND CONSULATES

Australia: Suite 1, Strand Centre, 870 Military Road, Mosman, Sydney, NSW 2088 (☎2/960 3565).

Austria: Karpfenwaldgasse 11-A1190, Vienna (☎1/321105).

Bangladesh: Lake Road, No. 2, Baridhara Diplomatic Enclave, Baridhara, Dhaka (☎2/601790).

Belgium: Nepal House, 149 Lamorinierstraat, B-4118 Antwerp (☎03/230 8800).

Denmark: 36 Kronpinsessagade, DK 1006, Copenhagen (☎01/143175).

France: 7 Rue de Washington, 75008 Paris (☎43.59.28.61).

Germany: Im-Hag 15, D-5300 Bonn, Bad Godesberg 2 (☎0228/343097).

Great Britain: 12a Kensington Palace Gdns, London W8 4QU (☎071/229 1594).

India: Barakhamba Road, New Delhi 110001 (☎11/381 484); 19 Woodlands, Sterndale Road, Alipore, Calcutta 700027 (☎33/452024).

Italy: Piazza Medaglie d'Oro 20, 00136 Rome (☎06/345 1642).

Netherlands: 687 Gelderland Bldg., NL-1017 JV Amsterdam (☎020/25 0388).

Norway: Haakon VIIs gt. 5, PO Box 1384 Vika, 0116 Oslo (☎2/414743).

Pakistan: 506 84th Street, Attaturk Avenue, Ramna G-6/4 Islamabad (☎5/823 642).

Sweden: Karlavägen, 97S - 115 22, Stockholm.

Thailand: 189 Soi 71, Sukhamvit Road, Bangkok-10110 (☎2/391 7204).

TREKKING PERMITS

A tourist visa is technically valid only in the fraction of Nepal served by roads. To visit anywhere more than a day's walk off a main road you need to get a **trekking permit** from Central Immigration — even if you don't intend to trek. The fee is Rs90 per week during the first month of your stay in Nepal, Rs112.50 during the second and third months, and again you have to exchange $10 a day. A trekking permit acts as an automatic visa extension, so you only have to apply for one or the other; bargain-hunters will spot that in the third month it's actually cheaper to apply for a trekking permit than a visa extension.

> A trekking permit isn't required for any of the places described in this book *except* the areas covered in Chapter Seven, *The Himalayan Trekking Regions*, where you'll find a more detailed discussion of trekking permits.

COSTS, MONEY AND BANKS

Your money goes a long way in Nepal. Off the tourist routes, it can actually be hard to spend US$5 a day, however willing you might be to pay more. On the other hand, Kathmandu and some of the other tourist traps can burn a hole in your pocket rather faster than you might have expected in a Third World city. While even in the capital it's still possible to keep to $5 a day, the figure can effortlessly balloon to $15–20 simply by trading up to slightly nicer hotels and restaurants. The cost of seeing Nepal, then, depends in large part on the proportion of time you spend on and off the beaten track.

The price of **accommodation** varies considerably, depending on where you stay and when. Really basic rooms can almost always be found for Rs50 ($2) or less. Prices aren't automatically higher in tourist areas, but most travellers take up the option of paying more for a few creature comforts: figure on at least Rs80 ($3) for a double room in the high season. Off-season rates can plummet by 50 percent or more, but it's up to you to bargain. Prices for single rooms are usually lower, and dorm beds are often available, but you generally save money by doubling up.

Food, cheap as it is, tends to be the biggest daily expense for travellers. *Daal bhaat*, the all-you-can-eat national meal of rice, lentils and a few veg, costs Rs15–20 everywhere in Nepal, and you can fill up on road snacks for just pennies. Normally, though, an *à la carte* Nepali or Tibetan dinner will run to Rs30–60 ($1–2), rising to Rs200 or more in a really posh place. Western food usually costs somewhat more.

As long as you stick to buses, the cost of **transport** is trifling. Most local bus journeys only come to Rs50 ($2) or so, and they're so uncomfortable that you probably won't want to move around very often anyway. However, the stakes go up dramatically if you fly (most internal flights cost $60 and up).

No matter how tight your budget, it would be foolish not to **splurge** now and then on some of the things that make Nepal unique: trekking on your own is quite cheap, but you might prefer to hire a porter for $3 a day, or even pay $20-plus a day for a fully-catered trek; rafting and wildlife trips also work out to be relatively expensive, but well worth it; and few will be able to resist buying at least something from Nepal's rich range of handicrafts.

A final point: some independent travellers make a wild show of pinching pennies, which Nepalis find pathetic — they know how much an air ticket to Kathmandu costs. Others throw money around too freely, which, to a Nepali, only

INFLATION AND PRICING

Trade disputes and political instability are pushing the prices of most things in Nepal up by 10–20 percent a year, so local prices quoted in this book should be adjusted accordingly. However, the steady devaluation of the Nepalese rupee is just about offsetting inflation, so prices in US dollars – the most coveted foreign currency in Nepal – tend to remain fairly constant from one year to the next; thus general costs, and the prices of more upmarket accommodation options, are **given in the *Guide* in dollars**. Many hotels and travel operators have wised up to this and now quote their prices in dollars, too.

proves they deserve to be parted from it. Bargain where appropriate, but don't begrudge a few rupees to someone who's worked hard for them, and try to spend your money where it will do the most good.

MONEY

Nepal's unit of currency is the **rupee**, which is divided into 100 paisa. The government sets the exchange rate, devaluing the rupee every few months as necessary – at the time of writing, the **official rate** was Rs29.5 to the US dollar (£1=Rs49), and 168 Nepalese rupees to 100 Indian rupees (where confusion might arise, it's common practice to refer to the two currencies as NC and IC respectively).

Almost all Nepali money is paper: notes come in denominations of Rs1 (barely 2p!), 2, 5 10, 20, 50, 100, 500 and 1000. Coins, not much used, are of 5, 10, 25 and 50 paisa and 1 rupee; 50 paisa is sometimes called a *mohar*. One of the minor annoyances of travelling in Nepal is **getting change**. In tourist areas it's no problem, but trying to pass a Rs100 (or larger) note to a village merchant or a riksha driver is sure to invite delays, since few Nepalis can afford to keep much spare change lying around. It gets to be a game of bluff between buyer and seller, both hoarding a wad of small notes for occasions when exact change is absolutely required.

If at all possible, **carry US dollars**, which are more widely accepted and command a premium on the black market (see below). Other hard currencies can be exchanged at major banks and luxury hotels. **US dollar travellers' cheques** aren't as liquid as cash on the black market, but they're obviously more secure, and they

command a slightly higher official exchange rate. A **credit card** is a handy back-up – in Kathmandu you can draw funds against *Amex*, *Visa* or *Access/Mastercard* (although the latter two charge hefty commissions) – and an increasing number of businesses now accept plastic in the tourist areas. In an emergency, you can have **money wired** to you in Kathmandu, a procedure that takes two or three working days.

BANKS AND THE BLACK MARKET

Using banks in Nepal is, by Asian standards, surprisingly hassle-free. The two national banks, *Rastriya Banijya Bank* and *Nepal Bank*, maintain tourist branches at the airport, at various strategic locations in Kathmandu and Pokhara, and at all the overland border crossings, as well as somewhat less efficient offices in every town of any consequence. No commission is charged on exchanging currency. Banking **hours** vary: the Kathmandu airport branch operates round the clock, and other tourist branches keep generous hours – refer to the *Guide* for specific timings – but the lesser branches generally change money only Sunday–Thursday 10am–2pm, Friday 10am–noon.

Hold onto all **exchange receipts**. You'll need them not only when applying for visa extensions or trekking permits, but also to **change money back** when you leave. You're allowed to change back up to 15 percent of what you've got receipts for. This can only be done at the airport or a border crossing, however, where you're likely to be told that they're out of sterling and you'll have to take yen, zlotys or some other currency you don't want; if entering India, it's easier just to change your NC into IC unofficially.

THE BLACK MARKET

Nepal's currency **black market** is a fast and rather shady business. Briefly, the dollars you change in a Kathmandu carpet shop are sent to Hong Kong where they buy gold ingots, which are then smuggled back through Nepal to India where they're used to redeem gold-backed mortgages and dowry loans. The mark-up on this gold, plus proceeds from cannabis sales, produces a glut of rupees which are laundered through you, the tourist. That said, changing on the black market involves no danger of arrest and very little of rip-off, and you can get 10–15 percent over the bank rate. Big bills – $100 or $50 – fetch the best rate, while small denominations, travellers' cheques and other currencies may not even be worth the effort. Let a tout take you to his boss the first time, and you can conduct future transactions direct with the dealer to cut out the middleman. The market fluctuates from day to day, and it goes without saying that moneychangers will always try to give less than the going rate. Shop around, bluff, and walk out of the door until you find the limit. Inspect all notes very carefully.

HEALTH AND INSURANCE

No **inoculations** are required for Nepal, but typhoid and meningitis jabs are recommended, and it's worth ensuring that you're up to date with polio and tetanus boosters. Most doctors also recommend a gamma globulin injection against hepatitis A – the protection given by this serum wears off quickly, though, so have it done as late as possible before departure. Although rabies is a problem in Nepal, probably the best advice is just to give dogs and monkeys a wide berth; there is a vaccination, but it's expensive and involves two shots four weeks apart, and even then you'll need two more doses if you get bitten: should this happen to you, get to the nearest doctor or hospital without delay. Don't bother with the cholera inoculation.

Malaria hasn't been eradicated in Nepal, as is sometimes claimed, but it's controlled, thanks to liberal sprayings of DDT. The risk of catching it is small, and then only in areas below about 1000m. The best prevention is mosquito netting or repellent, but for greater immunity take 500mg of chloroquine once a week and 200mg of *Paludrine* daily, starting just before entering the malarial area and ending four weeks after you leave it.

For advice on **altitude sickness** and other trekking hazards, see Chapter Seven.

STOMACH TROUBLES

A far more common complaint than any of the above, **stomach troubles** are caused by contaminated water or food, or sometimes just a change in diet. Usually it's flashy tourist restaurants and "Western" food that bring the most grief: more people get sick in Kathmandu than anywhere else. Nepali food is usually fine and you can probably trust anything that's been boiled or fried in your presence, although meat can sometimes be dodgy. The lack of sanitation in Nepal is sometimes overhyped – it's not worth getting too uptight about it or you'll never enjoy anything, and run the risk of rebuffing Nepalese hospitality.

A few common-sense **precautions** are in order, though, starting with the water: stick to tea or bottled drinks, or purify water with tablets (eg, *Puritabs*) or iodine. Many guest houses provide water in drip-filter units, but make sure it's been boiled. Raw, unpeeled fruit and vegetables should always be viewed with suspicion, nor can you ever be entirely sure about the iodine-soaked salads served in tourist restaurants. Wash your hands often.

If (or more likely, when) you come down with something, the first **treatment** is to starve the bug for 24 hours, taking care to replace fluids and salts – *Jeevan Jal*, sold in packets everywhere, is a cheap and effective rehydration formula. Diarrhoea tablets will at least plug you up if you have to travel, although this undermines the body's efforts to rid itself of the infection. **Food poisoning**, marked by vomiting and diarrhoea, is usually over in a day or less, while **simple diarrhoea** should clear up of its own accord in less than a week. If it doesn't, or if the symptoms are more severe, the problem may be **amoebic dysentery** or **giardia**.

Clinics in Kathmandu and Pokhara do **stool tests**; elsewhere, you'll have to rely on **self-diagnosis**, which is unreliable at best. Giardia is often recognisable by rotten-egg belches and farts, and can be treated with a single 2000g dose of *Tiniba*, an antibiotic. The symptoms of dysentery – diarrhoea, mucous or blood in the stool, sometimes constipation – are too varied for effective self-diagnosis, but the prescription is 2000g of *Tiniba* daily for three days, followed by 500mg of *Furamide* three times a day for ten days. For simple diarrhoea, some doctors prescribe *Nalidixic Acid* (two tablets every six hours for three days) or *Bactrim* (one tablet every twelve hours for three days), but there is resistance to these antibiotics, and they can also kill off beneficial bacteria and leave you susceptible to other bugs. These and other Indian-manufactured **medicines** are available without prescription in *pharmas* (chemists) in all major towns.

FINDING A DOCTOR

Almost all qualified **doctors** are based in Kathmandu – in the event of a serious injury or illness, contact your embassy there (see "Listings" at the end of Chapter One) for a list of recommended physicians.

Hospitals are listed in the Kathmandu and Pokara sections of the *Guide*; other hospitals are located in Patan, Tansen and many of the Tarai cities, though they're often poorly equipped.

INSURANCE

In the light of all this, **travel insurance** is too important to ignore; besides covering medical expenses and emergency flights, it also insures your money and belongings against loss or theft. Policies (around £35 per month; double if you're trekking) are sold by all travel agents: *ISIS* schemes, from *STA Travel* or branches of *Endsleigh Insurance* (97–107 Southampton Row, London WC1; ☎071/580 4311; other offices throughout the UK) are good value. You'll need to keep receipts for any medicines you have to buy, or treatment you pay for, to claim from your insurance company once you're home. Similarly, should you have anything stolen, report the theft to the police (see "Police and Trouble") as soon as possible, and keep a copy of your statement.

INFORMATION AND MAPS

Despite its unabashed advertorialism, *Nepal Traveller*, a free monthly magazine distributed to the big hotels and travel agencies, is the best source of **what's-on information**. You can also check the informal **noticeboards** in restaurants around Kathmandu's Thamel tourist quarter for news of upcoming events or to find travelling or trekking companions.

MAPS

Good **maps** of Nepal are rare. The most reliable is a three-sheet 1:500,000 set (Rs21) published by HMG's Topographical Survey Branch, available through *Maps of Nepal* in Naya Baneswar in Kathmandu (near the *Everest Hotel*). The *Police Mountaineering and Adventure Foundation*'s map makes a cruder but more portable alternative. The prettiest map of the country, published by *Nelles*, is appallingly inaccurate – much is pure fiction.

Inexpensive **city maps** of Kathmandu and Pokhara are sold everywhere, but those of other cities simply don't exist. *Geo-Buch*'s "Kathmandu Valley" is indispensable if you plan to do any serious exploring of that area. Free brochures containing sketch maps of **national parks** and

Nepal's Tourism Department runs on a shoestring budget, letting the free market fill the gap with a confusing welter of advertising. There are no tourist offices outside the country, and those few in Nepal are chronically starved of printed materials and completely bereft of maps. They can, however, be useful sources of information on festival dates, local bus schedules and the like.

A NOTE ON PLACE NAMES

Even though Devanagari (the script of Nepali and Hindi) spellings are phonetic, transliterating them into the Roman alphabet is an inexact science. Some places will never shake off the erroneous spellings bestowed on them by early British colonialists – for instance Durbar Square, which according to widely accepted phonetic rules (see *Contexts*) should be spelled "Darbaar". Where place names are Sanskrit- or Hindi-based, the Nepali pronunciation sometimes differs from the accepted spelling – the names Vishnu (a Hindu god) and Vajra (a tantric symbol) sound like "Bishnu" and "Bajra" in Nepali. This book follows local pronunciations as consistently as possible, except in cases where this would be out of step with every map in print. Having said that, it's often hard to get a consensus on pronunciation – some people say Hetauda, others Itaura; some say Trisuli, others Tirsuli – so keep an open mind while map-reading.

wildlife reserves are available from the *Department of National Parks and Wildlife Conservation*, Thapathali, Kathmandu, although the office is not used to dealing with tourist queries. *Tiger Tops*' Kathmandu office sells a useful map of Chitwan National Park. Maps are as common as hens' teeth in the parks themselves. **Trekking maps** are detailed in Chapter Seven.

All of the above maps are available in the bigger Kathmandu bookshops, although you'll save a little money by buying maps published in Europe before you go. **In Britain** you'll find a fair selection at *Stanford's*, 12–14 Long Acre, London WC2E 9LP (☎071/836 1321). Note, however, that maps produced in Nepal are vastly cheaper in the country.

GETTING AROUND

Travel in Nepal expands to fill the time allotted to it: no matter where you're going, it always seems to take all day to get there. Distances aren't great, but in a mountainous country there's no such thing as a straight line; roads are few, narrow and poorly maintained. The usual way to get anywhere is by bus, although the odd internal flight, if you can afford it, can save a good deal of time and discomfort. Apart from one short line around Janakpur, Nepal has no rail network. However, the best way to experience Nepal is to walk or cycle – which often doesn't take much longer than going by bus.

BUSES

Buses ply every paved road in Nepal – as well as quite a few of the unpaved ones. The bus network is completely and chaotically privatised – there seem to be as many bus companies as there are buses, and as many ticket sellers as tickets – but there is some method to all this madness. Except for the tourist services, all route prices are fixed. These depend less on distance than on the state of the road and the time it takes to make the journey; for day buses it works out to about Rs6 per hour, somewhat higher for night buses.

Timetables are nonexistent and departure times are only approximate: it's a good idea to always get a third opinion. You'll find details of the major bus routes listed at the end of each chapter in "Travel Details".

Few travellers are ever quite prepared for the sheer **slowness** of bus travel in Nepal. Allowing for bad roads, overloaded buses, tea stops, meal stops, police checks, constant picking up and letting off of passengers, and the occasional flat tyre or worse, the average speed in the hills is barely 25 kilometres per hour; in the Tarai you might touch 40kph.

STATIONS AND TICKETS

Open-air **bus stations** (*bas park* or *bas istand* in Nepali) are typically the smelliest, dustiest and muddiest parts of town. Each long-distance service will have a ticket booth or desk somewhere in the vicinity, though they're rarely marked in English – you just have to ask around, if you're not approached first. In Kathmandu and Pokhara you may find it easier to make arrangements through a ticket agent (but heed the warnings given in the "On from Kathmandu" section of Chapter One), while in other cities with inconveniently located bus stations you can ask your hotel to send someone to buy a ticket for you.

Tickets for longer journeys should be booked at least a day in advance, or you could end up in one of the torture seats over the rear wheels. Always check the seating chart, if there is one, to see what's available. Normally seats can be reserved only at the bus's point of origin; getting on midway is seldom a problem, but you'll probably have to stand, or ride on the roof.

PUBLIC BUSES

If nothing else, **public buses** are a terrific opportunity to meet Nepalis and experience their legendary good humour in the face of adversity. Two distinct public-bus services operate, one in the day and one at night.

Day buses are ancient, battered contraptions with seats designed for midgets. They try to cram as many passengers in the aisle as possible – indeed, a bus isn't making money until it's nearly full to bursting, and it can get awfully suffocating inside. This can lead to infuriating false starts, as the driver inches forward and the conductor runs around trying to round up customers, since no bus can leave the station with empty seats. Even so-called "express" buses stop to pick up all comers. On shorter routes, buses have no fixed departure times and simply leave whenever they fill up; tickets are purchased on board. Long-distance buses tend to set off in the morning in order to arrive at their destination before dark. Unless your bag is small, it will have to go on the roof, but it should be safe there so long as it's locked; ordinarily there's no baggage charge. Riding on the roof can actually be quite pleasant in good weather, but it's illegal and you'll only be allowed to do it in remote areas between checkposts.

Look out for the blue quasi-government **Sajha** buses, which run a limited day service between the major cities in central Nepal. Donated by Japan, these converted city buses have more room, are faster and a little safer than the rest. However, tickets are only bookable the day before departure. Luggage must be stowed inside.

Nepali **night buses** aren't as luxurious as those in other Asian countries, but for a few rupees more they do provide reclining seats and adequate legroom. Departures are in late afternoon or early evening, to arrive the following morning – on relatively short routes, this means taking long meal breaks at horrible waysides in the middle of the night. Don't expect to get any sleep.

TOURIST BUSES

The only regularly scheduled **tourist buses** run between Kathmandu and Pokhara. These depart from the tourist areas of both cities, and tickets (which cost roughly double the ordinary fare) are widely touted, all of which at least saves you the trouble of hoofing down to the bus station. The vehicles are usually in good nick, and they aren't supposed to take any more passengers than there are seats (they usually pick up a few anyway), so the ride is more comfortable and somewhat faster than in a public bus.

TRUCKS

If no buses are going your way, you can always flag down a **truck**. Mostly they're ungainly Indian-built Tatas, ferrying fuel to Kathmandu or building materials to hill boomtowns; many in the Tarai are "Public Carriers" – gaily decorated hauliers-for-hire from India. Almost all do a sideline in hauling passengers, and charge set fares comparable to what you'd pay on a bus. Fully laden, they go even slower than buses. The ride is comfortable enough if you get a seat in the cab, and certainly scenic if you have to sit in the back – either way, the trip is bound to be eventful. **Women** considering utilising truck transport will probably prefer to join up with a companion.

However, trucks aren't licenced as passenger vehicles, and so take little interest in passenger safety: watch your luggage. **Hitching** in the accepted sense of the term isn't feasible in Nepal, as there are so few private vehicles.

PLANES

Internal flights aren't such a bargain now that *RNAC* have started charging tourists inflated dollar prices on all routes. Even so, there may be times when $75 seems a small price to pay to avoid spending 24 hours on a bus, or a week retracing your steps along a trail.

Given Nepal's mountainous terrain, aircraft play a vital role in the country's transport network, especially in the west, where planes are often used to carry in food during the winter. Of the 40 towns and villages with **airstrips**, almost half are two or more days' walk from a road. Most flights begin or end in Kathmandu, but two other **airports** in the Tarai – Nepalganj in the west, Biratnagar in the east – serve as secondary hubs. *RNAC* flies 727s between these cities, as well as between Kathmandu and Pokhara, and uses 20-seat Twin Otters for the hops to STOL (Short Takeoff and Landing) airstrips. Popular flights, like the one to Lukla in the Everest region, are scheduled up to five times a day, while obscure airstrips may receive only one flight a week. Many operate only seasonally. For frequencies and flight times, see "Travel Details" at the end of each chapter in the *Guide*.

Booking tickets can be exasperating. *RNAC* isn't computerised, and many airstrips don't even have phones, which means their passenger lists are made up in Kathmandu and delivered to them a few days ahead of time. The Kathmandu *RNAC* office will only issue a confirmed seat for the return journey up to the time that the list is sent off. If you wait till you get to the other end to book a ticket back to Kathmandu, you'll probably be disappointed. During the trekking season, most flights out of airstrips along the popular trails are booked up months, even years, in advance by trek agencies. But at off-peak times or away from the trekking routes – in the Tarai, for instance – you shouldn't have any trouble getting a seat.

Buying a ticket is only half the battle, since any number of things can delay or cancel a flight, **weather** being the most common. *RNAC* pilots will not fly if they can't see the ground (sensibly enough, considering some of the places they're expected to land). When planes are grounded, or commandeered by VIPs, **delays** multiply throughout the system. Since clouds usually increase as the day wears on, delays often turn into **cancellations**. If your flight is cancelled, rather than putting you on the next available flight, *RNAC* puts you at the bottom of a waiting list; in busy times or during extended periods of bad weather, the wait can be several days.

CARS AND MOTORCYCLES

Self-drive **cars** are not generally for hire in Nepal. In any case, you're better off not having to grapple with Nepal's treacherous roads and daunting traffic laws: killing a cow carries the same penalty as killing a person, up to 20 years in prison. Arranged through a travel agent, a chauffeur-driven car will run to about $80 a day. It makes more sense to take taxis.

A more affordable alternative, **motorcycles** can be rented (in Kathmandu only) for about Rs300 a day; petrol is extra, and costs about Rs19 a litre. A serious drawback is that hired bikes carry no insurance – if you break anything, you pay for it, and parts are expensive. You'll be expected to leave an air ticket or a large sum of money as a deposit.

LOCAL TRANSPORT

Few cities in Nepal are so large that you're dependent on public transport. Where available, **local buses** and minibuses are usually too crowded, slow or infrequent to be worthwhile. Three-wheeled, pedal-powered **rikshas**, common in Kathmandu and the Tarai, are slow and bumpy, but handy for short runs when you've got heavy bags or aren't sure where you're going. Be sure to establish the fare before setting off (Rs2–5 per kilometre, depending on how touristy the place is).

Taxis are confined mainly to Kathmandu and Pokhara, and you'll find details on their idiosyncrasies in the relevant sections; a metered ride should cost about Rs5 per kilometre, but on popular tourist routes, fixed fares work out to be around twice that. **Motor rikshas** – three-wheeled scooters with room for two passengers – are more common than taxis, though only slightly cheaper. Motor rikshas that operate on set routes are known as **tempos**; they fit six (barely), set off when they're full, and usually charge only a few rupees per head.

Hiring a bicycle (*saikal*) spares you having to deal with any of the above. Indian-made *Hero* one-speeders are good enough for most around-town cycling: they're incredibly heavy, but sturdy;

in case of a breakdown, repair shops are everywhere. Cycles are rentable all over Kathmandu and Pokhara for about Rs15 a day, less if you haggle for a long-term discount. Elsewhere, hire shops are rare, but you may be able to strike a deal with a lodge owner or cycle repairman. Details on mountain-bike hire are given in "Outdoor Pursuits", below.

FINDING A PLACE TO STAY

Finding a place to sleep is hardly ever a problem in Nepal, although only the established tourist centres offer much of a choice.

GUEST HOUSES

Kathmandu and Pokhara have their own tourist quarters where fierce competition among **budget guest houses** (often called lodges) ensures great value for money. In these enclaves, even the cheapest places (Rs50 or less for a double) provide hot running water, flush toilets, foam mattresses and clean sheets. They're never heated – they can be very cold in winter – but most offer a garden or roof terrace, a supply of (supposedly) boiled and filtered water and a phone. Innkeepers speak excellent English, and can arrange anything for you from laundry to trekking-porter hire. **Upmarket guest houses** (for lack of a better term) are becoming increasingly popular. These tend to be more spacious, private buildings with carpeting and furniture in the rooms, and maybe a lobby of sorts; the better ones will provide an electric heater in winter. Most are registered with the government, which means they quote their prices in dollars (about $5–10 for a double with attached shower) and add 10 percent tax on top.

Off the beaten track, however, you may have to settle for something less salubrious: stark concrete floors (painted red to hide the betel stains), cold-water showers and smelly squat toilets are the rule, and often not much English is spoken. Sheets and kapok quilts are usually provided, but it's a good idea to bring your own sleeping sheet (a sleeping bag is seldom necessary). Noise is always a problem: earplugs are a godsend. In the Tarai, mosquito netting (or mosquito coils) and a ceiling fan that works are crucial. Sometimes, though, the most primitive lodges – the ones with no electricity, where you sit on the mud floor by a smoky fire and eat with your hosts – can be the most rewarding of all. **Trekking inns** are another matter altogether, and are described in Chapter Seven. Nepal has only one **youth hostel**, in Patan, and it doesn't even offer a discount for *IYHA* card holders.

The cheeriest and most efficiently run guest houses are highlighted in the *Guide*, but remember that recommendations are often self-defeating and can result in instant price hikes. Also, watch out for name-changes, a common ploy to dodge taxes.

HOTELS

It's hard to generalise about the more **expensive hotels**. Most – usually the bigger ones – are over-priced and insulate guests from the Nepal they came to see, but the *Guide* flags a few admirable exceptions which, in their own way, offer unique experiences of the country. After a trek or a long spell of roughing it, a night or two in one of these hotels can be just what the doctor ordered. A government rating system awards hotels from one to five stars, but this is a vaguer guide to quality than price. Rated hotels add 10–15 percent tax, according to their number of stars.

Jungle lodges and tented camps inside the Tarai wildlife parks are the most expensive hotels of all; a stay in one is indeed the experience of a lifetime, but if $100–200 a night is beyond your reach there are plenty of more affordable outfits just outside Chitwan National Park.

CAMPING

Perhaps surprisingly, **camping** doesn't come high on the agenda in Nepal. Much of the country is well settled, every flat patch of ground is farmed, and rooms are so cheap that camping offers no savings. It's a different story, of course, if you're rafting or trekking. Also, camping is (theoretically) permitted in the lesser wildlife parks, although not in Chitwan. Long-distance cyclists might find it useful to bring a tent along, to avoid spending nights in roadside flea-pits en route to more interesting places. Between October and May many terraces are left fallow, and farmers won't expect you to ask permission to camp so long as you're respectful. Set up well away from villages, unless you want to be the locals' entertainment for the evening. Don't burn wood. An unattended tent is *probably* safe if zipped shut, but anything left outside is liable to be pinched.

EATING AND DRINKING

is **Tibetan**, consisting of soups, pastas, potatoes and breads.

WHERE TO EAT

You're spoiled for choice in Kathmandu and Pokhara, where enterprising **tourist restaurants** show an uncanny knack for sensing exactly what travellers want and simulating it with the most basic ingredients. Some specialise in Italian, "Continental", Chinese, Mexican or even Japanese food, but the majority attempt to do a little of everything. Display cases full of extravagant cakes and pies are a standard come-on. Nepal's tourist restaurant scene has grown progressively more gross and surreal over the years, but there's no denying that the food is tasty – especially after a trek.

Nepal – specifically Kathmandu – is renowned as the budget eating capital of Asia. Sadly, the reputation is based not on Nepali food, but on the skilful aping of continental and other cuisines: pizza, chips, "buff" (buffalo) steaks and apple pie are the staples of tourist restaurants. Outside the popular areas, travellers' chief complaint is the blandness of the diet.

Yet Nepal lies at the intersection of two great culinary traditions, **Indian** and **Chinese**, and if you know what to look for you'll find good, native renditions of everthing from tandoori to stir-fried dishes. The simple cooking of the hills – Nepal's heartland – is essentially a regional variation of north Indian, comprising curried vegetables and meats, rice, chapatis and chutneys. In the Tarai, the vast range of Indian snacks and sweets comes into play, while in the mountains the diet

Nepali restaurants are traditionally humble affairs, offering a limited choice of dishes (or no choice at all). Menus don't exist, but the food will normally be on display or cooking in full view, so all you have to do is point. Utensils should be available on request, but if not, try doing as Nepalis do and eat with your hand – the *right* one only (see "Cultural Hints" for more on social taboos relating to eating). In towns and cities, eateries tend to be dark, almost conspiratorial places, unmarked and hidden behind curtains. On the highways they're bustlingly public and spill outdoors in an effort to win business. In hill villages, there's little discernible difference between a teahouse (*bhatti* or *chiya pasaal*) and a restaurant, both being humble operations run out of family kitchens. Tarai cities always have a fancy (by Nepali standards) restaurant or two, patronised by businessmen and Indian tourists. Confusingly, restaurants are often called "hotels"; hotels are called "lodges".

For fast food, **sweet shops** (*mithaai pasaal*) dish up not only sweets but also yoghurt (*dahi*) and savoury snacks, while **street vendors** sell fruit, nuts, roasted corn, fried bread and, in the Tarai, various fried specialties. When you're travelling, as often as not the food will come to you – at every bus stop, vendors will clamber aboard or hawk their dishes through the window.

Vegetarians will feel at home in Nepal, since meat is considered a luxury. Imaginative preparations are rare, though: rice, lentils, vegetable curry and noodles are the standard offerings everywhere. As a rule, vegetarian dishes get more interesting and varied the closer you get to India: some orthodox Hindu restaurants near the border bill themselves as vegetarian-only. Tourist menus invariably include meatless items, which are often excellent.

Nepalis generally start the day with nothing more than a cup of tea, eat a full meal in mid-morning, then carry on until the second big meal of the day at dinnertime. The Western concept of **breakfast** doesn't tie in very well. Again, tourist restaurants have this covered – many do excellent set breakfast deals, with eggs, porridge, muesli and the like – but out in the sticks you may have to make do with a greasy omelette or packet noodles.

NEPALI AND INDIAN FOOD

Special Nepali dishes are best sampled in a tourist restaurant, as it may be hard to find anything more than the basics elsewhere.

Daal bhaat tarkaari (lentil soup, white rice and curried vegetables) isn't just the most popular meal in Nepal – for many Nepalis it's the *only* meal they ever eat, twice a day, every day of their lives; indeed, in much of hill Nepal, *bhaat* is a synonym for food. It's a potentially boring dish, admittedly, and if you spend much time trekking or travelling off the beaten track you'll probably quickly tire of it. That said, a good *achhaar* (chutney) – made with tomato, aubergine, wild plum or whatever grows locally – can liven up a *daal bhaat* tremendously. One price covers unlimited refills.

Other traditional Nepali dishes are more localised, or reserved for special occasions, but well worth the effort of tracking them down. You'll often be able to supplement a plate of *daal bhaat*

with small side dishes of *maasu* (meat), marinated in yoghurt and spices and fried in *ghiu* (clarified butter), or *mismas*, mixed, mildly curried vegetables. *Daal* takes on an added buttery savouriness when it's fried (*taareko daal*). **Soups** (*surwa*) are sometimes available: *tama surwa*, made with bamboo shoots, is popular. You could make a meal out of rice and *sekuwa* (kebabs of spicy marinated meat chunks) or *taareko maachhaa* (fried fish), both common in the Tarai. The Kathmandu Valley has many specialties of its own, including *choyaala* (meat cubes fried with spices and greens) and various bean and vegetable mixtures. Nepali **desserts** include *sikarni* (thick, whipped yoghurt with cinnamon, raisins and nuts) and *khir* (rice pudding).

A full description of **Indian dishes** isn't possible here, and only a few pricey Kathmandu restaurants do them authentically anyway. In the Tarai the best bets are *masaala* (meaning spicey, although it isn't really) curries, and you generally can't go wrong with *kofta*, spicy vegetable balls in curry. *Chapatis* are always available in Indian restaurants, *nan* and *parathas* usually so. Ask for *papad*, not pappadums. And as for the incredible array of Indian **sweets**, well, that could fill a book in itself. A selection: *laddu*, yellow and orange speckled chewy balls; *jelebi*, deep-fried pretzels of sweetened batter; *barphi*, fudgy squares made from reduced milk, often decorated with edible silver leaf; *koloni*, a softer version of the same; *lal mohan*, brown spongy balls in sweet syrup; and *ras malai*, sweet spongy cakes in cream. Really good sweets are only found in the bigger Tarai towns – Nepali attempts just don't cut it.

TIBETAN FOOD

Strictly speaking, "Tibetan" refers to nationals of Tibet, but the people of the Nepal Himalaya, collectively known as Bhotiyas, together with the people of several other highland ethnic groups, all eat what could be called Tibetan food.

Momos, arguably the most famous and popular of Tibetan dishes, are available throughout hill Nepal. Distant cousins to ravioli, the half-moon-shaped pasta shells are filled with meat, vegetables and ginger, steamed, and served with hot tomato *achhaar* and a bowl of broth. Fried *momos* are called *kothe*. Put the same stuffing ingredients inside a flour pastry shell and fry it and you get *shyaphale*, a sort of Tibetan meat pie.

A GLOSSARY OF FOOD TERMS

The following list should give an idea of what to ask for in restaurants, although tourist places will usually have an English menu.

Basics

Bread	*Roti*	Innkeeper (male)	*Sahuji*	Rice (uncooked)	*Chaamal*
The bill	*Bil*	(female)	*Sahuni*	Rice (beaten)	*Chiura*
Butter	*Makhaan*	Knife	*Chhaku*	Salt	*Nun*
Chutney, Pickle	*Achhaar*	Milk	*Dudh*	Spoon	*Chamchaa*
Egg	*Phul*	Oil	*Tel*	Sugar	*Chini*
Food	*Khaanaa*	Pepper (ground)	*Marich*	Sweets, Candy	*Mithaai*
Fork	*Kanta*	Plate	*Plet*	Water	*Paani*
Glass	*Gilaas*	Rice (cooked)	*Bhaat*	Yoghurt, Curd	*Dahi*

Common Nepali Dishes

Daal bhaat tarkaari	Lentil soup, white rice and curried vegetables.	*Samosa*	Pyramids of pastry filled with curried vegetables.
Dahi chiura	Curd with beaten rice.		
Pakoda	Vegetables dipped in chickpea-flour batter, deep fried.	*Sekuwa*	Spicy, marinated meat kebab.
		Taareko maachhaa	Fried fish.

Common Tibetan Dishes

Momo	Pasta shells filled with meat, vegetables and ginger, steamed.	*Thukpa*	Soup containing pasta, meat and vegetables.
Kothe	The same, fried.	*Tsampa*	Toasted barley flour.

Vegetables (*Saabji* or *Tarkaari*)

Aubergine	*Bhanta*	Coriander	*Dhaniyaa*	Potato	*Alu*
Beans	*Simi*	Corn	*Makai*	Pumpkin	*Pharsi*
Cabbage	*Banda Khobi*	Garlic	*Lasun*	Radish	*Mulaa*
Carrot	*Gaajar*	Lentils	*Daal*	Spinach, Greens	*Saag*
Cauliflower	*Kaauli*	Mushroom	*Chyaau*	Tomato	*Golbheda*
Chickpeas	*Chaana*	Onion	*Pyaaj*		
Chili	*Khursaani*	Peas	*Kerau* or *Matar*		

Meat (*Maasu*)

Beef	*Gaiko maasu* (rare: taboo for most Nepalis)	Chicken		*Kukhuraako maasu*
		Mutton		*Khaasiko maasu*
Buffalo ("Buff")	*Raangaako maasu*	Pork		*Sungurko maasu*

Fruit (*Phalphul*) and Nuts (*Supaari*)

Apple	*Syaau*	Guava	*Ambaa*	Peanut	*Badaam* (Mambale near India)
Banana	*Keraa*	Lemon	*Kagati*		
Cashew	*Kaaju*	Lime	*Nibuwaa*	Pineapple	*Bhuikatahar*
Coconut	*Nariwal*	Mango	*Aaph*	Pistachio	*Pista*
Date	*Chhora*	Orange	*Suntalaa*	Raisin	*Kismis*
		Papaya	*Mewaa*	Sugarcane	*Ukhu*

Spices (*Masaala*)

Aniseed	*Soph*	Chili pepper	*Khursaani*	Ginger	*Aduwaa*
Cardamom	*Sukumel, Elaaichi*	Cinnamon	*Daalchini*	Saffron	*Kesari*
		Clove	*Lwang*	Turmeric	*Besaar*

Some common terms			
A little	*Alikati*	Delicious	*Mitho*
A lot	*Dherai*	Hot	*Taato*
Another	*Aarko*	Spicy	*Piro*
Boiled (water)	*Umaaleko*	Stir-fried	*Bhuteko*
Cooked	*Pakeko*	Sweet	*Guliyo*
Cold	*Chiso*	Vegetarian	*Sahakaari*
Deep-fried	*Taareko*	I don't eat meat	*Ma maasu khaana*

Tibetan cuisine is also justly celebrated for its excellent hearty soups, usually called *thukpa*, consisting of homemade pasta strips or noodles, meat and vegetables in broth.

For a special blow-out, try *gyakok*, a huge meal for two that includes chicken, pork, prawns, fish, tofu, eggs and vegetables, and which gets its name from the brass container it's served in; *gyakok* is only found in Kathmandu restaurants and has to be ordered several hours ahead. In trekking lodges you'll encounter frisbee-shaped items called **Tibetan bread** which, though unappealing on their own, are made more interesting by the addition of honey or peanut butter.

The average Tibetan seldom eats any of the above: the most common standbys in the high country are **potatoes**, boiled or made into pancakes (*riki kur*), and **tsampa** – toasted barley flour, mixed with milk or tea to make a sort of gruel, or eaten plain.

ROAD FOOD AND SNACKS

Road food is a genre in itself – there's certainly no need to go hungry when you're travelling. If you've time to sit down, ask for a plate of *pakodas*, fried, bready nuggets of chickpea flour and vegetables, served with hot sauce, or *tarkaari ra roti*, vegetable (usually bean) curry served with a few pieces of fried bread that in India would be called *puris*. Another refreshing possibility is *dahi chiura*, a mixture of curd and beaten rice that's reminiscent of muesli curd. If you're in more of a hurry, you can always grab a handful of *samosas*, fried pyramids of pastry filled with curried vegetables, or carry away fried lentil patties or other titbits on a leaf plate. If nothing else, there will always be packet **noodles**, which can either be boiled as a soup or stir-fried. Roadside vendors peddle roasted peanuts, peas and chickpeas, coconut slivers, corn on the cob, *sel roti* (doughnuts), and whatever **fruit** is in season – in winter, have a go at a length of sugarcane.

Imported **chocolates** are sold in Kathmandu and Pokhara, and waxy Indian substitutes can be found in most towns. **Biscuits** and cheap boiled sweets are sold at roadside stalls everywhere.

DRINKS

Tea (*chiya*), something of a national beverage in Nepal, comes with milk (*dudh*) and heaps of sugar (*chini*) unless you insist otherwise. Tibetans and Bhotiyas take it with salt and yak butter, which is definitely an acquired taste. Tourist establishments also do lemon tea and "hot lemon". **Coffee** (*kaphi*) is instant and undistinguished.

Water (*paani*) is automatically served with food in Nepali restaurants – needless to say, stick to the bottled stuff (*Bisleri* and *Star*, both about Rs20 a litre). **Soft drinks** are safe and sold in "cold stores" everywhere, but the price rises steadily (from about Rs5) as you move into roadless areas; many international brands are represented. Fresh lemon soda, made with lemon (or lime) juice and soda water, makes a good alternative if you want to cut out sugar. Tourist restaurants serve freshly-squeezed **fruit juices** – orange, apple, mango, guava and papaya, when they're in season – but they're not cheap. Tinned juice and fruit drinks in cartons are widely available. A **lassi**, a blend of yoghurt, water or ice (beware), sugar and fruit (or salt), always goes down a treat, and helps take the heat out of a curry.

Beer (*biyar*) makes another fine accompaniment to Nepali and Indian food. Two breweries set up with German assistance produce some serviceable lagers: *Iceberg* is full-bodied but heavy, *Leo* and *Golden Eagle* a bit lighter and less strong, while *Star*, the cheapest, is on the rough side. All are sold in 600ml bottles, which work out not too expensive if you share.

An amazing and amusing selection of ersatz **spirits** is bottled in Nepal, ranging from *Ruslan* vodka to *Ye Grand Earl* whiskey ("Glasgow – London – Kathmandu"). They're cheap and on the whole nasty, but tolerable if disguised by liberal quantities of soft drinks. *Khukuri 'XXX'* rum is actually quite palatable with Coke. Imported spirits and wine are exorbitant. Look out for regional specialties like the apricot and apple brandies of Marpha, north of Pokhara, and the aniseed-based *dudhiya* (so called because it goes milky when added to water) of the eastern Tarai. Unless you're absolutely desperate, give so-called "country liquors" such as *Urvashi* a miss. Shops sell spirits in convenient 1/4-size bottles, restaurants by the "peg" (measure). You can even get exotic **cocktails** in a few of Kathmandu's tourist bars.

Nepalis are avid home brewers and distillers. Cloudy (sometimes almost porridgy) **chhang** is the generic term for any beer made from rice or other grains, typically fermented in cast-off mountaineering expedition barrels. ***Raksi***, the most popular alcoholic drink in Nepal, is a distilled version of the same and bears a heady resemblance to tequila. Harder to find, but perhaps the most pleasant drink of all, is a brew-it-yourself Sherpa concoction called **tongba**. The ingredients are a jug of fermented millet, a straw, and a flask of hot water: you pour the water in, let it steep, and suck the mildly alcoholic brew through the straw until you reach the bottom; repeat four or five times. Two *tongbas* can easily lubricate an entire evening.

COMMUNICATIONS: POST, PHONES AND THE MEDIA

Due to Nepal's isolation, it's not hard to fall out of touch with the rest of the world while you're there. International telephoning is surprisingly easy – though expensive – but post is usually slow and patchy, and English-language newspapers and magazines are only available in two major cities.

POST

Mail takes at least ten days, sometimes a lot longer, to get to or from Nepal. Nepal's only **Poste Restante**, in Kathmandu, is reasonably efficient. Mail should be addressed: *Name, Poste Restante, GPO, Kathmandu, Nepal*. Letters are filed alphabetically in self-serve trays. To reduce the risk of misfiling, your name should be printed clearly with the surname underlined or capitalised; it's still always a good idea to check under your first initial, too. Oversized envelopes are filed in a separate tray. Parcels can be received, but they may not arrive intact, so anything of value should be sent registered. Mail is held for about two months, and can be redirected on request.

Likewise, **American Express** handles mail only in Kathmandu (see "Listings" at the end of Chapter One). You need to be carrying *Amex* cheques or a card to use the service.

When **sending** letters and cards, take them to the post office and have the stamps franked before your eyes. Never use a letterbox: the stamps will be removed and resold, and your correspondence will be used to wrap peanuts. Some guest houses and shops will take mail to the post office for you, but make sure they're reliable. **Post offices** in the major cities sell stamps and aerogrammes for overseas posting (see the "Listings" sections in the *Guide* for hours). Mail posted from smaller towns carries a higher risk of going astray, and in any case will take so much longer to be delivered that it's better to wait till you get back to Kathmandu to send it. Sending **parcels** is a whole other story – see "Shipping stuff home" in Chapter One.

PHONES

Public **phones** in Nepal are rare indeed, and usually broken, except for the ones in Kathmandu airport which are free for local calls. Tourist lodges will let you make local calls for a couple of rupees, trunk calls for about Rs15 per minute. Phone numbers change every other week: **directory enquiries** (☎197) might be able to help. Making **international calls** is easy from Kathmandu and Pokhara, where even lowly guest houses have direct-dialling facilities, but expensive (Rs250–375 for three minutes, counted by wristwatch). Booking a call through a *Central Telegraph Office* in one of the bigger cities is less convenient but can save 10–20 percent. It's not possible to reverse the charges.

Telegrams can be sent from the *Central Telegraph Office* in Kathmandu, but a 20-word message costs more than a three-minute phone call to the UK. Incoming telegrams can be collected at Poste Restante. The luxury hotels in Kathmandu have telex and fax machines.

THE MEDIA

Despite only 35-percent literacy, Nepal boasts an astonishing 460 **newspapers**. Of the handful printed in English, only the *Rising Nepal* is widely circulated, and outside Kathmandu it's always a day or more out of date. Formerly a toadying government mouthpiece, it has improved considerably since the recent restoration of press freedom, while the spunky new *Sunday Despatch* (available only in the capital) shows real promise. **Foreign publications** such as the *International Herald Tribune*, *Time* and *Newsweek* are sold widely in Kathmandu and Pokhara, but nowhere else. For British newspapers, try the *British Council* in Kathmandu.

Radio Nepal carries English-language news bulletins daily at 8am and 8pm. If you're travelling with a short-wave radio, you can pick up the **BBC World Service** on the 41-, 31- or 25-metre bands. **Nepal-TV**, with transmitters in Kathmandu, Pokhara and Biratnagar, broadcasts the news in English at 8.15am and 8.40pm.

OPENING HOURS AND HOLIDAYS

Shops in Nepal keep long hours, and in tourist areas usually open seven days a week. But when dealing with officialdom remember that Saturday, not Sunday, is the day of rest – and bureaucrats like to knock off early on Friday, too.

In theory, **government offices**, **post offices** and **museums** are open Sunday–Thursday 10am to 5pm, Friday 10am to 3pm; in winter (mid-February to mid-November), closing time is 4pm Sunday–Thursday. These schedules often get truncated at either end, though. **Banks** in tourist areas are generous with their hours (see the "Listings" sections in the *Guide* for hours), but

elsewhere you'll have to do your transactions between 10am and 2pm Sunday–Thursday, 10am to noon on Friday. **Travel agents** tend to work a five-day week, 9am or 10am to 6pm, Monday to Friday; airline offices are the same but they take a lunch break from 1–2pm. **Embassy** and consulate hours are all over the place: see Chapter One, *Kathmandu*, for a rundown.

Complicating matters is Nepal's hectic calendar of **festivals** and **holidays**, which can shut down offices for up to a week at a time. Dates vary from year to year – Nepal has its own calendar, beginning in mid-April and consisting of twelve months that are completely out of step

NATIONAL HOLIDAYS

Prithvi Narayan Shah's Birthday – January 10 or 11.

Basant Panchami – late January or early February.

Shiva Raatri – late February or early March.

Democracy Day – February 18 or 19.

Nawa Barsa (Nepali New Year) – April 13 or 14.

Guru Purnima – late June or early July.

Janai Purnima – late July or early August.

Dasain – a full week off in October.

Tihar – three days off in late October or early November.

Queen's Birthday – November 7 or 8.

Constitution Day – December 15 or 16.

King's Birthday – December 28 or 29.

with the Western ones. (The Vikram Sambat calendar began in 57 BC. Thus the Nepali year beginning in April 1991 is 2048 VS.) As if that weren't confusing enough, religious festivals are calculated according to the *lunar* calendar. Tibetan festivals follow yet a different calendar.

On **national holidays** (see above), all government offices are closed.

FESTIVALS AND ENTERTAINMENT

Stumbling, perhaps accidentally, onto a village festival may prove to be the highlight of your travels in Nepal (and given the sheer number of them, you'd be hard pressed not to). Though most are religious in nature, merrymaking, not solemnity, is the order of the day, and onlookers are always welcome. However, some celebrations, while public, are personal: don't photograph worshippers without asking permission. Other entertainments, such as music, dance and sports, are colourful, commonplace, and reveal the cultural variety of the country.

FESTIVALS

Festivals are a sophisticated brand of performance art in Nepal, as exotic as the religions that underlie them, which may be Hindu, Buddhist, animist or a hybrid of all three (see *Contexts*). **Hindu events** can take the form of huge pilgrimages and fairs (*mela*), or more introspective gatherings such as ritual bathings at sacred confluences (*tribeni*) or special acts of worship (*puja*) at temples. Many involve animal sacrifices and jolly family feasts afterwards, with priests and musicians usually on hand. Parades and processions are common, especially in the Kathmandu Valley, where idols are periodically ferried around on great, swaying chariots. **Buddhist festivals** are no less colourful, typically bringing together maroon-robed clergy and lay pilgrims to walk and prostrate around stupas (dome-shaped monuments, usually repainted specially for the occasion), chant from sacred texts and make splendid, otherworldly music.

Festival **dates** vary from year to year, as most are determined by the lunar calendar; consult a current Nepali calendar (sold in tourist bookshops) or, less reliably, a tourist information office.

Major festivals are highlighted below. The best of the **local festivals** are listed at the end of each chapter, but there are many others – and it's often the obscure and unexpected event that can be the most fun. A few worth trying to coincide with are: Patan's amazing *Rato Machhendranath Rath Jaatra* (about three weeks in April or May); Kathmandu's *Gai Jaatra* (late July or early August) and *Indra Jaatra* (September); *Mani Rimdu*, the Sherpa dance-drama held at Tengboche (November or December); and Janakpur's massive *Viveh Panchami* celebration (late November or early December).

Similarly jubilant (and public), Nepali **weddings** are usually held in the spring, and especially on *Basant Panchami*, the traditional celebration of the first day of spring, which falls in late January or early February. The approach of a wedding party is always heralded by the sound of a hired brass band – one of colonialism's stranger legacies, often sounding like a Dixieland sextet playing in a pentatonic scale – and open-air feasts go on until the early hours.

Funeral processions are understandably sombre and should be left in peace. The body is normally carried to the cremation site within hours of death by white-shrouded relatives; white is the colour of mourning for Hindus, and a man is expected to shave his head and wear white for a year following the death of a parent. Many of the hill tribes conduct special shamanic rites to guide the deceased's soul to the land of the dead.

NEPAL'S MAJOR FESTIVALS

Nepal doesn't have any truly national festivals, but the following are the most widely observed events.

Losar, or **Tibetan New Year** – Celebrated in February with drinking, dancing and feasting, this is the highlight of the calendar in Buddhist highland areas, as well as Tibetan refugee settlements near Kathmandu and Pokhara.

Shiva Raatri – Falling in late February or early March, "Shiva's Night" is marked by bonfires and evening vigils in all Hindu areas, but most spectacularly at Pashupatinath, where tens of thousands of pilgrims and holy men gather for Nepal's best-known *mela*. Using the old "penny for the Guy" technique, children collect firewood money by holding string across the road to block passersby; foreigners are considered easy prey.

Holi – Nepal's version of the spring water festival, common to many Asian countries, is an impish affair lasting a week in late March or early April. During this period, anyone – bus passengers included – is a fair target for water balloons and coloured powder (usually red: the colour of rejoicing), and it culminates in a general free-for-all on the full-moon day.

Nawa Barsa – **Nepali New Year** (April 13 or 14) is observed with local parades and the like; Bhaktapur's celebration, known as *Bisket*, combines religious processions with a rowdy tug-of-war.

Dasain – Although Hindu in origin, Nepal's greatest festival is enthusiastically embraced by members of almost all religious and ethnic groups. It stretches over ten days in October, but the liveliest action, as far as outside observers are concerned, takes place on *Durga Puja*, the ninth day, when animals are sacrificed to the goddess Durga in honour of her victory over demons. On *Vijaya Dasami* (the "Victorious Tenth Day"), elders bestow *tika*, an auspicious mark on the forehead, which on this day consists of a red paste mixed with rice. *Dasain* is a time for families to gather (buses can get very crowded), and you'll see swings and miniature ferris wheels set up to entertain the kids.

Tihar – Following *Dasain* by about a month, the "Festival of Lights" lasts for five days. On the first, crows are honoured as the messengers of death, while on the next three days dogs, cows and bulls are garlanded. More significantly, houses throughout the hills and Tarai are trimmed with hundreds of candles and oil lamps on the third night, called *Lakshmi Puja*, in the hope of attracting Lakshmi, the goddess of wealth; trusting in her, many Nepalis gamble during this festival. On the fifth day, *Bhaai Tika*, sisters give their brothers *tika* and sweets.

MUSIC AND DANCE

Music is as common as conversation in Nepal. In the hills, travelling minstrels (*gaine*) make their living singing ballads and accompanying themselves on the *saranghi*, a hand-carved, four-stringed fiddle. Teenagers traditionally attract the attention of the opposite sex by exchanging teasing verses. After-dinner singalongs are popular everywhere, even in sophisticated Kathmandu, and of course music is indispensable in all festivals. Instrumental backing typically consists of harmonium, tabla, *madal* (horozontally held drum) and *murali* (a sort of fife). Sherpas and other mountain people play crashing, Tibetan-influenced music with cymbals, horns, conch shells and long, telescoping trumpets called *zang dung*, which look like Swiss alpenhorns and produce a sound like a subsonic fart.

Traditional Nepali music is getting swamped by a rising flood of **Indian film music**, with its surging strings and hysterically shrill vocals. Yet **Nepali pop** also exists, and gets a good airing; in contrast, it sounds mercifully calm and villagey. Tapes are widely sold in street stalls. In tourist restaurants, you're more likely to hear dinosaur rock, reggae or New Age muzak.

Nepali music is almost inseparable from **dance**, especially at festivals. Nepali dance is an unaffected folk art – neither wildly athletic nor subtle, it depicts everyday activities like work and courtship. Each region and ethnic group has its own distinct traditions, and during your travels you should get a chance to join a local hoedown or two, if not a full-blown festival extravaganza. Look out, too, for the muscular stick dance of the lowland Tharus, performed regularly at lodges outside Chitwan National Park.

Staged **culture shows** in Kathmandu and Pokhara are a long way from the real thing, but they do provide an overview of folk and religious dances, and hint at the incredible cultural diversity contained in such a small country. Most troupes perform such standards as the dance of the *jhankri* (shaman-exorcists still consulted by many, if not most, hill Nepalis); the sleeve-twirling dance of the Sherpas; the flirting dance of the hill-dwelling Tamangs; the Tharus' fanciful peacock dance; perhaps a formal priestly dance, to the accompaniment of a clasical *raga* (musical piece); and at least one of the dances of the Kathmandu Valley's holiday-loving Newars.

CINEMA AND THEATRE

Nepal's love-hate relationship with India is perhaps best illustrated by its **cinema**: Nepalis might grouse about India's cultural imperialism, but that doesn't stop them rushing to see the latest schmaltz and pyrotechnics from Bombay. Nepali and Hindi are similar enough that films aren't usually dubbed. You don't need to understand the dialogue to follow the excruciatingly obvious plots, and in any case the audience is the primary entertainment. Tickets cost just pennies. **Video** rental shops are now commonplace in Kathmandu, where kung-fu epics from Hong Kong are almost as popular as Indian imports.

Theatre is poorly developed in Nepal. Occasional (and unpublicised) plays are performed at the National Theatre and, even less frequently, at the Royal Nepal Academy, both in Kathmandu.

SPORT

It's often said Nepalis are a martial race; certainly military parade grounds are more common than playing fields. **Martial arts** are popular among urban youth – Nepal's best shot at an Olympic medal in 1992, everyone agrees, is in karate. Team sports aren't big, although the Nepali **football** team periodically hosts other Asian clubs at the National Stadium in Kathmandu. Cricket, so enthusiastically followed in India, is largely unknown in Nepal.

The big tourist hotels in Kathmandu have **swimming** pools and **tennis** courts, and some of them allow outsiders to use their facilities for a fee (usually steep). There's also a health club in Kathmandu, as well as two **golf** courses in the Kathmandu Valley and a third in Dharan.

SHOPPING

Nepal's handicrafts scene is as rich and varied as its culture, having been influenced by centuries of trade and religious exchange with Tibet and India. The influx of Tibetan artisans since 1959 has enriched the marketplace immeasurably, while tourist demand, ironically, has helped fuel something of an artistic renaissance. You can pick up distinctive gifts, souvenirs and clothes for a song, or if your budget runs to it, spend a fortune on carpets and *objets d'art*.

WHERE TO SHOP

Ninety-nine percent of craft outlets are concentrated in the Kathmandu Valley and Pokhara: that's where the buyers are, and much of the mass-produced stuff is actually made there. Competition is intense. You can't stroll the tourist strips without being importuned by **curio sellers** cradling "priceless" dross in white cloths, or beckoned from the sidelines by operators of makeshift stalls; their overheads are low and so, at least in theory, should be their prices. More reputable **shops** and glass-fronted boutiques have better selections and aren't so hard-driving. Kathmandu has a couple of fixed-price "emporia", which are good for finding out the going rate for things, and in Patan (Nepal's handicrafts capital) you'll find **"factory" showrooms**, where you can watch the wares being made, and a number of excellent **non-profit outlets**.

Quite a few items sold in tourist areas are made elsewhere, though, and needless to say it's more fun (and cheaper) to pick them up at their source. Best buys are noted in the relevant sections of the *Guide*, along with a few local specialities that can't be found anywhere else.

Except where prices are clearly marked as fixed (and even then, sometimes), you'll be expected to **bargain**. Bargaining is very much a matter of personal style, but in Nepal it's always lighthearted, never acrimonious. There's no firm guide as to what to expect to have knocked off, although prices are always softer on the street. The initial asking price can be anywhere from 10 to 200 percent over the going rate, depending, to a certain extent, on how gullible you look. All the old chestnuts (never show the least sign of interest, let alone enthusiasm; walking away will always cut the price dramatically) still hold true; but most important is to know what you want, its approximate value, and how much you're prepared to pay. Never start to haggle for something you definitely don't intend to buy – it'll end in bad feelings on both sides. Sellers always speak English in tourist areas, but everywhere else you'll need some rudimentary Nepali to haggle properly.

No matter what the seller says, very few items are older than last week. Genuine **antiques** – anything over 100 years old, or anything customs officials might think is that old – have to be cleared for export by the *Department of Archaeology*, Ram Shah Path, Kathmandu. Get the dealer to take care of the paperwork.

NEPALI CRAFTS

Nepal is probably best known for its metal wares, especially *khukuris*, the deadly knives of Nepal's feared Gurkha soldiers; Bhojpur, in the eastern hills, is the traditional forging centre, but knives are heavily peddled in Kathmandu. So, too, are **metal statuettes** of Buddhist and Hindu deities, produced by the lost-wax process in Patan, as well as **jewellery** made of silver, white metal and semiprecious stones (often fake). Look out for *malla*, the many-stranded necklaces worn by all married hill women.

Nepali **woodcarving** reaches its apex in Bhaktapur, where you'll find everything from modest Buddha busts to exquisite, full-size window frames. The nearby town of Thimi is famous for its **papier mâché masks and puppets**. A couple of shops in Kathmandu sell nothing but **musical instruments**, including *saranghis* (Nepal's version of a fiddle) and *jhankri* drums.

Textiles are produced locally throughout Nepal. *Dhaka*, a brightly patterned cotton weave made on hand looms in the eastern and western hills, and *pashmina*, a cashmere-like wool made from goat's hair, are the best known. You'll also run across raw silk, block-printed cottons, synthetic sari material and *khadi*, traditional homespun cotton. All of these turn up in **clothes**, ranging from cheap pyjamas to quite stylish silk and *dhaka* readymades and *pashmina* shawls. *Dhaka* is also used to make **topis** (Nepali caps), while Nepali designers are starting to experiment with other fabrics in such contemporary crafts as cushion covers and place settings.

Handmade paper, produced from the bark of the *daphne* bush in many hill areas, is made into calendars, stationery and greeting cards for tourist consumption. **Batiks**, depicting typical Nepalese scenes, are an artform introduced in the past two decades as an income-generator for disabled people.

TIBETAN CRAFTS

India may have more Tibetans, but Nepal is the foremost market of Tibetan crafts in the world – including, these days, Tibet.

Kathmandu and Pokhara are thick with refugees-turned-entrepreneurs, selling a vast range of **curios**: prayer wheels, amulets, charm boxes, bracelets (usually inscribed with the mantra, *om mani padme hum*), prayer-flag printing blocks, *chhang* pots, wooden masks, turquoise and coral jewellery, musical instruments and many other bizarre artifacts. Much of it has been artifically aged, and the turquoise is often fake (bite it to see if the colour comes off).

Tibetan **carpets** are now reckoned to be Nepal's single biggest export item. These don't come cheap – a 3' x 6' carpet will cost about $100, although price is dependent on many factors. You can watch them being made in Patan and Pokhara; see these sections for details on their manufacture. Attractive sweaters, socks and other **woollens**, knitted in Tibetan settlements everywhere, are amazingly cheap, if scratchy. Bags and caps made of "Tibetan" wool go in and out of fashion.

Thankas – ceremonial scroll paintings – are, next to carpets, the most coveted and expensive Tibetan art (though to be accurate, many *thankas*, like most "Tibetan" items, are produced by other Himalayan ethnic groups). Kathmandu is the biggest *thanka* centre, and you'll find more information about them in that section.

EVERYDAY GOODS

Quite a few imported items are sold in tourist areas – for a price, naturally.

Film is now easily obtainable in Kathmandu for not much more than what it costs back home, but you'll be wise to bring all other camera hardware, including batteries. Many places process film.

No-frills Indian **toiletries** and tampons are easy enough to come by in Kathmandu; Western brands are exorbitant. Since it's little-used by

Nepalis, toilet paper has to be imported from China. Used **trekking gear** is always for sale, but probably better rented or brought from home; bring footwear, sunglasses, torch, canteen and pocket knife.

If you're short of cash you could try **selling things**: digital watches, personal stereos, cameras and calculators all generate interest, though you won't get their new price. T-shirts with logos can sometimes be traded for handicrafts.

OUTDOOR PURSUITS

It hardly needs to be said that Nepal is ideal for outdoor enthusiasts. Most come to trek, but activities such as rafting, cycling and wildlife- and bird-watching are also well developed. None requires any previous experience.

TREKKING AND HIKING

Even if you're not the outdoor type, **trekking** is a rare pleasure that shouldn't be passed up: it's the only way to get *into* the Himalaya, as opposed to looking at them from a distance, and is by far the best way to experience Nepal's constantly changing landscape and people-scape. A trek normally lasts at least a week, but you'll get more out of it if you can set aside two or more weeks. Most people don't trek with a group, and wait until they get to Kathmandu before making any arrangements, although those with lots of money and little time may want to book through a trekking agency in their home country. Equipment can be rented cheaply in Nepal, and it's no problem to store unneeded stuff while you're on the trail. Realise, though, that travel insurance is all the more essential if you plan to trek. In addition, **day hikes** – which offer many of the rewards of trekking with none of the red tape – are described throughout the *Guide*.

> For more on **trekking preparations and routes**, including a list of London-based trekking agencies, see Chapter Seven, *The Himalayan Trekking Regions*.

RAFTING

Compared to treks, **rafting** trips tend to be shorter, more expensive (per day), less work, not as cold nor as hot, more exciting at times, and culturally less interactive. Nepal's whitewater is fine for first-timers, and from the river you can

get fresh angles on villages and religious gatherings at sacred confluences. Most rafting companies offer a standard three-day trip, and provide all camping gear; some organise longer trips and raft-trek packages. Rafting is covered in **more detail on p.150**, and a listing of operators is given in the "On from Kathmandu" section of Chapter One.

MOUNTAIN BIKING

A **mountain bike** is the most appropriate technology of all for Nepal's rugged roads. Bikes are for rent at many outlets in Kathmandu and one or two places in Pokhara (Rs50–160 per day), and a growing number of companies run organised tours. Bring your own mountain bike (*not* a touring bike), if possible, to save money and avoid technical difficulties. Airlines will accept a bicycle as baggage at no extra charge, so long as it doesn't put you over the weight limit. No special container is needed, but you'll be expected to deflate the tyres and swivel the handlebars to be parallel with the frame. **For more on routes, equipment and techniques, see pp.141–3**.

WILDLIFE

Viewing **wildlife** in the Tarai is safari-ing with a distinctly Asian flavour: the animals most commonly seen include rhinos, monkeys, several kinds of deer and the occasional bear – tigers are spotted only rarely – and the most fun way to see them is atop an elephant. **Chitwan National Park** (p.182) is the easiest game reserve to get to, and the only one geared for budget travellers, although it's heavily used. **Bardia National Park** (p.203) and **Sukla Phanta Wildlife Reserve** (p.207) are untouristed alternatives, and for bird-watchers there's **Koshi Tappu Wildlife Reserve** (p.221). Don't forget binoculars. For **full details** on these parks see the relevant sections in the *Guide*, and for an overview of Nepal's wildlife see "Natural History" in *Contexts*.

CULTURAL HINTS

Customs and traditions run deep in Nepal. Few Nepalis get the chance to travel abroad, or even to see foreign films or media, so their only exposure to the outside world is through travellers. This puts a great responsibility on visitors to be sensitive to Nepali ways and values, and to project a favourable image of foreigners.

The dos and don'ts listed here aren't as inflexible as they sound. You'll make gaffes all the time and Nepalis will rarely say anything. The list is hardly exhaustive, either: when in doubt, do as you see Nepalis doing.

EATING

Probably the greatest number of Nepali taboos – to an outsider's way of thinking – have to do with **food**. One underlying principle is that once you've touched something to your lips it's polluted (*jutho*) for everyone else. If you take a sip from someone else's canteen, try not to let it touch your lips (and the same applies if it's your own canteen – you're expected to share). Don't eat off someone else's plate or offer anyone food you've taken a bite out of (with one exception: a wife may eat her husband's leftovers), and don't touch cooked food until you've bought it.

Another all-important point of etiquette is **eat with your right hand only**. In Nepal, as in most Asian countries, the left hand is reserved for washing after defecating; you can use it to hold a glass or utensil, but don't eat, wipe your mouth, pass food or point at someone with it. It's considered good manners to give and receive everything with the right hand – or, to convey respect, with both hands. Also remember that the family hearth is sacred, so don't throw rubbish or scraps into it.

HOUSES AND TEMPLES

Other rules have to do with **caste**. In a Hindu society, foreigners, however much they might be courted for their money, are technically casteless. In most places this isn't a big deal – and at higher elevations, people are mostly Buddhist and couldn't care less about caste – but in Hindu areas not geared up for tourists, especially in the far west, your presence will be polluting to orthodox Brahmans; don't expect to eat or sleep in a Brahman house.

Major Hindu **temples**, or their inner sanctums, are usually off-limits to non-Hindus (which in practice means foreigners). Respect this: what seems like elitism is just Hindus' way of keeping a part of their culture sacred in a country where nearly everything is open to inspection by outsiders. In most cases, you can see everything from outside anyway. Where you are allowed in, be respectful, take your shoes off before entering, don't take photos unless you've been given permission, and leave a rupee or two in the donation box. The same goes for Buddhist monasteries. Walk around Buddhist stupas and monuments clockwise – that is, keep the monument on your right.

CLOTHING AND THE BODY

Nepalis are innately conservative in their attitudes to **clothing**. Not a few are still shell-shocked from the hang-loose styles of the hippy era, and wary of all budget travellers as a result. A woman is expected to dress modestly, with legs and shoulders covered, especially in temples and monasteries: a dress or skirt that hangs to mid-calf level is best; slacks are acceptable, but shorts or a short skirt are offensive to many. A man should always wear a shirt in public, and long trousers if possible (men who wear shorts are assumed to be of a low caste). It's equally important to look clean and well groomed – travellers are rich, Nepalis reckon, and ought to look the part. You can flout these traditions, but you'll only shut yourself off from the happy encounters with locals that make travelling in Nepal so pleasant.

Still other conventions pertain to **the body**. In Nepal, the forehead is regarded as the most sacred part of the body and the feet the most profane. It's impolite to touch an adult Nepali's head, and it's an insult to kick someone. Take your shoes off when entering a private home, or follow the example of your host. When sitting, try not to point the soles of your feet at anyone. On a related note, it's bad manners to step over the legs of someone seated: in a crowded place, Nepalis will wait for you to draw in your feet so they can pass.

Nudity is a sensitive issue. When Nepali men bathe in public, they do it in their underwear, and women make a tent out of a sari or skirt.

Foreigners are expected to do likewise. Nepal has some idyllic hot springs, but most are heavily used as bathing areas; don't scare the locals off by stripping. Paradoxically, it's deemed okay to shit in the open, as in many villages there are no covered toilets – but out of sight of others, in the early morning or after dark. Men may pee in public at any time – discreetly, not wantonly – but women have to find a sheltered spot.

OTHER THINGS

Nepali views about **displays of affection** are the opposite of what most of us are used to. It's considered acceptable for friends of the same sex to hold hands or put their arms around each other in public, but not for lovers of the opposite sex. Straight couples shouldn't cuddle or kiss in public, or at least not in front of a Nepali host.

Be sensitive when **photographing people**. Ask first, and if they say no, don't press it. Don't offer money (see below). It helps if you can show pictures of your own family. Unless you've got a Polaroid, don't mislead people into thinking they'll get an instant portrait of themselves.

Finally, **be patient**. Nepal is a developing country and things don't always work or start on time. It's unrealistic to expect things to be like they are at home, even if the menu or brochure makes them sound like they will be. If a restaurant is slow in filling your order, you have to remember they've probably only got one stove. Getting angry or impatient will only confuse Nepalis and won't resolve the problem. The Nepali way of dealing with setbacks isn't to complain, or even to keep a stiff upper lip, but to laugh. It's a delightful, infectious, response. To get by with a minimum of disappointment in Nepal, the best strategy is to scale back your expectations, always double- and triple-check important arrangements, take all assurances with a pinch of salt (Nepalis will sometimes tell you what they think will make you happy rather than the truth), and find something fun to do while you're waiting.

POLICE AND TROUBLE

Nepal is one of the safest countries in the world, which is all the more remarkable when you consider the gulf between rich and poor. However, reports of theft seem to be on the rise, and political uncertainty may be bringing a general rise in lawlessness.

The only real concern still is **petty theft**, and then chiefly from fellow travellers. Common sense suggests a few precautions. Carry valuables in a money belt or pouch around your neck at all times. Bring along a padlock for securing your room and baggage; it doesn't have to be big – deterrence is the main thing. In a dormitory, keep your kit locked up and your camera gear with you. A bag stowed on the roof of a bus is probably safe, but place it well forward where it will be hidden under the luggage tarpaulin.

If you're robbed, report it as soon as possible to the local police. They're apt to be friendly and consoling, if not much help. For insurance purposes, go to the **Interpol Section** of the main police headquarters in Naksal, Kathmandu, to fill in a report, a copy of which you'll need to retain to claim from your insurer once you're back home. Bring a photocopy of the pages in your passport containing your photo and your Nepalese visa, together with two passport photos. Dress smartly and expect an uphill battle – they're jaded by stolen-travellers'-cheque scams.

Violent crime is extremely rare. Women probably shouldn't walk alone after dark, but the danger of getting raped or assaulted in a populated area is statistically insignificant. The countryside is equally safe, except for one or two stretches along the Tibetan border where the government still hasn't quite introduced law and order. In the light of a few isolated trekking incidents, it's advisable not to walk alone in remote parts (see Chapter Seven).

There are several ways to get on the wrong side of the law, none of them worth it. **Smuggling** is the usual cause of serious trouble – drugs and gold are the big no-nos, and if you get caught with commercial quantities of either you'll be looking at a more or less automatic five to twenty years in prison (see "The Jails" in Chapter One for a description of that edifying experience). Give a wide berth to anyone in Hong Kong or Singapore offering "courier" jobs to Kathmandu: smuggling illicit electronics into Nepal, or antiques out, could also put you behind bars.

While it would be incredibly stupid to go through immigration control with drugs, discreet **possession** inside the country carries virtually no risk; flash dope around, though, and you could conceivably get shopped by an innkeeper. If you're religious, don't try to convert anyone – **proselytising** is against the law and carries a sentence of up to six years. An American and a Canadian spent three months in jail in 1989 before being acquitted of distributing Christian pamphlets.

In Nepal, where government servants are poorly paid, a little **bakshish** sometimes greases the wheels.

Nepalese police don't make busts simply in order to get bribes, but if you're accused of something it might not hurt to make an offer, in a an extremely careful, euphemistic and deniable way. This shouldn't be necessary if you're the *victim*, although you may feel like offering a reward.

WOMEN'S NEPAL

Nepal is a relatively easy place for women to travel: Kathmandu and Pokhara are the only places where you're likely to run into Western-style hustlers, but even they are seldom sinister and easily shrugged off. The main reason you will be of interest is as a foreigner rather than a woman, and, as such, the atmosphere is tolerant and inquisitive rather than threatening or dangerous. However, it is important to be sensitive to local customs – shorts and skimpy clothes are considered offensive.

Outside the relative sophistication of Kathmandu, Hindu **Nepali women** are a long, long way from liberation. In remote rural areas, they're considered their husband's or father's chattel, given or taken in marriage for the price of a buffalo – a status reinforced by law. Orthodox Hindus, while in the minority, reveal the extent of female subjugation – they believe a woman is ritually unclean during menstruation and for ten days after giving birth, and that she must remain apart during that period and drink cow's urine to cleanse herself. Polygamy is widely practiced in the hills, and if a woman doesn't produce a son she's liable to be replaced. Sherpanis and other Buddhist women are treated much more equally, but the average Nepali woman does the work of ten men.

The **women's movement** is embryonic. Aid projects and agencies such as the *Nepal Women's Organisation* (Pulchowk, Patan) are chiefly concerned with setting up cottage-industry employment for women, so they can earn spare cash as a first step to some sort of self-determination. The *Centre for Women and Development*, PO Box 3637, Kathmandu, is a non-governmental organisation set up by a group of professional women in order to collect and disseminate information on women's issues and development projects.

For **further discussion of women's issues in Nepal**, and one Western woman's account of living and working in the country, see the Rough Guide Special *Women Travel: Adventures, Advice and Experience* (Harrap Columbus £6.95).

HARRASSMENT AND SAFETY

Sexual harrassment in Nepal is low-key and need rarely upset your travels. **Staring and catcalling** is on the increase in Kathmandu, mostly by groups of young lads who seem to have acquired the stereotype, gleaned from imported videos, of all Western women as sexually available – but it's nowhere near as bad as in India, or indeed most of Asia, and it doesn't go any further than words.

Nepali society is on the whole chaste, almost prudish. Men are almost universally respectful, and perhaps a little in awe, of foreign women. That said, enough trekking guides have apparently had liaisons with foreign females that a few have acquired a taste for conquest; if you suspect ulterior motives, let him down gently and he'll usually retreat gracefully.

A woman **travelling or trekking alone** won't be hassled so much as pitied. Going alone (*eklai*)

is most un-Nepali behaviour. Locals (of both sexes) will ask if you haven't got a husband – the question is usually asked out of genuine concern, not as a come-on – and teaming up with another woman stops the comments as effectively as being with a man. As a foreign woman, about the only other form of discrimination you'll encounter is during toilet stops on bus journeys, when you'll have to hunt around for a sheltered place while men are free to pee by the side of the road.

STAYING ON

The Nepalese government is making it a lot harder to stay on legitimately these days, although a few dodges still exist. The main obstacle is that you can't stay longer than three months at a time on a tourist visa, or four months in any twelve-month period.

It's against the rules to work on a tourist visa, but plenty of people do anyway – notably as **trekking and rafting guides**. However, you'd have to have made several trips to Nepal, or already be experienced and well-connected in the adventure-travel business, to find work as a guide. Guides are usually hired on a freelance basis, so the work is only seasonal.

If you haven't got any particular skills, and just want an open-ended arrangement for a few weeks or so, **teaching English** is a good way to become a temporary local. Language schools in Kathmandu and Pokhara take people on with no previous experience, although the pay is negligible.

Volunteer opportunities are where you find them. Tashi Palkhel, one of the former Tibetan refugee camps near Pokhara, welcomes help, and no doubt many other aid organisations wouldn't say no to a willing dogsbody. People with **medical qualifications** are always needed. The *Himalayan Rescue Association* accepts four doctors each autumn and spring to staff its high-altitude aid posts; the waiting list is two or three years long, but it can't hurt to send a c.v. to Dr David Shlim, Director, Himalayan Rescue Association, GPO Box 495, Kathmandu, Nepal.

Postings with **VSO (Voluntary Service Overseas)** abound, providing you've got the relevant skills and the bottle to stay two or more years. People with experience in education, health, nutrition, agriculture, forestry and other areas are needed. VSO doesn't instigate its own projects, but places volunteers in existing projects where technical help is needed; a small stipend is paid. VSO's UK address is 317 Putney Bridge Road, London SW15 2PN (☎081/780 2266). Many other aid agencies (eg Action Aid, Christian Aid and Oxfam) operate in Nepal and occasionally hire specialists. See "Development Dilemmas" in *Contexts* to get an idea of what you'd be dealing with.

STUDY

The only known way to turn a tourist visa into a resident visa is to **study** at Tribhuwan University's *Campus of International Languages* in Kathmandu. One-year courses in Nepali, Tibetan, Sanskrit and Newari begin in July, which isn't climatically convenient, although they're considering offering a six-month Nepali course starting in February. Classes run for two hours a day, five days a week, and a year's tuition is Rs2250. Apply no later than June with a letter of recommendation from your embassy or university to: Mr G. P. Upreti, Campus Chief, Campus of International Languages, Exhibition Road, Bhrikuti Mandap, Kathmandu, Nepal (☎226713). The university will sort out your visa. See "Listings" in the *Kathmandu* chapter for other schools offering intensive language courses. Other possibilities are listed in the "Meditation, Yoga and Massage" section in the same chapter.

DIRECTORY

ADDRESSES don't exist in Nepal: few streets even have names, and houses are never numbered. In cities, though, intersections or neighbourhoods (*tol*) usually have names and these are gradually lending themselves to the major streets nearby.

BAGS An internal-frame backpack is probably best for heaving your things around on buses and rikshas, especially if you're also travelling in other parts of Asia. A travel pack, with shoulder straps that can be zipped out of sight, will help dispel lingering "hippy" prejudices when dealing with officialdom; best of all is one in which all compartments can be secured with a single padlock. A lightweight daypack also comes in handy. For trekking, more specialised packs are easily rentable in Kathmandu.

BOOKS No need to lug a library along: Kathmandu and Pokhara each have dozens of bookshops that are devoted to travel, fiction and classics, new and used, in English and other European languages. Most will buy books or trade as well.

CHILDREN Travelling with children can be both challenging and rewarding – kids always help break the ice with strangers, and among Nepalis they unleash even more than the usual hospitality (although the lack of privacy may prove to be a problem). Poor sanitation, dogs, traffic and steep slopes are hazards parents have to watch out for. Disposable nappies and baby foods aren't available in Nepal. Older children might turn up their noses at some of the food.

CONTRACEPTIVES Condoms are available in pharmacies everywhere, but not the pill.

CUSTOMS officers are fairly lax on entry, but they might note fancy video gear in your passport so you can't sell it in Nepal. They check more thoroughly on departure, mainly to make sure you're not smuggling antiques out.

DISABLED TRAVELLERS will have a hard time with Nepal's steep slopes and uneven pavements; stairs and steps are a fact of life throughout the hills. However, a safari in one of the Tarai wildlife parks is perfectly feasible, and even a trek, catered to your needs by an agency, might not be out of the question.

DRUGS Cannabis grows wild throughout hill Nepal, and old folks sometimes smoke it as an evening tonic. Touts in Kathmandu – shady characters, but not informants – mostly peddle local hash, and also whisper offers of opium and heroin from the Golden Triangle. See the section on "Police and Trouble" for legalities.

ELECTRICITY is 220 volts AC, where you can get it. The bigger hill towns and most of the Tarai are electrified, but most villages aren't. Virtually all power is generated by hydroelectric projects, so "load shedding" (ie power cuts) is common in spring when water levels get low.

EMBASSIES AND CONSULATES are all in Kathmandu: see Chapter One for listings.

EMERGENCIES Where there's a phone, dial ☎100 for the police or ☎102 for an ambulance – but it's better to get a Nepali-speaker to do the talking. Registering with your embassy can expedite things in the event of an emergency.

GAY LIFE Nepalis will tell you gay sex doesn't happen, or it's "something that Indians do". For sure, there are no gay bars or meeting places or any support network whatsoever, even in the capital. Yet in a society where the sexes are kept well apart before marriage, and men routinely hold hands and sleep together, it obviously goes on – and often, it's said, among Buddhist monks. The only approach a gay traveller is likely to get is from touts who might offer, at the end of a long inventory of drugs, "nice Nepali girls", and if that doesn't work, boys. But it's nothing like the scene in Southeast Asia.

LAUNDRY Tourist guest houses generally take laundry, although the turn-around time depends on the weather. Rates are reasonable – a few rupees per item. If you're doing your own, detergent is sold in inexpensive packets in Kathmandu, although a concentrated liquid (like *Dylon Travel Wash*) is less messy.

LEFT LUGGAGE Guest houses will always store bags for you, an invaluable service if you go trekking or anytime you just want to travel light. The usual charge is Rs1 per item per day, although some places waive this if you take a room when you return.

ODD ESSENTIALS Earplugs are a must for shutting out the sound of barking dogs at night. In cheap lodgings, a sleeping sheet is an insurance policy against fleas and the like. Mosquitoes can be a problem in the Tarai: bring repellent, or buy coils locally. A small padlock (available locally) is an effective deterrent to would-be thieves. For trekking essentials, see Chapter Seven.

TIME in Nepal is 15 minutes ahead of India – just to be contrary, one suspects – and 5 hours 45 minutes ahead of GMT.

TIPPING isn't expected, except in the classier restaurants where service is often added to the bill, but a few rupees on a dinner at a budget tourist place is appreciated. Don't tip taxi drivers.

TOILETS, where they exist, range from "Western" (sit-down) flush jobs to two planks projected over a stream. In lodges – tourist ones aside – the norm is a squat toilet, usually pretty stinky and flyblown. A public toilet will often be nothing but a designated field; when in doubt, you should ask *Chaarpi kahaa chha?* (Where is the toilet?). Toilet paper is only provided in pricier hotels: Nepalis use a jug of water and the left hand.

PART TWO

THE
GUIDE

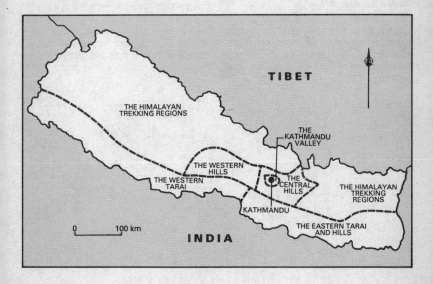

Map of Nepal showing:

TIBET

THE HIMALAYAN
TREKKING REGIONS

THE
KATHMANDU
VALLEY

THE WESTERN
HILLS

THE WESTERN
TARAI

THE
CENTRAL
HILLS

THE HIMALAYAN
TREKKING
REGIONS

KATHMANDU

THE EASTERN TARAI
AND HILLS

0   100 km

INDIA

CHAPTER ONE

KATHMANDU

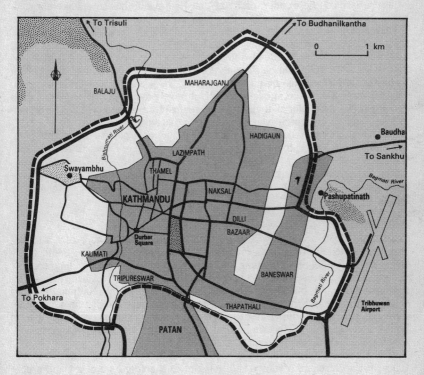

And the wildest dreams of Kew are the facts in Kathmandu ...

Rudyard Kipling "In the Neolithic Age" (1895).

Not even Kipling could have dreamed up buffalo sukiyaki with rum raisin cheesecake. **Kathmandu** has changed beyond recognition in the past two decades – or at least a small part of it has. Thamel, where most travellers congregate, is like a thumping, Third World theme park, all hotels and hoardings and promises, promises, with touts flogging carpets and hashish to holiday hippies, while the words "Cake and Pie" blaze from restaurant windows like a mantra. Yet Thamel is the exception to the rule. Walk one minute in any direction from the tourist quarter and you'll find yourself in the real Kathmandu: frenetic, filthy, otherworldly, an extravagant blend of chaos and dignity, breathtaking architecture, stunning pageantry, and history so alive you can smell it; of dark alleys, barefoot porters, vegetable sellers and sacred cows.

Nepal's capital is, moreover, a centre of great cultural sophistication. Despite a population of just 350,000 people, it is Nepal's biggest and most cosmopolitan city – a meeting place of a dozen ethnic groups, and the hometown of the Newars, Nepal's master craftsmen and traders extraordinaire. Trade, indeed, created Kathmandu – for at least a thousand years it controlled the most important caravan route between Tibet and India – and trade has always funded the city's Newar artisans. Little wonder, perhaps, that Kathmandu has so deftly embraced the tourist business, while keeping its art and culture fundamentally intact.

Kathmandu is likely to be your first port of call in Nepal – all international flights land in the capital, and most roads lead to it – and you're bound to spend at least a few days here. It's the obvious place to sort out your affairs: it has all the embassies and airline offices, the only Poste Restante in Nepal, and a welter of **trekking and travel agencies** for arranging treks, rafting and cycle trips. At least as important, in the minds of long-haul travellers anyway, are Kathmandu's **restaurants** – which, for all their hype, serve the cheapest and best Western food in Asia – and the amazingly easy **social scene** that surrounds them.

For mainly practical reasons, Kathmandu is the most popular base for seeing the Kathmandu Valley, though by no means the only one. Patan, Bhaktapur and the valley's other towns and sights are covered in Chapter Two, *The Kathmandu Valley*. Besides being worthy day trips, many of these places make excellent overnight bases for exploring the nether regions of the valley, or just escaping the bubble of Kathmandu.

A little history

People must have occupied what is now Kathmandu for thousands of years, but chroniclers attribute the city's founding to Gunakama Deva, who could have reigned anytime between the ninth and twelfth centuries – by which time sophisticated urban centres had already been established by the **Lichhavi** kings at Pashupatinath and other sites in the surrounding valley. Kathmandu was originally known as Kirtipur ("City of Glory"), but it later took its present name from the **Kasthamandap** ("House of Wood") that was constructed as a rest house along the main Tibet–India trade route in the late twelfth century, and which still stands in the city centre.

The city rose to prominence under the **Malla** kings, who took control of the valley in the thirteenth century and ushered in a golden age of art and architecture that lasted more than 500 years; all of Kathmandu's finest buildings and monuments, including those of its spectacular **Durbar Square**, date from this period. At the start of the Malla era, Kathmandu ranked as a sovereign state alongside the valley's other two major cities, Bhaktapur and Patan, but soon fell under the rule of Bhaktapur. The cities were again divided in the fifteenth century, and a long period of intrigue and rivalry followed.

Malla rule ended abruptly in 1769, when Prithvi Narayan Shah of Gorkha, a previously undistinguished hill state to the west, captured the valley as the first conquest in his historic unification of Nepal. Kathmandu actually did rather well out of the new order, being made capital of the new nation and seat of the new **Shah** dynasty. The Shahs rule to this day, although from 1846 to 1951 they were politically outmanoeuvred by the powerful **Rana** family, who ruled as hereditary prime ministers and left the capital with a legacy of enormous white (now mouldy grey) neoclassical palaces.

ORIENTATION AND ACCOMMODATION

Despite chaotic first appearances, Kathmandu is surprisingly easy to get to grips with; the touts, like everything else, become much more manageable once you've dumped your bags. The following should help with **orientation**.

Tradition has it that old Kathmandu was laid out in the shape of a *khukuri* knife. Positioned at what would be the hilt of the knife is **Durbar Square** – a non-stop carnival set amidst temples, monuments and the former royal palace – while the city's oldest neighbourhoods stretch northeast and (to a lesser extent) south-west. **New Road**, the city's best-known shopping street, runs east from the square. Kathmandu's budget hotels are concentrated in two areas: **Thamel**, north of Durbar Square in a new part of town, and Jhochhen, better known as **Freak Street**, immediately south of the square.

Suburban Kathmandu sprawls mainly east of **Kantipath**, the main north–south thoroughfare, and is dominated by two landmarks, the **Royal Palace** and the **Tudikhel** (parade ground). Most of the expensive hotels, restaurants and airline offices huddle along **Durbar Marg**, the broad boulevard running south from the palace gate. West of the Bishnumati River is not, strictly speaking, part of Kathmandu, but the hilltop temple of **Swayambu** is close enough to be reached easily on foot.

The **maps** provided in this chapter should suffice for most purposes, but for more detail you'll want to pick up a tourist map (sold everywhere) or, better still, HMG Survey Department's "Central Kathmandu" (sporadically available at bigger bookstores).

Arriving and getting around

Arriving by air at **Tribhuwan International Airport's** shiny new terminal, 5km east of the city centre, make straight for the **bank**, which offers the same (official) rate as everywhere else (but see "Costs, Money and Banks" in *Basics* for details of black-market moneychanging). To get into town, **taxi** fares are quasi-fixed at Rs60 (Rs80 for two people). Alternatively, take the **blue (Sajha) bus**, charging Rs15, from the terminal forecourt (daily 8am–10pm); once in town it heads north along Kantipath, and drops passengers off within a few minutes' walk of most guest houses and hotels. The crowded **local bus**, leaving from the far end of the airport drive and terminating at Ratna Park, north of Tudikhel, only costs Rs1.50, but it's murder if you're carrying lots of baggage.

Arriving **by bus from India**, you'll pull into the **main bus park**, about 1km from most lodgings. You could walk, assuming you know where you're going, but it's simpler to take a riksha – figure on Rs15 for the ride, which is longer than it looks because of the one-way system. Tourist buses **from Pokhara** deposit passengers either in Thamel or near the GPO at Bhimsen Tower, a five-minute walk from Freak Street. Night buses stop at Bhimsen Tower.

The telephone code for Kathmandu is ☎01

Getting around the city is easiest by bike or on foot. **Bicycles** are for hire literally everywhere in Thamel and Freak Street (roughly Rs15 a day), and many hotels have their own cycles for rent; bargain for a long-term discount. Kathmandu is the only place in Nepal where **mountain bikes** and **motorcycles** can easily be rented (see "Listings"). Vehicles with four wheels (or even three) make slow progress through the old part of town, but have their place for longer journeys. Pedal **rikshas** cruise for custom nearly everywhere; pay no more than Rs5 per kilometre and, needless to say, establish terms *before* setting off. **Taxis** and **motor rikshas** are metered, but after 8pm they add 50 percent to the indicated fare. They tend to hang out at the main Thamel intersection, along Durbar Marg and at the bus station, but get scarce after dark – try the night taxi service (☎224374). **Tempos** (fixed-route motor rikshas) shuttle from near the *Air India* office on Kantipath north to Maharajganj and Balaju, and from the GPO south to Patan. Cheapest, but slowest and most crowded, are the **public buses** and minibuses, which run along regular but unnumbered routes; details are given where relevant in this chapter and the next.

Finding somewhere to stay

Kathmandu is well-stocked with all kinds of **accommodation**. At the budget end of the spectrum, it's just a matter of hitting the guest houses: they're all cheek by jowl, so if one's full you can just try the next. In the autumn high season the prominent Thamel lodges fill up early, yet there'll always be vacancies at smaller places nearby. If arriving by air, free local phones at the airport are handy for making provisional bookings. Touts often offer a free ride if you stay at their lodge, but such places usually have little to recommend them (and they bump up their prices to pay for your ride).

Budget places

Budget tourism in Nepal was born on **Freak Street** (Jhochhen Tol) in the late 1960s, and, being the most run-down area now, its prices are the lowest (rooms for as little as Rs25). In the 1980s, **Thamel** emerged as a smarter, more respectable alternative (basic rooms here range upwards of Rs50). While Thamel's restaurants will probably remain top of the pops for a long while yet, its lodges are losing some ground to a new wave of more **upmarket guest houses** popping up around the fringes of Thamel; constructed to stricter building codes, these tend to quote their rates in US dollars, with rooms costing anything from $2 to $10.

Prices are influenced by supply and demand, and thus completely fluid. More and more guest houses are printing "tariff" cards, which is what prices given here are based on, but in slow times expect discounts of up to 50 percent. You should also be able to negotiate a better rate for longer stays. As a rule, Kathmandu innkeepers are tremendously helpful and good-humoured people. In winter, when Kathmandu can be cold and clammy, they'll provide kapok quilts, but only the most upmarket guest houses have heaters. Finally, try to get a room that doesn't overlook the street: Kathmandu's barking dogs and early-morning throat-clearing are enough to wake the dead.

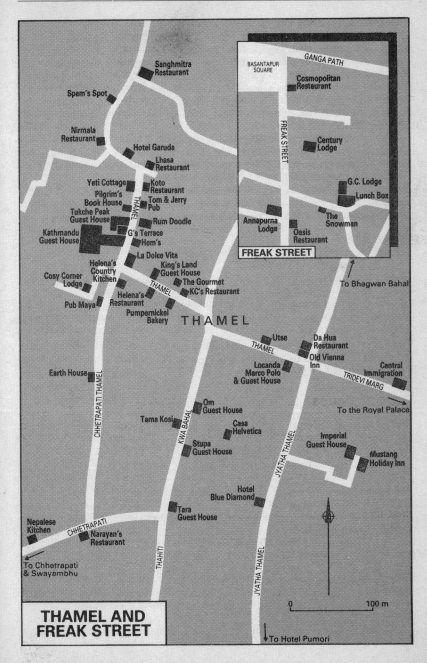

THAMEL

FREAK STREET

GANGA PATH

BASANTAPUR SQUARE

Cosmopolitan Restaurant

FREAK STREET

Century Lodge

G.C. Lodge

Lunch Box

Annapurna Lodge

Oasis Restaurant

The Snowman

Sanghmitra Restaurant

Spam's Spot

Nirmala Restaurant

Hotel Garuda

Lhasa Restaurant

Yeti Cottage

Koto Restaurant

Pilgrim's Book House

Tom & Jerry Pub

Tukche Peak Guest House

Rum Doodle

Kathmandu Guest House

G's Terrace

Hem's

La Dolce Vita

Helena's Country Kitchen

King's Land Guest House

Cosy Corner Lodge

The Gourmet

KC's Restaurant

Pub Maya

Helena's Restaurant

Pumpernickel Bakery

THAMEL

THAMEL

Utse

Da Hua Restaurant

To Bhagwan Bahal

THAMEL

Old Vienna Inn

Central Immigration

Locanda Marco Polo & Guest House

TRIDEVI MARG

Earth House

CHHETRAPATI THAMEL

Om Guest House

To the Royal Palace

Tama Kosi

KWA BAHAL

Casa Helvetica

JYATHA THAMEL

Stupa Guest House

Imperial Guest House

Mustang Holiday Inn

Hotel Blue Diamond

Nepalese Kitchen

CHHETRAPATI

Tara Guest House

Narayan's Restaurant

THAHITI

To Chhetrapati & Swayambhu

JYATHA THAMEL

0   100 m

THAMEL AND FREAK STREET

To Hotel Pumori

Rock bottom: Freak Street

Little remains to remind you of Freak Street's hippy heyday. Bona fide hippies have been an endangered species in Nepal ever since 1974, when the present king, then new to the throne, passed a series of immigration and drug laws that made life more difficult for them. But for a few oldtimers – and plenty of newcomers – Freak Street retains certain advantages. It may be scruffy, but it's very central, with loads more character than Thamel. Remember that lodge owners in this area come under periodic police pressure to check passports and snoop for dope.

Annapurna Lodge, (☎213684). The cleanest of the old Freak Street pack. Singles without bath Rs60, doubles Rs80; with bath, Rs100/120.

Century Lodge, (☎214341). The building, though dilapidated, features some fine traditional carved windows. Singles Rs30, doubles Rs45; Rs55 with bath.

G.C. Lodge, A real dive, mentioned here only for its knock-down prices. Singles Rs25, doubles Rs45.

Kumari Lodge, Right on Durbar Square, it's as grotty as they come but it might be worth the Rs100 for one of its triple rooms with a view in the front; don't bother with the Rs60 doubles at the back.

Cheap guest houses in Thamel

A budget travellers' pleasure dome, Thamel nevertheless ensures a comfortable and sociable stay, with a great choice of budget restaurants and a growing (but still tame) nightlife scene. On the other hand, it's a rather long, jostling walk to the sights of Kathmandu. The name Thamel is nowadays casually applied to everything from Paknajol in the west to Jyatha in the east. The lodges listed here are the grittier, mostly older ones in Thamel proper and along the three streets that extend southwards to Thahiti.

Cosy Corner Lodge, Thamel (☎417799). One of several cheap and cheerful outfits tucked away in a quiet yet central cul-de-sac. Singles Rs44, doubles Rs66.

Earth House, Chhetrapati Thamel. Idiosyncratic, its traditional architecture making a welcome change. Singles Rs66, doubles Rs99; Rs165/198 with bath.

King's Land Guest House, Thamel (☎417129). Perhaps the best deal on this street, the trendy heart of Thamel, but no sitting area. Singles Rs60, doubles Rs80; Rs80/100 with bath.

Marco Polo Guest House, Thamel (☎227914). Tidy and relaxing, excellent value for such a central location. Singles Rs60, doubles Rs90; Rs150 with bath.

Stupa Guest House, Kwa Bahal (☎226658). The best garden you'll find for the price; rooms are basic. Singles Rs50, doubles Rs70; Rs150 with bath. If it's full, *Tara Guest House* next door and *Om Guest House* further north are almost as good.

Tukche Peak Guest House, Thamel (☎215739). Has the advantage of the pleasant outdoor seating of its *Sungava Restaurant*. Singles Rs60, doubles Rs90; Rs105/125 with bath.

Yeti Cottage, north Thamel (☎417089). A funky old building shaped like a grand piano with a good restaurant and plenty of greenery, though somewhat monopolised by overland groups. Singles Rs60, doubles Rs80.

Upmarket guest houses in and around Thamel

These slicker budget places tend to quote their prices in dollars, though in most cases you can pay in rupees; 10 or 12 percent government tax is usually added.

Kathmandu Guest House, (☎413632). Thamel's original guest house is still the best, set well back from the noisy street, with efficient management and a gorgeous garden. It's a huge and social place: exciting or pretentious, depending on your outlook. Rooms are always

Rakesh Adhikari U2 collection
shop no - 314/325
21 century, super market

in demand, and booked up well ahead during the high season. Singles without bath in the old wing start at $2, doubles $3; $7/$9 and up with bath; $14/$17 in the new wing.

Hotel Garuda, north Thamel (☎416776). A smart new place with friendly staff. Singles with bath from $8, doubles $10.

Hotel Shrestha, Tahachal (☎270528; near the National Museum). Quiet and out-of-the-way, this might be a good choice if you've got kids. Singles Rs75, doubles Rs100; Rs150/200 with bath.

Marsyangdi Mandla Guest House, Chhetrapati (☎227988). Clean and well-run. Singles $3, doubles $4; $4/$6 with bath.

Mustang Holiday Inn, Jyatha Thamel (☎226538). Courteous, helpful staff and a pleasant garden. Singles start at $3, doubles $4.50; $5/$7 and up with bath. If it's full, try the nearby *Imperial Guest House* (☎229339) where rooms with bath are $7/10.

Sanghmitra, north Thamel (☎411991). Mainly a restaurant, but it has a few rooms and two exquisite, fragrant gardens. Singles Rs200, doubles Rs250 without bath.

Tibet Guest House, Chhetrapati. (☎214383) Friendly, and with a really lovely roof garden. Singles and doubles $9; $12.25/$13.25 with bath.

Moderate and expensive hotels

The posh hotels are more spread out, so it's advisable to have a particular place in mind before setting off. Most are members of the Nepal Hotel Association, which operates a reservation desk at the airport, but you could just as easily make your own phone calls. Tax of 12–15 percent (rising with the number of stars) isn't included in the prices given below.

Moderate

Hotel Ambassador, Lazimpath (☎410432). Two stars. All mod cons at a reasonable price. Singles with bath $19, doubles $22.

Hotel Blue Diamond, Jyatha Thamel (☎226392). Two stars. No great shakes, but the cheapest air-conditioning in Nepal. Singles $16, doubles $19.

Hotel Vajra, Bijeshwari (☎272719). Two stars. Unquestionably the best in its class: beautifully appointed, with a library, theatre and art gallery, and tremendous views of Swayambhunath from the roof terrace. Definitely worth a splurge. Singles with sink $11, doubles $13; with bath, $19/$23 and up.

Expensive

Everest Hotel, Baneswar (Airport Road; ☎220567). Five stars. Pool, tennis, gym, disco. Singles $100, doubles $110.

Hotel de l'Annapurna, Durbar Marg (☎221711) . Five stars. Pool, sauna, the works. Singles $80, doubles $90.

Hotel Malla, Lekhnath Marg (☎410320). Four stars. Small, with an excellent Chinese restaurant. Singles $78, doubles $92.

Hotel Shangrila, Lazimpath (☎412999). Four stars. Singles $65, doubles $80.

Hotel Shanker, Lazimpath (☎410151). Three stars. A fabulous converted Rana palace with an entrance that has to be seen to be believed. Singles $65, doubles $80.

Hotel Yak & Yeti, Durbar Marg (☎222635). Five stars. Pool, tennis, opulent restaurants. Singles $95, doubles $105.

Hotel Yellow Pagoda, Kantipath (☎220337). Three stars. Central. Singles $50, doubles $60 including breakfast.

— Bhishop - Market.

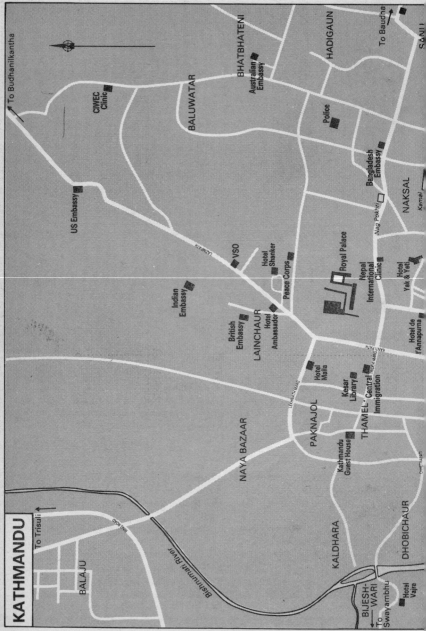

KATHMANDU

To Trisuli

BALAJU

Bishnumati River

Bhit Kulo

KALDHARA

DHOBICHAUR

BIJESH-WARI
To Swayambhu

Hotel Vajra

NAYA BAZAAR

PAKNAJOL

Kathmandu Guest House

THAMEL

Kesar Library

Central Immigration

Hotel Malla

LAINCHAUR

British Embassy

Hotel Ambassador

Indian Embassy

LEKHNATH MARG

KANTIPATH

Peace Corps

Hotel Shanker

VSO

LAZIMPATH

US Embassy

To Budhanilkantha

CIWEC Clinic

BALUWATAR

BHATBHATENI

Australian Embassy

HADIGAUN

To Baudha

Police

Bangladesh Embassy

NAKSAL

Nag Pokhri

Kamal

SANI

Royal Palace

Nepal International Clinic

Hotel Yak & Yeti

Hotel de l'Annapurna

DURBAR MARG

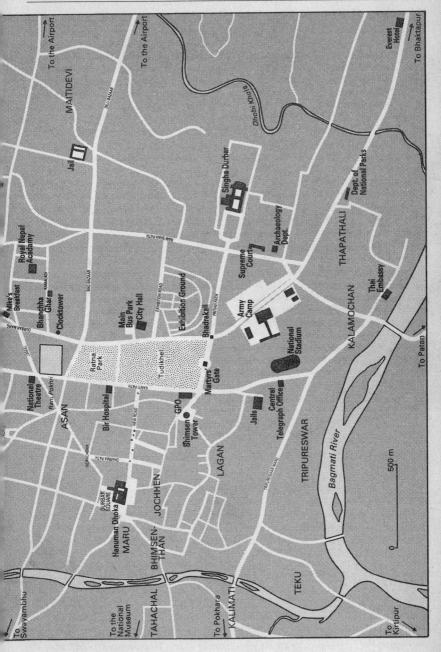

To the Airport

To the Airport

MAITIDEVI

Jail

Dhobi Khola

To Bhaktapur

Everest Hotel

Singha Durbar

Dept. of National Parks

Royal Nepal Academy

RAM SHAH PATH

Archaeology Dept.

THAPATHALI

Mike's Breakfast

Bhenchha Ghar

Clocktower

BAG BAZAAR

Exhibition Ground

PRITHVI PATH

Supreme Court

Thai Embassy

Main Bus Park

City Hall

EXHIBITION ROAD

Bhadrakali

Army Camp

KALAMOCHAN

DURBAR MARG

National Theatre

Ratna Park

Rani Pokhri

Tudikhel

National Stadium

To Patan

ASAN

KANTI PATH

Martyrs Gate

Bir Hospital

NEW ROAD

GPO

Jails

Central Telegraph Office

Bhimsen Tower

LAGAN

TRIPURESWAR

TRIPURESWAR MARG

Bagmati River

DHARMA PATH

DURBAR SQUARE

JOCHHEN

Hanuman Dhoka

MARU

BHIMSEN-THAN

500 m

0

To Swayambhu

To the National Museum

TAHACHAL

KALIMATI

To Pokhara

TEKU

To Kirtipur

To Swayambhu

THE CITY

The scene on Thamel avenue today: a very pretty pale-brown cow standing on the sidewalk, between a cigarette stand and an umbrella repairman, her head lifted straight up, perpendicular with the ground, while a ten-year-old boy heading home from school stood there, reaching up and scratching the animal's neck. Meanwhile all the tourists pointing to the fruit-bats hanging in the trees. The smell of bat shit and garbage and day-old murk, literally Another Shitty Day in Paradise. Shangri-la's getting wasted, but you can still stand on the street corner in Kathmandu and scratch her heavy velvet throat.

Jeff Greenwald *Mister Raja's Neighborhood*

The Kathmandu most travellers come to see is the **old city**, a tight tangle of narrow alleys and numerous temples immediately north and south of the central Durbar Square. It's a bustling, intensely urban quarter where tall, extended-family dwellings – built of traditional brick and wood or, increasingly, concrete – block out the sun, dark, open-fronted shops crowd the lanes, and vegetable sellers clot the intersections. Though the city goes to bed early, from before dawn to around 10pm there's always something happening somewhere. Early morning is the best time to watch people going about their daily religious rites (*puja*), adorning idols with red paste (*sindur*) and marigold petals. If you walk around after dinner, especially in the neighbourhoods of Indrachowk, Asan and Chhetrapati, you'll frequently run across mesmerising hymn-sings.

This is only one side of Kathmandu, though, and not necessarily representative of the rest. Across the Bishnumati River, just **west** of town, is a more newly settled area which is still rural in parts; the famous Swayambhu stupa, magnificently set on a conical hill here, has attracted a large community of expatriate Tibetans, whose culture is a world apart from that of Kathmandu's indigenous Newars.

Most commerce these days is conducted **east** of the old quarter: the boulevards around the Royal Palace are wide and businesslike, lined with airline offices and five-star hotels, while tinny, congested bazaars sprawl further to the south and east. The northeast is given over to quiet, tree-lined suburbs.

Durbar Square

Teeming, touristy **DURBAR SQUARE** is the natural place to begin sightseeing. The old Royal Palace (*durbar*), running along the eastern edge of the square, takes up more space than all the other monuments here combined. Kumari Chowk, home of Kathmandu's "living goddess", overlooks the square from the south. The square itself is squeezed by the palace into two parts: at the southern end is the Kasthamandap, the ancient building that probably gave Kathmandu its name, while the northern part of the square is taken up by a varied procession of statues and temples.

Hanuman Dhoka

The rambling **old Royal Palace** (Sun–Thurs 10.30am–4.15pm; 10.30am–3.15pm in winter; Fri 10.30am–2.15pm; Rs10) – usually called **Hanuman Dhoka**, after its main entrance – was built over the course of almost four centuries. Its oldest,

KATHMANDU CULTURE: THE NEWARS

Although only a minor ethnic group in national terms, the **Newars** account for three-quarters of Kathmandu's population and exert a cultural influence in Nepal far beyond their numbers. Some scholars make the Newars out to be descendants of the Kiratas, who ruled the Kathmandu Valley between the seventh century BC and the second century AD, while others say they go back even further than that; in any case, the Newar community has had to absorb successive waves of immigrants, refugees, traders and usurpers ever since, resulting in a complex cultural matrix.

Centuries of domination by foreign rulers have, if anything, only accentuated the uniqueness of Newar culture. For 1500 years the Newars have sustained an almost continuous artistic flowering: under the Lichhavis they produced acclaimed stone carvings, and under the Mallas and Shahs they've excelled in wood, metal and brick. They're believed to have invented the **pagoda**, and it was a Newar architect, Arniko, who led a Nepalese delegation in the thirteenth century to introduce the technique to the Chinese. The pagoda style of stacked, angled roofs finds unique expression in Nepalese (read Newar) temples, and if you look closely you'll see that it's echoed in the overhanging eaves of Newar houses, too.

The shape of Newar settlements goes right to the roots of Newar civilisation: farming and trade. As farmers, Newars build their **villages** in compact, urban nuclei to conserve the fertile farmland of the valley. As traders, they construct their houses with removable wooden shutters, so that the ground floor can double as a shop. Scattered, in part, by the shortage of land in the valley, Newar traders have colonised lucrative crossroads throughout Nepal, recreating bustling **bazaars** wherever they go.

But above all, Newars are consummate city-builders. The fundamental building-block of old Newar **cities** is the **bahal** – a set of buildings joined at right angles around a central courtyard. Kathmandu is honeycombed with *bahals*, many of which were originally built as Buddhist monasteries, but have reverted to residential use during the past two centuries as state-sponsored Hinduism has chipped away at Newar Buddhism. *Bahal* architecture was applied to palaces as well, as a look at a map of Durbar Square will readily

demonstrate. Another uniquely Newar invention is the *guthi* – a benevolent community trust that handles the upkeep of temples (*mandir*) and fountains (*hiti*), organises festivals and arranges cremations of deceased members. Strangely, for a people so advanced in urban planning, Newars are still fairly clueless about sanitation.

Newars are easily recognisable: one dead giveaway is that they carry heavy loads in baskets suspended at either end of a **shoulder pole** (*nol*), whereas other Nepali hill people carry things on their backs, supported by a tumpline from the forehead. As for **clothing**, you can usually tell a Newar man by his waistcoat, and a woman by her shawl (it used to be the fashion for Newar women to wear their saris in complicated pleats, requiring upwards of twenty-five metres of material, but these days most follow the Indian style). Newars still speak among themselves in **Newari**, a Tibeto-Burman language, and several Newari newspapers are published in Kathmandu; but with the lure of good government jobs strong, many young Newars are neglecting their native tongue for Nepali. For a detailed description of Newar **religion**, see *Contexts*.

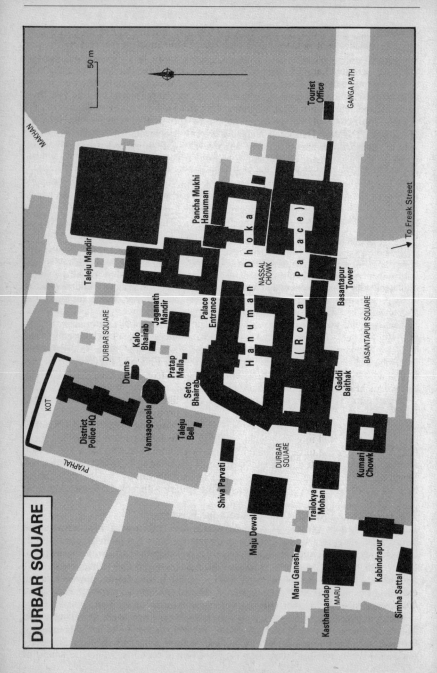

DURBAR SQUARE

eastern wings date from the mid-sixteenth century, but in all likelihood there was a palace on this spot before then. Malla kings built most of the rest by the late seventeenth century, and after capturing Kathmandu in 1768, Prithvi Narayan Shah added (in characteristically martial fashion) four lookout towers at the southeastern corner. Finally, the Ranas left their mark with the garish neoclassical facade along the southwestern flank. Nepal's royal family last lived here in 1956, before moving to the northern end of town.

Only a fraction of the palace is open to the public; entrance is through **Hanuman Dhoka** (Hanuman Gate), a brightly decorated doorway at the east side of the northern part of Durbar Square. The gate is named after the popular monkey god Hanuman, whose statue stands outside – you won't recognise him, smothered under a layer of *sindur*, but that's the way Nepalis like him. Rama's right-hand man in the Hindu *Ramayana* epic, Hanuman has always been revered by Nepalese kings, who, like Rama, are held to be incarnations of the god Vishnu. On the left as you enter is a masterful sculpture of another Vishnu incarnation, the man-lion Narasimha, tearing apart a demon. The entrance opens to **Nassal Chowk**, the large central courtyard that provided the setting for King Birendra's coronation in 1975, and which is still used for important royal functions. The brick wings that form its southern and eastern flanks date from the sixteenth century and boast painstakingly carved wooden doorways, windows and struts – check out the door jambs beaded with tiny skulls. At the northeast corner of the square, the five-tiered pagoda-like turret, notable for its round roofs, is the **Pancha Mukhi Hanuman Mandir**.

Two sights along the **outer walls** of the palace are worth mentioning. Just to the left of the entrance is a **stone inscription** in fifteen languages, carved in 1664 by King Pratap Malla, who fancied himself something of a linguist. The inscription is supposed to be a poem to the goddess Kali, and the story goes that if anyone can read the whole thing, milk will gush from the stone. Look for the two words in French and one in English.

Stuck onto the palace's southwestern end like a barnacle is the **Gaddi Baithak**, a ponderous addition from 1908 that pretty much sums up Rana-era architecture. If you didn't know Nepalese history you might say it had a whiff of the Raj about it, and in a way you'd be right: while India was under British rule, Nepal was labouring under its own home-grown colonialists, the Rana line of isolationist prime ministers. Purists bemoan the building's distorting effect on Durbar Square's proportions, but while it's admittedly out of step with traditional Nepalese architecture, it certainly peps up the square with a dash of mock bravado.

The Tribhuwan Museum and Basantapur Tower

Located inside the palace off Nassal Chowk, the **Tribhuwan Museum** (same hours as Hanuman Dhoka) is your only chance to get a peep at the interior. Featured here is a typically indulgent display of memorabilia from the reign of the present king's grandfather, Tribhuwan, who restored the monarchy in 1951 and opened up Nepal to the outside world. Genuinely interesting, however, is the exhibit of jewel-studded coronation ornaments, including elephant dressings, *howdahs* (elephant platforms) and a throne.

The museum leads to the massive eight-storey **Basantapur Tower**, the biggest of the four raised by Prithvi Narayan in honour of the four main cities of the Kathmandu Valley. You can ascend to a kind of crow's nest enclosed by pitched wooden screens to get fine views in four directions, while the sound of flute sellers drifts up from the square below. The highest mountains visible are those of the Ganja La Himal, a modest range whose peaks just touch 6000m. To take pictures from the tower, enter through a separate doorway at the south end of Nassal Chowk, since cameras aren't allowed in the museum.

Kumari Chowk

Immediately south of the Gaddi Baithak stands **Kumari Chowk**, the gilded cage of the Raj Kumari, Kathmandu's "living goddess". In case there was any doubt, Kumari Chowk proves Kathmandu is no stuffy, dead museum: no other temple better illustrates the living, breathing and endlessly adaptable nature of Nepalese religion, and its freewheeling blend of Hindu, Buddhist and downright bizarre elements.

The **cult of the Kumari** – a prepubescent girl worshipped as a living incarnation of Durga, the demon-slaying Hindu mother goddess – probably goes back to the early middle ages. Jaya Prakash, the last Malla king of Kathmandu, institutionalised the practice when he built the Kumari Chowk in 1757. According to legend, the king either committed some sexual indiscretion against a Kumari, or disbelieved a girl who claimed to be the goddess – in any case Jaya Prakash, who is remembered as a particularly paranoid and weak king, was so consumed by guilt that he erected the building as an act of atonement. He also established the tradition – continued to this day – that each September during the *Indra Jaatra* festival, the Kumari should bestow a *tika* (auspicious mark) on the forehead of the king who was to reign for the coming year. In 1768, the hapless Jaya Prakash was driven into exile on the eve of *Indra Jaatra*, and the conquering Prithvi Narayan Shah slipped in and took the *tika*.

Although the Kumari is supposed to be a Hindu goddess, she is chosen from the Buddhist Sakya clan of goldsmiths, according to a **selection process** reminiscent of the Tibetan Buddhist method of finding reincarnated lamas. Elders interview hundreds of Sakya girls, aged three to five, short-listing those who exhibit thirty-two auspicious signs: a neck like a conch shell, a body like a banyan tree, eyelashes like a cow's and so on. Finalists are placed in a dark room surrounded by freshly severed buffalo heads, while men in demon masks parade around making scary noises. The girl who shows no fear, can correctly identify belongings of previous Kumaris, and whose horoscope doesn't clash with the king's, becomes the next Kumari. She lives a cloistered life inside the Kumari Chowk – her feet are never allowed to touch the ground – and is only carried outside on her throne at *Indra Jaatra* and four or five other festivals each year. Durga's spirit leaves her when she menstruates or otherwise bleeds, whereupon she's retired with a modest state pension. The transition to life as an ordinary mortal can be hard, and she may have difficulty finding a husband, since tradition has it that the man who marries an ex-Kumari will die young. The present Kumari was installed in 1986, when she was four years old, so she's likely to reign well into the 1990s.

The Kumari Chowk's exterior has recently been restored to expose its original brickwork, long buried under Rana plaster. Non-Hindus aren't allowed past the **interior courtyard**, which is decorated with exquisitely carved (if weathered) windows, pillars and doorways. When she feels like it, the Kumari, decked out in exaggerated eye makeup and jewellery, shows herself at one of the first-floor windows, at which time one of her handlers generally whips round for donations.

She's believed to answer her visitors' unspoken questions with the look on her face. Cameras are okay inside the courtyard, but photographing the Kumari is strictly forbidden.

> For background information on the various gods, their symbols and styles of worship, see "Religion" in *Contexts*. Definitions of various Nepali religious terms are also given in the glossary at the end of *Contexts*.

The temples and monuments

Dozens of free-standing temples and statues litter Durbar Square; the following are the highlights.

The Kasthamandap
Standing at the southwestern end of the square, the **Kasthamandap** is Kathmandu's oldest building, if not the oldest wooden building in the world. It's said to have been constructed from the wood of a single tree in the late twelfth century (Simha Sattal, the smaller version to the south, was made from left-overs), but what you see is mostly the result of renovations in 1630. An open, pagoda-roofed pavilion, it served for several centuries as a rest house along the Tibet trade route, and probably formed the nucleus of early Kathmandu; this corner of the square, called Maru Tol, still has the look of a crossroads, with sellers hawking fruit and veg off bicycles.

The Shah kings converted the Kasthamandap into a temple to their protector deity*, **Gorakhnath**, whose statue stands in the middle of the pavilion. A Brahman priest usually sets up shop here to dispense instruction and conduct rituals. In four niches set around are shrines to Ganesh, the elephant-headed god of good fortune, which supposedly represent the celebrated Ganesh temples of the Kathmandu Valley (at Chabahil, Bhaktapur, Chobar and Bungamati), thus enabling Kathmandu residents to pay tribute to all four at once. The building to the southeast of the Kasthamandap is **Kabindrapur**, a Shiva temple mostly patronised by musicians and dancers.

The rest of the southern square
Immediately north of the Kasthamandap stands yet another Ganesh shrine, the unassuming but ever-popular **Maru Ganesh**. A ring on Ganesh's bell is usually the first stage in any *puja*, and the shrine is the first stop for people intending to worship at the other temples of Durbar Square, royalty included. Ganesh's trusty "vehicle" – a rat – is perched on a plinth of the Kasthamandap, across the way.

---

*A word about the confusing matter of royal deities. **Gorakhnath**, a mythologised Indian guru, is revered as a kind of guardian angel by all the Shah kings. **Taleju Bhawani**, to whom many temples and bells are dedicated in the Kathmandu, Patan and Bhaktapur Durbar Squares, played the same role for the Malla kings. The **Kumari** has been worshipped by the kings of both dynasties, but mainly as a public gesture to secure her *tika*, which lends credibility to their divine right to rule. Finally, the present king, Birendra, exercising the prerogative of all Hindus, has taken as his own family deity **Dakshin Kali**, whose shrine is at the southern edge of the Kathmandu Valley.

The three-roofed temple between the Kasthamandap and the Kumari Chowk is the seventeenth-century **Trailokya Mohan**, dedicated to Vishnu. The *Das Avatar* dance takes place here during the October *Dasain* festival, in which masked dancers portray the ten incarnations of Vishnu. A much-photographed statue of the angelic **Garuda**, Vishnu's man-bird vehicle, kneels in his customary palms-together *naamaste* position in front of the temple. The broad, bricked area east of here is **Basantapur Square**, where the souvenir sellers lie in wait.

Moving north, the huge seventeenth-century **Maju Dewal** sits high atop a pyramid of nine stepped levels. Climb to the top for a sweeping, god's-eye view of the square and all its hubbub, but don't expect to escape the roving bangle-sellers and students anxious to practice their English. From this height you can look straight across at the boxy **Shiva Parvati Mandir**, erected in the eighteenth century by one of the early Shah kings. Painted figures of Shiva and his consort Parvati lean out of the first-floor window, looking like they're about to toss the bouquet and dash off to Benidorm for their honeymoon.

Seto Bhairab and Kalo Bhairab

North of the Shiva Parvati temple, the square narrows and then opens out to another temple-clogged area. Ranged along the left (western) side are the **Taleju Bell**, the octagonal **Vamsagopala**, and a pair of ceremonial **drums** of the eighteenth century. To the right, set against the palace wall but not very visible behind a wooden screen, is the snarling ten-foot-high head of **Seto Bhairab** (White Bhairab), the terrifying, blood-swilling aspect of Shiva. One day a year, during the *Indra Jaatra* festival in September, the screen comes down and men jostle to drink rice beer flowing out of a pipe in Bhairab's mouth. The column nearby supports a gilded statue of **King Pratap Malla** and family, a self-congratulatory artform that was all the rage among the Malla kings of the late seventeenth century.

North of this, on the other side of the small Degu Taleju Mandir, the massive, roly-poly image of **Kalo Bhairab** (Black Bhairab) dances on the corpse of a demon. Carved from a single twelve-foot slab of stone, it was found in a field north of Kathmandu during the reign of Pratap Malla, but probably dates to Lichhavi times. It used to be said that anyone who told a lie in front of it would vomit blood and die; one story has it that when the chief justice's office stood across the way, so many witnesses died while testifying that a temple had to be erected to shield the court from Kalo Bhairab's wide-eyed stare.

The Jaganath and Taleju temples

Between Pratap Malla's column and his multilingual inscription stands the sixteenth-century, pagoda-style **Jaganath Mandir**, dedicated to the god whose runaway-chariot festival in India gives us the word "juggernaut". The struts supporting the lower roof of this temple contain Kathmandu's most tittered-about **erotic carvings**, although such carvings are actually quite common in Nepalese temples: once you know where to look, you start noticing them everywhere. Scholars can't seem to agree on the significance of these little vignettes, which often feature outrageous athletics, threesomes and bestiality. Some suggest that sex in this context is being offered as a tantric path to enlightenment. A more popular belief is that the goddess of lightning is a chaste virgin who wouldn't dare strike a temple so decorated. In any case, Hanuman, who guards the nearby palace entrance, is spared the sight by the globs of *sindur* over his eyes.

The massive temple northeast of the square is the sixteenth-century **Taleju Mandir**. Kathmandu's biggest, the temple looks down on you with haughty grandeur: it's open only on the ninth day of *Dasain*, and then only to Nepalis, who make sacrifices to Durga in the courtyard. Taleju Bhawani, a south Indian goddess imported in the fourteenth century by the Mallas, is worshipped by Nepalese Hindus as a form of the mother goddess Kali, while Buddhist Newars count her as one of the Taras, tantric female deities.

Other, minor temples dotting the northern square belong mainly to Shiva. Inside each, the god is worshipped as a *lingam* – a stone phallus, which to a *Shaiva* (follower of Shiva) is as potent a symbol as the cross is to a Christian. The infamous **Kot Courtyard**, which once lay northwest of the square, is now taken up by a walled police compound. It was here that the Machiavellian general Jang Bahadur Rana engineered a grisly massacre of fifty-five of the king's top brass in 1846, thereby clearing the way to proclaim himself prime minister and establish the hereditary line that was to rule Nepal until 1951.

North of Durbar Square

Kathmandu's oldest, liveliest streets lie north and northeast of Durbar Square. You could make a more or less circular swing through the area (as this section does), but you'll almost certainly be diverted somewhere along the way. At any rate, the sights described here are only a backdrop for the old city's fascinating street life.

Indrachowk and Kel Tol

The old trade route to Tibet passes through Durbar Square and becomes a narrow lane where it rounds the Taleju Mandir. Called **Makhan Tol** at this point, it runs a gauntlet of *thanka* (Buddhist scroll painting) sellers and then takes a northeasterly bearing through Kathmandu's traditional goldsmiths' neighbourhood. The first big intersection you reach is **Indrachowk**, named in honour of the original Hindu king of the gods: a sort of Asian Zeus, complete with thunderbolt, Indra fell from grace in India centuries ago, but in the Kathmandu Valley he's still revered as a rainmaker and has his own festival (*Indra Jaatra*). The gaudy house-like temple on the west side of the crossroads – its front decorated with European ceramic tiles, a common practice earlier this century – is that of **Akash Bhairab** (Sky, or Blue, Bhairab), who in the best anything-goes spirit of Hinduism sometimes trades places with Indra. The temple is out-of-bounds to non-Hindus, but you can see the scary silver mask of Bhairab paraded around Kathmandu during *Indra Jaatra*.

The tumultuous street heading north from Indrachowk is the direct route to Thamel, but the old Tibet road continues diagonally to the small square of **Kel Tol** and the seventeenth-century temple of **Seto Machhendranath** (White Machhendranath), one of two main shrines to the protector god of the Kathmandu Valley (the other is in Patan). Machhendranath's white mask, which you can see from the threshhold of the temple, is wheeled around the city on a chariot in late March or April. The well-concealed building boasts some beautiful gold and brass work on the outside, but an iron grille, installed to thwart temple thieves, robs it of any aesthetic appeal: the entrance is a gate at the west side of the square. Beyond

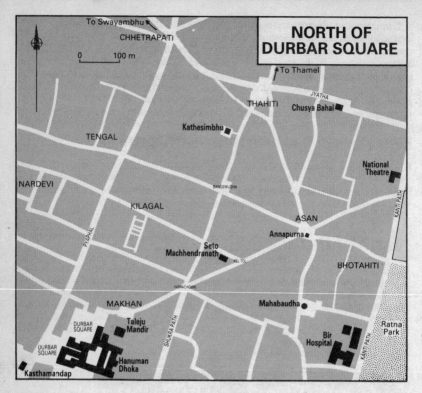

Kel Tol, a three-tiered octagonal building on the left is one of Kathmandu's oldest houses. Its ground floor was built as a rest house, probably in the early fifteenth century, and the upper floors were added later for overnight guests.

Asan, Mahabaudha and Bangemudha

The last and most exuberant intersection along this route is **Asan Tol**, north Kathmandu's principal fruit and veg market and the main gathering point and hiring centre for city porters (*kuli* in Nepali and Hindi – hence "coolie"). The brass-roofed pagoda at the south side of the square is the temple of **Annapurna**, the goddess of grain and abundance: a lavish little affair, the pagoda bristles with icons and imagery, and the roof is strung with electric bulbs like a Christmas tree. Annapurna is represented by a silver *kailash*, or vessel.

From Asan, the trade route angles up to Kantipath and the modern city, while an alley heading south leads to **Mahabaudha**. This plain white stupa, stuck in a rather unattractive square, takes its name from the big, harlequin-painted statue of Buddha in an adjacent shelter. Just east of Mahabaudha, Kathmandu's removal men wait for work: you see them all over town, pushing loads around on rubber-wheeled flatbed carts, almost always in bare feet and shorts – like porters, they are usually of the Tamang tribe.

If you walk westwards from Asan, you return to the main Indrachowk-Thamel lane at **Bangemudha**. Just south of this square is the odd shrine of Vaishya Dev, commonly (and misleadingly) billed as the **"Toothache Tree"** – it's actually the butt end of a log, embedded in the side of a building, and locals believe you can cure a toothache by nailing a coin to the log. Vaishya Dev's curative powers are now stronger than ever, thanks to the help of several nearby dentists. Fans of ancient sculpture might appreciate the tiny fifth-century figure of Buddha at the north end of Bangemudha; however, its tacky tile niche does it no favours.

Kathesimbhu, Thahiti, Thamel and Chhetrapati

Kathesimbhu, central Kathmandu's biggest stupa, stands in a square off to the left about 200m north of Bangemudha. The temple is only a modest replica of the more impressive Swayambhu stupa (its name is a contraction of "Kathmandu Swayambhu"), but for those too old or infirm to climb to Swayambhu, rites performed here earn the same merit. The square doubles as a playground for a local school and is best avoided during playtime.

Traffic circulates around another stupa at **Thahiti**, the next square north on the way to Thamel. Because they're continually replastered, stupas never look very old and are hard to date, but both this one and Kathesimbhu probably go back to the fifteenth or sixteenth century. One of Kathmandu's finest old *bahals*, the seventeenth-century **Chusya Bahal**, stands about two blocks east of Thahiti. You'll recognise it by the two stone lions out front and a meticulously carved wooden *torana* (decorative shield) above the doorway, both standard features of a *bahal*. The building is now privately owned, but you can get a look at the court-yard from the threshhold.

In the tourist zone north of Thahiti, old buildings are few and about the only sights are the goodies in the restaurant windows. To find a monument in the vicinity of **Thamel**, you could visit **Bhagwan Bahal**, a minor, apparently disused pagoda that lends its name to an area north of Thamel. A bizarre feature of this temple is the collection of kitchen pans and utensils nailed to the front wall, presumably placed there as offerings to the deity.

Playing a madal

At the southwestern fringe of Thamel lies boister-ous **Chhetrapati**, a musicians' neighbourhood. It's not an old area and there aren't any monuments (unless you count the Edwardian bandstand in the middle of the junction), but look out for the shops hiring out brass bands and band instruments for weddings. Religious processions and impromptu musical jamborees are almost daily occurrences here.

From Chhetrapati it's a straight run south to the Kasthamandap. Towards the lower end you get back into atmospheric eighteenth-century neighbourhoods, with several large *bahals* dating back as far as the fourteenth century tucked away down dark alleys. Keep an eye out on the east side of the street for the **Deshaya Marujhya** – literally, the "Country Nowhere Window" – a window grille of staggering complexity which, even in a country abounding in outstanding woodwork, is considered unique. Carved from a single block of wood, it predates the house in which it's now set.

South of Durbar Square

South Kathmandu – the old part, at least – is a smaller area, less medieval, less bustling, and much poorer. Except for the area from Freak Street across to the GPO, it's completely untouristed and a fair representation of reality in modern, urban Nepal.

Bhimsenthan and Jaisi Dewal

A small square southwest of the Kasthamandap, down a lane leading to the Bishnumati River, **Bhimsenthan** is named after one of Nepal's favourite gods. Bhimsen was one of the famous five brothers of the Hindu *Mahabharata*, a mortal hero who has been adopted as the patron saint of Newar merchants: you'll see pictures of him in shops everywhere. The Bhimsen temple here is supposed to have been built in the early eighteenth century, but has been renovated in off-putting modern colours: the shrine on the first floor is open only to Hindus, while the ground floor is, fittingly, occupied by shops.

Jaisi Dewal, a seventeenth-century Shiva temple, stands in a square several blocks south of the Kasthamandap down a different road. A three-tiered pagoda without much ornamentation, its size alone is impressive. *Lingam*-spotters can ogle at the eight-foot-high monster at the foot of the temple, which has to be the biggest in the kingdom (although only a raw, uncarved stone, it's nonetheless authentically proportioned). The road continues south, past Takan Bahal's fourteenth-century stupa – mossy and cracked, it looks like a mouldy orange – to **Tripureswar Marg**, an important east–west road.

Pachali Bhairab and the ghats

The most interesting part of south Kathmandu begins with **Pachali Bhairab**, an open-air shrine marooned in a light industrial area south of Tripureswar Marg (follow the path opposite the *Hotel Valley View*). The tiny gilded idol of Bhairab stands in a peaceful courtyard, dwarfed by a huge banyan tree and a brass, life-sized human figure laid out like a pharoah's casket. This is a *betala*, a likeness of death which, in Nepalese Hinduism, is believed to protect against death (the old principle of fighting fire with fire); *betalas* normally take the form of miniature skulls or skeletons at temple entrances, and this one is unusual for being so large. An esoteric parade involving Bhairab and other gods converges here on the fifth day of *Dasain*.

Things get weirder as you follow the path from Pachali Bhairab down to the **Bagmati River**. Derelict, languid but strangely mesmerising, the **ghats** (platforms by the rivers edge, used for Hindu cremation and worship) here stretch as far as the eye can see in either direction. Statues, temples and all manner of neglected artifacts are jumbled along the shore, and you could easily spend several hours picking around among them; cremations are held here quite often. A footbridge crosses the river to Patan.

The biggest riverside temples are more than a kilometre east of here. Lurking inside a crumbling courtyard, the massive pagoda of **Tripura Sundari** has been squatted by a collective of low-caste families, while further south, the marvellously hideous **Kalamochan Mandir** is a study in Rana excess and faded glory.

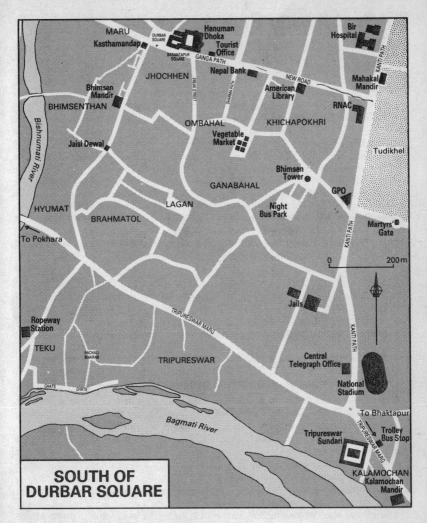

MARU
Kasthamandap
DURBAR
SQUARE
BASANTAPUR
SQUARE
GANGA PATH
Hanuman
Dhoka
Tourist
Office
Bir
Hospital
KANTI PATH
JHOCHHEN
Nepal Bank
NEW ROAD
Mahakal
Mandir
Bhimsen
Mandir
PRATAP STREET
DHARMA PATH
American
Library
RNAC
BHIMSENTHAN
OMBAHAL
KHICHAPOKHRI
Jaisi Dewal
Vegetable
Market
Tudikhel
Bhimsen
Tower
Bishnumati River
GANABAHAL
GPO
HYUMAT
LAGAN
Night
Bus Park
Martyrs'
Gate
BRAHMATOL
KANTI PATH
To Pokhara
0   200 m
Jails
Ropeway
Station
TRIPURESWAR MARG
TEKU
PACHALI
BHAIRAB
TRIPURESWAR
KANTI PATH
Central
Telegraph Office
GHATS   GHATS
National
Stadium
To Bhaktapur
Bagmati River
Tripureswar
Sundari
TRIPURESWAR MARG
Trolley
Bus Stop
KALAMOCHAN
Kalamochan
Mandir

SOUTH OF DURBAR SQUARE

Resembling a grotesque white wedding cake, it was built in 1852 by the first of the Rana prime ministers, the homicidal Jang Bahadur; the brass gargoyles snarling at its four corners are fitting symbols of his ambition. The way in is through the entrance marked "Nepal Association for the Welfare of the Blind".

New Road, Freak Street and Bhimsen Tower

Rebuilt after the disastrous 1934 earthquake, **New Road** (Juddha Sadak) cuts a swathe of modernity through the old city. Indian tourists (who number twice as many as any other nationality) swarm its shops for perfume and rice warmers, while Nepali peasants visiting the capital stand transfixed at the sight of holiday snaps rolling off automatic photo-processing machines. It's all heady stuff for Nepal – the "supermarket" here even boasts an escalator.

Freak Street (Jhochhen), like Thamel, isn't prime sightseeing territory, although nowadays tour groups come in search of the hippies that gave Freak Street its name – you still get the occasional sighting – or just to take a trip down memory lane. On a cultural note, the pair of *chaityas* in front of the *Paradise Restaurant* illustrate the unique synthesis of Hindu and Buddhist imagery that's so common in hill Nepal: Buddha would probably be appalled, but his images are carved around unapologetically phallic *lingams*, and set atop bases that symbolise the female genitalia (*yoni*).

The lane heading east from here leads to Kathmandu's main **vegetable market**, located in an unpaved compound: fish and other items are sold in the street in front. Further east, **Bhimsen Tower** ("Dharahara" in Nepali), the tall minaret-like tower overlooking the GPO, is of no earthly use to anyone except land surveyors. Three of Kathmandu's four **jails** are located south of here, down a side street off Kantipath – make a right at the *Mercantile Service Station*.

THE JAILS

One of the more thought-provoking, not to mention worthy, things you can do while in Kathmandu is to visit westerners held in the capital's four **jails**. Since families are expected to provide for most of the prisoners' needs, foreigners are particularly badly off. Most are held in one of the jails (Central, Badragol, Women's) south of the GPO; a fourth facility is located in Dilli Bazaar.

At any given time, a dozen or so **westerners** are imprisoned or awaiting trial in Kathmandu, mainly on charges of smuggling gold or drugs. Five years is a typical sentence, with no time off for good behaviour: a favourable appeal verdict usually doesn't result in freedom, only a shortened sentence, and every prisoner can tell a sorry tale or two about shady lawyers and indifferent embassy officials. At the height of the democracy movement in the spring of 1990, it was estimated that 8000 **Nepalis** were jailed as **political prisoners** – convicted criminals were even released to make room for political detainees – but presumably all have been released since the restoration of democracy.

Conditions in the jails are unsurprisingly grim. For food, inmates receive a half-kilo of "black" rice and *daal* each day, plus Rs3 with which to buy vegetables at the prison shop. They sleep on the floor, with up to fifty to a room. No clothes or bedding are provided.

Daily **visiting hours** are 7am–5pm (but check: times may vary). You must ask for prisoners by name – check posters around Thamel and Freak Street to find out who's being held where. Inmates appear at a barred doorway, while visitors stand behind a chain, so conversations are far from private. Most prisoners will be happy just to chat, but don't go without bringing something tangible: food, vitamins, toiletries, books, clothes and blankets are all appreciated.

Swayambhu

Even if temple-touring makes your eyes glaze over, don't miss **SWAYAMBHU** (or SWAYAMBHUNATH), perched on a hill 2km west of Thamel. To begin with, it's a great place to get your bearings, geographically and culturally, in your first few days in Nepal: the hill commands a sweeping view of the Kathmandu Valley, and the temple complex, overrun with pilgrims and monkeys, is a real eye-opener. But there's much more if you dig for it. The 2000-year-old stupa is the most profound expression of Buddhist symbolism in Nepal, and possibly the world.

Swayambhu is the source and central location of the valley's creation myth, and there's evidence to believe the hill was used for animist rites long before Buddhism arrived in the valley 2500 years ago. Tantric Buddhists consider it the chief "power point" of the Kathmandu Valley, and one chronicle states that an act of worship here carries thirteen billion times more merit than anywhere else. The place is so steeped in lore and pregnant with detail that you'll never absorb it all in a single visit. Try going early in the morning at *puja* time, or at night when the red-robed monks pad softly around the dome, murmuring *mantras* and spinning the prayer wheels. Make a final visit on your last day in Nepal and see how your perceptions of it differ from your initial trip.

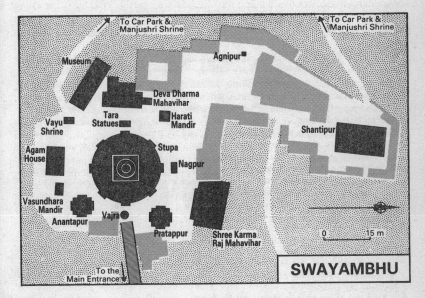

Getting there

The main entrance is at the eastern foot of the hill and **getting there** is a simple matter on foot or cycle. From Thamel the easiest way is via Chhetrapati, where a small road heads straight towards Swayambhu, passing the *Hotel Vajra* en route. From Freak Street or Durbar Square, take the rustic lane running northwestwards from the Kasthamandap. Either way, it should take about twenty minutes to walk it. If you're cycling, the local kids will expect you to cough up a few rupees' protection money – failure to comply invites a flat tyre. A city bus also runs at irregular intervals between Ratna Park and the entrance, and taxis drive up to a small carpark near the top, on the west side of the hill. Near the turning for the carpark you can get **food** at a couple of cafés, *Iko* and *The Hungry Horse*, sedate descendants of the hippy hangouts that once thrived here.

Since the Chinese invasion of Tibet in 1959, the area surrounding Swayambhu has been home to hundreds of **Tibetans in exile**. You'll see many of them making a full circuit around the hill, queueing up to spin the gigantic fixed **prayer wheels** around the eastern entrance at the hill's base, or twirling their own hand-held ones. Although there are several other ways up the hill, the steep main path, with its centuries-smoothed steps, is the most dramatic. The **Buddha statues** on the way up are from the seventeenth century, while the slates heaped up along the path are *mani* stones, inscribed in Tibetan script with the words *Om mani padme hum* ("Oh hail to the jewel in the lotus"), the ubiquitous Buddhist mantra .

Swayambhu's significance

According to Buddhist scriptures, the Kathmandu Valley was once a **snake-infested lake** (geologists agree about the lake: see "Natural History" in *Contexts*). Long ago – 91 eons ago, to be exact – a perfect, radiant lotus flower appeared on the surface of the lake, which the gods proclaimed to be Swayambhu ("Self-created"), the abstract essence of Buddhahood. **Manjushri**, the *bodhisattva* of knowledge, decided he wanted a closer look at the lotus, so he drew his sword and cut a gorge at Chobar, south of Kathmandu, to drain the lake. As the water receded, the lotus settled on top of a hill and Manjushri established a shrine to it, before turning his attention to ridding the valley of snakes and establishing its first civilisation. Another legend tells how, when Manjushri cut his hair at Swayambhu, the hairs that fell on the ground grew into trees, and the lice turned into monkeys.

The apparently simple structure of **the stupa** belies an immensely complex physical representation of Buddhist cosmology, and the purpose of walking round it – always in a clockwise direction – is to meditate on this. The solid, whitewashed dome symbolises the womb or creation. Set in niches at the cardinal points, statues of **dhyani (meditating) Buddhas** correspond to the four elements (earth, air, fire and water) and a fifth, placed at an angle, to the sky or space. Each represents a different facet of Buddhahood: the hand positions, colours and "vehicles" (the animal statues below) of each are significant. The *dhyani* Buddhas are the same characters who appear on virtually every *chaitya* around the Kathmandu Valley. At each of the sub-cardinal points sit **female counterparts**, which according to the tantric view of things represent the creative force that must be (sexually) united with the active/male force to achieve enlightenment.

The gilded cube surmounting the stupa is in fact the top of a thick wooden pillar, considered the phallic foil to the female dome. The **eyes** painted on it are those of the all-seeing Buddha, staring in all four directions; what looks like a nose is actually the Nepalese figure "one", conveying the unity of all things. A **spire** of thirteen gold disks stacked above the pillar represents the thirteen steps to enlightenment*. The *torana*, or gold plaques above the painted eyes, also show the five *dhyani* Buddhas, known collectively as the *Panchabuddha*. Finally, the umbrella at the top symbolises the attainment of enlightenment: some say it contains a bowl filled with precious gems.

Swayambhu's main **festivals** are *Losar* (in February or March) and *Buddha Jayanti* (April or May), when pilgrims throng around the stupa and monks splash arcs of saffron paint over it in a lotus-flower pattern.

---

*The spire was broken during a storm in 1816, which was considered a bad omen for the British residency, having only been established earlier that year.

Shrines around the stupa

The stupa is surrounded by an incredible array of shrines and votive whatnots, most of which have been donated over the past four centuries by merit-seeking kings and lamas. The bronze sceptre-like object at the top of the stairs is a vastly oversized **vajra**, a tantric symbol of power and indestructibility; its pedestal is carved with the twelve animals of the Tibetan zodiac. The bullet-shaped *shikhras* on either side of this, known as **Anantapur** and **Pratappur**, were installed in the seventeenth century for purely aesthetic reasons, and lack any religious significance.

Moving around clockwise, the brick hut to the south of Anantapur is **Vasundhara Mandir**, dedicated to the earth goddess Vasundhara, who's more or less synonymous with Annapurna and Lakshmi, the goddesses of grain and wealth respectively. Further on – past the priests'
quarters and a number of *chaityas* – is a small
marble-faced shrine to **Vayu**, the Vedic god of
wind and storms. The **museum** (Sun–Fri 10am–
5pm; donation), behind, contains a formidable
range of bas-relief statues of gods, Hindu as well
as Buddhist, which, though beautiful to look at,
are so tersely identified that they'll leave you
hopelessly confused by the Nepalese pantheon.
Next door and up a flight of steps, the **Deva
Dharma Mahavihar** is a small, uneventful
monastery that's open to the public, and in front
of this, close to the stupa, stand two acclaimed
bronze statues of the **White and Green Taras**,
princess wives of an eighth-century Tibetan king.

At the far side of the stupa squats the gilt-
roofed **Harati Mandir**, built to appease the
fickle protectress of children (often worshipped
interchangeably as Ajima, the goddess of small-
pox). A legend relates how Harati was originally
an abductor of children – when the people
complained to Buddha, he stole one of Harati's
own children, forcing her to realise the pain she
caused humans and repent of her ways. Harati's
shrine is extremely popular, and you'll see
queues of mothers with kids in tow, waiting to
make offerings.

A Chaitya

Agnipur, an insignificant-looking lump on the pavement in the northwest corner of the complex (marked by two tiny lions in front) is a seldom-visited shrine to the Vedic fire god Agni, the relayer of burnt offerings to heaven. **Nagpur**, a bathtub-sized tank at the north point of the stupa, propitiates the valley's snake (*naga*) spirits, and when it's not filled with water you can see the idol (looking more like a draught excluder than a snake) at the bottom. Finally, the **Shree Karma Raj Mahavihar**, an active monastery at the northeast corner of the compound, contains a big Buddha and numerous butter candles, which Tibetan Buddhists light in much the same way Catholics do; you can catch the sonorous chanting of the monks at around 3 or 4pm everyday.

Shantipur and Manjushri

A 1500-year-old mystery surrounds **Shantipur**, the otherwise plain, box-like building northwest of the stupa. Shanti Shri, a fifth-century holy man, is supposed to have sealed himself in a vault beneath the temple to meditate, vowing not to emerge until the valley needed him. Commentators write that he subsequently attained a mystic state of immortality, and locals believe he's still in there.

King Pratap Malla, who entered the chamber in 1658 to seek magical help in ending a drought, experienced adventures worthy of Indiana Jones. According to scholar Keith Dowman, the king recounted how he entered alone and descended to the second subterranean level. In the first room "bats as large as kites or hawks came to kill the light", while in the second room "ghosts, flesh-eating spirits and hungry ghosts came to beg", clutching at anyone who failed to pacify them. Of the third room he said, "if you cannot pacify the snakes by pouring out milk, they chase and bind you. Having pacified them you can walk on their bodies". Finally, Pratap Malla found the saint in an almost skeletal form, and was rewarded with a *naga* rain-making emblem. Shantipur, also known as Akashpur ("Sky-place"), completes a cycle of shrines to the five elemental spirits: earth, air, fire, water (snakes) and sky.

The **Manjushri Shrine**, located on a second hilltop west of the main one, comes second only to the main stupa in popularity and antiquity – the canopied *chaitya* is reckoned to be 1500 years old. Manjushri, the Buddhist god of wisdom and founder of civilisation in the valley, is traditionally depicted by an empty niche in the *chaitya*, but an image of Saraswati, the Hindu goddess of learning, was placed in the niche 300 years ago and so the shrine is now on the pilgrimage circuit for Hindus as well. Schoolchildren make a special trip here on *Basant Panchami*, in late January or early February, to have their books and pencils blessed.

The rest of the hilltop is littered with other obscure monuments. In addition, several **Tibetan monasteries**, which as a rule welcome visitors, have been built in the area since 1959. The morbidly amusing **Natural History Museum** (Sun–Fri, 10am–4pm; free), also lurks nearby, at the southern base of Swayambhu Hill. Its jumbled collection of stuffed birds and shrivelled animals in old-fashioned display cases looks like it was cobbled together from the trophy rooms of hoary old Rana hunters. The weirdness is fun for its own sake, though, and the specimens might give you an idea of what to look for when you get to the mountains or jungle. (See also "Natural History" in *Contexts*.)

En Route to Swayambhu: Bijeshwari

Bijeshwari, along the west bank of the Bishnumati on the way to Swayambhu, used to be Kathmandu's execution ground; Henry Ambrose Oldfield, one of the few Europeans allowed to tour Nepal in the last century, attended a beheading here and pronounced the place "a regular Golgotha". While Tibetan immigrants have broken the taboo against settling near the cursed ground, a fear of ghosts still lingers, as do two important but little-visited temples.

Bijeshwari Bahal, perched at the top of a flight of stairs above the river, is the centre of worship of an esoteric Buddhist goddess, Bijeshwari, who is also known as Akash (Sky) Jogini and sometimes counted as the fifth of the valley's Bajra Joginis, the wrathful aspects of the tantric Tara goddesses. The inner courtyard is thick with *chaityas* and stone figures, including a Lichhavi-era Buddha. Just upstream stands a new cremation pavilion, and beyond that, the Hindu **Shobha Bhagwati Mandir**. Bhagwati is another name for Kali, the flesh-eating mother goddess, and this idol of her is considered to be among of the most powerful in the valley: early in the morning you might see government ministers stepping out of chauffeur-driven cars to do *puja* to her.

South of Swayambhu: the National Museum

The **National Museum** (Sun–Thurs 10.30am–4.30pm; 10.30am–3.30pm in winter, Fri 10.30am–2.30pm; Rs10), 1km south of Swayambhu, is the most comprehensive in Nepal – or at least it will be when it's completed. The art building, which contains the *crème de la crème* of Nepalese statues and paintings, has been closed for remodelling since 1988, with no reopening date in sight. The history building's endless displays of weaponry do little to dispel the stereotype of the Nepalis as a "martial" race (although a pair of leather cannon, captured during a skirmish with Tibet in 1856, is a genuine rarity). More interesting than what's included, perhaps, is what's left out: this is Nepalese history as rewritten by the Shahs and Ranas, who've ruled Nepal for the past two centuries; the country's lower classes and ethnic groups, and any history prior to the Shah conquest, are given not a mention.

Eastern neighbourhoods

For travellers, the area east of Kantipath is mainly of interest for airline offices and restaurants, not sightseeing. But while you're in the neighbourhood it's worth stopping to take a closer look at a few odds and ends.

The Royal Palace, Kesar Library and Singha Durbar

An architectural travesty from the Sixties, the creepy new **Royal Palace** looks like something out of Buck Rogers, with echoes of the Mormon Tabernacle. The things that resemble black handbags dangling from the trees out front are bats; at dusk, they and about a million crows wheel overhead, creating an almighty racket.

The **Kesar** (Kaiser) **Library** (Sun–Thurs 10am–5pm, Fri 10am–3pm; free), located in the compound marked "Ministry of Education and Culture" east of Thamel, is your best shot at seeing the inside of a former Rana palace. The library of Field Marshal Kesar Shamsher Rana (1891–1964) is more or less what you'd expect: long shelves of European books, a suit of armour, a stuffed tiger and portraits of all the famous people the field marshal ever shook hands with.

Undoubtedly the most impressive structure ever raised by the Ranas, **Singha Durbar** dominates the governmental quarter in the southeastern part of the city. Once the biggest building in Asia, the Prime Ministers' palace of a thousand rooms was mostly destroyed by fire in 1973, but has been partially rebuilt. You can go right past the guards at the sweeping front gate to have a look at the luxurious gardens and the gleaming white colonnaded main wing. Numerous governmental ministries and departments are housed here and in crumbling old mansions nearby.

Rani Pokhri and Tudikhel

Rani Pokhri (Queen's Pool), the large square tank east of Asan, is older than it looks: it was built in the seventeenth century by King Pratap Malla to console his queen after the death of their favourite son; the shrine in the middle, which is opened one day a year during the *Diwali* festival, is more recent. East of the pool stands the Rana-era **clocktower** (like Bhimsen Tower, a landmark only in the functional sense) and Kathmandu's two **mosques**. Muslims first settled in Kathmandu as traders five centuries ago, and now represent only a tiny fraction of Nepal's half-million "Musalmans". Nearby Trichandra College, whose students have a reputation for militancy, was a flashpoint of anti-government riots in early 1990, when its walls were painted with such slogans as "Do or Die for Democracy".

Kathmandu's **Tudikhel** is the biggest military parade ground in Nepal; Percival Landon, an early-twentieth-century traveller, proclaimed it "level as Lord's", and indeed the expanse seems quixotically flat in so mountainous a country. An institution rooted in Nepal's warring past, the *tudikhel* is a feature of every town of consequence throughout the hills.

On the Kantipath side of Tudikhel stands the **Mahakal Mandir**, whose modern surroundings have in no way diminished the reverence of its worshippers: pedestrians and motorists passing by almost always touch a hand to the forehead. Mahakal ("Great Black One") – to Hindus a form of Bhairab, to Buddhists a defender of *dharma* – is depicted here trampling a corpse (signifying ignorance), holding a skull-cup of blood and wearing what look like glacier goggles. The **Bhadrakali Mandir**, at the southeast corner of Tudikhel, has been turned into a traffic roundabout but remains a popular wedding venue. The nearby **Martyrs' Gate** commemorates the four ringleaders of a failed 1940 attempt to restore the monarchy.

Dilli Bazaar, Baluwatar and Hadigaun

Kathmandu's eastern and northeastern neighbourhoods have absorbed the lion's share of recent city growth, and while these areas don't have much of scenic interest, they certainly provide insights into suburban Nepal. Crowded **Dilli Bazaar** pretty much sums up one end of the spectrum, with its typing institutes, lawyers' cubbyholes and shops selling office furniture and "suitings and shirtings".

The other extreme is found further north in the shady lanes of **Baluwatar** and **Maharajganj**, where old money, new money and foreign money hides in walled compounds, and caretakers water the flowers for highly paid absentee development consultants. Between the two lie the hopeful settlements of a burgeoning middle class, who build their houses one floor at a time, as funds allow, and send their children off in uniforms to "English boarding schools" with names like "Bright Future" and "Little Flower". An "English" education is almost universally viewed as the key to success in the capital: whether these children are being educated to think for themselves is a matter of debate, but they may well help Nepal escape its cycle of poverty.

Another world away, **Hadigaun**, stowed away on the edge of the northeastern suburbs, is the nearest place to Thamel to find typical Newar village life in action. You'll see better as you go further out into the valley, but Hadigaun's old brick houses, dirt streets and farm animals are remarkably well insulated from the hurlyburly of the city. Indeed, the settlement is probably as old as Kathmandu.

Evidence of Hadigaun's age comes from the overgrown shrine of **Dhum Barahi**, a further kilometre northeastwards (head north out of Hadigaun, and when in doubt always take the right fork). Inside the small brick shelter, which is completely engulfed in the roots of an enormous pipal tree, a whimsical fifth-century image illustrates the tale of Barahi (Vishnu in his incarnation as a boar) rescuing the earth goddess Prithvi from the bottom of the sea. Scholars rave about this sculpture because it dates from a time when there were no established rules for depicting Vishnu as a boar, nor for how a boar should look while fishing the earth from the sea. Locals say the shrine was built at the same time as the nearby stupa to appease Vishnu, who out of jealousy had caused the stupa's spire to collapse while under construction.

THE FACTS

There's no comparison between Kathmandu and other cities in Nepal: the capital has all the best restaurants, the only bars, the majority of entertainment, the broadest (though not the cheapest) selection of handicrafts, and several yoga and meditation centres – not to mention all the embassies and airline offices.

Eating out

Now secure in its reputation as a gastronomic oasis, Kathmandu continues to refine its technique. Scores of **restaurants and cafés** line the lanes of the tourist areas, and more spring up after each monsoon. Quite a few carry on in a tatty, student-coffee-house style – they're like time capsules from the early Seventies – but a growing number are emulating French bistros, American diners and even English pubs, sometimes with disorientating authenticity.

While **Tibetan**, **Chinese** and **Indian** food have long been taken for granted in Kathmandu, **European** cuisines are now almost faultlessly simulated; American-style **pies and cakes**, though overrated, are steadily improving; and even **Japanese** and **Mexican** dishes are beginning to come into their own. The best news of all is that gourmet **Nepali** food – traditionally only served in private homes* – is now available in several tourist restaurants, and is slowly taking its place among the other distinguished regional Indian cuisines.

As with lodgings, **Thamel** has all the newest, trendiest and most credible budget eateries – some are getting so stylish they're pricing themselves out of the budget category. **Freak Street**'s restaurants are noticeably cheaper, but most have seen better days; depending on your age and outlook, they'll fill you with either nostalgia or embarassment. Kathmandu's best and most expensive restaurants are generally found near, or sometimes inside, the deluxe hotels around **Durbar Marg**. Even at the top end, **prices** are reasonable. As a guideline, places decribed here as cheap will charge Rs50 or less for a full dinner; inexpensive restaurants will run to about Rs75, maybe Rs100 if you share a beer with someone; moderately priced ones will charge more like Rs100–200, and expensive ones Rs200–300.

*A tradition which helped create Kathmandu's Western-restaurant scene: early travellers and homesick Peace Corps volunteers, finding little to eat besides *daal bhaat*, promptly set about teaching Nepalis to make lasagna and apple pie.

It's all too easy to overemphasise food in Kathmandu – it can also be the greatest peril of staying here. An alarming number of travellers come down with **stomach upsets** or worse, even those who eat only in "reputable" restaurants. Indeed, Nepalese restaurants are arguably safer, since chefs know what they're doing when they prepare Nepalese food. Heed the words of caution given in "Health and Insurance" in *Basics*, and don't be taken in by an apparently clean dining room or shiny cutlery.

Nepali

The places listed here are all geared for tourists, and tend to be a bit on the expensive side. Many other Thamel restaurants offer less expensive (albeit less interesting) set Nepali meals. For extremely cheap Nepalese and Newari fare, try eating at one of the local taverns, which advertise themselves with a curtain (usually green) hung over the entrance. See "Eating" in *Basics* for a rundown of Nepalese dishes.

Bhanchha Ghar, Kamaladi (☎225172). Nepalese nouvelle cuisine, featuring such delicacies as venison, wild mushroom curry and buckwheat chapatis – truly wonderful. Book ahead for dinner. Expensive.

Naachghar, at the *Yak & Yeti Hotel* off Durbar Marg (☎413999). Top-flight Nepalese cooking; set dinner with culture shows on Tuesday and Sunday. Expensive.

Nepalese Kitchen, Chhetrapati, Thamel. A friendly establishment demonstrating that there's more to Nepali cuisine than *daal bhaat*. Moderately priced.

Tama Kosi, Kwa Bahal, Thamel. Nepali food, eastern-hills style: curries spiced with cardamom and served with creamy tomato *achhaar*. Inexpensive to moderate.

Tibetan and Chinese

Tibetan restaurants serve by far the cheapest food in Kathmandu; cheaper still are the many *momo* kitchens throughout the old city, notably around Mahabaudha. Again, see the comments on Tibetan food in *Basics*. Chinese food can be reasonably priced, although the best restaurants are found in deluxe hotels like the *Malla*.

Da Hua Chinese Restaurant, Thamel. Good all-round Chinese. Cheap to moderately priced.

Lhasa Restaurant, Thamel. Excellent Tibetan soups, fiery *momos* and – best of all – *tongba* (do-it-yourself millet beer). Cheap.

Mountain City, in the *Hotel Malla* north of Thamel. Delicious Chinese food; Sichuan a specialty. Moderate to expensive.

New Dish Restaurant, Khichapokhri. Excellent Tibetan food, fair Chinese. Cheap.

Solu Restaurant, Jyatha Thamel. A locals' hole-in-the-wall that does *tongba*. Practically free.

Utse, Thamel. Amazingly cheap Tibetan and Chinese food in a fun atmosphere.

Indian

Good Indian food comes dear in Kathmandu, but as with Nepalese restaurants there's an affordable alternative: try the tandoori diners along Lazimpath and in Kalamochan (around the corner from the *Blue Star Hotel*).

Amber, Durbar Marg. Live classical Indian music nightly. Moderate to expensive.

Ghar-e-Kebab, Durbar Marg. Superlative (north) Indian food, live music, strange nightclub interior. Expensive.

New Kebab Corner, in the *Hotel Gautam* just off Kantipath. Popular with expats. Moderately priced.

Shiva's Sky, New Road. Nepalese-inflected Indian food. Moderately priced.

European

Keep telling yourself: this is not what I came to Nepal for. . . Still, it's hard to pass up a beautiful lasagna dinner for less than a quid.

Casa Helvetica, Kwa Bahal, Thamel. Authentic Swiss fare, with some Tibetan dishes thrown in for good measure. Moderately priced.

G's Terrace, Thamel. High-cholesterol Bavarian specialties (would you believe *zwiebelrostbraten*?). Moderate to expensive.

La Dolce Vita, Thamel. Kathmandu's most upscale Italian. Moderate prices, except the wine.

Locanda Marco Polo, Thamel. Forget the rest, this place has the best lasagna in Kathmandu, and it's cheap, too.

Mike's Breakfast, Durbar Marg. Terrific pizza (Mon nights only). Moderately priced.

Old Vienna Inn, Thamel. Schnitzel and crèpes, tasty but marred by Muzak. Moderate to expensive.

Ristorante La Cimbali, Kwa Bahal, Thamel. A small café with a nice atmosphere and fair pizza. Cheap.

Japanese

Sushi is out of the question, but Nepalese sukiyaki comes fairly close to the mark. Try miso soup if your stomach's acting up.

Fuji, Kantipath. Good food, beautiful dècor. Expensive.

Koto, north Thamel and Durbar Marg. Probably the best value for money on the Japanese front. Inexpensive to moderate.

Kushi Fuji, Durbar Marg. More authentic, but more expensive.

Vegetarian

These are the only two all-vegetarian restaurants worthy of recommendation, but every restaurant serves at least a few meatless dishes; even Tibetan places will usually do vegetable *momos*.

Nirmala Restaurant, north Thamel. A somewhat dated concept of vegetarianism – crèpes and brown rice, mostly – but tasty. Inexpensive.

Sanghmitra Rajneesh Restaurant, north Thamel. Highly imaginative menu; run by the saturnine son of Boris Lissanevitch, Kathmandu's legendary Russian restauranteur. Moderately priced.

All-rounders

Most budget places fall into this catch-all category: jacks of all trades and usually masters of none. The old standbys are "buff" (water buffalo: cows are sacred, remember) steaks, pastas, cakes and pies.

Cosmopolitan Restaurant, Freak Street. The best pasta and steaks south of Durbar Square; salad with every dish. Inexpensive.

Helena's, Thamel. The cake display window here is Thamel's most popular tourist sight; the usual menu, but a gloomy dècor. Inexpensive.

KC's Restaurant & Bambooze Bar, Thamel. A perennial favourite: cozy surroundings, reliable menu, generous portions; big on "sizzling" dishes. Inexpensive to moderate.

Narayan's, Chhetrapati, Thamel. Very popular for pasta, steaks, pies and homemade ice cream. Inexpensive to moderate.

Rainbow Restaurant, at the *Yeti Cottage* in north Thamel. Good, stodgy food and plenty of it; mellow garden seating. Inexpensive.

Restaurant Oasis, Freak Street. The only patio dining on Freak Street. Inexpensive.

The Snowman, just off Freak Street. Classic subterranean hippy hangout, a real time warp – don't go for the food, though. Cheap.

Breakfast and lunch

Besides the places listed below, many all-rounders offer **set breakfasts**, which often represent great value for money (especially if you like eggs). For a **picnic lunch**, try *Pumpernickel Bakery* for bread and *Nepal Dairy* on Kwa Bahal for cheese. All cold stores sell biscuits, chocolate and the like, while a couple of speciality shops on Dharmapath (near Freak Street) carry imported items you won't find anywhere else. The *Bluebird Supermarkets* on Lazimpath and Tripureswar Marg also stock a wide range of goodies.

Big Bell Café, Durbar Square. Seating is on the roof of an unfinished building, but so close to the temples you can practically touch them. Cheap.

The Gourmet, Thamel. Spotless German deli, looking eerily out of place here, serving authentic wursts and paté. Moderately priced.

Hem's, Thamel. The rooftop terrace is ideal for sipping tea and writing postcards, although the food isn't much to write home about. Inexpensive.

The Lunch Box, just off Freak Street. Ever popular, but better for breakfast than lunch. Inexpensive.

Mike's Breakfast, Durbar Marg. Absolute bliss for breakfast – garden tables, classical music and spot-on food – Americans' eyes will mist over at the corn muffins, waffles and fresh coffee. Stiff competition for tables, though. Moderately priced.

Pumpernickel Bakery, Thamel. Immensely popular for croissant sandwiches and sticky buns, with seating in a pleasant garden out back. Inexpensive.

Desserts

Narayan's, *Helena's* and many other restaurants listed above produce spectacular confections, some of which actually taste as good as they look. If none of those hits the spot, try:

Helena's Country Kitchen, Thamel. Home of Kathmandu's most exotic (and expensive) cakes; under the same management as *Helen's*.

Nirula's, Durbar Marg and New Road. American ice cream parlour meets Indian bureaucracy. The ice cream's pretty good, though. Moderately priced.

Pancha's Pastries, Maru Tol. The last of the original hippy pie shops in a street that was once nicknamed "Pie Alley" – primarily of historical, rather than culinary, interest. Cheap.

Nightlife

For a capital, Kathmandu is pretty sleepy: most restaurants start putting up their chairs around 10pm, and drinking is supposed to stop at 11pm. **Bars** are still a speciality item, found only in Thamel and the big hotels. Attending a **culture show** is probably a more enlightening alternative, but perhaps the best idea of all is to retire early and rise early the next morning, when the city is at its best.

Bars

Thamel's **bar** scene is still very much in its infancy. About half a dozen places serve up beer, mixed drinks and uneven music; as with restaurants, they're more like a Nepali's imagination of what a bar must be like than the real thing, but there's nothing dark or heavy about them, and they're fine for meeting, mixing and prolonging an otherwise short evening. Unlike Thamel restaurants, which are frequented almost exclusively by travellers, the bars here attract a fair share of well-off Nepali lads, who aren't very representative of Nepalis in general. They'll latch onto any lone foreign female, but usually only to flirt. In the high season, bars often keep serving until the wee hours behind drawn curtains and locked doors. Don't forget to warn your innkeeper if you think you're going to stay out late.

Reputations rise and fall from season to season, but the following establishments appear to be in for the duration:

Pub Maya, Chhetrapati Thamel. Small space, loud music, "happy hour" from 3pm to 8pm.

Rum Doodle Restaurant's "40,000 1/2-Foot Bar", Thamel. Kathmandu's oldest, it cultivates a cluttered *après trek* atmosphere; cocktails are remarkably palatable, considering the improvised ingredients.

Spam's Spot, north Thamel. Going for the English pub look, with pint glasses and a few token horse brasses on the walls. Food includes bangers and mash and baked beans.

Tom and Jerry Pub, Thamel. Free popcorn, tasty cocktails and a "happy hour" from 5pm to 8pm.

All the expensive hotels feature sedate **cocktail lounges**, usually open to non-residents. Though it's hardly likely you came to Nepal to gamble, the *Soaltee Oberoi* lays on free buses from the other major hotels to its foreigners-only **casino** (admission free; show your air ticket within one week of arrival and you'll be given tokens worth Rs100).

Culture shows and cinemas

Music and dance are essential parts of Nepalese culture, and perhaps nowhere more so than in Kathmandu, where neighbourhood festivals and parades (not to mention weddings) are a daily occurrence. Touring other regions of the country, you'll encounter other, markedly different, styles of music and dance, and while it's more fun to see these performances in their native context, it's worth checking out a **culture show** before you leave the capital to get a taste of Nepal's folk and performing arts.

The **Pumori Cultural Centre** – really just a bamboo shack in the garden of *Hotel Pumori* in Jyatha Thamel – puts on the most spontaneous and heartfelt show (Wed–Mon 6.30pm; Rs30), and in truth, it's Nepal's only homegrown nightclub. Patronised by Nepalis and foreigners alike, the three-hour performance alternates between dancing and singing, and traditional and pop music. The admission charge includes a free cup of *raksi*; you can also get a Nepali meal. Shows at the big tourist hotels tend to be geared more for tour groups. The **New Himalchuli Cultural Group** does a fairly conventional performance in an auditorium beside the *Hotel Shanker*, north of the Royal Palace (daily 6.30–7.30pm in winter; 7–8pm in summer; Rs80). Ditto the show at the *Hotel de l'Annapurna* on Durbar Marg (daily 7–8pm; Rs100). During the high season **Hotel Vajra** puts on a culture show about once a week, as well as occasional full-length plays. Outside the tourist arena, scheduled performances of the arts are rare; groups allegedly hire out the *National Theatre* on Kantipath for dance, drama and musical events, although the box office seems to be perpetually shut.

Despite stiff competition from video, Kathmandu's several **cinemas**, showing the latest Indian blockbusters in Hindi, are still wildly popular. The easiest ones to get to are the *Jai Nepal Chitra Ghar*, one block east of the Royal Palace entrance, and the *Bishwa Jyoti* on Jamal. Showtime is generally noon, 3pm and 6pm daily and tickets cost between Rs1 and Rs12.

Shopping and shipping

Most traditional Nepalese **handicrafts** are sold in and around Kathmandu. Usually they'll be cheaper where they're actually made, but keen competition keeps prices low in the capital. The majority of wool, metal and wood items are made in the valley anyway, and many "Tibetan" items are imported from India. If you're in the market for **contemporary crafts**, visit *Mahaguthi II*, located just north of *Hotel de l'Annapurna* on Durbar Marg, or the *Nepal Women's Organisation Shop* on Lazimpath – or better still, go to Patan.

Souvenirs and curios

Khukuri knives, made in the eastern hills, are Kathmandu's most ubiquitous souvenir; an authentic one will have a moon-shaped notch at the base of the blade to channel the blood away, and the sheath will contain two smaller knives. Prices start at Rs150, but a fancy one with a bone handle will cost several times that. Vendors in Basantapur Square and Thamel flog vast arrays of **Tibetan curios**: prayer wheels, amulets, bangles, *dorjes* (thunderbolts), *mani* bracelets, snuff bottles, prayer chimes, prayer books, *pung* and *kere* (wooden flasks for water or *chhang*; called *teki* in Nepali), printing blocks and wooden masks, to name but a few. Most old items are Tamang, not Tibetan. Much of what is claimed to be silver, turquoise, coral or ivory is fake, and virtually none of it is antique. The same goes for **jewellery** sold in Thamel, which can nonetheless be quite attractive, and cheap.

Gem sellers are grouped mainly at the east end of New Road (although prices are better in Agra, India). Brass sets of **bagh chal**, Nepal's own "tigers and goats" game, rivalling chess in its complexity, are sold by shops and vendors all over Thamel (about Rs200). A couple of small shops in Thamel are devoted to Nepalese **musical instruments**. Hack minstrels around Thamel play bad renditions of "Frère Jacques" on *saranghis* (traditional fiddles) and in Durbar Square they peddle cheap bamboo flutes. Attractive caddies of **Ilam tea**, Nepal's answer to Darjeeling, are sold opposite the Tourist Information Office and in Thamel.

Certain handicrafts, though widely sold in Kathmandu, are better bought elsewhere in the valley: **metal statuettes** are a Patan specialty, **wood carvings** are best in Bhaktapur, and **papier mâché masks**, **puppets** and **pottery** are all better represented in Thimi and Bhaktapur.

Clothing, textiles and carpets

Thamel and Freak Street are awash with shops selling **wool sweaters**, jackets, mittens and socks, which are among Nepal's best buys. Prices vary with quality – sweaters start at around Rs250. Ask which grade of wool the garment is made from, and check that it isn't going to fall apart at the seams (literally). Similarly inescapable around here are **kit bags**, **caps** and other fashion items made from black wool with Tibetan rainbow fringes.

Hardly fashionable, though many people lap them up, are **T-shirts** and **ready-made clothes**; watch out when you wash them because the cheap fabrics shrink and the colours run. **Tailors**, usually found inside the same clothing shops, are skilled at machine-embroidering designs on clothing. Clothes made from **raw**

silk are sold in a few upmarket boutiques – try the *Cottage Handicrafts House* on Jamal. Shawls and scarfs made of **pashmina**, a fine goat's wool only a cut below cashmere, are cheapest at Indrachowk. **Topis**, the caps that Nepali men wear in much the same way Westerners wear ties, are sold around Asan Tol and in the daily outdoor market at Ratna Park. You'll find **sari material** in shops north of Indrachowk, although for discriminating textile buyers, Patan and Bhaktapur in the Kathmandu Valey (see Chapter Two) are the places to go.

A **Tibetan carpet** is a more serious purchase, requiring a lot of shopping around. Thamel carpet-sellers offer some good deals, but they'll take you to the cleaners if you haven't done your homework. Don't buy until you've had the chance to see carpets being made in Jaulakhel or Pokhara (see those sections in Chapters Two and Four respectively for more details on prices and designs). Similarly expensive are **chain-stitch tapestries**, sold by Kashmiri traders in Thamel: 3' x 5' wool hangings start at Rs1500, silk ones at Rs3000. Some of these are made by Kashmiris living in the Kathmandu Valley, but most are imported.

Thankas

Kathmandu is the biggest market in Nepal for **thankas**, exquisite religious paintings made on paper or silk. *Thanka* subjects are similar to those found on the walls of Tibetan Buddhist monasteries – the Wheel of Life, Lokeshwar the thousand-handed Lord of Compassion, *mandalas*, and various benign and menacing deities – and are designed to work on many levels: as a literal picture of a deity, as a symbolic representation of Buddhist concepts, and as a meditation tool. On the last, highest level, a Buddhist is supposed to meditate on the *thanka*'s deity and either identify with its godly attributes or recognise its demonic ones in him or herself.

A halfway decent *thanka* will start at around Rs500, and an intricate one, using microscopic brushstrokes and a generous amount of gold paint, can cost Rs5000 or more. To test if the paint contains real gold, press a moist finger against it – if no gold comes off on your skin, it's genuine. It's hard to say where to look for a bargain, since *thankas* are all different and don't lend themselves to comparison-shopping, but the biggest grouping of dealers is in Makhan Tol, north of Durbar Square. To get an idea of a fair price for *thankas* and other items, pay a visit to the *Cottage Industries and Handicrafts Emporium* at the east end of New Road. As with carpets, don't commit yourself to a *thanka* until you've shopped around and seen them being painted in Patan or Bhaktapur.

Shipping stuff home

Sending purchases home is never foolproof. The cheapest, most reliable, but thoroughly exasperating method is to take it yourself to the **Foreign Post Section**, around the corner from the GPO on Kantipath (Sun–Fri 10.15am–2pm). Bring the parcel packed, but open for inspection. You begin by filling out a yellow customs form and paying 1-percent tax on the value of the item (no prizes for being truthful). Then a wizened old man stitches the parcel up in cheesecloth (Rs15–50, depending on size) and you have it officially sealed with wax (Rs5), and finally the parcel is weighed (surface rates are Rs250–350 for the first kilo and about Rs60 for each additional kg). The whole business takes an hour and a half even if there's no queue, and you're wise to set aside the whole morning.

Shipping agents, found in Thamel and Freak Street, will do all this work for a service charge of around Rs200 (including packing), but there's always the slight risk of getting conned. Don't entrust shipping to a handicrafts shop unless it's tied to a reputable hotel.

Meditation, yoga and massage

Not surprisingly, Kathmandu is an important centre for spiritual pursuits. This section sketches out the general opportunities, concentrating on established outfits that cater specifically for westerners, but for current happenings check out posters in the popular lodges and restaurants. Opportunities also exist for individual study under Tibetan lamas – see "Baudha" in Chapter Two.

Buddhist meditation

The **Himalayan Yogic Institute** (PO Box 817, Kathmandu; ☎413094), located in Baluwatar, holds weekly teachings on *dharma*, conducts meditation courses and workshops on acupressure massage, *thanka* painting and Tibetan medicine, and has a library and meditation room (daily 9am–6pm). The HYI is affiliated with Kopan Monastery, north of Baudha, where it offers seven- to ten-day meditation courses during the autumn and spring (Rs875, including food and lodging) .

Nepal Vipassana Centre (PO Box 133, Kathmandu; ☎214209) runs ten-day courses on Vipassana meditation, the practice Buddha is said to have followed to achieve enlightenment, at its retreat near Budhanilkantha. These courses aren't for the frivolous: daily meditation begins at 4.30am, and silence is kept for the full ten days. To register or pick up a pamphlet on the course, visit the centre's Kathmandu office (Mon–Fri 5.30pm), well hidden in an unmarked building off a courtyard behind the Honda dealership on Kantipath. All courses are funded by donations.

The **Kathmandu Western Buddhist Centre** conducts one- and two-day courses in Buddhism and meditation at the *Hotel Asia*, Kwa Bahal, during the autumn and spring high seasons.

Yoga and massage

Patanjali Yoga Centre (☎272321), located east of the National Museum in Chhauni, offers classes and residential courses in pure *astanga* yoga, a balance of the eight traditional systems of yoga. The director, Yogacharya Sushil Bhattacharya, is highly respected in yoga circles. Meditation/*hatha* yoga sessions are held daily at 7am and 4pm (Rs75). One- to three-month residential courses in *hatha* yoga, yoga philosophy, diet and health cost $10 per day.

The **Himalayan Yogic Institute** (see above) also does one-day beginners' workshops on *hatha* yoga. For information on free classes in *sahaja* yoga, based on the teachings of guru Sri Mataji Nirmala Devi, ask at the *Gourmet Deli* in Thamel.

Signs around Thamel advertising "yoga" are, very often, misleading attempts to lend credibility to the otherwise suspect profession of **massage**. Masseurs come and go in Kathmandu: some are quite good, but ask to see their credentials. Nepalese massage, done correctly, is a vigorous, all-over operation involving pressure points; a full-body massage takes an hour and costs about Rs100–200.

On from Kathmandu: some travel practicalities

Life in Kathmandu is easy – too easy. Get out before you start gathering moss; later, you'll wonder why you stayed so long. Various **daytrips** to Patan, Bhatapur and other towns and villages of the valley are described in Chapter Two, and with a little extra preparation, **overnight trips** to Dhulikhel, Nagarkot and other hill resorts, or the Tibetan border at Kodari, are all quite feasible (see Chapter Three).

Eventually, you'll want to travel **beyond** the immediate central hills. Pokhara, six to eight hours west of Kathmandu along the sinuous Prithvi Highway, is deservedly the most popular destination (see Chapter Four). All other roads lead to the Tarai, which presents a wealth of possibilities, but unless you're in a hurry to get somewhere, Chitwan National Park (Chapter Five) would be a sensible first stop. **Trekking** is covered in Chapter Seven.

Ticket agents and travel agencies

With their funfair signs advertising "Bus and Train to India" and "Exciting Jungle Safari", **ticket agents** are the used-car salesmen of Nepal, preying on travellers' faith in the apparently limitless possibilities of Kathmandu. Though they make themselves out to be budget travel agencies, they're not registered with the government and they offer very limited services. Many are inept, and some are downright dishonest. Even the honest ones too often make promises they're in no position to fulfil. Naturally, they all mark up the price of the tickets they sell.

For seats on **local buses**, a ticket agent can save you the trouble of making an extra trip to the bus station, and his commission may be money well spent. However, for tickets to Pokhara or India, it's advisable to deal directly with the ticket-issuing company (see sections below) – using a middleman only increases the chances of something going wrong. The Chitwan packages that agents are are always so keen to push are poor value: do it yourself.

Go to a proper **travel agency** to arrange air tickets, car rental or anything involving telexes and suchlike. Some of the more reputable ones are:

Everest Travel Service, Ganga Path (☎220759).
Marco Polo Travels, Kamal Pokhri (☎414192).
Natraj Tours & Travels, Durbar Marg (☎222014); also has a branch in the *Kathmandu Guest House* forecourt.
Nepal Travel, Ram Shah Path. (☎412899)
Peace Travel & Tours, Kantipath (☎226146).
Yeti Travels, Durbar Marg (☎211234).

Tourist buses to Pokhara

Five companies operate regular tourist-bus services to Pokhara. Tickets cost Rs110; book as far in advance as possible during the busy seasons. The buses depart from near Central Immigration on Tridevi Marg, and take six or seven hours. The bus companies are:

Memorie Tours & Travels, Thamel (☎414270).
Paradise Tours & Travels, Jyatha Thamel (☎225898).

Shikhar Nepal Tours & Travels, Chhetrapati (☎215555).
Student Travels & Tours, Chhetrapati (☎221348).
Swiss Travels & Tours, Thamel (☎222231).

Rafting operators in Kathmandu

Unlike trekking, **rafting** in Nepal must be arranged through a company. Most rafting operators are based in Kathmandu; there are a few inexpensive outfits in Pokhara, but their trips are run on a more sedate stretch of river. Smaller Kathmandu companies tend to offer only three-day trips on the Trisuli River for around $20 a day, but for reasons explained in the rafting section (p.150), companies in this price bracket are hard to recommend. The ones listed here are more reputable, hence more expensive:

Great Himalayan Rivers, Lazimpath (☎410937). Experienced company offering Trisuli trips for $35 a day and Sun Kosi trips for $40 a day.

Himalayan Encounter, in the forecourt of the *Kathmandu Guest House* (☎413632). Trips encourage group participation and appeal to gung-ho types. Three-day Trisuli trip costs $99; they also do the Sun Kosi.

Himalayan River Exploration, Naksal (☎418491). Nepal's most reliable and expensive rafting operator, handling mainly overseas bookings.

Karnali River Tour & Exploration, Kamaladi (☎226130). Has the most experience on off-the-beaten-track rivers, but charges $60 a day.

White Magic, Jyatha Thamel (☎226885). Regularly rafts the Trisuli and Sun Kosi, and occasionally the Seti, Karnali and Kali Gandaki. Around $45 a day.

Overland to India

Many travellers get burned by scams involving **tickets to India**. Given that a typical bus/train package involves three different tickets and as many as six companies or agents, the chances of something going wrong are high. Ticket sellers in Kathmandu know that few travellers will come back to complain.

All **bus/train packages** to India involve travelling by regular bus to the border at Sunauli, and then by Indian bus to Gorakhpur, the nearest broad-guage railway station to Kathmandu. It's probably worth paying double in Kathmandu to have a confirmed sleeper out of Gorakhpur, since tickets are hard to obtain there, but Kathmandu ticket sellers require at least a week to arrange train tickets and they demand money up front. When you return to pick up your ticket, you may be told that it's being held at the border – and when you get to the border, you may be told it's in Gorakhpur. If the ticket isn't ready when it was promised, demand your money back and take your chances with the ticket scalpers in Gorakhpur. Be particularly careful when booking first-class sleepers, as there's a racket in replacing them with second-class sleepers or first-class seats. Never surrender your receipt to anyone – without it, you've got no proof of what you paid for.

Bus/bus deals to Darjeeling, Delhi and a few other Indian cities are less chancey. On the other hand, there's less reason to book an Indian bus so far in advance; if you want to save money, buy the Indian bus ticket in India. A Darjeeling **permit** is required to enter India via Kakarbitta in eastern Nepal – this is obtainable at the Indian embassy at no extra charge (ask for it specifically when applying for a visa), but *not* at the border.

Seven companies package tickets to India from Nepal, and all other agents deal through them. Of the seven, the most reliable appear to be *Student Travels & Tours* (☎221348) on Chhetrapati and *Yeti Travels* (☎221234) on Durbar Marg. Many travellers have complained about *New Annapurna Travel Service* and *Sidha Baba Overland Service*.

Travelling to Tibet

At the time of writing, China wasn't allowing individual travellers into Tibet. A few Kathmandu travel agents arrange **group tours** (minimum size three people), but these are strictly chaperoned by *CITS* guides and there's little chance of being allowed to leave the group to travel independently. They're also expensive: around $1000 for ten nights. Allow at least a week for a visa to be issued, and try these agencies:

Natraj Tours & Travels, Durbar Marg and Thamel (☎222014).
Nepal Travel, Ramshah Path (☎412899).
Tibet Travels & Tours, Tridevi Marg (☎410303).

Visas for other Asian countries

If you're moving on to other parts of Asia, the following embassies and consulates in Kathmandu issue **visas**:

Bangladesh, Naksal (☎414943). Apply Mon–Fri 9–10.30am, visa ready at 4pm the next day.
Burma, Chakpat, Patan (☎521788). Visas issued only through travel agents.
India, Lainchaur (☎410900). Apply Mon–Fri 9.30am–noon, visa ready in two days.
Pakistan, Panipokhri (☎410565). Apply Sun–Thurs 2–3pm, visa ready the next day.
Thailand, Thapathali (☎213910). Apply Mon–Fri 9.30am–12.30pm, visa ready in 24 hours.

Listings

Airlines Except for *RNAC*, they're all near the Royal Palace. *Air India*, Kantipath (☎212335); *Biman Bangladesh*, Durbar Marg (☎222544); *British Airways*, Durbar Marg (☎222266); *Indian Airlines*, Durbar Marg (☎223053); *KLM*, Durbar Marg (☎224895); *Lufthansa*, Durbar Marg (☎224341); *Pan Am*, Durbar Marg (☎411824); *PIA*, Durbar Marg (☎223102); *RNAC*, corner of Kantipath and New Road (☎220757 for international; ☎214491 for domestic); *Singapore*, Durbar Marg (☎220759); *Thai*, Durbar Marg (☎223565); *TWA*, Kantipath (☎226704).

American Express c/o *Yeti Travels Pvt Ltd.*, Hotel Mayalu, Ground Floor, Jamal Tole, Durbar Marg (Sun–Fri 10am–1pm & 2–5pm; ☎13596). As usual, you can receive mail at the office if you can produce an *Amex* card or travellers' cheques.

Banks *Nepal Bank*'s main exchange counter is on New Road (daily 7.30am–7.30pm). *Nepal Bank* and *Rastriya Banijya Bank* have branches on Kantipath and Lazimpath and inside the Central Immigration office (Sun–Fri 10am–4pm).

Black market Kathmandu is the only place in Nepal where changing money on the black market is worthwhile. The most common fronts are carpet shops and shipping agents in Thamel and Freak Street; touts prowl incessantly during opening hours. Rates fluctuate, but large-denomination dollar notes should fetch 15 percent over the official rate. Lodge owners and shopkeepers will usually be eager to accept hard currency, but at slightly less than the black market rate.

Books Kathmandu has a great collection of English-language bookshops, and browsing them is one of the city's main forms of nightlife – many stay open till 10pm. Thamel has the lion's share. Still the best, especially for hard-to-find tomes on Nepal, Tibet and Buddhism, is *Pilgrim's Book House*, north of the *Kathmandu Guest House*. Used paperbacks are bargains; most sellers will buy back books for 50 percent of what you paid for them.

Car hire is exorbitant: a Toyota Corolla with driver costs $80 a day; self-drive cars, available only through *Gurans Travel* in Patan (☎524232), cost $115 a day. Better to hire a taxi.

Central Immigration is on Tridevi Marg, just east of Thamel. For general information on trekking permits and visa extensions, see "Red Tape and Visas" in *Basics*. Application hours are Sun–Thurs 10am–2pm and Fri 10am–noon – the queue can be distressingly long in the busy seasons, so get there early. You can retrieve your passport later the same day. Beware the week-long *Dasain* holiday in October. Nearby studios do instant passport photos for Rs50.

Credit cards *Visa* and *Mastercard* are accepted only at major hotels; *Amex* is accepted by boutiques around Durbar Marg. You can draw **cash** against a Visa card at *Grindlays* in Naya Baneswar.

Drugs of all kinds are sold by the same sallow touts who change money. Foreign buyers are invariably overcharged, but the price is still low by any standard.

Embassies and consulates *Australia*, Bhatbhateni (Mon–Thurs 10am–1pm & 2–4pm, Fri 10am–1pm; ☎411578); *Britain*, Lainchaur (Mon–Fri 9am–noon; ☎414588); *Canada*, Lazimpath (Mon–Fri 9am–noon; ☎415193); *France*, Lazimpath (Mon–Fri 8.30am–12.30pm; ☎412332); *Germany*, Kantipath (Mon–Fri 9am–noon; ☎221763); *Israel*, Lazimpath (Mon–Fri 9am–3pm; ☎411811); *Netherlands*, Kumaripati, Patan (Mon–Fri 10am–noon; ☎522915); *US*, Panipokhari (Mon, Wed, Thurs & Fri 8.30am–12.30pm & 1.30–5pm; ☎411179). For visas, see "On from Kathmandu".

Emergencies Police ☎226988; Ambulance ☎211959; Red Cross ☎228094.

Fitness *Kathmandu Fitness Centre*, Lazimpath (☎412473) offers aerobics classes (Rs50) and weight-training sessions (Rs60).

Hospitals, clinics and pharmas For emergencies, *Bir Hospital* (☎221988) on Kantipath is the most central; *Patan Hospital* (☎522278) in Lagankhel is further afield but very professional. For inoculations, stool tests and other diagnoses, make for the *CIWEC Clinic* in Baluwatar (☎410983; 24-hour line; consulting hours Mon–Fri 9am–noon and 1–3.30pm), or *Nepal International Clinic*, a block east of the Royal Palace entrance (24 hours; consulting hours Sun–Fri 10am–5pm; ☎412842). Both offer Western-standard facilities, but are expensive. *CIWEC* also sells some excellent information sheets on health matters. *Kalimati Clinic* (Mon & Fri 1–2.30pm, Wed 10–11.30am;☎270923;) in southwest Kathmandu is cheaper for inoculations, and your fee helps subsidise a local immunisation programme. Pharmas are in every neighbourhood; *Sajha Swastha Sewa*, opposite the Mahakal Temple on Kantipath, is open 24 hours.

Information The *Tourist Information Office* on Ganga Path (the western portion of New Road) is friendly enough, but handicapped by an almost total lack of literature. Hours are Sun–Fri 9am–6pm in summer; 9am–5pm in winter; Fri 4pm closing. Notice boards outside the *Kathmandu Guest House* and elsewhere are useful for finding trekking partners, selling or buying equipment, or hearing about events.

Language courses *Speed Language Institute* (☎220999) in Bag Bazaar runs intensive courses in Nepali; *Karma Group* (☎418049) arranges village stays; *Universal Language Institute* (☎418599) offers courses in Nepali, Newari and Tibetan. See also "Staying On" in *Basics*.

Laundry Cleaners are everywhere around Thamel, and most lodges will send laundry out – in by 9am, back by 6pm.

Libraries The *British Council* on Kantipath has an admirable little collection, where you can pore over recent UK papers and magazines (Mon–Fri 10.30am–6.30pm in summer; 10am–5.30pm in winter). On New Road, the *American Cultural Center*'s library is smaller, but features Kathmandu's only copies of the *New Yorker* (Mon–Fri 11am–6pm).

Maps Best selection of tourist-friendly maps is at *Pilgrim's Book House* in Thamel. For avid cartographers, *Maps of Nepal*, 300m west of the *Everest Hotel* on the road to Bhaktapur, carries an intriguing range of political and resource maps.

Motorcycles Operators in Thamel and Freak Street hire out 200cc bikes for about Rs300 a day, Rs2000 a week. You'll need to leave a plane ticket or some travellers' cheques as a security, and you're supposed to show a driving licence.

Mountain bikes, for hire from several shops in Thamel, range from Rs50 (for a Taiwanese ten-speed) to Rs160 a day (for an eighteen-speed American model). See p.141 for tips on touring.

"Mountain flights" *RNAC* lays on hour-long scenic flights towards Everest, costing $95. Book through *Yeti Travels* on Durbar Marg for the best seat allocation.

Newspapers and magazines The *Rising Nepal* sells out early at *Pilgrim's* and shops along New Road. The *International Herald Tribune, Time, Newsweek* are available at most bookshops.

Photography Print and slide film is widely available at only slightly higher than western prices; shops along New Road are competitive. High-quality processing labs in Thamel and on New Road handle print and E6 transparency films.

Post The GPO is open for franking and stamps Sun–Thurs 9am–4.30pm & Fri 9am–3pm, and for Poste Restante Sun–Thurs 10.15am–4pm (3pm closing in winter) & Fri 10.15am–2pm. Many lodges will run letters down to the GPO, but make sure they have them franked. Pilgrim's sells stamps for a 10-percent fee. Send parcels from the Foreign Post Section (see "Shipping stuff home").

Radio and TV Radio Nepal reads English-language news bulletins at 8am and 8pm. Nepal TV broadcasts the news in English at 8.40pm.

Sports Football matches at the *National Stadium*, at the southern end of Kantipath, can be good fun: watch the Nepalis grapple with various Asian national teams. The Soaltee Oberoi, Everest Hotel and Yak & Yeti all have tennis courts, open to non-residents for a fee. For golf, see Gokarna Safari Resort in Chapter Two.

Swimming pools and saunas *Hotel de l'Annapurna* charges non-guests Rs100 to use its pool and Rs65 for the sauna, while use of the *Yak & Yeti*'s pool costs Rs115. *Hotel Woodlands'* facilities are less appealing (Rs60 for the pool, Rs100 for the sauna).

Telephones and telegrams The *Central Telegraph Office* is open 24 hours a day, seven days a week; the queue can range from a few minutes to over an hour. International calls cost Rs85 per minute. Most lodges with a phone will let you dial direct overseas (adding a service charge of 20–25 percent) and make local calls for a couple of rupees each.

Trekking equipment Almost anything can be rented in Thamel or Freak Street, including climbing gear. Figure on Rs10 per day for a good sleeping bag, pack or parka. Bring small items like water bottles and sunglasses from home, where they're cheaper, and don't bother hiring boots since it's no good trying to break them in on the trail. As for woollens, you might as well buy.

Wiring money to Nepal takes two to three working days. Have funds transferred to *Nepal Bank*, New Road (☎225904; telex 2220 LUXMI NP); *Nepal Arab Bank*, Kantipath (☎220089; telex 2385 NABIL NP); *Nepal Indosuez Bank*, Durbar Marg (☎228229; telex 2435 INDOSU NP); or *Nepal Grindlays Bank*, Naya Baneswar (☎212683; telex 2531 GRINDLY NP).

festivals

Your chances of coinciding with a festival while in Kathmandu are good, since the capital spends about a month out of every year partying. The festivals listed here are just the main events; neighbourhood festivals happen all the time. Dates are determined according to the lunar and Nepalese calendars, and vary from year to year – enquire at the tourist office for dates, or consult a Nepalese calendar, available in tourist bookshops.

Basant Panchami Spring festival, marked by a VIP ceremony in Durbar Square, while children celebrate *Saraswati Puja* on the same day at Swayambu (late January or February).

Losar Tibetan New Year, observed at Swayambu but more significantly at Baudha, described in Chapter Two (February).

Shiva Raatri "Shiva's Night" is celebrated with bonfires in Kathmandu, but the most interesting observances are at Pashupatinath, described in Chapter Two (late February or early March).

Holi Popular week-long water-splashing festival, reaching a climax on the full moon in March (sometimes early April).

Seto Machhendranath A flamboyant four-day procession in which the white mask of Machhendranath is placed in a towering chariot and pulled from Jamal to an area south of Freak Street (late March or April).

Ghoda Jaatra Equestrian displays at Tudikhel (March or April).

Nawa Barsa Nepali New Year (April 13 or 14): Kathmandu holds parades, but Bhaktapur's festivities are more exciting (see Chapter Two).

Buddha Jayanti The anniversary of Buddha's birth, enlightenment and death, celebrated at Swayambu (May).

Ghanta Karna Demon effigies are burned on street corners throughout the city (late July or early August).

Naga Panchami A day set aside for the propitiation of snake spirits with offerings and worship (late July or early August).

Gai Jaatra The Cow festival, marked by processions led by garlanded boys costumed as cows (late July or August).

Indra Jaatra A week of chariot processions and masked-dance performances; on the last day, the king receives a special *tika* from Kathmandu's "living goddess" and beer flows from the mouth of Seto Bhairab in Durbar Square (September).

Dasain A mammoth ten-day festival celebrated in most parts of Nepal; in Kathmandu, mass sacrifices are held at the Kot courtyard near Durbar Square on the ninth day, *Durga Puja*, and the king bestows *tikas* to all and sundry at the Royal Palace on the last day (October).

Tihar The Festival of Lights, celebrated here (as in most places) with masses of oil lamps throughout the city and five days of special observances (late October or November).

travel details

Buses

For bus services within the Kathmandu Valley, see "Travel Details" in Chapter Two. As for long-distance buses, you've three kinds to choose from:

Tourist buses leave from Tridevi Marg to Pokhara (2-7 daily, depending on season; 6-7hr).

Sajha buses leave **from Bhimsen Tower** to Bhairawa (2 daily; 8-9hr); Birganj (2 daily; 10hr – stops at Tadi Bazaar for Chitwan); Hetauda (1 daily; 8hr – via Rajpath) and Janakpur (1 daily; 10hr); Pokhara (2 daily; 7-8hr) and Trisuli (2 daily; 4hr). Tickets go on sale the day before at a booth east of Bhimsen Tower.

Public buses generally depart **from the main bus station**. Buying tickets is confusing, since several companies operate out of a score of booths, and seats often sell out the day before. Services to Banepa (frequent; 1hr 30min); Bhairawa/Sunauli (8 daily; 9-10hr); Bharabise (6 daily; 5hr); Biratnagar (7 night buses; 16hr); Birganj (4 daily; 10hr); Butwal (7 daily; 8hr); Dharan (6 night buses; 16hr); Dhulikhel (frequent; 2hr); Gorkha (2 daily; 7hr); Janakpur (6 night buses; 12hr); Jiri (3 daily; 9-13hr); Kakarbitta (8 night buses; 20hr); Nepalganj (6 daily; 15hr); Pokhara (8 daily; 8-9hr); Tadi Bazaar (3 daily; 6hr) and Tansen (1 night bus; 12hr). **From Paknajol**

(the intersection 300m north of *Kathmandu Guest House*) buses leave for Trisuli (4 daily; 4-5hr).

Additional **night buses** run **from Bhimsen Tower** to Birganj (4 nightly; 10-12hr); Hetauda (4 nightly; 9hr – via Rajpath); Pokhara (8 nightly; 8-9hr) and Sunauli (4 nightly; 10hr).

Planes

RNAC connects Kathmandu to over 30 domestic airstrips. Only a few routes are worth mentioning here.

From Tribhuwan Airport to Biratnagar (daily; 1hr 30min); Dhangadhi (2 weekly; 2hr); Janakpur (3 weekly; 40min); Jumla (1 weekly; 1hr 40min); Lamidanda (2 weekly; 45min); Lukla (up to 5 daily; 45min); Mahendranagar (1 weekly; 2hr 45min); Manang (seasonal; 1hr); Nepalganj (daily; 1hr 30min); Phaplu (2 weekly; 40min); Pokhara (4 daily; 40min); Silgadhi Doti (weekly; 2hr); Taplejung (1 weekly; 1hr 15min) and Tumlingtar (4 weekly; 1hr).

Boy dressed as a cow during the *Gai Jaatra* festival

CHAPTER TWO

THE KATHMANDU VALLEY

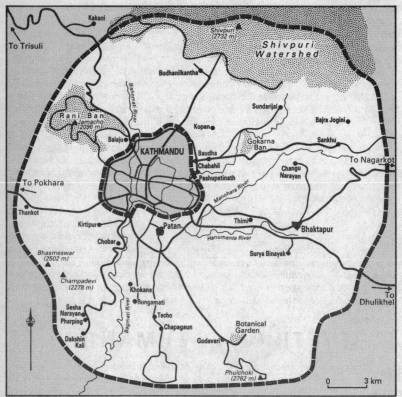

F ew places on earth can rival the **Kathmandu Valley**'s combination of
natural and man-made beauty. Despite the capital's encroachments, the
fertile, terraced valley maintains its traditional, rural ways in a hundred
huddled brick villages, few of which ever see foreigners; most of the valley
floor shimmers in an undulating patchwork of paddy fields – brown, golden or
brilliant green, depending on the season – crisscrossed by rutted paths and
country lanes. Viewed from any point along its rim, with snowy peaks behind, it
seems almost magically preserved. But above all it's the valley's incredible wealth
of art and architecture that overwhelms visitors, just as it did the early explorers.
"The valley consists of as many temples as there are houses, and as many idols as
there are men", gushed William Kirkpatrick, the first Englishman to reach

Kathamandu, and generations of travellers since have accurately (if patronisingly) described it as a "living museum". If most of this chapter is devoted to temples and holy sites – there are no forts, you'll notice – it's because religion is the best and most fascinating window on Nepalese culture.

Until two hundred years ago, this protected bowl *was* Nepal (and for many hill people outside the valley, it still is). At that time, Kathmandu was only one of three major city-states constantly battling for dominance: **Patan**, just across the Bagmati River, controlled the southern part of the valley, while **Bhaktapur** ruled the east. The historical divisions are profoundly ingrained in valley society, and they live on in religious practices, festivals and even dress. This chapter divides the valley into three sections, as much for practical reasons as historical ones, since roads and transport have developed out of the old patterns of settlement.

The sheer density of sights in the valley is phenomenal. Roads radiate out to dozens of towns and villages, and you won't go wrong with any of them. Hindu holy places abound: the great pilgrimage complex of **Pashupatinath**, the sleeping Vishnu of **Budhanilkantha**, the sacrificial pit of **Dakshin Kali** and the hilltop temple of **Changu Narayan** are the most outstanding. If Buddhism is your main interest, head for the great stupa of **Baudha**, the centre of Tibetan Buddhist worship and study in Nepal, or the *bahals* of **Patan**, the valley's most Buddhist city. For medieval scenes, try **Kirtipur**, **Bungamati** or, best of all, **Bhaktapur**. For views, you're spoilt for choice – the protected areas of **Shivpuri**, **Rani Ban** and **Godavari** stand out, but almost any hill will do.

Getting around the valley is generally easiest by **bike** (see p.141 for tips on mountain-bike touring). In the sections that follow, bus routes are mentioned where they exist (fares are usually Rs5 or less), but unless it's stated otherwise, take it as given that the quickest way to get there is with your own wheels. **Walking**, on the other hand, is often more rewarding: distances are small, trails are everywhere, and locals are always happy to give directions. The *Geo-Buch* colour **map** of the valley is by far the best for serious walking, although *Mandala*'s much cheaper dyeline job will probably suffice: see "Information and Maps" in *Basics* for further details .

NORTH OF KATHMANDU

Chapter One covers Kathmandu inside the Ring Road; this section deals with the remainder of the northern valley. Most people will treat the sights described here as **day trips** from Kathmandu – some places are even within walking distance of town – but if you're interested in Buddhism, or you're just getting fed up with Thamel, an **overnight stay** in Baudha would be a smart move.

Pashupatinath, Gorakhnath and Ghujeshwari

Often likened to Varanasi in India, **PASHUPATINATH** (pronounced Posh-*potty*-not) is Nepal's holiest Hindu pilgrimage site: a time-warp enclave of exotic temples, cremation ghats, ritual bathers and half-naked *sadhus*. The sacred complex lies just beyond the Ring Road east of Kathmandu – incongruously close

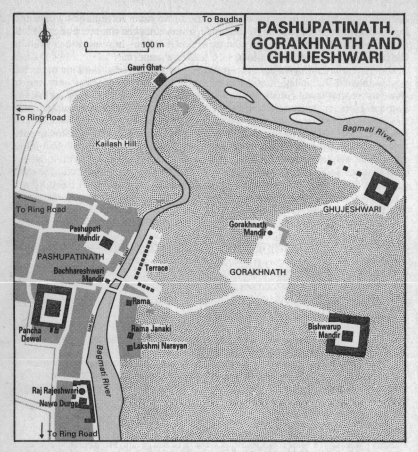

to the modern airport, but fortunately sheltered from it in a wooded ravine. Pashupatinath, together with the associated temples of Gorakhnath and Ghujeshwari, is a heady cocktail of Hindu – and to a lesser extent Buddhist – proceedings, spiked with some of the most bizarre mythology in the world.

Buses from Kathmandu's Ratna Park drop you off at a busy, modern intersection on the Ring Road, southwest of the temple area. The site's layout favours an anti-clockwise circuit on foot, first around Pashupatinath's temples and ghats, then up to Gorakhnath, on to Ghujeshwari and back. Instead of returning to Pashupatinath, however, you might want to continue on to Baudha, which is only a kilometre or so further northeast along a rough track.

The Pashupatinath complex

The **temples of Pashupatinath** straddle the Bagmati River, which is thought by Hindus to be the holiest in the Kathmandu Valley, and this specific stretch the most sacred of all. To die and be cremated here is to be released from the cycle

Mitra park - Chowk

of rebirths, according to tradition. Wives used to commit *sati* on their husbands' funeral pyres here, and although the practice was outlawed a century ago, it's still widely believed that husbands and wives who bathe here together will be remarried in the next life. Bathing is considered especially meritorious on full-moon days and on *Magh Sankranti* (usually January 14), and for women, during the festival of *Tij* in late August or early September. Foreigners are free to observe most of these rituals, but it's essential to respect the privacy of bathers and worshippers. Be especially sensitive about photographing people and crema-tion pyres.

Shiva is the principal deity here, in one of his more benign forms: **Pashupati, Lord of the Animals**, in whose name the King of Nepal ends all his public addresses. Several tales are told of how Shiva came by this title. Nepali schoolchildren are taught that Shiva took his wife Parvati to this spot for their honeymoon and exhausted her with so much lovemaking that she turned herself into a deer to escape; by transforming himself into a stag to pursue her, Shiva gained dominion over the animals of the forest.

SADHUS, YOGINS AND GANJA

Sadhus, those dreadlocked, ashen waifs usually seen lurking around Hindu temples, are essentially an Indian phenomenon. However, Nepal, being the setting for so many of Shiva's amorous and ascetic exploits, is a favourite *sadhu* stomping ground, and nowhere more so than Pashupatinath, which is rated as one of the four most important *Shaiva* pilgrimage sites. On *Shiva Raatri* (held on the new moon of late February or early March), Pashupatinath hosts a full-scale *sadhu* convention, which draws pilgrims from all over the subcontinent. The government lays on free firewood for the festival.

Shaiva sadhus follow Shiva in one of his best-loved and most enigmatic guises – the wild, dishevelled **yogin**, the master of yoga, who sits motionless atop a Himalayan peak for eons at a time and whose hair is the source of the mighty Ganga (Ganges) River. *Sadhus* live solitary lives, always on the move, subsisting on alms and owning nothing but what they carry. They bear Shiva's emblems: the *trisul* (trident), *damaru* (two-sided drum), a necklace of seeds, and perhaps a conch shell (*sankha*) for blowing haunting calls across the cosmic ocean; they smear themselves with ashes, symbolising Shiva's role as the destroyer, who reduces all things to ash so that creation can begin anew; and on their foreheads usually paint a trident-shaped *tika*. (In addition to the trident, *sadhus* employ scores of other *tika* patterns, each with its own cult affiliation and symbolism.)

A Sadhu

Given Shiva as a role model, *Shaiva sadhu* theology – insofar as it exists – is a bloody-minded business. As befits followers of a mountaintop ascetic who is also the god of the phallus, *sadhus* practice celibacy, performing diverse contortions and mortifications of the flesh to free themselves from sensual passions, yet radiate a smouldering sexuality. They're forbidden to take intoxicants, but blithely get stoned out of their heads on **ganja**, whose transcendental powers were supposedly discovered by Shiva. Marijuana, which grows wild throughout hill Nepal, is smoked by *sadhus* in a *chillum*:, and with each toke on the vertical clay pipe they intone *"Bam Shankar"* –

Pashupati Mandir

From a terrace high above the east bank of the river you can look directly across to the gilded roofs of the main **Pashupati Mandir**, the holy of holies for Nepali followers of Shiva. Like many orthodox Hindu temples, it's only open to Hindus (in practice, anyone who looks Asian). From the outside, though, you can glimpse two symbols that are found in front of almost every Shiva temple, their gargantuan proportions here a measure of the temple's sanctity: the prongs of a two-storey-high *trisul* are just visible from the terrace; while by peering through the main entrance at the other (west) side of the temple you can see the enormous, brass (and anatomically correct) backside of Nandi, Shiva's faithful bull, who is yet another reminder of the god's procreative power.

Hidden inside, the famous **Pashupati lingam** is believed to display four carved faces, one of which, Buddhists claim, is that of Buddha. Hindus associate this *lingam* with one of the most famous myths of Shiva, in which the god transformed his phallus into an infinite pillar of light and challenged Brahma and Vishnu – the other members of the Hindu "trinity" – to find the ends of it. Brahma flew heavenward, while Vishnu plumbed the depths of hell; both were forced to abandon the search, but Brahma falsely boasted of success, only to be caught out by Shiva. *Shaivas* claim that this is why Brahma is seldom worshipped, Vishnu gets his fair share, and Shiva is revered over all.

The gold-clad pagoda dates from the late seventeenth century, but inscriptions indicate that a temple has stood here since at least the fifth century, and some historians suspect it goes back to the third century BC, when the ancient village of Deopatan, which once occupied the rise just to the west, is said to have been founded. The temple apparently emerged as a hotbed of tantric practices in the eleventh century and remained so for 400 years, until the Malla kings reined things in by importing conventional Brahman priests from south India – an arrangement that continues to this day.

Along the west bank

Many of the buildings around the main temple, including the tall, whitewashed ones overlooking the Bagmati's west bank, are *dharmsalas*, rest houses set aside for devout Hindus approaching death. Cremations are held continuously on two **burning ghats** along the embankment: Arya Ghat, north of the footbridges, is reserved for the royal family and VIPs, while Ram Ghat, to the south, is used by other members of the higher castes. The barbecue stench around here is sure to put you off lunch.

The small pagoda between the two footbridges is the **Bachhaleshwari Mandir**, dedicated to Shiva's consort Parvati in one of her mother-goddess roles. Next to it stands a ten-foot terracotta freize of Vishnu and other sculptures of Ganesh and Gauri (alias Parvati). Running south along the west bank is another string of metal-roofed *dharmsalas*, which you can explore in a limited way; behind them broods the gothic bulk of **Pancha Dewal** (which has now become a home for the destitute), whose five Mughal-style cupolas are visible from high up on the opposite bank. Sticking out of the embankment in front of the second-to-last *dharmsala* is a small but priceless seventh-century **Buddha statue**, looking rather out of place in this Hindu Lourdes. The southernmost building shelters two temples in its courtyard, the oval **Raj Rajeshwari** and the gilded pagoda of **Nawa Durga**.

The east bank

Crossing over to the east bank here, the first thing you'll reach is a pockmarked slope: a **burial ground**, which also doubles as the local latrine, where plots are reserved for *sadhus*, infants and people too poor to afford wood for a funeral pyre.

Moving northwards and uphill, you'll enter a wide, paved enclosure which during *Shiva Raatri* is chock-a-block with *sadhus* doing mysterious and sometimes gruesome penances. Two small temples are found here: the one with a statue of Garuda in front is called **Lakshmi Narayan**, in honour of Vishnu (aka Narayan) and his wealth-bringing wife Lakshmi; the other is the **Rama Janaki**, which contains statues of Rama – Vishnu's incarnation as a mortal in the *Ramayana* epic – and his whole family, including Hanuman the monkey king, who helped rescue Rama's wife Sita from the clutches of a Sri Lankan demon. Sita is popular among Nepali Hindus, since she was born in Janakpur in the eastern Tarai. These temples, along with the **Rama Mandir** in the next compound and the eleven great *shivalayas* (box-like *lingam* shelters) along the river further north, are disappointingly recent and un-Nepalese. The temples at Pashupatinath are built and rebuilt often – renovations are the standard way of winning favour with gods and men – and wealthy Indian patrons are among the principal contributors to the development fund.

Gorakhnath and Ghujeshwari

The main stairway up the east bank carries on to the mellow **Gorakhnath Mandir** at the top of the hill. Visiting this compound, after the sensory overload below, is like entering a sound-proofed room. The temple itself, a medium-sized *shikhra* structure, isn't interesting – what will amaze you is the sight of hundreds of **shivalayas** arranged in crumbling rows in the forest, mottled by shade and shafts of sunlight. The place has the romantic, ruined feel of an overgrown cemetery, with broken statuary lying undisturbed and stone inscriptions recording long-forgotten decrees. You could easily mistake the *shivalayas* for tombs, but their iconography – the *trisul*, statues of Nandi and Shiva (always with an erection), the *lingam* atop the *yoni* – proclaims them to be Shiva shrines. It's a fine spot for a picnic, though you have to watch out for the thieving monkeys. The onion dome rising above the trees to the southeast of Gorakhnath is the **Bishwarup Temple**, dedicated to Vishnu in his "universal form" (entrance only to Hindus).

The **Ghujeshwari** (or Guhyeshwari) **Mandir** sits at the bottom of the path that continues downhill from Gorakhnath. Here, too, non-Hindus can only peek from outside, but the legend behind this temple is one of the all-time masterpieces of Hindu surrealism. The story goes that Shiva's first wife, Sati, offended by some insult, threw herself onto a fire (thus the term *sati*, or *suttee*); Shiva retrieved her corpse and, blinded by grief, flew to and fro across the subcontinent, scattering parts of the body in 51 sacred places. Ghujeshwari is where Sati's vagina (some say her anus) fell. As a consquence, the temple here represents the female counterpart to Pashupatinath and is held to be every bit as sacred, its chief focus being a well into which worshippers throw offerings. Buddhists consider Ghujeshwari to be one of the valley's four mystic Bajra Joginis – powerful tantric goddesses – and the site to be the seed from which the Swayambhu lotus grew.

From Ghujeshwari a lane follows the river back around to Pashupatinath, passing **Gauri Ghat**, a peaceful spot where the river enters the Pashupatinath ravine and monkeys leap from branches and cliffs into the water. The road crosses the river here and circles around to the village of Pashupatinath, while a trail after the river crossing takes a more direct route up and over **Kailash Hill**. This grassy knoll, named after the Tibetan mountain where Shiva does his meditating, gives good views of the mountains as well as the Pashupatinath area.

Baudha

To ancient travellers along the Kathmandu–Tibet trade route, the ten-kilometre corridor from Pashupatinath to Sankhu was known as the zone of *siddhi* (supernatural powers), where guardian deities dwelt and all wishes were granted. The biggest, most auspicious landmark along this route was – and still is – the great stupa at **BAUDHA** (or BODHNATH), about 5km east of downtown Kathmandu.

One of the world's largest stupas, Baudha is generally acknowledged to be the most important Tibetan Buddhist monument outside Tibet – Tibetans simply call it *Chorten Chempo* or "Great Stupa" – and since 1959 it has become the Mecca of **Tibetan exiles** in Nepal. Tibetans now run most of the businesses along the main road and around the stupa, while the construction of monasteries is creating a regular suburban sprawl to the north: despite the coach parties and souvenir sellers, Baudha gives you a thorough dunking in Tibetan culture, both its proud past and anxious present. Dusk is the best time to be here, after the daytrippers have gone, when the resonant chanting of monks and the otherworldly cacophony of their music drifts from the upper rooms of the houses that ring the stupa, and pilgrims shuffle and prostrate their way around the dome. If you want an extra helping, go during **Losar** in February, when Baudha hosts the biggest celebration of Tibetan New Year in Nepal.

The stupa

Assigning a reliable age to the stupa is impossible, and historians are left at the mercy of legends, which seem to fix Baudha's origins around the fifth century AD.

A **Tibetan text** relates how a daughter of Indra stole flowers from heaven and was reassigned to earth as a lowly poultryman's daughter, yet prospered and shamed the valley's wealthy folk by building a gigantic stupa to honour the Buddha of the Previous Age. Tibetans attach great importance to this tale because it's attributed to Guru Padma Sambhava, Tibet's first and best-loved evangelist. Interestingly, in the same manuscript the guru warns of an invasion by a giant enemy, which would scatter the Tibetan people south into Nepal and India.

The **Newar legend** has a firmer historical grounding, involving a drought that struck Kathmandu during the reign of the early Lichhavi king, Vikramajit. When court astrologers advised that only the sacrifice of a virtuous man would bring rain, Vikramajit commanded his son Mana Deva to go to the royal well on a moonless night and decapitate the shrouded body he would find there. Mana Deva obeyed, only to find that he had sacrificed his own father, and so to expiate his guilt he erected the Baudha stupa.

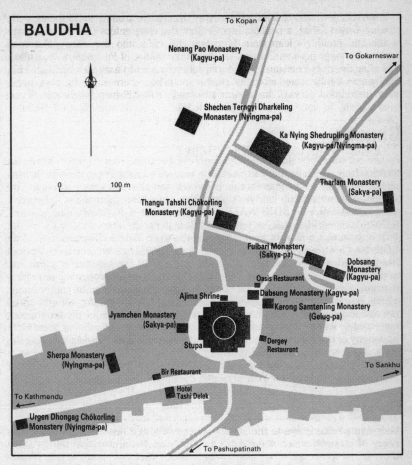

While less embellished than Swayambhu, Baudha is in its own way more interactive: you can climb up onto **the stupa**'s base, and during the windy autumn months kids fly kites from it. The dome is elevated on three *mandala*-shaped plinths of decreasing size, which reinforce the notion of the stupa as a meditation tool. As usual, Buddha's searching blue eyes are painted on the four sides of the central spire, and above them rise the thirteen golden steps to *nirvana*. Instead of five *dhyani* Buddhas, however, 108 (an auspicious number) much smaller images are set in niches around the dome.

The small **Ajima Shrine** at the far side of the stupa shelters the image of a nasty goddess dining on a hapless victim; Newars consider this ghoul to be Harati, the protectress of children. Next door is a room-sized prayer wheel – all are welcome to spin it – and on the other side of the shrine you'll see the tanks where whitewash is mixed during festivals.

Baudha's **pilgrims** are arguably its greatest attraction, as the stupa is famed throughout the Himalayan region for its wish-fulfilling properties. Prayer wheels, heavy silver jewellery and rainbow-striped aprons are good general indicators of Tibetan origins. You can tell the men of Kham, in eastern Tibet, by the red tassels in their long hair. Nomads from the central Tibetan plateau wear sheepskin coats with extra-long sleeves. Bhutanese men and women keep their hair cropped short and wear distinctive embroidered robes. Ladakhi women are distinguished by their velvet dresses, and high-crowned silk hats with small wings on either side. In addition, Nepali Tamangs and Bhotiyas (see Chapters Three and Seven) visit Baudha in force, although the stupa has no special attraction for Buddhist Newars.

The monasteries and back lanes

The past decade has seen an unsettling spate of monastery-building at Baudha, and there are now more than a dozen *gompas* (monasteries) scattered around the neighbourhood. All four of the major Tibetan Buddhist sects (see "Religion" in *Contexts*) are represented at least twice, and there's even a Sherpa *gompa* – for a full listing of names and sects, refer to the Baudha map.

The older **monasteries around the stupa** keep their doors open most of the time, and welcome spectators during their morning and evening services. Furnishings and icons are broadly similar in each. The gilded statues at the front of the assembly hall will usually represent Buddha, *bodhisattvas* or the founder of the monastery's sect. Spread out in front of these are likely to be butter lamps, which monks and pilgrims continually replenish; heaps of rice piled onto three-tiered silver stands, which are objects of meditation; conical dough-cakes symbolising deities; and offerings of fruit, coins, flowers and incense. Frescos on the walls depict four temple guardians or, like *thankas*, express the complex cosmology of Tibetan Buddhism.

If you follow either of the two lanes heading **north of the stupa**, the romance evaporates in short order: this is Baudha the boomtown, an unplanned quagmire of garbage-strewn lanes and unlovely new buildings. It's a disturbing picture of the bittersweet present – and very likely the future – of the Tibetan diaspora. The monasteries here, secluded behind high walls and iron gates, have been deliberately named after *gompas* in Tibet that were destroyed by the Chinese, and it's hoped that, besides keeping the flame of Tibetan Buddhism alight, they'll help bring about the resurrection of their namesakes. Money is pouring into Baudha from all over the world to build them, but looking at the results you might wonder whether the Tibetans are being driven down the infamous road of good intentions.

Further afield

Boom town aside, Baudha makes a good springboard for several walks and bike rides in this part of the valley. **Kopan Monastery**, occupying a beautifully leafy ridge about 3km due north of the stupa, is an easy target. From there, it's a delightful three-hour hike north along the ridge to NAGI GOMPA, and another hour's descent to Budhanilkantha. In the opposite direction, Pashupatinath is only about a half-hour's walk south of Baudha. The path – revoltingly smelly at first – sets off from the main road almost opposite the entrance to the stupa. Sankhu, Gokarneswar and Sundarijal, described in the next section, all make fine excursions on a bike.

THE DHARMA SCENE

Baudha's western community is well-established but perceptibly aloof. To become a part of it you need either an introduction or a lot of time, since serious western students of *dharma* tend to regard tourists as spiritual interference; the ones who'll deign to talk with you may not shed much light on things. Many westerners rate Baudha as the **best place in the world to study Tibetan Buddhism**, for although Dharmsala in India is better known because the Dalai Lama is based there, the presence of the Tibetan government-in-exile creates a politically charged atmosphere that can distract from serious spiritual study. Moreover, Dharmsala is heavily dominated by the Dalai Lama's *Gelug-pa* order, whereas at Baudha all four sects are well represented, making it easier to sample the different traditions.

The Chinese occupation of Tibet killed or drove away an entire generation of teachers, and Baudha's line-up of **lamas**, though formidable, reflects this: most are either very old or rather young. By far the most popular among the *dharma* set is **Chokyi Nyima**, abbot of the Ka Ning Shedrupling Monastery, who speaks excellent English and runs meditation courses during the tourist season (For more on Chokyi Nyima see "Tibetan Exiles in Nepal" in *Contexts*). Some westerners study at Shechen Terngyi Dharkeling Monastery under **Dingo Khyentse**, a leading light from Bhutan and one of the Dalai Lama's teachers. **Choge Trichen**, who runs the Jyamchen Monastery, is also abbot of the Tibetan *gompa* at Lumbini, Buddha's birthplace in the Tarai. Curiously, a young Spanish boy is being groomed as the reincarnation of Kopan Monastery's Yeshe Lama.

Western monks wear the same maroon robes and have taken the same monastic vows as Tibetan monks but, partly because of visa restrictions, aren't expected to make the same commitment to a monastery. While Tibetan monks live at their monastery, maintaining the building and making visits to the local community, westerners are free to come and go. Given a three-month visa, most cram as much personal instruction as possible into their time, and then try to maintain a long-distance teacher-disciple relationship from home. Some follow their lama on speaking tours overseas, which are conveniently scheduled during the soggy monsoon months. In any case, a lifestyle with one foot in the West and the other in the East requires either sponsorship or independent means.

A separate wing of the *dharma* crowd consists of westerners living in Baudha for a season of **individual study**. Some are just trying Buddhism on for size, others are earnestly shopping around for a lama. Most lamas and teachers at Baudha give occasional open talks – with or without English translation – and will normally agree to one-on-one meetings with anyone who shows a keen interest. To find out about upcoming teachings, check out the notice board at the *Bir Restaurant*, or try asking some of the regulars there. But if you've had no prior experience with Buddhism, you'd probably want to test the waters first by enrolling in a **meditation course**. The week-long retreats run by *Himalayan Yogic Institute* at Kopan Monastery are the usual place to start; Kopan also holds a month-long course each November (see "Meditation, yoga and massage" in Chapter One).

Practicalities

The coach-party crush is worst between mid-morning and late afternoon – Baudha is much pleasanter after hours. It also has the widest range of budget and moderately priced accommodation in the valley outside Kathmandu, so it's well worth staying overnight. If you're not on a bicycle, **buses** leave frequently from Ratna Park in front of the *Air India* office.

Although western **meals** are available, you'd be foolish to miss trying Tibetan specialities such as the ravioli-like *kothe* and *momo*, chunky *thukpa* soup, and *tongba* (hot millet grog) – check out the many cheap and cheerful local eateries along the main road. The *Bir Restaurant*, west of the stupa on the main road, is *the* meeting place for westerners in Baudha, with a cozy atmosphere and inexpensive (but unremarkable) food. In the stupa area itself, the tiny *Oasis Restaurant* is good for breakfast, tea and Tibetan snacks, while the *Dergey Restaurant and Coffee Shop* does Chinese and Tibetan food and espresso coffee.

Of Baudha's **budget lodges**, the *Bir Restaurant*'s rooms are closest to the heart of things, but often full up with long-term *dharma* types (singles Rs50, doubles Rs75). Across the street, *Hotel Tashi Delek*'s (☎471380) south-facing rooms have balconies that overlook a garden and paddy fields (singles Rs80, doubles Rs110). *Snowlion Lodge* (☎4470341) is comparable, but further from the stupa – it's on the main road about 400m east of the entrance and offers rooms with attached baths for Rs80.

Moderately priced hotels are less conveniently situated. *Maya Guest House* (☎470266), east of the *Snowlion*, has a gorgeous garden (singles Rs350, doubles Rs450, including breakfast and transport from Kathmandu). *Hotel Stupa* (☎470385), even further east, is large and efficient, but on the sterile side (singles $9, doubles $13). The government-run *Tara Gaon Resort Hotel* (☎410409) is a strange affair with self-catering rooms, nearly 1km west of the stupa (singles $15.50, doubles $21).

Tibetan **souvenirs** at Baudha are notoriously overpriced, and the hard bargaining that's required isn't really worth it unless you're seeking genuinely obscure or antique items. Look out for Tibetan trumpets (*ka-ling*), flasks (*pung* or *kere*), butter-tea churns, festival masks and prayer-flag printing blocks. For **books** on Buddhism, try *Dharma Books* on the main road west of the stupa; near the entrance you can buy **film**.

The Sankhu road

The paved road past Baudha – the old trade route to Tibet – begins at Chabahil on the Ring Road and rolls eastwards as far as Sankhu. It's a gentle ride on a bicycle, the only hazard being the sheaves of rice and wheat that farmers spread out during harvest time. From Ratna Park, an erratic **minibus** service plies the whole way to Sankhu; four buses a day go as far as Gokarna Ban, and dozens cover the stretch to Chabahil and Baudha.

Chabahil

Just off the Ring Road, **CHABAHIL** is part Kathmandu suburb and part Baudha Tibetan spillover – a cluster of shops and concrete buildings without much character, though it's one of the valley's oldest settlements. Tibetans have been drawn to Chabahil's **stupa**, which despite its newish appearance possibly predates the stupas of Baudha and Swayambhu. Its construction is generally attributed to Charumati, who settled here and married a local prince after accompanying her father Ashoka on his well-documented pilgrimage to the Kathmandu Valley in the third century BC. The prince, Devapala, is credited with founding Deopatan, one of the valley's ancient capitals, which stood just south of here near Pashupatinath. Chabahil's Nepalis rally round the **Chandra Binayak**, one of the valley's four principal Ganesh temples, located west of the main Chabahil intersection.

Gokarna Ban

GOKARNA BAN, 3km east of Baudha, looks and feels more like an English country estate than a **Royal Game Reserve** (October to March daily 8am–5.30pm; April to September daily 7am–6pm; Rs15); the "game" consists mainly of tame deer, monkeys, plenty of birds and a few tigers safely penned up in a three-acre enclosure, so promises of "safari adventure" are pure hyperbole. On Saturdays the park is mobbed with picnicking locals. *Gokarna Safari Resort* (☎410063) manages all activities – which include golf, elephant rides and horse rides – and also operates a hotel (doubles $30). Opposite the park entrance is the headquarters of the *Nepal Disabled Association*, which runs a roadside sales shack specialising in wicker items. Five kilometres beyond here, a trail sets off southwards and up the ridge to Changu Narayan.

Sankhu

An important trade and spiritual centre in ancient times, **SANKHU**, 20km east of Kathmandu, now drifts on as a Newar backwater in a far corner of the valley. You could easily pedal out here on a one-speeder, but Sankhu is best thought of as a stopover along the back route down from Nagarkot, which is only possible on a mountain bike. A few shops sell cold soft drinks, but food is scarce.

Sankhu's abiding claim to fame is its temple to **Bajra Jogini**, whose gilded roof glints from a grove of trees on the barren hillside above town. To make the two-kilometre hike, follow the dirt road northwards out of town and then bear left on a stony path that heads straight for the temple. Sankhu Bajra Jogini is the most senior of a ferocious foursome of tantric goddesses unique to the Kathmandu Valley: to Buddhist Newars, her main devotees, she represents the wrathful, corpse-trampling, female aspect of Buddhahood; her implicitly sexual role in a supernatural union of opposites earns her the esoteric "tantric" label.

The slightly dilapidated **temple** dates from the seventeenth century, but inscriptions elsewhere record that a shrine stood here a thousand years earlier. Next to it stands a small shrine containing a replica of the Swayambhu stupa. The compound is pleasantly shaded, but overrun by monkeys – the place literally stinks of them. Animal sacrifices performed in front of a triangular stone representing Bhairab, just below the temple, sadly don't include monkeys.

The Sundarijal road

Branching off from the Sankhu road a kilometre east of Baudha, a second road rumbles along even more rurally as far as Sundarijal in the extreme northeastern corner of the valley. The paved surface soon gives out, but it's still delightful cycling country, with handsome three-storey brick houses, feathery bamboo forests and a steady stream of pedestrians. Four **buses** a day leave from Ratna Park for Sundarijal.

Gokarneswar

Despite UNESCO conservation efforts, the sixteenth-century temple of **GOKARNESWAR** (also known as GOKARNA MAHADEV) appears slightly worse for wear, but it does occupy a tranquil spot. Located 4km up the Sundarijal road, it overlooks the Bagmati River where it cuts through a low ridge (Gokarna Ban game reserve is just across the river, but there's no access from here). The temple's most unusual feature is its outdoor gallery of stone **sculptures** representing an unorthodox cross-section of the Nepalese pantheon – you'll see a bearded Brahma, a skeletal Chamunda (a form of Kali) and a snake-hooded Buddha, among others. Inside the temple stands a beefy *lingam*, while nearby there's a smaller temple to Shiva's consort Parvati. The highlight of the **festival** calendar here is *Gokarna Aunsi*, Nepali Father's Day, held in late August or early September.

You can **hike** up onto the long ridge to the west and follow it northwards to NAGI GOMPA, or continue westwards to KOPAN.

Sundarijal

The scenery wanes somewhat beyond Gokarneswar. Although **SUNDARIJAL**, 15km from Kathmandu, isn't a brilliant destination in itself, it's the most accessible trailhead for **treks in the Helambu** region. The steep climb up alongside the cascading Bagmati River – no more than a stream here – would be much prettier without the hulking iron pipe that crisscrosses the trail: much of Kathmandu's water supply comes from the upper Bagmati. There are no lodges in Sundarijal.

Budhanilkantha and Shivpuri

A paved road leads 8km north from Kathmandu to **BUDHANILKANTHA**, site of the Sleeping Vishnu, one of the valley's most impressive reminders of its semi-mythic early history. There's a small row of shops nearby, but the Vishnu statue, set in a walled compound, is the only attraction of the place. **Buses** to Budhanilkantha leave from Rani Pokhri every half-hour or so. You can walk from here to the summit of Shivpuri, the second-highest point of the valley rim.

The Sleeping Vishnu

The five-metre **Sleeping Vishnu** reclines in a recessed water tank like an oversized astronaut in suspended animation. The figure's origins are obscure: locals say it was unearthed by a farmer several centuries ago, having been carved and dragged here at some remote point in time, but most art historians believe its style pinpoints it to the seventh or eighth century AD. In the fields to the east, piles of bricks and a lone statue provide further evidence that this must have been a substantial settlement in ancient times.

Budhanilkantha's **name** has been a source of endless confusion and not a little religious rivalry. No one seriously claims it has anything to do with Buddha, but that doesn't stop Buddhist Newars from worshipping the image as Lokeshwar, the *bodhisattva* of compassion. The real puzzler is why Budhanilkantha (literally "Old Blue-Throat"), a title which unquestionably refers to Shiva, has been

The sleeping Visnhu

attached here to Vishnu. The myth of **Shiva's blue throat**, a favourite in Nepal, relates how the gods churned the ocean of existence and inadver-tently unleashed a poison that threatened to destroy the world. They begged Shiva to save them from their blunder and he obliged by drinking the poison. His throat burning, the great god flew up to the range north of Kathmandu, struck the mountainside with his trident to create a lake, Gosainkund, and quenched his thirst – suffering no lasting ill effect except for a blue patch on his throat. *Shaivas* claim a reclining image of Shiva can be seen under the waters of Gosainkund during the annual Shiva festival there in August, which perhaps explains the asso-ciation with the waterborne figure of Budhanilkantha.

Nonetheless, the Budhanilkantha sculpture bears all the hallmarks of **Vishnu** or, as he's often called in Nepal, Narayan (pronounced Nuh-*rai*-n): "having waters for his abode". It depicts Vishnu at his most cosmic, floating in the ocean of exis-tence upon the snake Ananta (Infinity); from his navel will grow Brahma and the rest of creation. Each year Vishnu is said to "awaken" from his summer slumber during the *Haribondhini Ekadashi* **festival** around the full moon of late October–early November, an event which draws thousands of worshippers. One person who never puts in an appearance, as a matter of policy, is the king of Nepal: some say the boycott goes back to the seventeenth-century king, Pratap Malla, who was visited by Vishnu in a dream and warned that he and his successors would die if they ever visited Budhanilkantha; others say it's because the king, who is half-heartedly held to be a reincarnation of Vishnu, must never gaze upon his own image.

Up to Shivpuri

At 2732m, **SHIVPURI** (or SHEOPURI) offers outstanding views of the Himalaya, from Jugal and Ganesh Himal all the way west to Himalchuli. The summit can be reached in about four hours by one of two trails (at least) – you'll need to pack a lunch and sufficient water, and the vertical gain, nearly 1300m, shouldn't be taken lightly. You can **camp** on the flat, grassy summit to catch the best views first thing in the morning; clouds often move in by lunchtime.

From Budhanilkantha, follow the paved road straight uphill until it veers to the right and crosses a stream, where the more **direct trail** to the summit leaves the road and continues up the west side of the stream before entering the walled Shivpuri Watershed. After passing through a doorway, it climbs steadily, crosses a dirt road, enters a forest and meets the ridge; from here, a less-used trail branches off from the main one and follows the ridge eastwards for another two hours to the top. The **other route** sticks to the paved road until the main Shivpuri Watershed gate, and from there follows the dirt road to the right, contouring around and up the ridge to the east – where the road finally rounds this ridge, take a trail up to **Nagi Gompa**, a former Tamang monastery now run by Sikkimese nuns, and continue along the ridge to Shivpuri. Another trail leads back down from Nagi Gompa, following the ridge south to Baudha or Gokarneswar.

The Shivpuri Watershed contains some superb, and still largely untested, **mountain biking** possibilities. From the main entrance, the dirt road to the left snakes generally eastwards for at least 15km, from which point the hill resort of KAKANI (see Chapter Three) is about 2km further east along the ridge by trail.

AGRICULTURE IN THE VALLEY

Agriculture employs two out of three valley residents, so it merits a brief digression here. Valley **farmers** are a mixture of Newars, Brahmans, Chhetris and Tamangs (see Chapters One and Three for background on these ethnic groups). Newars dig their fields with a two-handed spade called a *kodaalo* (*ku* in Newari) – it's back-breaking work – and live in close, brick settlements, while the other groups tend to use bullock ploughs and build detached, mud-walled houses. Many are tenant farmers, and are expected to pay half their harvest as rent.

Low enough to support two or even three main crops a year, and endowed with a fertile, black clay – *kalimati*, a by-product of sediment from the prehistoric lake – the valley floor has been intensely cultivated and irrigated for centuries. **Rice** is seeded in special beds shortly before the first monsoon rains in June, and seedlings are transplanted into flooded terraces no later than the end of July – normally women do this job, using their toes to bed each shoot in the mud. The stalks grow green and bushy during the summer, turning a golden brown and producing mature grain by October. **Harvest time** is lazily anarchic: sheaves are spread out on paved roads for cars to loosen the kernels, and then taken to the nearest available open area and threshed against rocks. The grain is gathered in bamboo trays (*nanglo*) and tossed in the wind to winnow away the chaff. That done, the terraces are planted with **winter wheat**, which is harvested in a similar fashion in April or May. A third crop of pulses or maize can often be squeezed in after the wheat harvest, and vegetables are raised year-round at the edges of plots. The important thing is never to let any land go to waste – Newars will sooner "farm" bricks from the clay soil than let a field lie fallow.

The lot of valley farmers has improved in recent years. Land reform in the 1950s and 1960s, which didn't work too well in most parts of the country, was more rigorously implemented near the capital, helping to get landlords and moneylenders off the backs of small farmers. However, Kathmandu's prosperity is bringing problems. In the past decade, housing has been chewing up farmland at an alarming rate – a trend which threatens to accelerate, as ever more hill people flock to the valley for a piece of the action.

Balaju and Rani Ban

If **BALAJU**'s "Water Garden" isn't as ravishing as its name suggests, neither is the Balaju Industrial Estate as awful as it sounds. The Water Garden is where Kathmandu comes to picnic and paddle on Saturdays, and for the jaded traveller it can provide some welcome relief from the commotion of the city. The park is only 2km northwest of Thamel along the road to Trisuli, behind a municipal-looking fence at the foot of a wooded hill: Trisuli-bound buses will drop you off here, and tempos follow a fixed route from the north side of Rani Pokhri, but it's easier to cycle or even walk. Admission is Rs1, bicycle parking Rs2.

In the northeast corner of the grounds lies a **Sleeping Vishnu** which might be as old as Budhanilkantha's, though the smaller Balaju statue is probably only a copy commissioned in the seventeenth century by King Pratap Malla when he was barred from visiting Budhanilkantha. Balaju's other claim to fame – for Nepalis, at least – is **Baisedhara**, a *hiti* (bathing tank) fed by twenty-two stone spouts, which really rocks with bathing worshippers on the day of the full-moon in April.

Once in Balaju, you might as well continue on up the road another kilometre to the entrance of **RANI BAN** (or NAGARJUN BAN), a large and surprisingly wild royal forest preserve (daily 7am–10pm; pedestrians 25 paisa, cyclists 50 paisa, cars Rs10). A road winds to the summit of the 2096-metre **Jamacho**, but you can hike straight up the ridge along a five-kilometre trail starting at the entrance. The north side of this ridge is riddled with limestone **caves**, including one where the famous second-century Buddhist saint Nagarjuna meditated and died, or so it's said. At the summit, a **stupa** decorated with fluttering prayer flags and penetrating eyes marks the spot where Buddha sat during an apocryphal visit to the Kathmandu Valley and a small **lookout tower** commands a panoramic view of the valley and the Himalaya, notably Ganesh Himal.

Several **alternative routes** return to the valley below. If you can find it, the most interesting one is an obscure trail that starts from the road southeast of the lookout tower and descends in a southeasterly direction through thick forest past several limestone caves, one of which contains a large image of Buddha. The trail eventually meets the Jamacho road, which you can either follow back to the entrance (3km), or part of the way until a military post (1km), from which you can leave the forest reserve to the village of RANI BAN and muddle back down to Balaju or Swayambhu. Another trail from Jamacho makes for the slightly higher summit 1km to the west, then curves south down to the rather seedy temple of **Ichangu Narayan**, from which a rough road leads east to the Ring Road behind Swayambhu.

PATAN AND THE SOUTHERN VALLEY

The southern valley is as well-endowed with sights as the north, and no less accessible. Once you cross the Bagmati River you're in **Patan** – even the cows commute. Good roads fan out from Kathmandu and Patan to the hilltop outpost of **Kirtipur**, the holy places of **Chobar** and **Dakshin Kali**, and the wilds of **Godavari**, while rougher roads make for a dozen other rural settlements. Although everything is within daytripping range of Kathmandu by bus or bike, staying in Patan will give you a head start; it may not be so geared up for overnight guests, but the valley's second city – a world apart from Kathmandu – deserves more than just an afternoon's visit. Accommodation isn't available anywhere else in the southern valley, however.

Patan

PATAN (*Paa*-tun) likes to recall its old name Lalitpur ("City of Beauty"), and although now largely absorbed by greater Kathmandu, this once-powerful, independent kingdom still maintains a defiantly distinct identity. Compared to Kathmandu it's quieter, less frenetic and more Buddhist (there may be a correla-

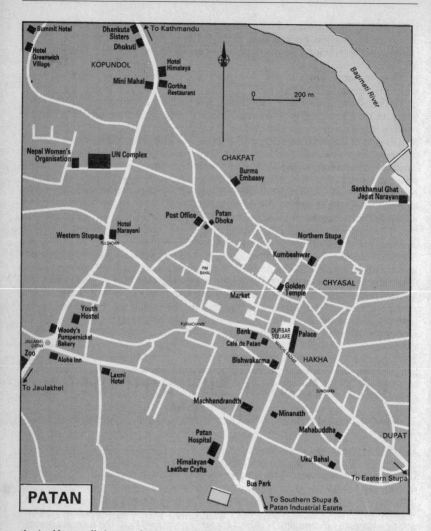

PATAN

tion). Above all, it remains a proud city of **artisans**: Patan produces nearly all Nepal's fine metalwork (the sounds of tapping and filing ring out from workshops all over town), and its craftspeople have created some of the most extraordinarily lavish temples, *hitis* and *bahals* in the country. *Bahals* – their doorways always guarded by cuddly stone lions with timid gnashers – are a particular feature of Patan, and a few still function as active monasteries. In the past two decades, Patan has also emerged as the de facto **foreign aid** capital of Nepal: the UN delegation and diverse smaller organisations are scattered around the western suburbs, as are the residences of many expats who commute to the big USAID headquarters just across the river.

In legend and fact, Patan is the oldest city in the valley. **Manjushri**, the great lake-drainer, is supposed to have founded Manjupatan, the forerunner of Patan, right after he enshrined Swayambhu, while the so-called Ashokan stupas, standing at four cardinal points around Patan, seem to confirm the legend that the Indian emperor **Ashoka** visited the valley in the third century BC (historians are sceptical). By the seventh century Patan had emerged as the cultural and artistic capital of Nepal, if not the entire Himalayan region. It maintained strong links with the Buddhist centres of learning in Bengal and Bihar – thereby playing a role in the transmission of Buddhism to Tibet – and when these fell to the Muslims in the twelfth century, many scholars and artists fled to Patan, setting the stage for a **renaissance** under the later Malla kings. Patan existed as part of a unified valley kingdom until the late fifteenth century, then enjoyed equal status with Kathmandu and Bhaktapur as a sovereign state until 1769, when Prithvi Narayan Shah and his Gorkhali band conquered the valley and chose Kathmandu for their capital. One of Patan's charms is that its historic core is frozen much as it was at the time of defeat.

Getting there and finding your way around

Frequent **minibuses** shuttle from Ratna Park and Martyrs' Gate in Kathmandu to Lagankhel, Patan's main bus park, or you could **cycle** from Kathmandu in a few minutes. Patan itself has few rikshas and no bicycles for hire, but within the old part of town you can easily get around on foot.

Old Patan developed along two intersecting axes, which extended out to the four **Ashokan stupas**. The northern route, now pedestrianised, takes in Patan's **Durbar Square** and also the famed **Golden** and **Kumbeshwar temples**. Patan's western axis (known as **Mangal Bazaar** where it meets Durbar Square) serves as the main way into town from Kathmandu. The busy southern road runs past the **Machhendranath Mandir** and the **bus park**, while the eastern road skirts the temple of **Mahabuddha**. Coming from Kathmandu, you can enter the city via the Western Stupa or more directly via **Patan Dhoka** (Patan Gate) – taking the latter route you're sure to get lost, though. The Tibetan crafts centre of **Jaulakhel** is located at the southwestern edge of the city.

Durbar Square

Patan's **Durbar Square**, while smaller and less monumental than Kathmandu's, comes across as more refined, not to mention less touristy. Maybe it's because the city of artisans has a better eye for architectural harmony; or because Patan, which hasn't been a capital since the eighteenth century, has escaped the continuous meddling of monument-building kings. Having said that, the formula is similar to that in Kathmandu, with a solemn royal palace looming along one side and assorted temples grouped in the remaining public areas of the square.

The Royal Palace

Patan's richly decorated **Royal Palace** was largely constructed during the second half of the seventeenth century, but substantially rebuilt after the Gorkhali invasion of 1769 and the 1934 earthquake. It consists of three main courtyards, each with its own entrance.

The small, southernmost courtyard, **Sundari Chowk**, contains what must surely be one of the grandest bathtubs in the world: **Tusha Hiti**, the seventeenth-century sunken royal bath, is done up like a hall of fame of Hindu gods and goddesses. Its brass spout, the only bit of metal here, is decorated with Shiva and Parvati, while the bath itself is shaped like a *yoni*, the symbol of female sexuality. At one end of the basin stands the obligatory statue of Hanuman the monkey god, plus a "holy stone" – a nearby guard will ensure that you don't touch it – and at the other end a replica of the Krishna Mandir, one of the temples outside. Among the ornate woodwork that surrounds the courtyard, be sure to see the window carved with Surya, the sun god, riding across the heavens in a horse-drawn chariot.

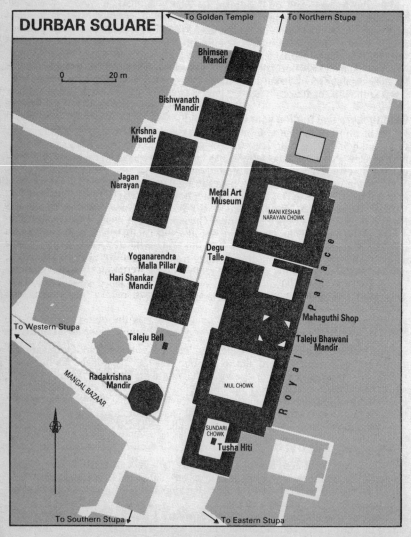

DURBAR SQUARE

To Golden Temple
To Northern Stupa

Bhimsen Mandir

0   20 m

Bishwanath Mandir

Krishna Mandir

Jagan Narayan

Metal Art Museum

MANI KESHAB NARAYAN CHOWK

Degu Talle

Yoganarendra Malla Pillar

Hari Shankar Mandir

Royal Palace

Mahaguthi Shop

To Western Stupa

Taleju Bell

Taleju Bhawani Mandir

MANGAL BAZAAR

Radakrishna Mandir

MUL CHOWK

SUNDARI CHOWK

Tusha Hiti

To Southern Stupa

To Eastern Stupa

Mul Chowk, the next courtyard to the north, served as the actual royal family residence. A sadly deteriorated gilded door in the right-hand wall, leading to the private Taleju Shrine, is flanked by statues of the Indian river goddesses **Ganga** and **Jamuna**, the latter riding a *makana* – a mythical cross between a crocodile and an elephant, whose curling snout decorates almost every public water spout in Nepal. Behind and to the left of Mul Chowk rises the octagonal, three-tiered **Taleju Bhawani Mandir**.

Yet a third temple to Taleju, the monolithic **Degu Talle**, towers just north of Mul Chowk. Seven storeys high and the tallest building on the block, this seventeenth-century temple had to be completely rebuilt after being razed in the 1934 earthquake, and is only open during the October *Dasain* festival. Behind it, just off a small *chowk* once used for courtly performances, you'll find the excellent *Mahaguthi* handicrafts shop (see "Shopping").

The northernmost courtyard, **Mani Keshab Narayan Chowk**, contains Patan's **Metal Art Museum**, which has lately been closed for renovations. If it's reopened by now, you'll find in it an impressive exhibit of idols, *toranas* and other temple decorations, although it's widely acknowledged that all the best Nepalese bronzes (a generic term for works cast from copper, brass and various alloys) were long ago bought up – or stolen – by foreign collectors.

The temples

Starting at the newer – eighteenth-century – southern end of Durbar Square, the stone, octagonal **Radakrishna Mandir** in front of Sundari Chowk is the lesser of the square's two Krishna temples. The cast-iron **Taleju Bell** was the first to be erected in the valley (1736); keen civic rivalry between the three valley capitals prompted Bhaktapur and Kathmandu to follow suit with their own bells. North of here, the finely carved **Hari Shankar Mandir** is dedicated both to Vishnu (sometimes called Hari) and Shiva (alias Shankar), while the statue mounted on a pillar and praying to the Degu Talle depicts **King Yoganarendra Malla**, during whose reign much of the royal palace and square were constructed. An angry cobra rears up like a halo above Yoganarendra: like all god-fearing kings of the valley, he would have made sure to appease the *nagas*, animist snake spirits who deliver or withhold the valley's rains.

If the two-tiered **Jagan Narayan**, built in 1565, is the oldest temple in the square, the most unusual one is the seventeenth-century **Krishna Mandir**. Its central structure, a Mughal-style *shikhra*, is girdled by three levels of stone verandas, with minutely carved scenes from the *Mahabharata* along the lintels. An incarnation of Vishnu, Krishna is one of the best-loved characters of the epic *Mahabharata*: superhuman baby, mischievous lad, seducer of milkmaids and heroic slayer of the evil king Kamsa. Devotees flock here on Krishna's birthday in August or early September.

The **Bishwanath Mandir** contains a copy of the Shiva *lingam* of the same name in Varanasi, India. Last but not least, the seventeenth-century **Bhimsen Mandir** is dedicated to the ever-popular god of Nepalese traders, who habitually pitch coins into the windows of the gilded first floor.

North and west of Durbar Square

Some of Patan's most interesting sights – the Golden and Kumbeshwar temples and the ghats – lie north of Durbar Square, but there's also plenty of serendipitous exploring to be done among the back alleys west of the square.

Hiranyavarna Mahavihara (Golden Temple)

Dark and masonic (if it weren't for the sign, you'd never think of entering), the **Hiranyavarna Mahavihara** – commonly dubbed the "**Golden Temple**" – is the most opulent little temple in Nepal. The three-tiered pagoda occupies one side of the cramped courtyard of Kwa Bahal, a still-active twelfth-century Buddhist Newar monastery and the spiritual hub of old Patan. During early-morning *puja*, the *bahal* is a fascinating theatre of Nepalese religion in all its perplexing glory. Note that you're not allowed to bring anything made of leather inside.

The temple's brass-clad facade, embossed with images of Buddhas and Taras, is regarded as the pre-eminent example of large-scale repoussé **metalwork** in Nepal, while in the middle of the courtyard a small, lavishly ornamented shrine contains a priceless silver and gold *chaitya*. Both the shrine and the main temple are draped with what look like long brass neckties; these *patakas* are supposed to provide a slide for the gods when they descend to answer the prayers of their worshippers. Buddha is the main image in the temple, and various Buddhas and *bodhisattvas* are represented in alcoves around the courtyard.

Kumbeshwar

The **Kumbeshwar Mandir**, Patan's oldest temple and one of only two free-standing five-tiered pagodas in Nepal (the other is in Bhaktapur), was built as a two-roofed structure in 1392, and despite the addition of three more levels it remains well-proportioned and to all appearances sturdy. Shiva is the honoured deity here: inside you can see a stone *lingam* and a brass one with four faces; Nandi, Shiva's patient mount, waits outside. The temple apparently owes its name to an episode in which a pilgrim at Gosainkund, the sacred lake high in the mountains north of Kathmandu, dropped a pot (*kumbha*) into the water there. Much later, the same pot appeared in the water tank here, giving rise to the belief that the tank is fed by an underground channel from Gosainkund, and adding to Shiva's roll of titles that of Kumbeshwar – the Pot God.

Thanks to this connection, Kumbeshwar's water tank is regarded as an alternative venue during Gosainkund's great annual **festival**, *Janai Purnima*. Falling on the full moon day of late July or early August, *Janai Purnima* is the ceremony in which Brahmans and Chhetris formally change the sacred thread (*janai*) that distinguishes them as members of the "twice-born" castes. At Kumbeshwar, thousands come to pay respect to a *lingam* erected in the middle of the tank, and a big part of the festivities is for bathers to see how much water they can splash at spectators. Elsewhere in the temple courtyard stands the shrine of **Sakunimukhi** ("Vulture Head"), an obscure goddess whose tiny idol is encased in an ornate silver frieze.

The Northern Stupa . . . and on to the ghats

Just northeast of the Kumbeshwar Mandir, the **Northern Stupa** is the nearest and smallest of the Ashokan mounds, and the only one that's been sealed over with plaster. Although it doesn't look wildly interesting for a 2200-year-old monument, you can let your imagination dwell on what treasures or relics Ashoka might have buried here – the contents are unlikely ever to see the light of day, since archaeological digs are prohibited.

The stupa stands at the abrupt edge of the city: the road south plunges back between brick tenements and neglected temples to Durbar Square; northwards, it wends through farmland towards Patan's **Sankhamul Ghat**, a kilometre-long embankment near the junction of the Manohara and Bagmati rivers (confluences are regarded as auspicious locations). Though a holy place, it's also rather sombre: funeral processions arrive bearing bodies to the cremation platforms, and across the river – under the shadow of the *Everest Hotel* – are some of Kathmandu's most destitute dwellings. Atop the bank behind the ghats stands the brick *shikhra* of **Jagat Narayan**.

Points west

From **Mangal Bazaar** – these days selling mainly cloth and tourist odds-and-ends – central Patan's main drag heads out towards the **Western Stupa**. Though little more than a grassy mound beside a busy intersection, on one day a year the stupa comes to life as the starting point of the great chariot procession of Rato Machhendranath (see below). A shelter just south of here displays retired *ghamas* – long, upward-curving chariot yokes – from past festivals.

The northwestern quarter of old Patan is a jumble of *bahals*, none particularly worth singling out; the lane leading from the Golden Temple west to **Patan Dhoka** takes you past quite a few. The next lane further south, which parallels the main road to the Western Stupa, contains Patan's small fruit and veg **market** and eventually opens out into Pim Bahal, a large and less than glamorous square that contains what some hold to be a **fifth Ashokan stupa**, although no records mention it before the fourteenth century.

South and east

South of Durbar Square you essentially have two choices. The southbound street passes the Machhendranath temple and other sights en route to the Lagankhel bus park, while the continuation of Mangal Bazaar leads southeastwards to Mahabuddha. The area directly east of Durbar Square, though short on guide-bookish sights, is an active artisans' quarter.

Machhendranath

Outwardly, Patan's **Machhendranath Mandir** resembles many others: a huge seventeenth-century pagoda adorned with beautifully carved struts, elegant *toranas*, and an ill-advised layer of modern tiles. It stands in an extra-large grassy compound called Ta Bahal about 300m south of Durbar Square, reached by following a flagstoned path west from the main street.

Scene during the *Rato Machhendranath* festival

What makes this temple so extraordinary, however, is its idol, **Rato Machhendranath** (Red Machhendranath), a painted shingle of sandalwood which, for several weeks beginning in late April, is the object of the most spectacular festival in Nepal. Older than his white counterpart in Kathmandu, Rato Machhendranath is a god of many guises. To Budd'iists he's Avalokiteshwara or Lokeshwar, the *bodhi-*

sattva of compassion, or Bunga Deo, the androgynous god of agricultural prosperity. As Machhendranath, he's the spirit of a noted Hindu guru who once taught the Shah kings' beloved saint, Gorakhnath. Legend has it that Gorakhnath once visited the valley and, offended that he wasn't accorded a full reception, caused a drought by rounding up all the rain-bringing snakes. The locals sent a posse to fetch Machhendra from Assam, who came to their rescue in the form of a bee. Wishing to pay tribute to his guru, Gorakhnath had to release the snakes, whereupon the rains returned and Machhendranath came to be seen as a rain-maker.

Machhendranath's **festival** is an electric event in which the god's image is pulled through Patan in a tremendously unwieldy chariot crowned by a 20-metre-high swaying tower of poles and vegetation; special blessings are promised to anyone whose house gets bashed by the wayward spire. Lurching along in stages, the chariot takes days or weeks to travel from the Western Stupa to the bus park at Lagankhel. Since the procession is held just before the monsoon, Machhendranath always obliges with rain: bring an umbrella.

Minanath, Bishwakarma and the Southern Stupa
Across the street, the smaller sixteenth-century **Minanath Mandir** is dedicated to yet another mythologised Indian saint. Historically supposed to have been Machhendra's guru, Mina has been transmuted by popular tradition into his brother, son or even daughter, and follows Machhendranath in a smaller chariot of his own during the great procession.

One of Patan's most charming streets runs east–west roughly halfway between Durbar Square and Machhendranath. This is an area of metalsmiths and sellers, which perhaps accounts for the **Bishwakarma Mandir**'s facade of hammered brass and froggy copper lions standing guard, Bishwakarma being the god of artisans.

It's not really worth travelling a kilometre south of Durbar Square to visit the grassy **Southern Stupa** – the biggest of the four – although anyone bound for the Patan Industrial Estate (see "Shopping") will pass right by it.

Mahabuddha
Nicknamed "Temple of a Thousand Buddhas", **Mahabuddha** is not your average Nepalese temple. Constructed entirely of terracotta tiles – each one bearing Buddha's image – this remarkable rococo structure mimics the famous Mahabodhi Temple of Bodh Gaya in India, where its builder, an enthusiastic sixteenth-century Patan architect, had previously meditated for several years. Although the likeness is only approximate, the temple introduced to Nepal the Indian *shikhra* form, which to this day remains prevalent around Patan. Reduced to rubble during the 1934 earthquake, it was put back together rather like Humpty Dumpty; the smaller temple beside it was built from the spare parts.

Mahabuddha stands just off a brick-paved street about 500m southeast of Durbar Square, with a narrow passage on the right providing an entrance; so tightly is it hemmed in by residences, the temple is like a casket that's been upended to fit in a hole. For the best view, follow a sign to the top floor of one of the surrounding buildings, which – surprise, surprise – is a metal handicrafts studio.

Other eastern sights
Uku Bahal lies just south of Mahabuddha, behind an arch guarded by large, curly-maned lions. The now-defunct Buddhist monastery, believed to be one of

Patan's oldest, has undergone a recent renovation. Known as **Rudravarna Mahavihara**, its ornate principal temple is surrounded by a small menagerie of bronze animals and mythological beasts.

North and east of Mahabuddha, **Dupat** is a poor and not altogether welcoming neighbourhood whose close, dark alleys are nevertheless crawling with atmosphere. The **Eastern Stupa** is way out in the sticks, beyond the Ring Road.

Jaulakhel and the zoo

Patan's Tibetan ghetto, **Jaulakhel** is arguably the best place in the valley to watch carpets being made, although as a cultural experience it doesn't compare with Baudha or even Swayambhu. Tour groups tend to spoil the atmosphere. Everything revolves around the weaving and sales centre, a kilometre south of the Western Stupa (Sun–Fri 9am–noon & 1–6pm); see "The Tibetan villages" in Chapter Four for more information on carpet-making, and "Shopping", below, for more on carpet-buying.

Tibetans started pouring into the Kathmandu Valley immediately after the Chinese annexation of Tibet and the flight of the Dalai Lama in 1959. By 1960 their plight prompted the International Red Cross to set up a transit camp at Jaulakhel, later assigned to the Swiss Red Cross, which in turn formed the Swiss Association for Technical Assistance (offices just north of here) to help Tibetans on a long-term basis. SATA encouraged carpet-making and other cottage industries, and by 1964 the Jaulakhel "transit camp" was a registered company, whose increasing sales have brought wealth and a degree of self-determination to the Tibetan community here. No one calls Tibetans "refugees" anymore. A generation on, those with enough money have left the centre to establish businesses and live closer to the Buddhist holy places, while the 1000 Tibetans remaining here are, sadly, the ones who can't afford to leave; Jaulakhel is not a jolly place, and the shoddy brick residences across the road seem to be the work of people determined not to put down roots.

The zoo

Nepal's only **zoo** (daily 10am–5pm; 50 paisa) – often rendered "jew" by Nepali-speakers – lies en route to Jaulakhel, just past the big Jaulakhel Chowk roundabout. Conditions for the animals leave much to be desired, but a visit might be in order for close-up views of species that can otherwise only be glimpsed in the mountains or the Tarai. Highlights include almost-tame rhinos, far-from-tame tigers, graceful blackbuck antelope, ungainly nilgai, beautiful clouded leopards, and a bevy of birds (for an account of Nepal's wildlife, see "Natural History" in *Contexts*). For Rs20 you can take a spin around the grounds on an elephant, and women in red saris in front of the entrance will tell your fortune.

Shopping

Even if you're not in the market to buy anything, Patan is the best place in Nepal to watch **handicrafts** actually being made. The Patan Industrial Estate does a little of everything, Jaulakhel mainly produces carpets, while Patan's many non-profit shops, supported by the earnest local aid community, stock some excellent contemporary crafts made by disadvantaged workers.

Patan Industrial Estate

Despite its forbidding name, the **Patan Industrial Estate** is industrious in the nicest possible way. Located just beyond the Southern Stupa, the laid-back "estate" consists of a dozen or so factory showrooms – they're mainly pitched at coach parties, so independent travellers are generally left to mosey round the work areas without any pressure. The fixed prices are rarely undercut anywhere else (a prayer wheel will be as little as half what it costs at Jaulakhel), but the money isn't going to a good cause.

Perhaps the most fascinating **workshops** are those of the metalsmiths, who mass-produce statuettes by the lost-wax process, and repoussé and filigree work with a hammer and punch. You can also watch craftspeople painting *thankas* and chiselling wood statuettes, doors and windows.

Jaulakhel and around

For **carpets**, the obvious place to start is the Tibetan centre, where you can observe the actual weaving process, although you'll find the fixed prices here higher than in the shops along the road outside, where they'll do deals.

Carpet manufacture is now fairly standardised. Most carpets are made from chemically dyed sheep wool or a sheep-yak blend (vegetable-dyed, all-yak carpets have to be ordered specially) and come in three grades, based on 60, 80 or 100 **knots** per square inch. Make sure the ratio of vertical to horizontal knots isn't less than 2:3. Earthy, pastel **colours** like pale blue, khaki and salmon are the most common these days, although traditional Tibetan carpets can feature rich russet, gold or navy. **Designs** are bold and simple – usually a geometric border and a central *mandala* or pair of dragons against a plain background, which are further highlighted by trimming and embossing (see "The Tibetan villages" in Chapter Four for more on the production process). Compared to other Oriental makes, Tibetan carpets are quite well made and hard-wearing, but their knot density is at the low (poor) end.

Tibetan carpets made outside Tibet have no investment value to speak of, but they're more likeable – and cheaper – than the machine-made stuff on offer back home. Typical **prices**: Rs250 for an 18"x18"; Rs1200 for a 2'x3'; Rs3500 for a 3'x6'.

Patan's non-profit shops

One of the most encouraging developments in recent years has been the rise of non-profit handicrafts shops in Patan. By providing outlets for **women, handicapped people** and **workers' cooperatives** in some of Nepal's remotest hill areas, they increase employment and channel money where it's most needed. They also appear to avoid the pitfalls of other development projects in the hills, where lavish foreign aid has often led Nepalis to expect something for nothing.

Most of the items sold in these shops can't be found anywhere else. **Textiles** include unusual forms of *dhaka* (a traditional cotton weave with a simple, repeating geometric pattern) from the eastern hills; *khadi* (hand-spun cotton cloth) from the eastern Tarai; sari cotton from Bhaktapur, usually in the classic black with red trim; and *allo*, a wool-like material woven from nettle stems by a women's project in the eastern hills. Greeting cards of **handmade paper**, produced by a UNICEF project in Bhaktapur, are of stunning beauty. **Leather** goods and **batiks** are made by local lepers, while other groups produce **toys, ready-made clothes**, and ingenious articles out of **bamboo** and even **pine needles**. Except for *Dhukuti*, all are closed on Saturday.

Dhankuta Sisters, Kopundol, 400m south of the bridge to Kathmandu. An outlet for village women in the eastern hills, it carries *dhaka* clothes and place settings, wicker baskets, hand-knit cotton sweaters and *malla*, the bead necklaces worn by almost all hill women.

Dhukuti (☎272676), Kopundol (just south of *Dhankuta Sisters*). Run by a village and low-income project marketing association, Patan's biggest non-profit shop stocks a wide variety of cotton and quilted-cotton crafts (place settings, cushion covers, etc), toys, ceramics, paper and kids' clothes.

Himalayan Leather Crafts (☎521622), Lagankhel, just south of Patan Hospital. Run by the Nepal Leprosy Trust, it sells leather goods (handbags and wallets, mostly), ceramics, batiks and pine-needle place mats.

Mahaguthi (☎521493), Durbar Square, behind the Degu Talle Temple; with another branch on Durbar Marg in Kathmandu. Aided by Oxfam, it supports a home for destitute women, and has the best selection of textiles, plus paper and toys. Women weave in the courtyard outside.

Women's Skills Development Project (☎521904), Pulchowk, just west of the UN Complex; with a branch on Lazimpath in Kathmandu. The sales outlet for the Nepal Women's Organisation (offices behind) specialises in block-printed cottons, with some quilted cotton items (potholders, tea cosies), woollens, toys and paper.

Accommodation, food and other things

While Patan welcomes daytrippers, it seems less keen on visitors staying, particularly travellers on a **budget**. The cheapest option is the *Mahendra Youth Hostel*, just north of Jaulakhel Chowk, a lonely but quiet place with dormitory beds for Rs25 (with or without an *IYHA* card). *Café de Patan* in Mangal Bazaar is planning to build a budget lodge, and in the meantime might be able to arrange a private room near the Golden Temple (about Rs100) – this is the only accommodation in old Patan. Pass up *Laxmi Hotel* (☎523968), east of Jaulakhel Chowk, unless you're really desperate (singles Rs100, doubles Rs130; Rs110/150 with bath).

The picture is better for hotels at the **middle** and **high end**, all of which are located comfortably close to the aid offices northwest of town:

Aloha Inn, Jaulakhel Chowk (☎522796). Two stars. Small and functional. Singles $18, doubles $24.

Hotel Oasis, Pulchowk (☎522746). Two stars. Dumpy, but with tennis courts and use of a pool. Singles $17, doubles $22.

Hotel Greenwich Village, Kopundol (☎521780). One star. Idiosyncratic, with a good view. Singles $25, doubles $35.

Summit Hotel, Kopundol (☎521894P). Two stars. Beautiful Nepalese architecture, terrific view, swimming pool. Singles $27.50, doubles $42.

Hotel Himalaya, Kopundol (☎523900). Four stars. Really posh, with a swimming pool. Singles $85, doubles $100.

When it comes to **eating**, daytrippers are catered for by the *Café de Patan* in Mangal Bazaar, serving consistently good food and phenomenal lassis, and *Woody's Pumpernickel German Bakery* at Jaulakhel Chowk, which does passable sandwiches, croissants and cakes. Stay longer, though, and you'll probably start missing the variety of Kathmandu. At the cheap end, *Youth Green Garden Restaurant* in front of the youth hostel serves palatable Nepali-style Chinese and Indian food, while several nearby dives do simple snacks, espresso coffee and that odd local specialty, roast chicken. The *momo* shops near Patan Dhoka are always good for a quick bite. For a more upmarket meal, try the *Gorkha Restaurant* in Kopundol for Chinese and Japanese dishes, or the excellent *Mini Mahal*, just across the street, for Indian fare; the flash hotels listed above also have their own competent restaurants.

Patan's one **bank** with foreign-exchange facilities is located at the west end of Mangal Bazaar (Sun–Thurs 10am–2pm, Fri 10am–noon). The **post office** is at Patan Dhoka (Sun–Thurs 10am–5pm, Fri 10am–3pm), but you'd be better off using the one in Kathmandu.

Kirtipur

Once-proud **KIRTIPUR** occupies a long, low battleship of a ridge 5km southwest of Kathmandu. An historic stronghold commanding a panoramic view of the valley, the town is ideal for wandering, yet seldom visited – locals seem genuinely flattered whenever an outsider turns up. Poor Kirtipur is still shunned and pitied in the Kathmandu Valley, more than two centuries after its spirit was broken by an act of spectacular cruelty and humiliation.

Established as a western outpost of Patan in the twelfth century, Kirtipur had gained nominal independence by the time Prithvi Narayan Shah began his final conquest of the Kathmandu Valley in 1767. The Gorkha king, who had himself been born and raised in a hilltop fortress, considered Kirtipur the **strategic lynch-pin** of the valley and made its capture his first priority. After two separate attacks and a six-month seige, with no help forthcoming from Patan, Kirtipur surrendered on the understanding it would receive a total amnesty – instead, in an **atrocity** intended to demoralise the remaining opposition in the valley, Prithvi Shah

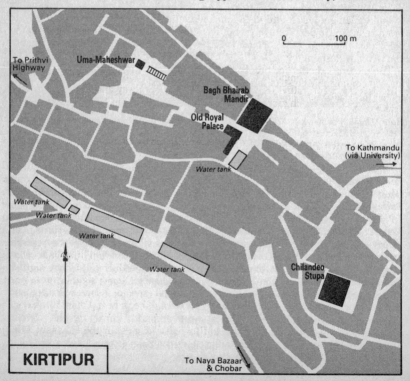

ordered his troops to cut off the noses and lips of every man and boy in Kirtipur. "This order was carried out in the most exact way," wrote the early twentieth-century traveller Percival Landon, "and it adds rather than detracts from the savagery of the conqueror that the only persons spared were men who were skilled in playing wind instruments. The grim statistic is added that the weight of the noses and lips that were brought to Prithwi Narayan in proof that his order had been obeyed amounted to no less than eighty pounds." The rest of the valley fell within a year.

Kirtipur's hilltop position, once a strategic asset, has become a serious handicap to development, for although a road was belatedly pushed up to the neglected upper town, almost all of Kirtipur's commerce has shifted to NAYA BAZAAR (New Market) at the south-

Shiva

ern base of the hill. Considering its nearness to Kathmandu, the town remains shockingly backward (and none too sanitary); the population of 10,000 is served by only one part-time doctor. Many residents are *jyapus*, who work the fields below the town and in spring and autumn haul their sheaves up and thresh the grain in the narrow streets. Others walk to jobs in Kathmandu, and quite a few produce handicrafts behind closed doors.

The easiest way **to get there** is via Tribhuwan University. Frequent minibuses run from Ratna Park to the university gate, from which it's a 15-minute walk up to the village. Cycling entails a steep, uphill slog at the end. Other footpaths lead to Kirtipur from the Prithvi (Kathmandu–Pokhara) Highway and Chobar. For **food**, you can't expect much more than an omelette or *pakodas* in Naya Bazaar.

Bagh Bhairab

The road from the university ascends to the saddle of Kirtipur's twin-humped ridge, depositing you in a weedy square outside the old royal palace, dubbed the "Coca-Cola Durbar" by locals after the sign on its crumbling brick front. Just off the square looms the prodigious **Bagh Bhairab Mandir**, which serves double duty as a war memorial and a cathedral to Bhairab in his tiger (*bagh*) form. Mounted on the outside is a collection of rusty weapons captured during the seige of Kirtipur – either by the Gorkhalis or the defenders, depending on whom you ask. Local musicians perform early in the morning and around dinnertime near a shrine on the left side of the temple, and on Tuesday and Saturday they sacrifice animals to it. Also kept in this courtyard is an image of Indriani, the Cinderella of the Hindu pantheon, who was bossed around by the other goddesses until she miraculously turned a pumpkin into gold. Kirtipur's biggest **festival** is in early December, when Indriani and Ganesh are paraded through town on palanquins.

Wandering around Kirtipur – and beyond

A pleasantly confusing maze of stony alleys, Kirtipur is great for wandering, and navigating isn't hard so long as you stick to the ridgeline. The north end of town is predominantly Hindu, the south end Buddhist.

At the top of the northern, Hindu hump stands the elephant-guarded temple of Uma-Maheshwar, mainly of interest for its sweeping **view** of Kathmandu, Swayambhu and the distant whitecaps of Jugal Himal. Kathmandu's quaint **aerial ropeway** runs just north of here; built in 1925, before any roads connected the valley to the outside world, it's since been upgraded and is still used for ferrying heavy freight. The atmospheric **Chilandeo Stupa** crowns the southern hill, its exposed brickwork lending a hoary antiquity generally lacking in better-maintained stupas. Chilandeo (also known as Chilancho Bahal) is commonly believed to have been erected by Ashoka (though if Ashoka really built every stupa attributed to him he would have had little time for anything else). The ridge that rears up so impressively to the southwest is **Chandragiri**, one of the high points along the valley rim.

You can **walk** to the crest of Chandragiri in three to four hours by following the dirt road southwest from Naya Bazaar and then west to MACHHEGAUN ("Fishville"), where a trail switchbacks up to a saddle on the ridge just north of **Bhasmeswar** (2502m); the views of the high Himalaya from this knoll are excellent. To return you could follow the ridge eastwards, up and over Champadevi and down to the Dakshin Kali road at several points (see below); however, flagging down full-to-bursting buses along this road isn't great fun and the full circuit is more easily done in reverse.

The Dakshin Kali road

The longest and most varied of the valley's roads begins in Kathmandu and ends at the famous sacrificial shrine of Dakshin Kali, a distance of 18km. En route it passes several temples, some beautiful stretches of forest, pleasant rest stops and fine views as it rises more than 300m above the valley floor. Minibuses depart from Martyrs' Gate in Kathmandu roughly every hour, more often on Saturday. Kathmandu travel agents offer guided coach tours every Tuesday and Saturday morning (Rs100 and up). For real independence, though, go by mountain bike.

Chobar Gorge
When Manjushri drained the Kathmandu Valley of its legendary lake, **Chobar Gorge** was one of the places he smote with his sword to release the waters, and as the Bagmati River slices through a wrinkle in the valley floor here it really does look like the work of a neat sword stroke. A path along the west bank scrambles up to two caves housing Shiva momentoes, for those who like dark, confined spaces.

Jal Binayak, a seventeenth-century Ganesh temple, stands where the Bagmati – swollen with the accumulated gunge and sewage of the valley – emerges from the gorge. Built on a rocky outcrop, the tip of which is worshipped as Ganesh, it's full of the usual bells and bell-ringing. A footbridge high above the river gives a good view of the chasm and Jal Binayak; the vista would be better if it weren't for the unfortunate siting of the Himal Cement Factory (the source of so much of the valley's modern concrete construction) just downstream from the temple.

Chobar village
Various paths lead from the main road up to **CHOBAR**, a former outpost of Patan at the top of the deceptively tall hill west of the gorge. The walk begins unpromisingly – the lower slopes look like they're being carried away by earth-movers – but higher up the northern valley spreads out handsomely. Chobar huddles around its

idiosyncratic **Adinath Mandir**, the front of which is completely decorated with pots, pans and jugs. No one has yet proposed an entirely credible explanation for the practice of offering kitchen utensils to Lokeshwar, the temple's deity, but like so many traditions the act has become independent of the original intention; perhaps it goes back to a time when metal implements were new technology and decorating a temple with them was a way to keep it looking spiffy and up-to-date – just as other temples are often graced by mirrors, photographs and European tiles. Lokeshwar is worshipped here in the form of a red mask, which bears more than a casual resemblance to Patan's Rato Machhendranath.

Taudah and hikes to Champadevi

Beyond the cement plant, the road begins climbing through attractive country-side and after 2km passes **Taudah**, the Kathmandu Valley's only lake of note. According to legend, when Manjushri drained the valley he left Taudah as a home for the snakes, and the belief persists that the serpent king Karkatoka still lives at the bottom, coiled around a heap of treasure. Jung Bahadur Rana, prime minister in the middle of the last century, is said to have tried to dredge the lake for booty but gave up because of its depth. Nowadays Taudah is considered sacred and is off-limits to hunters and fishermen.

The road ascends steadily for another 6km to its highest point, a little beyond PIKHEL. The villages of Khokna and Bungamati rest in tight whorls on the plateau across the river. **Trails to Champadevi**, the summit to the west, start from near Taudah, Pikhel and Pharping (see below). A hike up one and down the other will take four or five hours, not including time spent at the top. The first trail begins where the road makes an abrupt bend beyond Taudah, climbing steeply southwestwards to gain the ridge and then more gradually along this to Champadevi (2278m). From Pikhel, a trail heads north to the ridge, passing through a splendid pine forest, then tracks northwest to join the other trail up Champadevi. The Pharping route (best taken going down if you intend to get a seat on the bus) follows a dirt road up a valley south of the ridge as far as a duck pond, where it veers northwards straight up to Champadevi. From the stupa-marked summit, the valley spreads out magnificently and the peaks of the Ganesh and Langtang Himal stud the horizon. You can continue westwards along the ridge to the even higher knoll of Bhasmeswar (2502m), and from a saddle beyond that, down to Kirtipur.

Sesha Narayan

Cool, quiet and shady, **SESHA NARAYAN** crouches under a wooded hillside 2km beyond Pikhel and is regarded as a holy spot by both Hindus and Buddhists. Hindus worship Vishnu here as the mighty creator, who formed the universe out of the cosmic ocean; the snake Sesha (or Ananta), the "remainder" of the cosmic waters after Vishnu's creation, is symbolised by the four tranquil **pools** beside the road. Steps from there lead to Narayan's **temple** at the base of a limestone overhang, whose serpentine rocks and roots no doubt inspired *Vaishnavas* to make the Sesha connection. Buddhists, meanwhile, call this grotto Yanglesho and hold it to be the place where Guru Padma Sambhava, the eighth-century founder of the *Nyingma-pa* sect of Tibetan Buddhism, wrestled with a horde of *nagas* and turned them to stone. This episode marked a turning-point in Padma Sambhava's career – allegorically, it probably refers to the saint's struggle to introduce his brand of tantric Buddhism from India – which accounts for the presence of a **gompa** next to the Sesha Narayan temple.

Pharping

PHARPING is located a few hundred metres beyond Sesha Narayan, straight ahead up a side road where the main road swerves left. Unexpectedly large and lively for this distant corner of the valley, the town is only just beginning to register the changes of electricity and concrete construction. A 15-minute walk uphill brings you to the golden-roofed **Pharping Bajra Jogini**, one of the valley's four tantric temples dedicated to the angry, female aspect of Buddhahood. You can go upstairs – a rare privilege – and view the two prancing images of Bajra Jogini, each holding a skull cup and knife.

A short path leads further up the hill to a small monastery sometimes used as a retreat by Buddhist westerners. Introduce yourself and the monks will happily show you the **Padma Sambhava Cave** in the courtyard; the irrepressible guru, whose image stands among butter candles, apparently meditated in this grotto as well as at Yanglesho. Buddhists say the handprint to the left of the cave entrance and the "footprints" in the centre of the couryard are those of Padma Sambhava.

Dakshin Kali

The best and worst aspect of **DAKSHIN KALI** is that everything happens out in the open. The famous sacrificial pit of Southern Kali – the last stop for hundreds of chickens, goats and pigs every week – lies at the bottom of a steep, forested ravine, affording a rare opportunity to observe Nepalese religious rituals; unfortunately, the public bloodbath also attracts busloads of camera-toting tourists. For the full show in all its technicolor gore, go on a Saturday or Tuesday morning – but if you're squeamish or wish to avoid the tourist crush, try visiting in the afternoon or on another day. Whenever you go, respect the privacy of worshippers, especially if you're taking pictures.

The road from Pharping switchbacks down into the ravine, ending at a small bazaar of stalls selling **food**, drinks and sacrificial accessories. The **shrine** is directly below, positioned at the auspicious confluence of two streams. Tiled like an abattoir (for easy hosing-down) and covered with a brass canopy, the sacred area consists of little more than a row of short statuettes, Kali being the heavily decorated one on the right. You can get a good view of the whole area from a secondary shrine on a promontory high above the far side of the ravine.

Dakshin Kali is as much a picnic area as a holy spot. The sacrifice done, families make for the pavilions that surround the shrine and merrily barbecue the remains of their offerings.

A NOTE ON HINDU SACRIFICES

Hindu animal **sacrifice** is superficially similar to what the Old Testament patriarchs did, but Hindus don't kill animals to prove their loyalty to a deity so much as to propitiate it. Kali, the usual recipient, doesn't care about the *personal* sacrifice her worshipper has made in order to get an animal, all she wants is the blood. Nepalis lead their offerings to the slaughter tenderly, often whispering prayers in the animal's ear; they believe that the death of this "unfortunate brother" will give it the chance to be reborn as a higher life form. Only uncastrated males, preferably dark in colour, are used. At Dakshin Kali, men of a special caste slit the animals' throats and let the blood spray over the idols. Brahman priests (referred to as *bahun*, *pandit* or *pujari*) oversee the butchering and instruct worshippers in all the complex rituals that follow – the priests like to keep things obscure to keep themselves in demand. However, you don't need to speak Nepali to get the gist of the explanations.

The Bungamati and Chapagaun roads

Two minor roads south of Patan make for some easy, off-the-beaten-track cycling through rustic villages and countryside. The first, mostly unpaved road leads directly to delightful **Bungamati**, summer home of Rato Machhendranath; the second is paved as far as **Chapagaun** and its nearby forest temple. You can pedal to either town on a one-speed *Hero* cycle, but with a mountain bike you'll be able to make a circuit of both as well as roam all over the southern end of the valley. Buses also run along both roads.

Bungamati and Khokana

From a distance, you could almost mistake **BUNGAMATI** for a well-preserved Tuscan village: scrunched together on a hillock, its tall, block-like brick houses look distinctly Romanesque, with their tiled roofs sloping in different directions. Irregular **buses** from Patan's Jaulakhel drop you off along the road a short walk northeast of the town.

Close up, Bungamati is quintessentially Newar: what at first looks like a tiny village quickly envelops you in its self-contained world. All alleys eventually lead to the broad, teeming central plaza and the great white *shikhra* of **Machhendranath**, whose more ancient name is Bunga Deo. No one seems to be able to work out whether the town was named after the god or vice versa. According to legend, Bungamati marks the spot where Machhendranath, having arrived in the valley in the form of a bee to save it from drought, was "born" as the valley's protector-rainmaker. Each summer at the end of Patan's Rato Machhendranath festival, the god's red mask is brought to the Bungamati temple for a six-month residency, while every twelfth year (the next time will be in 1992) Machhendranath's lumbering chariot is pulled all the way to Bungamati.

One kilometre to the north, **KHOKANA** resembles Bungamati in many ways, but somehow lacks the character and magnetism of its neighbour. Its pagoda-style **Shekali Mai Mandir**, a massive three-tiered job, honours a local nature goddess. Midway between Khokana and Bungamati stands the poorly maintained **Karya Binayak**, another of the valley's four Ganesh temples. Marijuana grows in profusion around here.

Thecho and Chapagaun

THECHO, 8km south of Patan, is the largest town in this rural, undulating end of the valley, while **CHAPAGAUN**, 1km further south, is a smaller but similarly brick-built settlement. Thecho has a touch more atmosphere, Chapagaun more to eat. Hourly minibuses from Patan's Lagankhel serve both towns. Strangely, Chapagaun boasts the only bicycle rental shop in the valley outside Kathmandu.

More attractive than either town, the seventeenth-century **Bajra Barahi Mandir** is secreted in a small wood 500m east of Chapagaun. Despite Shiva imagery, the temple is dedicated to a tantric goddess; like the Bajra Joginis, Bajra Barahis represent the female, creative power of divinity. This goddess gets her share of worship, but most visitors come to picnic in the park.

From Chapagaun, you've several options for **pedalling on**. The Bajra Barahi track continues eastwards and eventually meets the Godavari road (see below), while a trail heading west from Chapagaun crosses the pretty Nakhu Khola and bends north to join the Bungamati road. The main Chapagaun road carries on to the mildly interesting Lele Valley.

The Godavari road

The greenest, most pristine part of the valley is its southeastern edge, where you'll find something now all too rare in Nepal, or at least around the Kathmandu Valley: virgin forest, once the dominant feature of the middle hills, which has come under increasing pressure in recent years by an exploding population desperate for fuel and farmland (see "Development Dilemmas" in *Contexts*). One way to take in the greenery is by visiting the **Royal Botanical Garden**; another is to hike or ride up **Phulchoki**, the highest point on the valley rim. The starting point for both is GODAVARI, 10km southeast of Patan near the end of a straight, paved road. Hourly minibuses from Patan's Lagankhel bus park go as far as the Jesuits' St Xavier School in Godavari; since the road gains more than 200m along the way, cyclists will want something with gears.

The Royal Botanical Garden

To reach the **Royal Botanical Garden** (daily 10am–5pm; Rs2), follow the main road to the left of the St Xavier School for 1km, then turn left again down to the carpark and main gate. Despite their modest size, the grounds contain some idyllic paths, streams and picnic areas; highlights are the orchid house and fern shed. If you're expecting well-labelled plants and trees you'll be disappointed, but the Department of Medicinal Plants publishes a map (Rs2 at the ticket booth) and guide booklet in English (Rs10) that are of some help in identifying species. The garden receives fairly enthusiastic support from the government – not surprising, perhaps, in a country where flowers play a major part in worship and medicine is largely based on plants.

Another pleasant spot nearby is the spring-fed water tank of **Godavari Kunda**, 300m past the botanical garden turning on the Godavari road. Alternatively, you can leave the garden via a back way on the western side, and keep following it for a **long walk** around the small valley to the north. The three- or four-hour circuit takes you past Bishanku Narayan, a *Vaishnava* pilgrimage cave high up in a notch at the far end of the valley. Kathmandu seems incredibly far away.

Phulchoki

The road bearing straight ahead to the right of the St Xavier School switchbacks and spirals right to the top of **Phulchoki** – a 1200-metre ascent on mostly loose gravel, making it hard going for mountain-bikers. The trail to the summit starts behind the **Phulchoki Mai shrine**, 500m up the road and just opposite the entrance to an unsightly marble quarry. This hike takes about three hours, and crosses the road a few times; the trail can be very slippery. Set off as early as possible to beat the afternoon clouds.

Phulchoki means **"place of flowers"**, which is entirely apt. If you know what to look for, you'll see orchids, morning glories, corydalis and, of course, rhododendrons; March–April is best for catching them in bloom. The whole mountain is covered by tall, luxuriant **forest**, and as you climb from its subtropical base to its temperate summit you pass through mixed stands of oak, chestnut, walnut, bamboo, laurel and rhododendron. It's a great place for **birdwatching** – a trained eye is supposed to be able to spot a hundred or more species in a day – and even better for **butterflies**, which are apparently attracted to the flowers during spring.

If the **summit** (2762m) isn't wreathed in clouds, you'll have a magnificent view of a wide swathe of the Himalaya (notably Gauri Shankar) and practically the entire Kathmandu Valley. The effect is only slightly marred by the presence of a microwave relay station, erected with Canadian assistance, which is the summit road's *raison d'être*.

BHAKTAPUR AND THE EASTERN VALLEY

The valley's eastern arm maintains a discreet cultural, as well as geographical, distance from Kathmandu. Perhaps because it lay off the main India–Tibet trade route all those years, its Hinduism has scarcely been diluted by Buddhism. Creeping westernisation has been slower to take root here, too, and concrete has made few inroads against native brick. If you look closely, you'll see that even the women's saris are different: called *patasi*, they're wrapped around the waist in tiers, giving the effect of a flamenco skirt, and are traditionally black with a red trim.

Everywhere is within daytripping range of Kathmandu, but for more detailed exploration a night in the medieval time capsule of **Bhaktapur** is a must. Trails radiate in all directions from here – the temple complex of **Changu Narayan** makes an immensely rewarding excursion, particularly for fans of Nepalese sculpture; Bhaktapur is also a staging post for Nagarkot, and can serve as a springboard for trips up the Arniko Highway to Dhulikhel and beyond (see Chapter Three). For some reason, the "bye-bye one rupees" mobs at this end of the valley are particularly insufferable – your best defence is a dogged sense of humour.

Bhaktapur (Bhadgaun)

In the soft, dusty light of evening the old city of Bhaktapur, with its pagoda roofs and its harmonious blend of wood, mud-brick and copper, looked extraordinarily beautiful. It was as though a faded medieval tapestry were tacked on to the pale tea-rose sky. In the foreground a farmhouse was on fire, and orange flames licked like liquescent dragon's tongues across the thatched roof. One thought of Chaucer's England and Rabelais's France; of a world of intense, violent passions and brilliant colour, where sin was plentiful but so were grace and forgiveness . . .

Charlie Pye-Smith, *Travels in Nepal*

Kathmandu's field of gravity weakens somewhere east of the airport; beyond, you fall inexorably into the rich, heady atmosphere of **BHAKTAPUR (BHADGAUN)**. A medieval world unto itself ("remote – willingly remote – from her neighbours, and one of the most picturesque towns in the East", wrote Percival Landon), Bhaktapur is Nepal's most perfectly preserved city. Bricks everywhere, streets paved with bricks in herringbone and parquet patterns, houses built of bricks and carved wood: brick and wood, the essential media of Newar city-builders. Well clear of the Ring Road, with no industrial zone, no diplomatic enclave and few suburbs, Bhaktapur feels more like a big village than a small city. Its streets and alleys are all the more suited for wandering, thanks to recent restoration and sanitation work by the German-funded Bhaktapur Development Project – there are some "medieval" features, like open sewers, that everyone can do without.

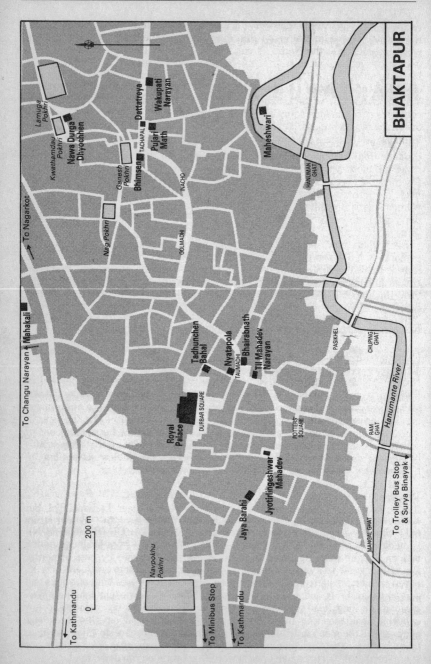

BHAKTAPUR

To Nagarkot

To Changu Narayan

Mahakali

Lamuga Pokhri

Kwathandau Pokhri

Nawa Durga Dhyochhen

Ganesh Pokhri

Bhimsen

Nag Pokhri

TACHAPAL

Dattatreya

Wakupati Narayan

Pujari Math

Maheshwari

TACHO

GOLMADHI

HANUMAN GHAT

Tadhunchen Bahal

Nyatapola

Bhairabnath

Til Mahadev Narayan

TAUMADHI

PASIKHEL

CHUPING GHAT

Hanumante River

Royal Palace

DURBAR SQUARE

POTERS' SQUARE

RAM GHAT

Jaya Barahi

Jyotirlingeshwar Mahadev

Navpokhu Pokhri

To Trolley Bus Stop & Surya Binayak

MANGAL GHAT

To Minibus Stop

To Kathmandu

To Kathmandu

0   200 m

The "City of Devotees" was probably founded in the ninth century, and by 1200 it was ruling Nepal. In that year Bhaktapur witnessed the launch of the Malla era when, according to the Nepalese chronicles, King Ari Deva, upon being called out of a wrestling bout to hear of the birth of a son, bestowed on the prince the hereditary title *Malla* ("wrestler" – to this day, beefy carved wrestlers are the city's trademark temple guardians. Bhaktapur ruled the valley until 1482, when Yaksha Malla divided the kingdom among his three sons, setting in train three centuries of continuous squabbling. It was a Bhaktapur king who helped to bring the Malla era to a close in 1766 by inviting Prithvi Narayan Shah, the Gorkha leader, to aid him in a quarrel against Kathmandu. Seizing on this pretext, Prithvi Narayan conquered the valley within three years, Bhaktapur being the last of the three capitals to surrender.

Bhaktapur drapes across an east-west fold in the valley, its southern fringe sliding down towards the sluggish Hanumante River. Owing to a long-term westward drift, the city contains two centres (residents of the two halves stage a boisterous tug-of-war during the city's annual *Bisket* festival) and three main squares. In the west, **Durbar Square** and **Taumadhi Tol** dominate the post-fifteenth-century city, while **Tachapal Tol** presides over the older, east end.

You'll **arrive** by one of two routes. The handy **trolley bus**, departing from the National Stadium south of Kathmandu's GPO every fifteen minutes or so, drops you on the main road about ten minutes' walk south of town, as do buses coming down from Dhulikhel and points east. Arriving by **minibus** from the main Kathmandu bus park, you'll be deposited near Sidha Pokhri, about five minutes west of Durbar Square; buses to Nagarkot leave from here. Bhaktapur has no rikshas or resident taxis, but it's compact enough to be explored on foot.

Durbar Square

Bhaktapur's **Durbar Square** hasn't got quite the same gusto as its namesakes in Kathmandu and Patan. Isolated near the city's edge, it's neither a commercial nor social focal point, and consequently the only locals you see here are either preying on tourists or cutting across the square to somewhere else. The 1934 earthquake, which knocked the stuffing out of Bhaktapur, claimed a number of the square's temples and left a great void in its middle. Despite all that, the square boasts one of Nepal's proudest artistic achievements – the Golden Gate – plus the National Art Gallery.

The Royal Palace

Bhaktapur's R**oyal Palace** originally stood further east, near Tachapal Tol, but was shifted westwards (like the city) in the fifteenth century; the present structure, dating from the eighteenth century, was renovated and greatly scaled down after 1934. Its superbly carved eastern wing, known as the **Palace of Fifty-Five Windows**, was raised around 1700 by Bupathindra Malla, Bhaktapur's great builder-king, whose *namaaste*-ing figure kneels on a stone pillar opposite.

While the **Golden Gate** (*Sun Dhoka*) probably wouldn't be so famous if it were made of wood or stone – it is, in fact, made of brass – its detail and sheer exuberance raise it to the level of a masterpiece. The *torana* above the door features a squat Garuda and a ten-armed, four-headed Taleju, the Mallas' guardian deity; but to locals, the most powerful figures are those of Bhairab and Kali, situated chest-high on either side of the gate. Upon entry, you follow an outdoor passage around to another impressive doorway, depicting Taleju and her heavenly host in wood, beyond which lies the ornate and sacrosanct **Taleju Chowk** (entrance forbidden to non-Hindus). Ask the guard to point the way to a vantage-point overlooking **Sundari Chowk**, Bupathindra Malla's regal bathing tank, once the centrepiece of a now-obliterated palace section.

The palace's western wing houses the excellent **National Art Gallery** (Sun–Fri 10am–5pm; Rs5), containing an extensive permanent exhibit of tantric Hindu paintings and *thankas* of the eighteenth and nineteenth centuries, plus a small collection of oblong book covers and illuminated pages of religious texts. Stone friezes at the entrance portray Vishnu Varahi and Narasimha, Vishnu's boar and man-lion *avatars*.

The square

The square itself won't detain you for long. Near the main gate at the west end you can admire a pair of multiple-armed statues of **Bhairab** and **Ugrachandi**, whose sculptor reportedly had his hands cut off by order of the Bhaktapur king to ensure that he wouldn't reproduce the images in Kathmandu or Patan. Among the clutch of minor temples opposite, a Shiva *shikhra* showcases the overlooked Newar art of brickwork.

In the entire square, only the fifteenth-century **Pashupati Mandir** at the busier, more touristy eastern end receives much in the way of reverence. The oldest structure extant here, the temple houses a copy of the exalted Pashupatinath *lingam* and its roof struts sport some wildly deviant erotic carvings. Next door stands the stone *shikhra* of **Batsala Durga** and the obligatory **Taleju Bell** (nicknamed "the Bell of Barking Dogs": its toll evidently inflicts ultrasonic agony on local curs), both from the mid-eighteenth century. Behind the bell rises the **Chyasilin Mandap**, the Pavilion of the Eight Corners, erected in 1990 as an exact replica of an eighteenth-century structure destroyed in the 1934 quake. East of here are the platforms of other demolished and half-heartedly rebuilt temples.

A rare Buddhist remnant in predominantly Hindu Bhaktapur, the well-preserved **Tadhunchen Bahal**, east of the square, is a gathering place for neighbourhood metalsmiths in the evening; you might also hear languorous music performed on harmonium and tabla.

Taumadhi Tol

One hundred metres southeast of Durbar Square, **Taumadhi Tol** is a livelier place to linger, if only to admire the view from the balcony of *Café Nyatapola*. In mid-April this square serves as the assembly point for the high-spirited *Bisket* festival, Nepal's foremost New Year celebration.

Dominating Taumadhi and all of Bhaktapur, the graceful, five-tiered **Nyatapola** is Nepal's tallest and most classically proportioned pagoda. So obscure is its honoured deity, a tantric goddess named Siddhi Lakshmi, that she apparently has no devotees, and the sanctuary has been locked ever since its completion in 1702. The Nyatapola's five pairs of temple guardians – Malla wrestlers, elephants, lions, griffins, and two minor goddesses, Baghini (Tigress) and Singhini (Lioness) – are as famous as the temple itself. Each pair is supposed to be ten times as strong as the pair below, with Siddhi Lakshmi herself, presumably, being ten times as strong as Baghini and Singhini. *Bisket* chariot components, including the solid wooden wheels, are stored in an empty lot behind the temple.

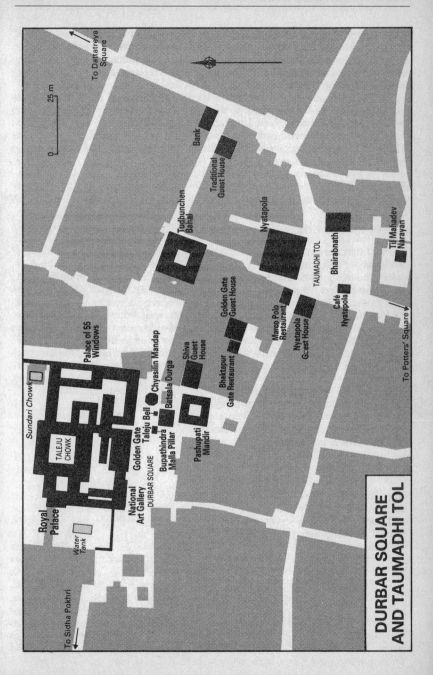

DURBAR SQUARE AND TAUMADHI TOL

To Dattatreya Square

0   25 m

Bank

Traditional Guest House

Tadhunchen Bahal

Nyatapola

Til Mahadev Narayan

TAUMADHI TOL

Bhairabnath

Golden Gate Guest House

Café Nyatapola

Marco Polo Restaurant

Nyatapola Guest House

Bhaktapur Gate Restaurant

To Potters' Square

Palace of 55 Windows

Chyasilin Mandap

Shiva Guest House

Batsala Durga

Taleju Bell

Sundari Chowk

Golden Gate

TALEJU CHOWK

Bupathindra Malla Pillar

Pashupati Mandir

Royal Palace

National Art Gallery

DURBAR SQUARE

Water Tank

To Sidha Pokhri

The heavy, thick-set **Bhairabnath Mandir** is as different from the slender Nyatapola as one pagoda could possibly be from another. The funniest thing of all about this hulk of a building, in fact, is that its Bhairab idol is just six inches tall, mounted on a sort of mantel on the front of the temple. A story is told that Bhairab, travelling incognito, once came to Bhaktapur to watch the *Bisket* festivities. Divining the god's presence and hoping to extract a boon, the priests bound him with tantric spells, and when he tried to escape by sinking into the ground they chopped off his head. Now Bhairab, or at least his head, gets to ride in the *Bisket* parade every year – inside a locked box on board the chariot.

Hidden behind recent buildings southeast of the square, the seventeenth-century **Til Mahadev Narayan Mandir** displays all the iconography of a Vishnu temple: a gilded *sankha* (conch), *chakra* (wheel) and Garuda are all hoisted on pillars out front in a manner clearly imitating the great temple of Changu Narayan, 5km north of Bhaktapur.

The western city

Like a brick canyon, Bhaktapur's main commercial thoroughfare runs from Taumadhi west to the city gate. Roughly 150m along, you'll reach a kind of playground of sculptures and shrines, and a *shikhra* that rejoices in the name of **Jyotirlingeshwar Mahadev**, freely translatable as "Great God of the Resplendent Phallus" – a reference to a myth in which Shiva challenges Brahma and Vishnu to find the end of his organ. Further west, where the street's brick cobbles temporarily give way to flagstones, the **Jaya Barahi Mandir** commemorates the *shakti* (consort) of Vishnu the boar; you have to stand well back from this broad edifice to see its pagoda roofs. Non-Hindus aren't barred from entering the upstairs sanctuary, but this intimate space wasn't designed for spectators.

Dark, damp alleys beckon on either side of the main road – north towards Durbar Square and south to the river. The most promising destination in this area is the **potter's square**, a sloping open space southwest of Taumadhi Tol. Although you may be buttonholed by the occasional potter's wife angling for a sale, for the most part this low-key production centre has few retail pretentions.

Like potters all over Nepal, the men of Bhaktapur employ primitive techniques: spurning even simple foot treadles, they use a pole to spin their solid wooden wheels to a dervish pitch, allowing four or five minutes' working time before the wheel gradually winds down to a slow wobble and needs to be cranked up again. The output here consists mainly of simple water vessels and stove pipes – for more decorative items, pay a visit to nearby Thimi.

Throwing pots

Tachapal Tol

From Taumadhi, the eastern segment of Bhaktapur's main artery snakes its way to the original and still-beating heart of the city, **Tachapal Tol**. Here again a pair of temples looms over the square, older than those of Taumadhi if not as eye-catching. More notably, though, Tachapal conceals Nepal's most celebrated masterpiece of woodcarving, the Pujari Math's Peacock Window, and a superb woodcarving museum. You'll also find the finest **woodwork studios** in Nepal here: well worth a browse, even if you haven't got room in your rucksack for an eight-foot, Rs50,000 peacock-window reproduction. Smaller items – mantel-sized gods and Malla wrestlers, boxes, miniature windows and temple struts – start at Rs150; a twelve-inch bust of Buddha will cost about Rs1000. Most pieces are made from *sal*, a rich, dark wood that's being systematically looted from the Tarai, so you'll have to wrestle with your conscience before buying.

Just north of Tachapal, a second open space around Ganesh Pokhri is equally busy with *pasaals* (shops) and street vendors. South of the square is even better for exploring, as Bhaktapur's medieval backstreets spill down the steep slope to the river like tributaries.

Dattatreya and Bhimsen

Rearing up behind an angelic pillar-statue of Garuda, the **Dattatreya Mandir** (accent on the second syllable) is Bhaktapur's oldest structure. The temple was raised in 1427 during the reign of Yaksha Malla, the last king to rule the valley from Bhaktapur, and like the Kasthamandap of Kathmandu, which it resembles, it was allegedly built from a single tree (the front portico was probably added later). Dattatreya, a sort of one-size-fits-all deity imported from southern India, epitomises the religious "syncretism" (as anthropologists call it) that Nepal is famous for: to *Vaishnavas* Dattatreya is an incarnation of Vishnu, while *Shaivas* hail him as Shiva's guru and Buddhists even fit him into their pantheon as a *bodhisattva*. Christians need not feel left out – decorated with tinsel and ornaments, the idol calls to mind a Christmas tree.

The oblong temple at the opposite end of the square belongs to **Bhimsen**, the patron saint of Newar merchants, whose territory Tachapal is. As usual for a Bhimsen temple, the ground floor is open and the shrine is kept upstairs.

Pujari Math and Bhaktapur's museums

Behind and to the right of the Dattatreya temple stands the sumptuous eighteenth-century **Pujari Math**, one of a dozen priests' quarters that once ringed Tachapal Tol. Given the nature of the caste system, perhaps it's not surprising that the grandest houses in the city traditionally belonged to priests. The *math*'s awesome windows can be seen on two sides; the often-imitated **Peacock Window**, overlooking a narrow lane on the building's far (east) side, has for two centuries been acclaimed as the zenith of Nepalese window-lattice carving.

At all costs don't miss the small **Woodcarving Museum** (Wed–Mon 10am–5pm; Rs5) inside the Pujari Math. Well displayed and lit, it enables you to inspect exquisite temple carvings which are often too high up to fully appreciate *in situ*. Highlights of the collection are a marvellously alluring Nartaki Devi of the fifteenth century and struts from the temple at Changu Narayan.

Somewhat misleadingly, the **Brass and Bronze Museum** (Wed–Mon 10am–5pm; Rs5) across the square contains none of the flamboyant religious art that one might expect, consisting instead of household vessels and implements; for statues and suchlike, go to Patan's *Metal Art Museum*.

Around Tachapal Tol

North of Tachapal, the **Nawa Durga Dyochhen** looks like a haunted house, Nepalese style. A tantric temple only open to initiates, it honours the nine manifestations of Durga, who are especially feared and respected in Bhaktapur. According to legend, the Nawa Durgas used to eat solitary travellers, turning the area east of Bhaktapur into a Bermuda triangle, until a priest managed to cast a tantric spell on them. Bhaktapur's once-famous Nawa Durga dancers aren't too active these days, but **Nawa Durga puppets** are popular around Durbar Square. (If you want to buy puppets, however, they're cheaper in Thimi – see below – where they're made.)

East along the main road from Tachapal, the **Wakupati Narayan Mandir**, where local *jyapus* worship Vishnu as a harvest god, displays no fewer than five Garudas mounted on pillars in a line.

The ghats – and beyond

The Hanumante River is Bhaktapur's humble tributary of the River Ganga, its name deriving from the monkey god Hanuman who, locals like to think, stopped here for a drink on his way back from the Himalaya after gathering medicinal herbs to heal Rama's brother in an episode from the *Ramayana*. Several bathing and cremation ghats flank the river as it curls along the city's southern edge, although unfortunately there's no riverside path connecting them. The most active one is **Hanuman Ghat**, located straight downhill from Tachapal Tol: morning *puja*, bathing and tooth-brushing are a daily routine for many, while old-timers come here just to hang out. A peaceful spot, the ghat packs an eyeful of cluttered *lingams*, statues and trees into a small area; a priest is usually set up in front of the main Hanuman image to prescribe the Hindu equivalent of Hail Marys.

Downhill from Taumadhi Tol, **Chuping Ghat's** array of temples and statuary is more of the mouldering-ruins school. The long, sloping area above the ghat is the focal point on New Year's Day (*Nawa Barsa*) in April, when a 25-metre *lingam* pole is ceremonially toppled by the throng. **Ram Ghat**, below the potters' square, has little to offer beyond a run-of-the-mill Ram temple, but **Mangal Ghat**, further downstream, boasts a more atmospheric selection of neglected artifacts, and by following the trail of *lingams* across the river you'll end up at a forbidding Kali temple in one of Bhaktapur's satellite villages.

Once south of the Hanumante, a ramble up to the densely forested ridge overlooking Bhaktapur might be in order, and **Surya Binayak** makes a worthy target. This most pleasantly situated of the valley's four main Ganesh shrines – catching the valley's first rays of the sun – is reached by a steep, 1km paved road from the trolley bus stop. The temple itself is just an ordinary plaster *shikhra*, surrounded by usual Ganesh trappings; smeared with red *sindur*, the god's image looks like a warm fire in an ornate Victorian hearth. Ganesh is regarded as a divine troubleshooter: this image specialises in curing children who are slow to walk or speak.

Sleeping and eating

Although Bhaktapur is usually regarded as a daytrip from Kathmandu, it has perfectly adequate facilities for an overnight stay.

Bhaktapur's **lodges** all fall into the budget category. The newest and cleanest is the cavernous *Golden Gate Guest House* (☎610534), between Durbar and Taumadhi squares (singles Rs45, doubles Rs75; Rs100/125 with bath), but *Shiva Guest House* (☎610741), overlooking the Pashupati Mandir in Durbar Square (singles Rs40, doubles Rs80), is cheaper and slightly more cheerful. East of Tadhunchen Bahal, *Traditional Guest House* doesn't quite live up to its name, but its rooms are clean (singles Rs35, double Rs70). The stoop-shouldered *Nyatapola Guest House* is really a last resort, though its location on Taumadhi Tol and its authentic lattice windows are both attractions (singles Rs30, doubles Rs60).

Food is likewise basic, but sufficient: if nothing else, you can always load up on thick, sweet **yoghurt** (Bhaktapur's "king of curds"), available by the glass from local sweet stalls. For ambience, you can't beat *Café Nyatapola* and *Marco Polo Restaurant*, both with balconies overlooking Taumadhi Tol; the latter is Bhaktapur's best bet for a main meal. *Bhaktapur Gate Restaurant*, adjacent to *Golden Gate Guest House*, serves palatable *kothe* and other pasta dishes. The food is less appetising at *Shiva Guest House*'s "Rooftop Café'" (which isn't on the roof, although it commands a fine vantage of Durbar Square). If you're waiting for a bus, *Pond Corner Restaurant* is only one of several spartan eateries near the mini-bus stop. As for **nightlife**, forget it.

Changu Narayan

Art and history buffs will get the most out of **CHANGU NARAYAN**, but this beautiful, tranquil site, reached by a delightful walk, is a must for anyone. Perched at the abrupt end of the ridge north of Bhaktapur, the ancient temple complex commands an extraordinary view of the valley in three directions – especially in late afternoon, when the meandering Manohara River turns into a golden ribbon.

The site

"One remembers all the wealth of carving of the rest of the Valley," wrote Percival Landon in 1928, ". . . but when all is recalled it is probably to the shrine of Changu Narayan that one offers the palm. Perhaps one drives back home from Bhatgaon more full of thought than from any other expedition to the many outlying places of this crowded centre of holiness and history and art." Protected by its remote location, Changu Narayan has changed little since Landon's day, with relatively few travellers, or even worshippers, making the effort to visit it. It is, on the face of it, just another pagoda – yet Changu Narayan's palpable age and its collection of the finest, oldest statues outside the National Museum seem to make it the *archetypal* Nepalese pagoda. Ideally, you should see it before you've burned out on all the others.

The valley's **oldest Vaishnava site**, Changu Narayan's documented history goes back to the fourth century AD, and its sculptures attest to continuous worship here ever since. Some historians even postulate a greater antiquity, speculating that Changu Narayan and Swayabhu were built on the foundations of prehistoric animist shrines which originated when the valley floor was still under water.

The **main temple**, rebuilt around 1700, stands in a quiet quadrangle of resthouses and pilgrims' shelters. A measure of the temple's importance is the exaggerated size of the four traditional emblems of Vishnu – the wheel (*chakra*), conch (*sankha*), lotus (*padma*) and mace (*gada*) – mounted on pillars at its four corners. The brass repoussé work on the front (west side) of the building is as intricate as any you'll find in Nepal, as are the carved, painted struts supporting the roofs. The *torana* above the main door depicts Vishnu in his *sridhara* posture (see below), brandishing the four emblems in his four hands. A gold-plated seventh-century image of Vishnu is allegedly kept inside the sanctuary, but only the temple priests are allowed to view it – from time to time, the statue is said to miraculously sweat, indicating that Vishnu is battling with the *nagas*, and the cloth used to wipe the god's brow is considered a charm against snake bites. **Smaller temples** in the compound are dedicated to Lakshmi (the goddess of wealth, Vishnu's consort), Kali and Shiva.

The **oldest inscription** in the valley covers the base of the *chakra* pillar. Dated 454 AD and attributed to the Lichhavi king Mana Deva, it apparently waxes sentimental about his dowager mother. Mana Deva was the legendary builder of Baudha, and any Oedipal undertones might be explained by the belief that the king erected the stupa to atone for killing his father. Perhaps significantly, the inscription records that Mana Deva persuaded his mother not to commit *sati* on her husband's funeral pyre.

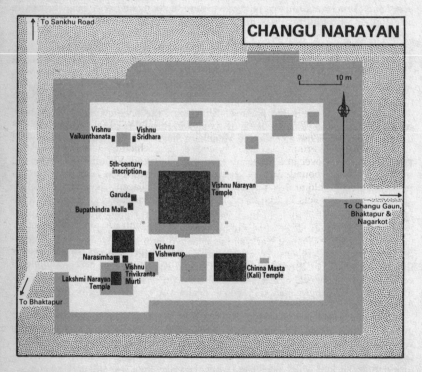

CHANGU NARAYAN

To Sankhu Road

0   10 m

Vishnu Vaikunthanata
Vishnu Sridhara
5th-century inscription
Garuda
Bupathindra Malla
Vishnu Narayan Temple
Narasimha
Vishnu Vishwarup
Vishnu Trivikranta Murti
Lakshmi Narayan Temple
Chinna Masta (Kali) Temple
To Changu Gaun, Bhaktapur & Nagarkot
To Bhaktapur

The statues

The courtyard of Changu Narayan is an outdoor museum of priceless works of art, almost offhandedly displayed and all the more exciting for it. You'll find the oldest, famous statues grouped around the front of the temple (see map) plus loads of other, more recent (but still centuries-old) pieces roundabout. With few exceptions, they all pertain to Vishnu or his faithful carrier Garuda, who gives his ancient name, Changu, to the site.

Probably dating from the seventh or eighth centuries, Changu Narayan's celebrated **Garuda** kneels before the temple, looking human but for a pair of wings and a cobra scarf. Garuda's association with snakes is legendary. It's said that when his mother was kidnapped by his step-mother, Garuda appealed to his serpentine step-brothers to free her, which they did on condition that Garuda brought them ambrosia from Indra's heaven. Although Indra later flew down and reclaimed his pot of nectar (leaving the snakes to split their tongues as they licked up the few drops spilt on the grass), Vishnu was so impressed that Garuda hadn't been tempted to consume the ambrosia that he immediately hired him as his mount. The brass statues inside a screened cage next to Garuda commemorate **King Bupathindra Malla** of Bhaktapur and his queen, who ruled during the late seventeenth and early eighteenth centuries.

Though damaged, the eighth-century image of **Vishnu Vishwarup** (Vishnu of the Universal Form) is an awesome example of Hindu psychedelia. The lower portion of this composite image shows Vishnu reclining on the snake of infinity in the ocean of existence, echoing the sleeping statues of Budhanilkantha and Balaju. Above, the god is portrayed rising from the waters before a heavenly host, his thousand heads and arms symbolising sheer omnipotence. The latter image is borrowed from an episode in the *Mahabharata* in which the warrior Arjuna lost his nerve and Krishna (an incarnation of Vishnu) appeared in this universal form to dictate the entire *Bhagavad Gita* by way of encouragement.

Two notable statues rest on the platform of the Lakshmi Narayan temple. The eighth-century **Vishnu Trivikranta Murti**, Vishnu of the Three Strides, illustrates a much-loved story in which the god reclaimed the universe from the demon king Bali. Disguised as a dwarf (another of his ten incarnations), Vishnu petitioned Bali for a patch of ground where he could meditate, which need only be as far as the dwarf could cover in three strides; when Bali agreed, Vishnu grew to his full divine height and bounded over the earth, sky and heavens (an even older version of this statue is held in the National Museum). The adjacent eleventh- or twelfth-century image depicts Vishnu in yet another of his incarnations, that of the man-lion **Narasimha**.

At the northwest corner of the compound, the twelfth- or thirteenth-century **Vishnu Vaikunthanata** – reproduced on the Nepalese ten-rupee note – shows a purposeful Vishnu riding Garuda like some sort of hip space traveller. Nearby stands a **Vishnu Sridhara** of the ninth or tenth century, an early example of what has since become a stereotypical Vishnu representation.

Getting there and back

You can approach the temple complex from Bhaktapur, the Sankhu road or Nagarkot – time permitting, the ideal itinerary is to walk from Nagarkot to Bhaktapur via Changu Narayan. Food is available only at CHANGU GAUN, the village immediately east of the temple, and there only *daal bhaat* and noodles; there's no place to spend the night.

From Bhaktapur, an asphalted **road** climbs right up to Changu Gaun; it's too steep for a one-speed bike, though if you push the bike up you can freewheel back down. The five-kilometre **trail** to the top passes through rural villages before a final steep ascent; two paths north of Bhaktapur soon converge, the brick-paved, easternmost one passing a hilltop Mahakali shrine and a sleeping Vishnu water tank en route.

The **trail from the Sankhu road** is only 2km long, but it's hard to find at its lower end and the bridge over the Manohara River is only seasonal. Descending is no problem, although you'll probably end up walking halfway to Baudha before a minibus comes along to take you back to Kathmandu.

The ten-kilometre **hike from Nagarkot** should take two to three hours, and despite a few road crossings the route along the forested ridge is immensely satisfying, with great views all the way. Stick to the trail nearest the ridgeline; the only tricky part is where it dips down into a gap near the halfway mark.

Thimi

Squalid **THIMI**, the valley's fourth-largest town, lies on a plateau 4km west of Bhaktapur. The name is said to be a corruption of *chhemi*, meaning "capable people", a bit of flattery offered by Bhaktapur to make up for the fact that the town used to get mauled every time Bhaktapur picked a fight with Kathmandu or Patan. Its mainly Newar inhabitants are indeed very capable craftspeople, and Thimi is *the* place to go for papier mâché masks and pottery.

The Bhaktapur trolley bus will drop you off at the southern end of Thimi, but you'll get a far more favourable introduction by cycling along the old road to Bhaktapur, which skirts the town to the north. Minibuses from Bhaktapur and Kathmandu's Ratna Park also ply this back route. Several **handicrafts shops** – Thimi's only real attraction – are located along the north road. The **papier mâché masks** seen all over Kathmandu are made in Thimi and you can count on getting the best deal here: medium-sized masks cost about Rs25, large ones Rs50. Snarling Bhairab, kindly Kumari and elephant-headed Ganesh are most commonly represented by the masks, which are based on those worn by dancers in Kathmandu's *Indra Jaatra* festival. Nawa Durga **puppets**, normally associated with Bhaktapur, are also made and sold here for a fraction of their usual price.

Pottery is an even older local speciality, and you can watch potters at work in alleys and courtyards all over the north end of town. The process is the same as in Bhaktapur, except that the capable people of Thimi have traded in their traditional wooden wheels for concrete-filled truck tyres. Pottery doesn't travel well, but you might be tempted by the elephant-shaped flower pots.

The remainder of Thimi is grotty and unglamorously primitive – it's one of the few places in the valley where poverty isn't offset by quaintness, but it gives an insight into what life is like for millions of Nepalis beyond the valley. Thimi's only temple of note is that of **Balkumari**, a sixteenth-century pagoda located near the southern end of the main north-south lane. The temple is the focus of frenzied New Year's festivities in April, when dozens of deities are ferried around on palanquins and red powder (red being the colour of rejoicing) is thrown like confetti.

festivals

Some of the festivals listed in the Kathmandu chapter are also celebrated in the valley. Again, most are reckoned by the lunar calendar, so check locally for exact dates.

Magh Sankranti The first day of *Magh* (January 14 or 15), marked by ritual bathing at Patan's Sankhamul Ghat; more bathing takes place at Sankhu on the day of the full moon of *Magh*.

Losar Tibetan New Year, celebrated at Baudha with processions, horn-blowing and *tsampa*-throwing on the big third day (May).

Shiva Raatri The Pashupatinath *mela* (fair) attracts tens of thousands of pilgrims and holy men, while children everywhere collect money for bonfires on "Shiva's Night" (late February or early March).

Bisket Bhaktapur's celebration of Nepali New Year (April 13 or 14), in which chariots are pulled around the city for several days and a *lingam* pole is ceremonially toppled to mark the start of the new year.

Balaju Jaatra Ritual bathing at the Balaju Water Garden on the full-moon day in April.

Machhendranath Raath Jaatra Nepal's most spectacular festival: thousands gather to watch as a swaying, 20-metre-high chariot is pulled through old Patan; it moves only on astrologically auspicious days, taking three weeks or more to complete its journey (April or May).

Dalai Lama's Birthday Observed informally at Baudha (July 6).

Janai Purnima The annual changing of the sacred thread worn by high-caste Hindu men, involving bathing and splashing at Patan's Kumbeshwar Mandir (late July or early August).

Krishna Jayanti Krishna's birthday, commemorated with an all-night vigil at the Krishna Mandir in Patan (late August or early September).

Gokarna Aunsi "Nepali Father's Day", observed at Gokarneswar with bathing and offerings (late August or early September).

Tij A day of ritual bathing for women, mainly at Pashupatinath (late August or early September).

Haribondhini Ekadashi Bathing and *puja* at the Vishnu sites of Budhanilkantha, Sesha Narayan, Bishanku Narayan and Changu Narayan (late October or early November).

Bala Chaturdashi All-night vigil at Pashupatinath, involving candles and ritual seed-offerings to dead relatives (late November or early December).

Indriani Jaatra Deities are paraded through Kirtipur on palanquins (early December).

travel details

Buses and minibuses

From Kathmandu

Leaving from Ratna Park to Pashupatinath (frequent; 20min); Baudha (frequent; 30min); Sankhu (approximately 4 daily; 1hr); Sundarijal (4 daily; 1hr); Patan (frequent; 20min) and Tribhuwan University/Kirtipur (frequent; 30min).

Leaving from Rani Pokhri to Budhanilkantha (frequent; 30min) and Balaju (hourly; 20min).

Leaving from Martyrs' Gate to Patan (frequent; 15min) and to Dakshinkali (approximately every 30 min; 1hr).

Leaving from the main bus park to Bhaktapur (frequent; 45min) and Thimi (frequent; 30min).

The **trolley bus** to Bhaktapur leaves from Tripureswar (about every 15min; 45min).

From Patan

Leaving from Lagankhel to Thecho/Chapagaun (hourly; 20min); Godavari (hourly; 45min) and Bhaktapur (hourly; 45min).

Leaving from Jaulakhel to Bungamati/Khokana (2–3 daily; 20min).

From Bhaktapur

Leaving from Sidha Pokhri to Nagarkot (3 daily; 1hr).

Buses stop at the trolley bus terminus on their way to Banepa (24 daily; 45min); Dhulikhel (24 daily; 1hr 30min); Panauti (4 daily; 1hr) and Bharabise (6 daily; 4hr).

CHAPTER THREE

THE CENTRAL HILLS

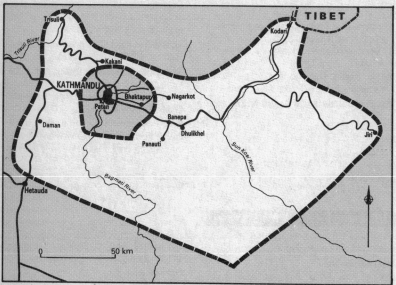

Beyond the Kathmandu Valley, major roads meander in three directions, making the **central hills** the most accessible – though not necessarily the most travelled – section of Nepal's jumbled, 700-kilometre band of foothills. To the northeast, the **Arniko Highway** follows the old Kathmandu–Lhasa trade route through broad valleys and misty gorges to the Tibet border; northwestwards, the **Trisuli Road** snakes its way down into a subtropical valley nearly 1000m lower than Kathmandu; and south, the **Tribhuwan Rajpath**, Nepal's first highway, cuts a tortuous cross-section through the hills on its way to the Tarai. If the scenery here is a shade less dramatic than what you'll encounter further west, the land is nonetheless varied and rugged, tamed only in pockets by defiant terraces. It's only when you leave the Kathmandu Valley that you appreciate how atypical it is of the region.

The majority of places described here can be treated as easy overnights from Kathmandu. The most popular are those that involve mountain views and hill-walking: **Nagarkot** and **Dhulikhel**, with well-developed budget accommodation, are acknowledged classics; **Kakani** is equally scenic, though lacking in cheap lodgings, while **Daman** is splendidly off the beaten track. These vantage points can't compare with what you'll see on a serious trek, but they come into their own in winter, when trekking can be a chilly business. Although cultural attractions are relatively few outside the Kathmandu Valley, **Panauti** and **Nuwakot** are among Nepal's most intriguing villages – all the more because they're so rarely visited – and even while the most alluring destination of all, Tibet, remains closed to independent travellers, **the border** still beckons.

To an extent, the boundaries of this chapter are dictated by travel formalities: towns and **day hikes** are described here, while backcountry areas requiring a trekking permit are saved for Chapter Seven. Despite a relative abundance of roads, **buses** in the central hills are slow and infrequent, and indeed few travellers brave them except to get to the start of the Langtang/Helambu and Everest treks. On the other hand, the region contains Nepal's most popular and rewarding **mountain-biking** destinations – an overview of the possibilities is given at the end of the chapter.

Nagarkot

Like many of Nepal's best highways, the road to **NAGARKOT** serves mainly strategic, not scenic, purposes: Nagarkot was originally developed as an army post – tourist facilities came later, with government encouragement. Set on a ridge northeast of Bhaktapur at about 2000m, it commands a classic panorama of the Himalaya from Langtang Himal to Gauri Shankar, and on a good day from the view tower you can see from Annapurna South to Everest. The best thing about Nagarkot is that you don't have to stay in an expensive hotel to get a view right out of your window. Hiking and mountain biking routes up and back down are particularly worthwhile, although it has to be said that there's not much to do once you're there. Nagarkot's biggest drawback is that, except for a couple of moderately expensive places, its lodges have no electricity or running water, which means you should remember to bring a torch and, in winter, a sleeping bag.

The layout and lodgings

Erase from your mind any picture of a quaint hilltop village. There's no such town as Nagarkot – it's only a loose affiliation of lodges stretching for 2km along the cultivated ridgetop. The lodges at the north end of the ridge – the ones with the best views – are reached along a dirt road that forks off to the left at the first bus stop. Two landmarks in this vicinity are a tiny **Mahakal shrine** and a small-scale **cheese-making project**. The **army barracks** and *Tara Gaon Hill Resort* stand further south, near the last bus stop. The road continues south for another 2km to a **lookout tower** (2164m), where you get the full 360-degree experience of the Himalaya, the Kathmandu Valley and everything in between. Since the army only lets you walk this stretch in the morning, you might as well be hard-core about it and set off in time to catch the sunrise over the mountains.

Staying in one of Nagarkot's **budget lodges** is a lot like being on a trek. Bedtime comes early, and what social life there is goes on in lantern-lit dining rooms; meals take a long time to prepare and usually don't live up to expectations. Most lodges will provide hot water for washing, but you should decline the offer because the use of wood to heat water contributes to deforestation. The best views are to be had from *Niva Home* (singles Rs30, doubles Rs40) and *Peaceful Cottage* (singles Rs25, doubles Rs40), both at the plunging north end of the ridge, or for real ambience try *New Pheasant Lodge*'s bamboo bungalows (Rs100) and its

"Restaurant at the End of the Universe" (they make a welcome hot toddy). While they have poorer immediate views, lodges further south are at least closer to the observation tower. Of these, *Star Guest House* looks the most inviting (dorm beds Rs15, singles Rs30, doubles Rs50) and *Mount Everest* (or *Didi's*) *Lodge* the homiest (rooms for Rs30).

If you want electricity and running water, you're up into the **moderately priced** category. *Tara Gaon Hill Resort* (Kathmandu office ☎01/211008), Nagarkot's original government-run outfit, seems the best deal, despite befuddled service. Single rooms in the rather colonial old building are $13 and doubles are

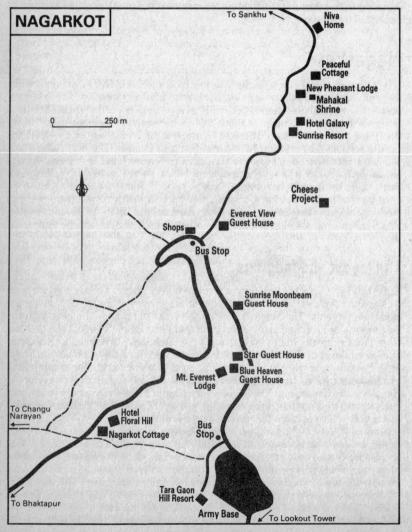

$18 (discounts for longer stays); in the smart new building singles are $20, doubles $26. *Nagarkot Cottage*'s rustic bungalows are $14 each, but they're a twenty-minute walk from good views. *Hotel Floral Hill*, (Kathmandu office ☎01/ 226893) next door, seems overpriced (singles $30, doubles $38).

Getting there – and back down again

The only public **buses** to Nagarkot depart from Bhaktapur's Sidha Pokhri (3 daily; Rs5); if you're coming from Kathmandu, don't expect an instant connection. (Kathmandu tour operators run direct **tourist coaches** most afternoons, which cost Rs125 and up for a return trip.)

Considerably more fun, however, is to walk up – or better yet, ride up and **walk back** the next morning. The main trail **to Changu Narayan**, a two- or three-hour hike, descends from the *Tara Gaon Hill Resort*, recrossing the Nagarkot road after about 600m. If you're starting from the north end of the ridge, a more convenient trail leaves from the big hairpin turn below the lower bus stop and joins up with the main trail 1km later. From there you keep descending, parallelling the road and for a while walking beside it, until the trail starts dropping into a notch – at which point you take a trail to the right and follow it along the wooded ridgeline to Changu Narayan. From there it's another hour down to Bhaktapur, or less to the Sankhu road. (According to the *Geo-Buch* "Kathmandu Valley" map, there are other, more direct trails from the Nagarkot view tower to Bhaktapur.)

A second option is to hike down **to Nala**, which also takes about two or three hours. From the view tower, one trail heads south to GHIMIREGAUN, then zigzags east and south again to follow a spur down to Nala; the other route leaves from the end of the view tower road, following a different spur south to Nala via TUKUCHA. From Nala it's an easy walk to Banepa, with buses to Kathmandu.

If you're **cycling**, the logical itinerary is to ride up the main road from Bhaktapur and return the back way to Sankhu; this allows you to take in Bhaktapur, Nagarkot, Sankhu and Baudha in a simple two-day ride. The ascent is consistently steep for the last 12km – the vertical gain is 650m – but paved all the way and agreeably devoid of traffic. The dirt road to Sankhu, which isn't marked on the *Geo-Buch* map, is simply a continuation of the road past Nagarkot's northern lodges. It's very steep, rutted and good fun – vehicles can't use the track in its present state, although there are signs it might eventually be upgraded. Pedalling up it would be more challenging.

Banepa, Nala and Panauti

The Kathmandu–Bhaktapur highway leaves the Kathmandu Valley through a gap at its eastern edge. Nepal's only road to the Tibet border is officially known as the Arniko Rajmarg (Arniko Highway), appropriately named after the thirteenth-century Nepali architect who led a delegation to Beijing and taught the Chinese how to build pagodas. Three ancient Newar towns, which once comprised a short-lived independent kingdom, lie just east of the valley rim.

BANEPA, 30km east of Kathmandu, was for centuries an important staging post to Tibet, and now – such is progress – it's an obligatory pitstop for buses heading up the Arniko Highway. The roadside buildup is pretty unattractive, and unfortunately there's not much left of the old bazaar: a fire burned most of it down in the 1960s, and earthquakes have sorely weakened the rest. Cheap cotton cloth, woven here on semi-mechanised looms, is an important local industry. *Banepa Guest House*, near the main roundabout on the highway, is the only place to get a **room** or a **full meal** in these three towns. One kilometre northeast of town, the three-tiered **Chandeshwari Mandir** overlooks a set of bathing and cremation ghats at the bottom of a steep ravine, and is best known for the psychedelic fresco decorating its exterior.

It's a three-kilometre walk northwestwards along a gravel road from Banepa to **NALA**, a quiet, parochial village near the head of the meandering Punyamata Valley. Fanning out at the base of a hill, its classically Newar houses look like a landslide of bricks, frozen in mid-tumble. Nala's main temple, dedicated to Ugrachandi Bhagwati (Angry and Wild Bhagwati, a cousin of Kali), is unusual for having four tiers – even numbers are usually avoided as they're considered unlucky. See if you notice a trend in the colour of married women's clothing here. From Nala you can continue west along a wide dirt track, passing a Lokeshwar temple on the outskirts of town, and reach Bhaktapur in 10km. The walk from here to Nagarkot is described in the Nagarkot section.

More charming still, **PANAUTI** leads a sleepy, self-sufficient existence in its own small valley 6km south of Banepa. The most pleasant way to get there is by bike – the paved road from Banepa follows the lovely Punyamata Khola – or on foot from Dhulikhel, but there are also minibus services from Kathmandu, Bhaktapur and Banepa.

Wedged between the Punyamata and Roshi streams, Panauti forms the shape of a triangle, with a serpent (*naga*) idol standing at each of its three corners to protect against floods. Buses pull up at the newish northwest corner, but the oldest and most interesting sights are concentrated at the streams' confluence at the east end of town. Pride of place goes to the massive, three-tiered **Indreshwar Mahadev**. Some authorities believe this to be the original structure (albeit restored) that was raised here in 1294, which would make it the oldest surviving pagoda in Nepal; the graceful and sensuous roof struts have been dated to the fourteenth century, although they may have been recycled. Unhappily, the building is showing its age, especially since the 1988 Dharan earthquake – which caused minor damage up to the edge of the Kathmandu Valley – shivered its timbers.

Carving from the Indreshwar Mahadev temple

The shrine area at the sacred confluence, called the **Khware**, is one of those tranquil spots that can waylay a dreamer for hours. The large *sattal* (pilgrims' house) here, a favourite hangout for local pensioners, sports an eclectic range of frescos depicting scenes from Hindu (and some Buddhist) mythology: Vishnu in cosmic sleep, Rama killing the ten-headed demon-king Ravana, and even Krishna being chased up a tree by a pack of naked *gopis* (milkmaids). Krishna is the honoured deity of the temple next door, too, where he's shown serenading his *gopi* groupies with a flute. Beside the river, the tombstone-shaped ramps laid into the ghats are where dying people are laid out, allowing their feet to be immersed in the water at the moment of death, and on the opposite bank stands the recently restored seventeenth-century **Brahmayani Mandir**. The Khware has been regarded as a *tirtha* (sacred power place) since ancient times, and on the first day of the month of *Magh*, which usually falls on January 14, it draws hundreds of people for ritual bathing.

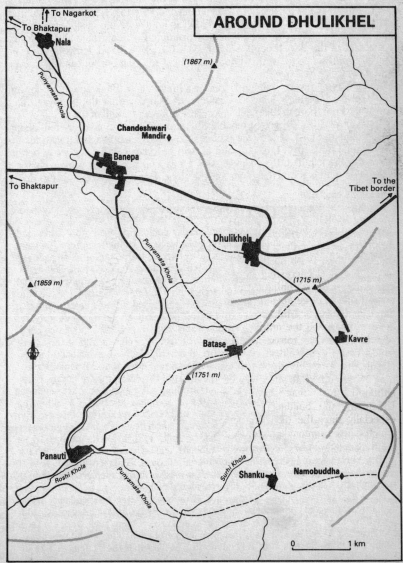

Dhulikhel

A well-preserved town as well as a mountain viewpoint, **DHULIKHEL** can keep you happily occupied for days – especially if you're into walking or biking. It sits in a saddle 5km east of Banepa, just off the Arniko Highway, at the relatively low elevation of 1550m; you get a restricted view of the Himalaya from several places around the town, but for the full vista you have to walk to a small nearby summit. Perhaps more than for its views, Dhulikhel is known as the customary starting point of the Namobuddha walk, a heavily promoted yet enjoyable all-day circuit. At the end of the day, though, what makes the place so addictive is the ever-popular *Dhulikhel Lodge*, without doubt the most relaxing port of call within overnight distance of Kathmandu.

Direct **buses** (every half-hour from Kathmandu or Bhaktapur's trolley-bus stop) are exasperatingly local and usually set you down on the highway. It's a short walk from there to the main square at the new, east end of town.

First impressions are pretty terrible: the square is surrounded by tall, dismal brick buildings that look like warehouses. Suspend your disbelief, make for the **Dhulikhel Lodge** (☎011/61114) and all will be revealed. Tucked away behind one of the brick hulks, the lodge boasts a peaceful patio with wicker chairs, a retro-1960s dining room (cushions on the floor, leave your shoes at the door),

PARBATIYAS AND TAMANGS

Nepal's **human geography** gets hideously confusing once you leave the Kathmandu Valley: over the course of millenia, waves of immigrants from Tibet and India have produced a complex overlay of cultures. Nearly half of all Nepalis are members of ethnic minorities and maintain distinct languages, customs and dress. The rest – the majority – are relative newcomers, descendents of Hindus who fled the Muslim conquest of northern India beginning in the twelfth century; they are collectively referred to as **Parbatiyas** or, more generically, **Hindu castes**. In India, Hindus are divided into four primary castes, but nearly all the migrants to Nepal were of the two highest orders, Brahmans and Kshatriyas (called the "twice-born" castes as males are symbolically "reborn" through an initiation rite at the age of thirteen and thereafter wear a sacred thread (*janai*), changed annually during the festival of *Janai Purnima*), since these had the most to lose from a Muslim regime.

Although **Brahmans** belong to the highest, priestly caste, they're not necessarily the wealthiest members of society, nor are they all priests. Many are landlords and moneylenders, earning a reputation (by all accounts deserved) for subjecting their borrowers to crippling interest rates and swift foreclosures. Priests, who generally follow their fathers into the vocation, make a living administering rites for fixed fees. Most Brahmans observe a range of rules to maintain the purity of their caste (certain foods and alcohol are prohibited), and orthodox Brahmans won't eat with lower castes or permit them to enter the house; Brahman women have it especially hard, as they have to keep strict seclusion during menstruation and for ten days after childbirth, when they're considered polluted.

The majority of Nepali Hindus are **Chhetris**, who correspond to Indian Kshatriyas, the caste of warriors and kings. While Nepali Brahmans usually claim pure bloodlines and exhibit the classic Aryan features of their caste, Chhetris are a more racially mixed lot and easily mistaken for members of other ethnic minorities. Many in fact are the offspring of Hindus with the hill tribes they subjugated, or in passable food, entertaining management, hot running water, electricity and a phone (international calls are possible); singles start at Rs35, doubles Rs70. Arrive early to get a room, especially during October and November – this is the *only* budget lodging in Dhulikhel.

For a splurge, try the *Himalayan Horizon Sun-n-Snow Hotel* (Kathmandu office ☎01/225092), along the highway about 1km west of Dhulikhel (singles $30, doubles $40). Even if you're not staying there, breakfast on the spectacular back terrace is a real treat. The *Hotel Vajra* (☎272719) in Kathmandu maintains a cottage near Dhulikhel where rooms are $15 per person, including meals. Dhulikhel's **bank** is just off the highway at the east end of town (Sun–Thurs 10am–2.30pm, Fri 10am–noon).

In welcome contrast to the soulless eastern entrance to town, **old Dhulikhel** is a close, traditional Newar settlement of remarkable architectural consistency, its four- and even five-storey brick mansions, many with ornate wooden lattices in place of glass windows, affecting a stern, almost Victorian elegance. These huge houses are extended-family dwellings: some Dhulikhel clans number 80 or more members. The older buildings, which are only held together by mud mortar, show some fairly serious cracks from Kathmandu's infamous earthquake of 1934; Dhulikhel also experienced some damage during the 1988 'quake centred near Dharan in the eastern Tarai. Wandering around Dhulikhel is basically a matter of

---

some cases of compliant hill dwellers who converted to Hinduism and were made honorary Chhetris: in the early days, Brahmans were willing to bend the rules to gain allies. Those of pure Kshatriya blood – notably the Thakuri subcaste of the far west, who are related to the king – can be as twitchy about caste regulations as Brahmans. Significantly, it was a Chhetri who unified Nepal and gave the country its abiding martial character, and the old warrior-caste mentality remains a key in understanding the politics of modern Nepal, for Chhetris occupy the palace and command the army to this day.

The lack of lower-caste Hindus in Nepal rather defeats the object of the caste system, and the result, frequently, is a case of all chiefs and no Indians. Communities of so-called **occupational castes** – leather-workers, blacksmiths and so on – occur in pockets in the hills, and often ethnic minorities fill the gaps (Newars, for instance, usually take over the shopkeeping); but in many hill villages, especially in the far west, Brahmans and Chhetris have to shed their dogma and do the menial work themselves.

While Hindu castes tend to monopolise the lower elevations throughout Nepal, **Tamangs** dominate the central hills between about 1500m and 2000m and constitute, numerically, the largest hill tribe in Nepal. Despite their numbers, they're also Nepal's most exploited people: Tamangs haven't profited from trade like the Newars, nor been recruited into the Gurkha regiments like the other hill groups. Most are peasant farmers, tilling marginal lands, or day labourers, typically seen hulking enormous loads around Kathmandu and in the hills. Skilled artisans, they produce much of what passes for Tibetan handicrafts in Kathmandu, though sadly they seldom get the credit for it. The tribe is thought to have originated in Tibet and migrated south in prehistoric times, which accounts for their Mongoloid features but leaves the significance of their name, which means "horse trader" in Tibetan, intriguingly unexplained. Tamangs follow a form of Buddhism virtually indistinguishable from Lamaism – religious texts are even written in Tibetan script – but they also worship clan deities, employ *jhankris* (shamans) and observe major Hindu festivals.

following your nose (and sometimes *holding* your nose – some alleys are used as public latrines), but highlights include the central square of **Narayanthan**, containing a temple to Narayan and a smaller one to Harisiddhi (both emanations of Vishnu), and the **Bhagwati Mandir**, set at the high point of the village for a fine view of the mountains.

Be advised that the schoolchildren in Dhulikhel take a malevolent delight in taunting foreigners, and will sometimes even spit or throw stones at them. It's a game you cannot win – just don't betray any exasperation, and if you know any Nepali, tease them back.

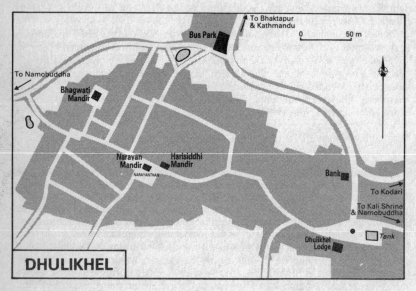

To Bhaktapur & Kathmandu
Bus Park
0   50 m
To Namobuddha
Bhagwati Mandir
Narayan Mandir
NARAYANTHAN
Harisiddhi Mandir
Bank
To Kodari
To Kali Shrine & Namobuddha
Dhulikhel Lodge
Tank

DHULIKHEL

The sunrise walk

The done thing in Dhulikhel is to hike to the high point southeast of town in time for sunrise over the peaks. To get to the top, take the road leading east from town until the pavement ends, then bear right and follow a gullied path straight up the hill; allow about forty-five minutes altogether. The peaks from Annapurna to (supposedly) Everest are visible from the summit (1715m) marked by a small **Kali Shrine**, – and the sight of Dhulikhel's brick houses, salmon in the dawn light and perhaps wreathed in mist, is pretty special, too. If you're running behind schedule or otherwise flagging, the view from the playing field near the end of the paved road might suffice.

On the way back down you can call in at a small, mossy temple complex, hidden down a flagstone path where the paved road gives out. The main **Shiva temple** contains a large bronze *lingam*; the adjacent **Ram temple**'s marble statues have been lopped off at the ankles by temple-robbers – a persistent problem in Nepal, and one that's not helped by demand for such treasures from foreign collectors.

To Namobuddha and Panauti

Dhulikhel Lodge has elevated the so-called **Namobuddha circuit** into something of an institution, and almost everyone who stays there ends up doing it. The walk has perhaps been overhyped: it certainly isn't in the same league as a proper trek, although it remains a fine introduction to the byways of rural hill Nepal. With the rapid construction of roads and grading of paths in the area, it actually makes much more exciting country for **mountain biking** than walking.

The full circuit takes five or six hours to complete, and tea is available at villages along the way, but bring food. There's no point in describing the route here – just ask at *Dhulikhel Lodge* for **the map** and they'll give you a diagram, complete with landmarks and walking times. It's possible to combine Namobuddha with a sunrise walk to the Kali shrine, although this requires a degree of organisation that most people won't be able to manage first thing in the morning.

NAMOBUDDHA (or NAMRO) itself won't detain you for long, although to Tibetans it ranks right up there on the hierarchy of holy sites in Nepal. About two-and-a-half hours south of Dhulikhel on foot, the stupa rests on a red-earth ledge near the top of a jungley ridge. It's like a hick version of Swayambhu – smaller and pretty uneventful, except during the February-March pilgrimage season, when Tibetans and Bhotiyas arrive by the vanload to circumambulate it. Among the houses surrounding the stupa is a dinky Tamang *gompa*, which you can enter. A trail leads up to a bigger Tibetan *gompa* on top of the prayer-flag-festooned ridge behind, and in one of the outbuildings is preserved a famous stone relief **sculpture** depicting the legend of Namo Buddha. According to the fable, Buddha, in one of his previous lives as a hunter, encountered a starving tigress and her cubs here, and moved by compassion, offered his own flesh to her, a sacrifice that helped pave the way for his eventual rebirth as the historical Buddha. The stupa is supposed to contain the hunter's bones and hair.

Although the *Dhulikhel Lodge*'s map recommends returning to Dhulikhel by a different route, carrying on **to Panauti** is equally enjoyable. The Panauti trail veers off to the left at SHANKU – a sign points the way in English – and enters Panauti from the east after about an hour and a half. From there you can catch a minibus to Kathmandu or back to Dhulikhel (change at Banepa).

To Jiri and the Tibet border

Traffic along the **ARNIKO RAJMARG** (ARNIKO HIGHWAY) drops off drastically beyond Dhulikhel. Built by the Chinese in the mid-1960s – to India's great distress – the road was once a busy conduit for lorry loads of Chinese goods by way of Lhasa, but landslides north of the border have slowed trade to a trickle*. In 1985, Tibet was opened to individual travellers and the Arniko Highway briefly flourished as a back-door route, but at the time of writing only expensive tour groups were being allowed in (officially, at least: some travellers with nothing more than a Hong Kong-issued Chinese visa have been waved through).

---

*Why this has been allowed to happen is unclear. One of the prime reasons for building the highway was to ensure an alternate source of goods so Nepal wouldn't be so dependent on Mother India. Yet the state of the highway (together with martial law in Tibet) prevented China from coming to Nepal's rescue during the 1989 Indian trade

Nowadays, the vast majority of travellers passing this way are bound for Jiri, the starting point of treks in the Everest region, located on a tortuous side road off the Arniko Highway. Public transport along the highway north of the Jiri turning is unreliable on account of the poor state of the road, and few but the hardiest mountain bikers make it to the border – which, if anything, only enhances the journey's mystique. There are no views of the high peaks along the Arniko Highway past Dhulikhel, and only fleeting ones from the Jiri road.

After Dhulikhel, the road drops 600m into the broad Panchkhal Valley, a lush, irrigated plain cultivated with rice paddy, sugar cane and tropical fruits. The village of PANCHKHAL is a springboard for treks in the Helambu region. The highway reaches its lowest (and hottest) point at **DOLALGHAT** (634m), a small market town clumped at either end of the bridge across the impressively vast and braided Indrawati River. Rafting parties put in here for the ten-day trip on the Sun Kosi, which joins the Indrawati just around the corner. CHAUTARA, high on the ridge to the north, is the headquarters of a big Australian reforestation project.

The scenery changes abruptly after Dolalghat, as the highway bends northeastwards up the deep, terraced **Sun Kosi Valley**. Nepal's terraces, while they're marvellous feats of engineering, are a sign of agricultural desperation: with so little flat land available and a growing number of mouths to feed, hill people have no choice but to farm ever steeper and less productive slopes. Terraces make good farming and environmental sense – they stabilise the topsoil, and form a stopgap against erosion on deforested slopes – but maintaining them is a tremendously labour-intensive chore that detracts from the actual business of growing food, and building more terraces inevitably brings about further deforestation.

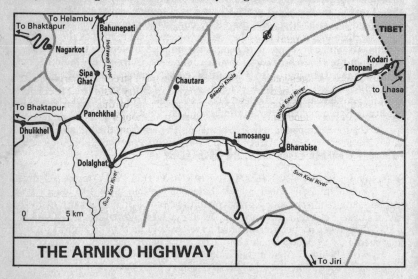

THE ARNIKO HIGHWAY

To Jiri

Kathmandu to Jiri is a wretched bus journey, taking anything up to thirteen hours to cover just 190km. Be wary if stowing luggage on the roof, as there have been reports of thefts along this route.

The **Jiri Road** breaks off from the Arniko Highway at the 78-kilometre mark, passing close to a hydroelectric station built by the Chinese. The road climbs a merciless 1800m out of the Sun Kosi Valley, reaching an elevation of 2540m, then contours around two more small basins to the Newar pitstop of CHARIKOT from which it's a long descent to the Tamba Kosi (800m), a steep climb to a forested ridge (2500m) and finally a dip into the Jiri Valley at 1900m. Completed in 1985, the road was financed by the Swiss government to provide easier access to their long-term development works at Jiri. The presence of these Australian, Chinese and Swiss projects isn't unusual in the Nepalese hills, although as you approach the Everest region you'll be struck how the most beautiful places often seem to attract the greatest number of aid workers.

Once an insignificant hamlet, **JIRI** has somehow been singled out by fate and politicians to receive a booster shot of western charity. Charlie Pye-Smith, in his book *Travels in Nepal*, has called Jiri "the half-caste offspring of an impoverished Nepalese mother and a wealthy Swiss father". In 1958 the Swiss established the Jiri Multi-Purpose Development Project, a ground-breaking scheme based on the now widely accepted view that development needs – health, agriculture, education and so on – are interrelated and can't be tackled separately. The programme established a hospital, technical school, experimental farm and other facilities; some have since been handed over to HMG, and their subsequent deterioration raises troubling questions about development in Nepal (see *Contexts*). The road, in turn, has transformed Jiri into a busy little boomtown, where lorries constantly drop off supply shipments and porters assemble to carry them on to hill villages (it has all but put nearby THOSE, once the area's main bazaar and an important iron-smithing centre, out of business). Trekkers obviously add a few pennies to the local economy, although most are too eager to hit the trail or get back to Kathmandu to spend more than a night here.

Practicalities

At least a dozen **lodges** jostle on either side of the main street, all charging a standard Rs5 for dormitory beds – *Cherdung Lodge and Valley Restaurant* is comfortable enough, with a reasonable choice of food. Shops in the bazaar flog some trekker-orientated food and even rent clothing, although prices are naturally higher than in Kathmandu. Book **return bus tickets** from the hut about halfway down the main street on the same side as the *Cherdung* – tickets go on sale at 6pm for the following day, and you need to queue up early.

To the border

Two kilometres past the Jiri turning, LAMOSANGU (740m) is distinguished by a magnesite processing plant and a wasteland of castings. **BHARABISE**, 8km north, is as far as buses from Kathmandu go. The highway and electricity have turned Bharabise, like Jiri, into an uncharismatic boomtown of tall, slapdash buildings and shops selling cassette tapes and readymade clothes. Several lodges let rooms for Rs15–25 and serve noodles and *daal bhaat*. North of town you can visit a small mill producing traditional Nepalese paper, which is often confused with rice paper but is actually made from the bark of the native *daphne* bush.

The pavement ends north of Bharabise and the steep gradient to the border begins a few kilometres later. As dirt roads go, this one is pretty well engineered, but it does its best to self-destruct with each monsoon. Afternoon rain is common up here, even in the dry season, and despite a general scarcity of trees near the river (here called the **Bhote Kosi**), everything is intensely green, with waterfalls splashing down cliff faces at every turn. The gorge is much deeper than it looks from the road.

Minibuses make sporadic runs from Bharabise to Tatopani, 23km further on. Most passengers are bound for Khasa, the first town in Tibet, which is as far as Nepalis can go without travel documents, to do a little innocent **smuggling**. They return the same day, after dark, laden with milk powder, Chinese training shoes and bolts of linen – all of which are considerably cheaper on the Tibetan side – and attempt to sneak them past the customs checkpost just south of Tatopani: if someone asks you to stow a bag of white powder in your rucksack "for a few minutes", it's probably only milk.

Tatopani

Ten years ago, **TATOPANI** (1530m) enjoyed a small following among westerners, who came to gaze into Tibet and soak in the village's hot springs (*taato paani* means "hot water"), but has fallen out of fashion now that Tibet is occupied and the Arniko Highway has gone to hell. It remains a quiet, relaxing place – possibly too dull and "native" for some, but a real find if you're into offbeat locales.

The village stretches along the highway for at least a kilometre, in two parts. Bhotiyas (see Chapter Seven) are a visible minority at this altitude, and they maintain a small **gompa** five minutes' walk above the southern bazaar. The building is modest, but it looks out on a fine view of the valley and, up at the head of it, a smidgen of Tibet. The **hot springs** are at the northern end of the village, behind a wooden entrance and down steps towards the river. A hot tub it's not: the water splashes out of pipes into a concrete pool and is used strictly for washing. If you take the waters, remember that nudity offends in Nepal.

Western menus have all disappeared, but a few **lodges** limp on from the good old days. *Kesang Lodge*, near the north end, is friendly (Rs10 for a dorm bed). Hints of China's nearness are everywhere: you'll see chopsticks and thermos flasks in every kitchen, and some places even sell Tsingtao beer (for a ridiculous price).

Kodari and the border

Disabuse yourself of any visions of high, snowy passes into Tibet. The border village of **KODARI** (1640m), 3km on from Tatopani, is just another bedraggled roadside bazaar at the bottom of a deep valley, with nary a yak in sight. The lowest point along the Nepal-Tibet border, Kodari has always been the preferred crossing for traders between Kathmandu and Lhasa. Its balmy elevation isn't so extraordinary as it might seem, though: the main Himalayan chain, which the border generally follows, is breached in several places by rivers that are older than the mountains themselves (the watershed, in fact, runs not along the highest peaks but as much as 100km to the north). In the case of Kodari, the border was actually shifted further south after an ill-advised war with Tibet in 1792.

Shared taxis ply between Tatopani and Kodari. Another long, drawn-out bazaar, Kodari is the Nepalese equivalent of a service strip along a highway bypass, while old Kodari, a scattered village with a small *gompa*, perches on the ridge above. Bunk **accommodation** is available for Rs10–15 at a few lodges along the road. Tatopani is the better bet, but if you're crossing into Tibet you'll want to stay here to get an early start.

The **border** is marked by the so-called **Friendship Bridge**, which spans the Bhote Kosi at the top end of town, guarded at either end by lackadaisical Nepali and Chinese soldiers. Up at the head of the valley, 600m higher than Kodari, the Chinese buildings of Khasa cling to the side of a mountain – that's the extent of the view of Tibet from here.

Should you be crossing the border, the 9km between the Kodari and Khasa immigration posts is a **no-man's-land** which can only be traversed on foot. The road is permanently washed out in places – several old-fashioned Chinese lorries have been stranded between the landslides – and all goods are ferried up and down by porters along steep shortcut trails; you can hire a porter to carry your pack for about Rs50. If you were wondering how all that pink Chinese toilet paper gets to Kathmandu, here's your answer. Remember that Tibet time is two hours and fifteen minutes *ahead* of Nepal time, so you have to set off early to catch the bank in Khasa before it closes. Guards at the Chinese customs post have orders to confiscate any pictures of the Dalai Lama.

The Trisuli Road

One of Nepal's earliest forays into road-building, the **TRISULI ROAD** was constructed in the mid-1960s as part of a hydroelectric scheme on the Trisuli River, northwest of Kathmandu. That's the official story, anyway, although the road probably owes its existence as much to historical nostalgia as progress: the route retraces the triumphal approach of Prithvi Narayan Shah, founding father of Nepal, from his fortress of Nuwakot to the Kathmandu Valley two centuries ago. It's since been extended north to a mining area in the Ganesh Himal. Most travellers passing this way are only concerned about getting to Dhunche, the usual starting point for treks to Langtang and Gosainkund, yet Nuwakot is sorely underrated as a stopover, and Kakani makes a serviceable destination in itself. **Buses** from Kathmandu (Paknajol) go to Trisuli Bazaar. For Dhunche, change at Trisuli.

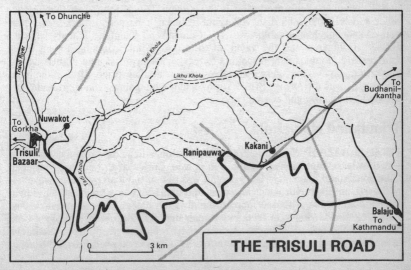

THE TRISULI ROAD

Kakani

KAKANI (*Kaa*-kuh-ni), the closest mountain viewpoint to Kathmandu, straddles the Kathmandu Valley's northwest rim at an elevation of 1980m. Like Nagarkot, Kakani is essentially a tourist phenomenon, as opposed to a town, with a view but not much else. Unlike Nagarkot, it has only one hotel, and it's not cheap – but you don't necessarily have to spend the night.

Trisuli-bound **buses** drop you off at the pass west of Kakani. From there, follow a side road signposted "Telecom Repeater Station" for 3km (there are shortcuts), passing a large army barracks en route. In the days of Prithvi Shah, the Kakani pass was the Kathmandu Valley's Achilles' heel – by controlling it, he was able to beseige the valley for two years – but this hilltop post, like the one at Nagarkot, now seems a quaint throwback to the days of hand-to-hand combat. If you get to Kakani early enough, you can **walk back** to Balaju in three or four hours by following the dirt road east from Kakani past an agricultural station, then contouring beneath the ridge through thick oak and rhododendron forest before bending south and down along a spur (great views); after passing a set of stupas, look for a fork to the left leading to DHARAMTHALI and Balaju. **By mountain bike**, you can cycle up via Budhanilkantha (see Chapter Two) and back down along the Trisuli Road or vice versa.

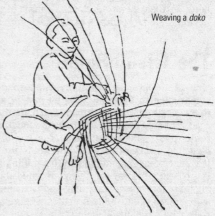

Weaving a *doko*

Kakani's only **accommodation** is the *Kakani Tara Gaon Resort* (Kathmandu office ☎01/410409), a bit dishevelled but featuring a marvellous back lawn where you can lounge like a sahib, with the Ganesh and Langtang Himals splashed across the horizon and the valley of the Likhu Khola coursing 1000m below (singles $13, doubles $18; discounts for stays of more than one night). Even if you're not staying, they serve palatable lunches at a fair price. The yellow building next door is the former British Ambassador's bungalow, whose grounds once boasted a miniature golf course.

Trisuli and Nuwakot

TRISULI BAZAAR (540m) is 17km from Kathmandu as the crow flies, or 70km – and at least four hours – as the bus crawls. Curled at the bottom of a deep, subtropical (and once malarial) valley, it was put on the map by the construction of the Trisuli River hydroelectric project and flourished for a time as the trailhead for Langtang treks. The development bandwagon has moved on, and nowadays most trekkers don't stop in Trisuli for longer than it takes to swill a bottle of Coke and board the bus to Dhunche. Indeed, there's little to see in this ramshackle township, with the possible exception of the old, stair-stepped **bazaar** (reached through a passage at the west end of the bridge) and a small **stupa** perched above the opposite bank. That said, staying overnight at Trisuli permits a visit to nearby Nuwakot, which, if you find yourself with an extra day at the end of a trek, is a good deal more enjoyable than killing time in Dhunche or returning to Kathmandu early. The trek to Gorkha and Pokhara begins here, following the lovely Samri Khola to the west.

For **accommodation**, the best of a bad lot is *Kerong Restaurant and Lodge* (dorm beds Rs15, rooms Rs20–30); their *thukpa* (soup) is gorgeous, though. To return to Kathmandu, **ticket offices** for both private and *Sajha* buses are located across the street from the *Kerong* (*Sajha* buses are faster).

Nuwakot

One of Nepal's proudest historical monuments, Prithvi Narayan Shah's aban-doned fortress looms like a forgotten shipwreck on a ridge above Trisuli, casting a poignant, almost romantic spell over the tiny village of **NUWAKOT**. The **walk** from Trisuli takes less than an hour, although the trail is a tad tricky to find: climb a flight of steps from the water tap near the east side of the Trisuli Bazaar bridge to the Dhunche Road, walk up the road for about two minutes and make a right at the first group of houses. The path becomes wide and eroded as it climbs through a spindly forest of *sal* trees – their leaves are gathered to make tradi-tional (biodegradable) leaf plates – and reaches Nuwakot on the crest of a ridge about 300m above the valley floor. To **cycle**, take the dirt road that leaves the main road about 1km south of Trisuli.

The **fortress** stands to the right as you enter the village, consisting of three brick towers rising like Monopoly hotels within a walled compound: the tallest one is open to the public, though you may have to track down the caretaker to unlock it for you. The views from the top-floor windows are stupendous, looking out on Ganesh Himal and the pastoral Trisuli and Tadi valleys.

It was from this command centre that **Prithvi Narayan Shah**, the unifier of Nepal, directed his dogged campaign on the Kathmandu Valley in 1744–69, and gazing out these windows you can gain some insight into the mind of this obses-sive but brilliant military tactician. In his determination to conquer the valley, Prithvi Shah had **three other towers** built in the name of the three valley capi-tals, perhaps hoping to bring about their downfall by a kind of voodoo; the Kathmandu and Patan towers share the main compound, while the crumbling Bhaktapur tower stands on a rise just outside. After Kathmandu's fall, Nuwakot had just one more moment in the limelight. In 1792, attempting to extend Nepal's territory into Tibet, Prithvi Shah's successor pushed his luck too far and was driven all the way back to BETRAWATI, the next village north of Trisuli. In the resulting **peace treaty**, signed at Nuwakot, Nepal ceded to Tibet the lucrative trading posts of Kyirong (north of Trisuli) and Khasa (north of Kodari), account-ing for two southward lunges in the border that remain to this day.

Nuwakot's old main street runs south from the fortress along the spine of the ridge and suddenly dead-ends, the land falling away to reveal a vast **panorama** of the Tadi and Trisuli valleys. In the late eighteenth century, when Nuwakot enjoyed a brief flowering as the winter residence of the Kathmandu court, the houses along this boulevard must have looked considerably posher. The only building of note now is a two-tiered **Bhairabi Mandir**, which hosts a festival in honour of Bagh Bhairab in April.

The Rajpath

Nepal's most magnificent and hair-raising highway, the **RAJPATH** (officially the TRIBHUWAN RAJPATH) heads west out of the Kathmandu Valley and then hurls itself, through an astounding series of switchbacks, straight over the Mahabharat Lekh to the Tarai. En route it passes through lush stands of rhododendron and takes in superb views of the Himalaya. Mountain bikers regard the road, culminating at the incredible Daman view tower, as something of a holy pilgrimage.

Built by Indian engineers in the mid-1950s, the Rajpath was the first highway to link Kathmandu to the outside world – before that, VIPs were carried to the capital by palanquin, and the prime ministers' automobiles had to be portered from India, fully assembled, by 200-strong teams of coolies. Since the construction of the Narayanghat–Mugling road, most drivers prefer to miss out the harrowing Rajpath and go the long way around. Only one **bus** a day (*Sajha*) travels along the Rajpath in each direction, taking about eight hours to cover 133km (several night buses also make the journey, but you'd have to have a real death wish to take one). A slower but more adventurous alternative is to hitch a ride with one of the many **trucks** taking wood and fuel to the capital; they take on passengers for the return journey at Kalimati in south Kathmandu. Hardest, but most exhilarating, is to go by **mountain bike**: though some diehards claim to have pedalled from Kathmandu to Daman in seven hours, the average mortal can expect to take from dawn to dusk and be utterly shattered by the end of it. Keep an eye out for approaching trucks, as the road is narrow and many corners are blind.

For its first 26km, the Rajpath follows the upgraded (and heavily used) Prithvi Highway towards Pokhara. Leaving the Kathmandu Valley through its most industrial corridor, it slips through a low point in the rim and descends to **NAUBISE** (945m), near the bottom of the deep, wrinkled Mahesh Khola Valley. Nepalese lodges and restaurants are plentiful in Naubise; if you had to spend the night, *Hotel Janak* (rooms Rs40) would probably be the quietest of the available options.

At Naubise the Rajpath branches off to the left and climbs 34km to TISTUNG (2030m) before descending to **PALUNG** at 1745m, a Newar village spread out amid tidy terraces (potatoes are a local speciality). Very basic food and lodging can be arranged here, but unless you're desperate it's worth toiling up the final, tough 11km to spend the night in Daman. A hardy cyclist could take the dirt track  south from Palung to BHIMPHEDI, which rejoins the Rajpath 10km north of Hetauda, and return to Kathmandu via Daman.

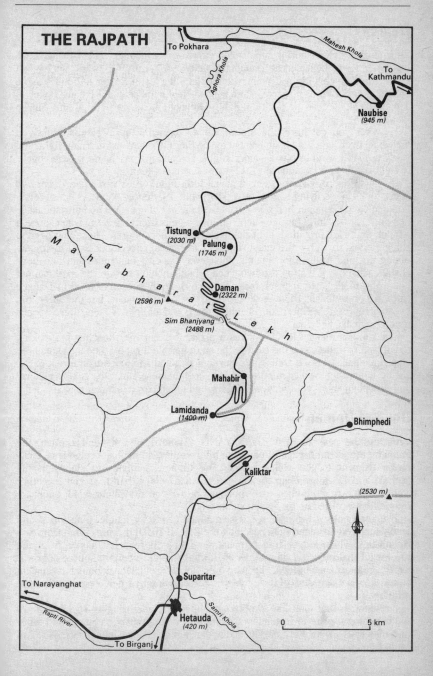

THE RAJPATH

To Pokhara

Mahesh Khola

Aghora Khola

To Kathmandu

Naubise
(945 m)

M a h a b h a r a t   L e k h

Tistung
(2030 m)

Palung
(1745 m)

Daman
(2322 m)

(2596 m)

Sim Bhanjyang
(2488 m)

Mahabir

Lamidanda
(1400 m)

Bhimphedi

Kaliktar

(2530 m)

0   5 km

To Narayanghat

Rapti River

Suparitar

Samri Khola

Hetauda
(420 m)

To Birganj

Daman

With fantastic views and a ramshackle viewtower-cum-lodge, **DAMAN** (2322m) has been a well-kept secret among the fat-tyre fraternity for years. Sitting just below the Rajpath's highest point, the hamlet – it's just a cluster of houses and a couple of agricultural research stations – overlooks the peaceful Palung Valley to a magnificent spread of peaks, notably Himalchuli, Ganesh Himal and Shisha Pangma.

However you get here, the mountains will probably be in clouds when you arrive: an overnight stay is obligatory to see them in their best morning light, and you'll probably want to stay a second night. To continue on, the daily *Sajha* buses to Kathmandu and Hetauda stop at Daman at around 10am.

Certainly one of Nepal's more unusual **lodgings**, the *Everest View Tower and Lodge* looks like a flying saucer on a pillar, with 360-degree windows, an observation deck and coin-operated telescopes (usually out of order). The futuristic facilities don't, however, extend to such comforts as electricity, running water or even a toilet; quilts are provided, but bring a sleeping bag in winter. There's no need to bring a book, though – the guest registers are virtual encyclopedias of mountain-biking tips and lore. Unfortunately, the tower has only one room and four beds (Rs30 each), but if it's full the two truck-drivers' haunts beside the road can put you up in rustic style. These places are also the only source of **food** in Daman. Both are pretty basic: the one on the right does better meals, but the other, run by an irrepressible Sherpani, is much more welcoming. No one here speaks much English.

The **gompa** above Daman makes a pleasant excursion. Reach it by walking about twenty minutes up the road to the sixth hairpin turn, marked by a small red sign in Nepali, where a trail winds through oak and rhododendron forest to the shrine in another twenty minutes. Run by a Bhutanese lama, the *gompa* is small and unembellished, but the view from its meditation perch is awesome.

Beyond Daman

Crossing the pass of SIM BHANJYANG (2488m), 3km beyond Daman, the Rajpath enters a landscape of plunging hill country and begins a relentless, 2200-metre descent to the valley below. The higher, south-facing slopes of the Mahabharat Lekh are dramatically greener and wilder than those on the other side – they wring much of the moisture out of the prevailing winds, and are frequently wreathed in fog by afternoon.

The road passes through successive zones of mossy jungle, pine forest and finally terraced farmland until reaching the BHIMPHEDI turning, 40km from Sim Bhanjyang. The electric transformers seen near here relay power from the Khulekani hydroelectric dam north of Bhimphedi, an important source of power for the region, and, indeed, the whole of Nepal. (See "Development Issues" in *Contexts* for a discussion of the problems surrounding hydroelectric development schemes.)

The devices that look like ski lifts are ropeways, one bringing rocks down to the big cement plant in Hetauda and the other taking finished cement and other raw materials up to Kathmandu. Hetauda, described in Chapter Six, is 10km further on.

MOUNTAIN BIKING: HOW, WHAT, WHERE AND WHEN

Nepal was made for **mountain bikes**: the roads are uncrowded and spectacular, the cycling is challenging, and the alternative – buses – is unpleasant. On a bike you can stop where you like, enjoy the scenery, make detours, amaze the locals, and reach your destination in only twice the time it takes by bus. A degree of fitness is required, but if you can handle a *Hero* cycle you'll have no trouble with a mountain bike.

If you haven't brought your own machine (see "Outdoor Pursuits" in *Basics*), you can easily **rent** one in Kathmandu; at the time of writing mountain bikes were still rare around Pokhara, but this is bound to change. Prices vary considerably, depending on the make, number of gears and condition of the bike. Ten speeds are probably all you'll need for day trips around the Kathmandu Valley, but if you're making a longer excursion you'll want eighteen gears. Make sure the saddle is comfortable, as some can be excruciating. Give brakes, gears, tyres and other moving parts a thorough checking-over before handing over any money – the last thing you want is for something to break on a remote mountain road. It's worth paying more (up to $5 a day) for a new, well-maintained bike.

One serious hitch with renting is that bike shops seldom provide **equipment** (though this, too, may change). Bring:
• Panniers (a light rucksack might suffice)
• Helmet
• All relevant tools, patch kit and spare inner tubes
• First-aid kit, including iodine for water purification (can be cobbled together in Kathmandu)
• Security cable
• Breathable waterproof clothing (eg Gore-Tex)
• Cycling gloves and shorts
• Bungie cords (spiders)
• Bell

Camping is strictly optional, but a sleeping bag, rentable in Kathmandu, often comes in handy for draughty lodges.

If you can't be bothered with logistics, join a **cycle tour**. Prices are comparable to organised treks, as are the pros and cons – you can count on good food, reliable equipment, companionship whether you want it or not, and a certain loss of freedom. The original and most reputable cycle outfitter is *Himalayan Mountain Bikes* (☎01/413632; PO Box 2769, Kathmandu), located in the forecourt of the *Kathmandu Guest House*, whose tours range from one to thirteen days; two- and three-day trips (costing $80–130) are frequent, but book ahead for longer ones (which cost up to $1945). *Discover Nepal* (☎01/224142), on Durbar Marg, runs ad hoc tours along obscure trails southeast of the Kathmandu Valley for about $14 a day, and also runs a twelve-day catered tour for $850, although the latter is aimed at a French clientele. *Makalu Trekking* on Jyatha Thamel is planning to get into cycle tours.

The chart below should help you find a **route** that's about your speed. If you're more adventurous, the possibilities for exploring off the beaten track, especially in the Tarai, are almost unlimited. **Cycle trekking** is yet another option, though one likely to appeal only to the most hard-core enthusiasts: riding a mountain bike on trekking trails requires great technical skill, and entails carrying the bike a good deal of the time (cycle trekkers rate trails according to the percentage of carrying they require). If you do it, be sure to give other people and livestock priority on the trail. Likely spots for cycle trekking include Helambu and the Trisuli–Gorkha–Pokhara trail; mountain bikes aren't allowed in Langtang and Sagarmatha (Everest) national parks, and the Annapurna region is considered only marginally cyclable.

MOUNTAIN BIKING ROUTES IN NEPAL

Circuits ex-Kathmandu	Distance–return (km)	Cycling days	Elevations (m)	Best time to go
Nagarkot/Sankhu	60	1–2	1300–2000	Oct–Dec, Feb–April
Dhulikhel/Namobuddha/Panauti	75	1–2	1300–1700	Oct–May
Kakani/Trisuli	150	2–3	540–2070	Nov–March
Daman	155	2–3	900–2320	Oct–Dec, Feb–April
Kodari (Tibet border)	230	3–4	630–1640	Nov–April
Chitwan/Hetauda/Daman	380	4–5	180–2490	Nov–March
Pokhara	400	4–5	280–1500	Nov–March
Pokhara/Butwal/Chitwan/Hetauda/Daman	600+	10+	180–2490	Nov–Dec, Feb–March
Circuits ex-Pokhara				
Birethanti	70	2	700–1600	Nov–April
Tansen	240	2–4	350–1400	Nov–March
Routes to/from India	Distance–one way (km)			
Kathmandu–Birganj	185	2	90–2490	Nov–Dec, Feb–March
Kathmandu–Sunauli	300 (380)	3 (4)	90–1500 (2490)	Nov–March
Kathmandu–Kakarbitta	540	5–6	80–2490	Nov–March
Pokhara–Sunauli	185	2	90–1300	Nov–March

Comments

Brisk ascent takes the better part of an afternoon; stay overnight for views; bumpy dirt road back via Sankhu.

Main road is easy and unspectacular, but Namobuddha–Panauti is first-class fat-tyre country.

Can take back roads to Kakani via Budhanilkantha, followed by 1500-metre descent; numerous dirt roads east of Trisuli. Road to Dhunche is a steep, rough, 900-metre ascent; a trekking permit is required, and cyclists report being turned back.

Nepal's classic: a punishing, dawn-to-dusk ride, involving two steep climbs totalling 1660m – you might want to rest a day before returning. Traffic is light, scenery is magnificent.

Pretty tough: two days up and two days back for most people, with nights spent at Dhulikhel (book ahead).

A varied, strenuous trip – approaching Daman from the south, you climb nearly 2200m without a break.

Fairly scenic route following rivers much of the way; long days but not too many steep pitches; traffic is heavy, however. Possible side trip to Gorkha.

A grand tour with many variations, which could also include side trips to Gorkha, Tansen and Lumbini.

Road expected to be passable by late 1990, though continuing construction may spoil the effect for some time to come.

A winding road with little traffic and challenging terrain, including a 1000-metre climb at the end.

A tremendous introduction to Nepal if you're coming from India; pity about Birganj, though.

Not very exciting via Mugling; figures in parentheses are via Chitwan and Daman, a superb route combining the best of all worlds.

Possible side trips to Janakpur, Hile and Ilam.

Possible side trips to Tansen and Lumbini.

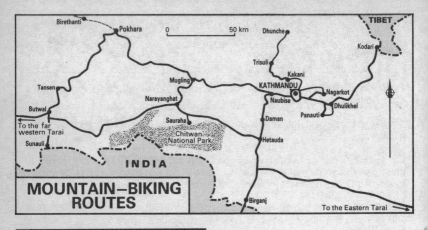

festivals

The festivals of *Dasain*, *Tihar* and *Holi* are celebrated everywhere in the central hills, while Dhulikhel and other Newar bazaars join in many of the Kathmandu Valley's holidays. In addition, look for these local events:

Magh Sankranti The first day of the month of *Magh*, traditionally observed with ritual bathing in the Punyamata Khola at Panauti (January 14 or 15).

Losar Tibetan New Year, celebrated at Namobuddha; Tibetans make pilgrimages to the stupa during the month that follows (February).

Bagh Bhairab Jaatra The festival of Bhairab in his tiger form, held at Nuwakot (April).

travel details

Buses
Most of the buses to destinations in this region either begin or end their journeys in **Kathmandu**:

Sajha buses from Kathmandu's Bhimsen Tower to Trisuli (2 daily; 4hr) and Daman (1 daily; 5hr).

Public buses from Kathmandu's main bus station to Banepa (frequent; 1hr 30min); Bharabise (6 daily; 5hr); Dhulikhel (frequent; 2hr) and Jiri (3 daily, 9–13hr).

From Paknajol in Kathmandu to Trisuli (4 daily; 4–5hr).

Night buses from Kathmandu's Bhimsen Tower to Daman (4 nightly; 4hr).

From Bhaktapur's Sidha Pokhri bus park to Nagarkot (3 daily; 1hr).

From Bharabise to Tatopani (infrequent; 1hr).

From Trisuli to Dhunche (2 daily; 4hr).

CHAPTER FOUR

THE WESTERN HILLS

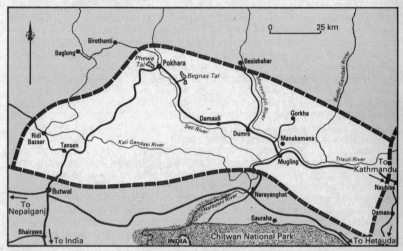

The **western hills** are Nepal at its most outstandingly typical: roaring gorges, precariously perched villages and terraced fields reaching to unsupportable heights, with some of the most graceful and accessible peaks of the Himalaya for a backdrop. •

In this, Nepal's most populous hill region, people are the dominant feature of the landscape. Magars and Gurungs, the most visible ethnic groups, live in their own villages or side by side with Tamangs, Hindu castes and the usual smattering of Newar merchants. Life is traditional and close to the earth, but relatively prosperous: the oval houses are tidy and spacious, and hill women are festooned with the family gold. The prosperity comes, indirectly, from an unlikely quarter, as the western hills were the original – and still are the most important – recruiting area for **Gurkha soldiers**. It's an often-quoted statistic that Gurkha salaries and pensions are Nepal's biggest foreign-exchange earner after tourism; in this part of the country, Gurkha wages are *bigger* than tourism, and the major source of development financing. Ex-Gurkhas command the highest respect within their communities, and young men look up to them as role models. They also speak English; wherever you go, there will probably be an ex-Gurkha to help you over the language barrier.

History, too, figures prominently here: the foundations of modern Nepal were laid in the western hills. While the kings of the Kathmandu Valley were building temples, the princes of the hills built forts – many of which still stand – and it's the hillmen who rule Nepal today.

HILL CULTURE: GURUNGS AND MAGARS

Leavened with nothing but the water of God
Comes from Rumjatar the flour of millet pounded,
Gurungs have mastered the knowledge of God
And Brahmans are left astounded.

Nepali poet Jnandil (c 1821–1883)

Hardy, self-sufficient peasant farmers, Gurungs and Magars are the "aboriginals" of the western hills. Both groups exhibit Mongoloid features and speak Tibeto-Burman dialects – signs that their ancestors probably migrated here from Tibet, though nobody's sure when. Together, they form the backbone of the Gurkha regiments, and also account for a fair proportion of the Nepalese army.

Although **Gurungs** are a common sight around Pokhara – where many have invested their Gurkha pensions in guest houses and retirement homes – their homeland remains the middle elevations from Gorkha to the southern slopes of the Annapurna Himal (those living in the Gorkha area call themselves Ghale). The majority who don't serve in the military herd sheep and raise wheat, maize, millet and potatoes; Gurungs were once active trans-Himalayan traders, but the Chinese occupation of Tibet has put a virtual stop to that, while other traditional pursuits such as hunting and honey-gathering are being encroached upon by overpopulation. Their unique form of **shamanism** is coming under pressure, too, as Hinduism advances from the south and Buddhism trickles down with Tibetan settlers from the north. Gurungs employ shamans to propitiate ghosts, reclaim possessed souls from the underworld, and guide dead souls to the land of their ancestors – rituals that contain clear echoes of "classic" Siberian shamanism, and are believed to resemble those of the ancient Bon priests of pre-Buddhist Tibet. Some authorities see the ongoing power struggle between Tibetan lamas and Gurung shamans as a modern re-enactment of Buddhism's battle with Bon in seventh-century Tibet; in that instance, Buddhism won.

A somewhat less cohesive group, **Magars** are scattered throughout the lower elevations of the western hills (recently they've colonised parts of the eastern hills as well). A network of Magar kingdoms once controlled the entire region, but the arrival of Hindus in the fifteenth century brought swift political decline and steady cultural assimilation. Nowadays, after centuries of coexistence with Hindu castes, most employ Brahman *pujaris* (priests) and worship Hindu gods just like their Chhetri neighbours, differing only in that they're not allowed to wear the sacred thread of the "twice-born" castes. Similarly, with farming practices, housing and dress, Magars are an adaptable lot and not easily distinguished from surrounding groups – the velvet blouses, coin necklaces and *malla* (thin strands of glass beads) worn by many Magar women, for instance, are also common to Gurungs and Chhetris. Even the Magar language varies from place to place, consisting of at least three mutually unintelligible dialects (most Magars speak Nepali). Despite the lack of unifying traits, group identity is still strong, and will probably remain so as long as Magars keep marrying only within the clan.

The chief destination here – by far – is **Pokhara**, a restful lakeside retreat as well as Nepal's major trekking hub (treks are described in Chapter Seven). On the way there, you can detour northwards to the magnificent hilltop fortress of **Gorkha**, seat of the tiny kingdom that brought down Kathmandu and unified Nepal. Beyond Pokhara, on the road to the Indian border, lies the even less publicised backwater of **Tansen**. All three are, above all, excellent bases for **day hikes**

– which can be almost as rewarding as trekking, without the commitment and red tape. Since **rafting** in the Trisuli River also brings many travellers to the western hills, a special section on operators and rivers is given early in the chapter.

Two main roads cut a swathe through the hills: the **Prithvi Highway**, running west from Kathmandu to Pokhara, and the **Siddhartha Highway**, which carries on from Pokhara to the Indian border. They're in poor condition these days, but they support frequent **buses**, which is more than can be said for the region's few other roads: elsewhere, most journeys are made on foot, and you don't have to go far in this area to appreciate how blurry the distinction between travelling and trekking can be.

HEADING WEST: THE PRITHVI HIGHWAY AND GORKHA

If you take one of the **tourist buses** between Kathmandu and Pokhara you might think there's nothing worth stopping for en route, for there are few towns of any consequence along the 200-kilometre Prithvi Highway. Travelling by **local bus**, however, you get a healthy dose of roadside villages, while going by **bike** allows you to explore a few offbeat sights along the way. Certainly the side trip to Gorkha makes a strong case for breaking the bus journey, even though it will mean giving up your seat.

Other activities might bring you in contact with the Prithvi Highway: **rafting** trips on the Trisuli River follow the road for about 50km, and **treks** around the Annapurna Circuit start on a side road from Dumre.

Along the Prithvi Highway

Bobbing and weaving through the heart of the hills, the **PRITHVI HIGHWAY** is most visitors' initiation into the pain and pleasure of Nepalese bus travel. You may find yourself on it several times, in fact, since besides linking Kathmandu and Pokhara it's also the first leg between both cities and the Tarai. Sublime views are rare, though, since the road careers along the bottom of deep valleys most of the way. Nepal's second trunk road when it was built by the Chinese in 1973, the Prithvi Highway has played a crucial role in modernising the country, opening up the western hills and enabling Pokhara to develop into Nepal's second tourist city. After seventeen monsoons, however, the road has deteriorated badly, and repairs are under way between Naubise and the Marsyangdi Dam – expect disruptions and a rough ride for at least another two years. It's often said that Nepal and its foreign-aid bankers are too quick to build new roads and too slow to maintain them; time will tell whether this project disproves that notion.

After parting with the Rajpath at Naubise (see Chapter Three), the highway descends steadily along the south side of the Mahesh Khola, which soon joins the **Trisuli River**. Keep an eye out for magnificent, spidery suspension bridges and precarious ropeways spanning the Trisuli; you might also spot funeral pyres on the sandy banks, and rafting parties running the rapids. The solid, three-story farmhouses seen here belong to Brahmans and Chhetris, while the humbler mud-and-thatch huts are typical Tamang or Magar dwellings. Tourist buses usually make a mid-morning fuel stop at MALEKHU, 70km from Kathmandu, where the remarkably well-provisioned *Blue Heaven Restaurant* serves everything from chips to Foster's tinnies.

Mugling and the Marsyangdi Project

All buses break for lunch at **MUGLING**, 110km from Kathmandu, whose wide main street and wood-fronted buildings give it the look of a wild-west town. Drivers get free meals for parking in front of certain **restaurants** – you can always check out the others (there are dozens), but there's little difference between one *daal bhaat* and another here. With buses coming and going twenty-four hours a day, Mugling would be an awful place to spend the night, and in any case only a few eateries have **rooms**; try *Hotel Laligurans & Lodge* (rooms Rs40) or *Lumbine Hotel & Lodge* (rooms Rs35, beds Rs15), or splash out on *Motel du Mugling* (Kathmandu ☎01/225242), located across the bridge and commanding a grandstand view of Mugling's latrines (singles $23, doubles $33). At 280m, Mugling is the lowest point along the Prithvi Highway – sugarcane is cultivated on a small scale around here, and you'll also see *simal*, a tall, angular Tarai tree that produces red flowers in February and pods of cotton-like seeds in May. Traffic bound for the Tarai turns left at Mugling and continues along the Trisuli River, making the gradual 34-kilometre descent to Narayanghat (see Chapter Five).

The Prithvi Highway crosses the Trisuli just past Mugling and heads upstream along the Marsyangdi River, passing the massive **Marsyangdi Hydroelectric Project** powerhouse 2km later. The dam and reservoir are 12km further on; water is diverted through a tunnel to the powerhouse and then channelled down to the turbines. Completed in 1990, the project is the single most expensive thing ever built in Nepal, costing $210 million of German, Saudi and World Bank money, and it's expected to generate 30 percent of the country's electricity. This diversion is just a puddle compared to some of the others on the World Bank's drawing board: the Arun III project, southeast of Everest, would be six times bigger, and the Karnali project in the far western Tarai, now shelved, would have been the biggest hydroelectric scheme in the world (see "Development Dilemmas" in *Contexts*).

Manakamana, Dumre and Damauli

The spur road to Gorkha (p.152) leaves the highway at ABU KHAIRENI, 7km west of Mugling. If you're into really off-the-beaten-track oddities, you can walk from here up to **MANAKAMANA** (Maan-*kaam*-na), a beautiful four-hour hike along a forested trail that begins on the right about 1km up the Gorkha road. Every day scores of pilgrims make the journey to worship at Manakamana's **Bhagwati Mandir**, revered as one of Nepal's five great wish-fulfilling temples – it's especially popular with newlyweds, who come to pray for sons. Animal sacrifices are an essential part of the ritual, and locals raise goats and chickens specifically for the sacrificial market. Tea and simple food is available in the nearby bazaar. Mountain views from here are good, but they're better from a small *puja* spot another two hours further up the ridge.

Trekkers tackling the Annapurna Circuit usually stop at **DUMRE** (450m), a drab roadside bazaar 18km past Mugling, but few spend the night here now that they can continue on to BESISAHAR by truck. If you're cycling from Kathamandu to Pokhara, however, this would be a marginally quieter place to stay than Mugling; *Mustang Lodge* (rooms Rs40) is one of many trekkers' inns left over from Dumre's heyday as a trailhead.

Children swinging during the October *Dasain* festival

West of Dumre, the hills get gentler and more heavily cultivated. Most Nepalis live in countryside like this, and the **farming** methods seen here are fairly representative of those practiced throughout the hills. The land is used intensely but sustainably: trees and bamboo are pruned for fodder; livestock, fed on fodder, pull ploughs and provide milk and manure (and fuel at higher elevations); and manure, in turn, is dolloped onto the fields as fertiliser. Goats, chickens and pigs recycle scraps into meat and eggs, and even pariah dogs are tolerated because they eat faeces. Most farmers barter surplus grain for odd essentials – salt, sugar, pots and pans – and have little to do with the cash economy, though growing numbers near the highway are starting to raise vegetables for cash. Several research stations here are experimenting with improved seeds, but tractors and chemical fertilisers will probably never be appropriate for the vast majority of Nepalese farms.

It's an eight-kilometre trek uphill and 8km down from Dumre to **DAMAULI** (350m), a nondescript administrative town overlooking the confluence of the Madi and Seti rivers. A paved road runs south for a kilometre to **Vyasa Gupha** (Vyasa's Cave), a popular *sadhu* hangout where the author of the *Vedas*, Hinduism's oldest and most sacred texts, is supposed to have meditated. After traversing the Madi, the highway rises and then descends gradually to rejoin the broad and featureless Seti Valley, finally reaching Pokhara some 54km from Damauli.

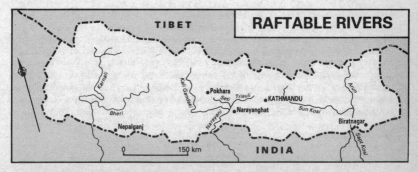

TIBET

RAFTABLE RIVERS

Karnali

Kali Gandaki

Bheri

Pokhara

Seti

Trisuli

Narayani

Narayanghat

KATHMANDU

Sun Kosi

Arun

Nepalganj

Biratnagar

Sapt Kosi

0   150 km

INDIA

RAFTING

Of all the outdoor activities on offer in Nepal, **whitewater rafting** probably tops the list for excitement (and sometimes, too, for wetness). Two popular rivers within reach of Kathmandu are well paced for novices – there's usually a quiet stretch to recover after each set of rapids – while more distant ones will challenge experienced river-runners.

Unfortunately, rafting is also the single biggest source of disappointment for many travellers, who too often get duped by shady or inexperienced river **operators**. Trip prices and quality vary enormously – as a rule, the only difference between cheap companies and expensive ones is that the latter usually can be relied on to do what they promised. A few of the more reputable operators are listed in the "On from Kathmandu" section of Chapter One; these deal mainly with groups booked from overseas, but they'll take "walk-ins", and if you can muster a party of four or more you can arrange your own customised trip. Some of the cut-price outfits in Kathmandu and Pokhara aren't bad, but making recommendations would be misleading – guides come and go, and standards rise and fall from one season to the next. Shop around, and press operators hard on the following criteria.

COSTS AND RED TAPE

Trips **cost** from $15 to $75 a day, depending on the river, number of people in the party, and standard of service. For trips on the Trisuli (Nepal's most popular river), upmarket companies typically charge $30–40 a day, which should include transportation to and from the river by private van and good, hygienic meals. Budget outfits offer this trip for around $20 a day, but at that price you can expect to travel by local bus and be served pretty unappetising food; anyone charging less than $20 is likely to make you buy your own bus tickets and meals. These prices assume full rafts, which hold up to seven paying passengers each – smaller group sizes mean a higher price per head. Other rivers cost $10 or more a day extra. If you pay in dollars, remember to get an official exchange receipt for the amount.

The rafting company is responsible for arranging the trip **permit**, which costs $5 per person and is normally included in the package (one passport photo required). Fly-by-night operators sometimes collect permit fees and pocket the money – a risky proposition, since as far as the government is concerned, unpermitted trips don't exist and therefore don't need rescuing. In theory, you're supposed to be **insured**.

SAFETY

No one has been killed rafting in Nepal yet, but lack of **safety** is a perennial complaint. Make sure the company supplies life vests, helmets (not required in "oar" rafts – see below) and a full first-aid kit, and satisfy yourself that the rafts are in good running order and that there will be a safety demonstration before entering the river. The minimum number of rafts is two, in case one capsizes. Most important of all, **guides** must be experienced and speak adequate English – ask what sort of training they've had and how many times they've guided the stretch of river in question (there should be an opportunity to meet guides before departure). The *Nepal Association of Rafting Agents* is supposed to be setting standards for guide training and certification, and may eventually establish minimum prices for trips; companies not belonging to *NARA* are unregulated, so you've no recourse if things go wrong .

EQUIPMENT

Most companies use "paddle" rafts, in which everyone paddles and the guide steers from the rear; on less exciting "oar" raft trips, the guide does all the work. The company should provide tents, sleeping bags, foam mattresses and kit bags, and each raft should come with a waterproof "ammo" box for storing clothes, cameras and valuables. It's up to you to bring two sets of clothes (one to remain dry) and shoes (training shoes are best), a bathing suit, towel, hat, sunglasses, suntan lotion and torch. Binoculars are invaluable for birdwatching.

WHEN TO GO
For the most thrilling whitewater, the **best time** to go is right after the monsoon in October. The water is still reasonably swift in November, and the spring snowmelt beginning in February also brings moderately high water. March and April are the best months for a pleasant combination of long, warm days, brisk rapids and excellent birdwatching. Winter can be chilly, though not so bad as you might think: most raftable river sections are below 500m elevation. The water is too low in May and June, and too high from July to September.

THE RIVERS
Perhaps ninety percent of all raft trips are done on the **Trisuli River**, west of Kathmandu. The normal itinerary is **three days**: given that it takes three or four hours to drive each way, two-day trips are an utter waste of time, and four-day trips are often just three-day trips done in slow motion. Companies put in at various points depending on the time of year (with a fast current, you have to put in higher up to reach the endpoint in the same time), and generally pull out between Mugling and Narayanghat. The Trisuli contains a good mix of whitewater and scenery, although it's hardly wilderness – a road follows it the entire way. In October and November you'll have to share it with many other parties, and there may be competition for campsites. When operators boast of "road support", that means the overnight gear is kept in a van and you can't camp on the less crowded north side of the river. All the best rapids are above Mugling, and many Pokhara-based companies miss these out. Many operators misleadingly advertise rafting trips to Chitwan National Park, but these actually end at Narayanghat; still, it's a pleasanter way to reach the Tarai than by bus.

Next in popularity comes the **Sun Kosi**, an eight-to eleven-day run (depending on the time of year) beginning at Dolalghat, three hours east of Kathmandu, and ending at Chatara in the eastern Tarai. Only a few companies do scheduled trips on the Sun Kosi, so you're unlikely to see any other rafting parties. Traversing a remote, roadless part of the country, the river flows through a varied landscape of jungle-clad canyons, arid, open valleys and sparse settlements. The water is too rough for beginners in early October, but after that it settles down to an easy float with a few brisk rapids and long stretches of flat paddling.

Other rivers are harder to get to – budget operators don't run on them, and the few companies that do charge through the nose. The lower **Kali Gandaki** makes a fairly easy three-day float from Ramdi Ghat, south of Pokhara, to Narayanghat (the upper section, beginning at Kusma, is very rough and requires special boats, but could be combined with a trek in the Annapurna region). Starting at Damauli, east of Pokhara, the **Seti** is a fairly tame river that can be run only in high water, taking two days to Narayanghat. Rafting the **Karnali** in far western Nepal is a serious expedition, involving an expensive flight and a five-day walk-in. A tributary of the Karnali, the gentle **Bheri** can be run from the Surkhet road to Bardia National Park. The **Arun**, reached by flying to Tumlingtar in the eastern hills and raftable from Tumlingtar to Chatara, passes through dramatic country but the water isn't very challenging.

Gorkha

Despite being midway between Kathmandu and Pokhara, **GORKHA** (Gor-*kaa*) remains strangely untouristed, probably because of the longstanding difficulty of getting there. However, the surfacing of the 24-kilometre road up from Abu Khaireni now makes it a relatively painless half-day ride from Pokhara, Kathmandu or Tadi Bazaar (Chitwan). The government is devoting a big chunk of its tourism budget to sprucing up Gorkha's monuments, and there seems to be a vague notion of putting the town on the tourist map; but for the time being, Gorkha is suspended in a happy halfway state, with just enough basic facilities for comfort, yet primitive enough to keep the crowds away.

Cradle of a nation and the ancestral home of the Nepalese royal family, Gorkha occupies a place in Nepalese history second to none. The village itself is miniscule, but hunched on the hilltop above is its link with that splendid past, the **Gorkha Durbar** – an architectural tour de force worthy of the flamboyant Gorkha kings and the dynasty they founded. Unless you're setting straight off on a trek or just finishing one (the Pokhara–Trisuli trail passes through Gorkha), you'll have to spend the night here. Think about staying two: the Durbar and environs could easily soak up a day, and hikes around the area could keep you busy for a further day or two. The hill climate is agreeable, the pace is easy and, for the moment at least, there's not an apple pie or pizza in sight.

Though direct **buses** to Gorkha are few, you can get off at ABU KHAIRENI on the Prithvi Highway and catch any bus or lorry chugging up the spur road from there. If you're pedalling, the last 10km is a tough 900-metre climb.

Some history

In a sense, Gorkha's history is not its own. A petty hill state in medieval times, it was occupied and transformed into a sort of Himalayan Sparta by outsiders who used it as a base for a dogged campaign against Kathmandu and then, having won their prize, restored Gorkha to obscurity. Yet during those two centuries of occupation, it raised the nation's most famous son, **Prithvi Narayan Shah**, and somehow bred in him the audacity to conquer all of Nepal.

Prithvi Shah's ancestors had come to Gorkha in the mid-sixteenth century, driven into the hills from their native Rajasthan by the Muslim advance, and soon gained a reputation as a singlemindedly martial lot. His father launched the first unsuccessful raid on the Kathmandu Valley in the early eighteenth century, and when Prithvi ascended the throne in 1743, at the age of twenty, he already had his father's obsession fixed in his mind*. Within a year, he was leading Gorkha in a war of expansion that was eventually to unify all of present-day Nepal, plus parts of India and Tibet. Looking at the tiny village and meagre terraces of Gorkha today, you can imagine what a drain it must have been to keep a standing army fed and supplied for 27 years of continuous campaigning. The hardy peasants of

---

*An odd legend confirms Prithvi Shah's destiny, but also puts the scale of his accomplishment into perspective. When still a prince he was approached by an old man, who took the boy's hand and spat in it. The spittle turned to yoghurt and the man ordered Prithvi to eat it; Prithvi, not unreasonably, flung the curd on the ground at his feet. At that, the old man revealed himself to be Gorakhnath, the demigod protector of the Shah kings, and pronounced that Prithvi would go on to rule wherever he placed his feet – but had he eaten the curd, he could have ruled the world.

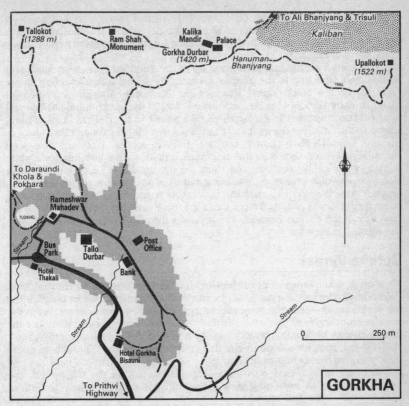

Gorkha got little more than a handshake for their efforts. After conquering the valley in 1769, Prithvi Shah moved his capital to the bright lights of Kathmandu, relegating Gorkha to a mere garrison from which the later western campaign was directed. By the early nineteenth century, Gorkha had been all but forgotten, even as a mispronounced form of the name – Gurkha – was becoming a household name around the world.

Settling in and exploring the village

Finding **accommodation** in Gorkha is fairly straightforward – the best by a long shot is *Hotel Gorkha Bisauni,* 400m back down the road from the bus stop, which has the only hot showers and English-speaking proprietor in town. Room rates are on the high side for a budget lodge – Rs75 with a common bathroom or Rs100 with attached bath – but dormitory beds are Rs20. If money is the only object, there are a half a dozen dives around the bus stop and along the path up to town. *Hotel Thakali's* rooms are Rs30 each, some of which have impressive views out across the valley. For **food**, the choice is similarly limited. The *Gorkha Bisauni's* little diner does remarkably good western fare, including seasonal fresh vegetable soups; everywhere else, it's the usual all-you-can-eat *bhaat*.

You can't get lost in Gorkha, but try anyway. Nestled on a shelf beneath a steep ridge, most of the village stretches along a single main path – the layout, with buildings huddled close together to save space for farming, calls to mind villages in the north of England.

A dirt road from the bus park leads up to the Tudikhel (parade ground) and immediately after that to the temple precinct. The gilded figure kneeling atop a pillar facing the onion-domed **Rameshwar Mahadev Mandir** is Prithvipati Shah; an early Gorkha king, he established most of the temples and shrines still in use around the town, including the Kalika temple in the Durbar. West of here, where the main street opens up to a small plaza, an inconspicuous lane leads to the old **Tallo Durbar** (Lower Durbar). Built in around 1750, this imposing Newar-style edifice served as the kingdom's administrative headquarters, while the upper Durbar housed king and court. Seen from above, Tallo Durbar indeed looks like a mini-Pentagon. Its fine brick and woodwork is now getting a facelift – peacock windows and all – and the building is supposed to be opened up as a museum of Gorkha history. You can also get there by a trail climbing up from the driveway of the *Gorkha Bisauni*, which passes through a schoolyard and enters the village the back way.

Gorkha Durbar

It's a brisk, 300-metre ascent to the **Gorkha Durbar** along the main trail from Pokharithok, the junction just east of Tallo Durbar; figure on half an hour. At the top of this route – once the royal approach to the palace – you can marvel at the massive front stairway that's the Durbar's most distinctive feature: pure ostentation or cheeky bluff, either way it must have cowed visiting vassals into submission – a neat trick for a tinpot realm that could barely muster 150 soldiers at the time of Prithvi Shah's first campaign.

The climb repays itself with more than history: set on the ridge crest, the Durbar commands a **sweeping view** of the Himalaya from Dhaulagiri to Ganesh Himal, with Baudha and Himalchuli of Manaslu Himal occupying centre stage. Although the warlike Gorkhalis picked the site for its strategic position, they can't have been unmoved by the scenery.

Conceived as a dwelling for kings and gods, the fortress remains a religious place, and first stop in any visit is the **Kalika Mandir**, probably the most revered shrine this side of Kathmandu. Occupying the left (western) half of the Durbar building, its interior is

The Gorkha Durbar

closed to all but priests and the king of Nepal (others would die upon beholding Kali's terrible image, say the priests), but plenty of action takes place outside: sacrifices are made in the alcove in front of the entrance, and during the twice-monthly observance of *Astami* – celebrated with special gusto in Gorkha – the paving stones are sticky with blood. Most worshippers arrive cradling a trembling goat or chicken and leave swinging a headless carcass. *Chaitra Dasain*, Gorkha's biggest annual **festival**, brings processions and more blood-letting in late March.

The east wing of the Durbar is the historic **palace**, site of **Prithvi Shah's birth-place** and, by extension, the ancestral shrine of the Shah kings. This accounts for King Birendra's regular visits (his helipad is just east of the Durbar) and the government's spare-no-expense renovation of the Durbar's exceptional eight-eenth-century woodwork. Though predating the Gorkhali conquest of Kathmandu, the palace bears the unmistakable stamp of Newar craftsmanship: the Gorkhalis, who never pretended to have any art or architecture of their own, imported workmen from Kathmandu. Upstairs are said to be Prithvi Shah's **throne** and an **eternal flame** that's been burning ever since he unified Nepal. Sentries discourage photography in the courtyard and bar the interior to all foreigners – a vandal could kick out the fire and cast a serious hex on Nepal's monarchy.

The remaining space within the fortress walls is fairly littered with other Hindu shrines. By the main entrance is a small temple built around the holy **cave of Gorakhnath**, the centre for worship of the shadowy Indian guru who gave Gorkha its name and is regarded as a kind of guardian angel by the Shah kings.

Upallokot and Tallokot

The notch in the ridge just east of Gorkha Durbar is known as **Hanuman Bhanjyang** (Hanuman Pass), after the valiant monkey king who guards the crossroads from a niche above the popular shady *chautaara* (rest stop). Cross the main trail (a branch of the Pokhara–Trisuli porter route) and follow a steep, stone-paved path up the ridgeline. Just above the crossing is a vantage-point where you can stand in the stone "footsteps" of Rama, hero of the *Ramayana* epic and Hanuman's best mate, and snap a postcard picture of the Durbar.

From Hanuman Bhanjyang it's another half-hour hike to **Upallokot** (Upper Fort), a 1520-metre eyrie at the highest, easternmost point of the ridge. Except for the slight intrusion of a microwave relay tower, the panorama here is total. If you can manage it, **sunrise** is the best time to visit: to the east, the ridge abruptly plunges 500m to misty depths while the sun's first rays play across the peaks. Late afternoon is pretty special, too, as the sun slants behind the Durbar and fills the Daraundi Valley to the west with a golden haze. From this angle, looking down the spine of the ridge, the Durbar looks like Nepal's answer to Mad Ludwig's castle. The one thing lacking is a sense of wilderness: nearly every hill and valley is cultivated and tamed, except for **Kaliban**, the forest covering the northern crest of the ridge. Spookily alive with rhesus monkeys, this sacred grove supplies wood for the Durbar's eternal flame. Upallokot itself is more a hut than a fort, its thatched roof long gone. The small walled pen contains an old grinding wheel and a set of stones laid out in the shape of a reclining human figure – obscure icons of Bhairab and Kali.

At the other end of the ridge stands **Tallokot**, a watch post with more limited views north and west. You can easily stroll there from the Durbar's front entrance, passing a small but active Kali temple and a new monument to Ram Shah, the seventh-generation ancestor of Prithvi Narayan Shah who is reckoned by some to have been the progenitor of the Shah title. A rough track descends directly from Tollokot to Gorkha, tripping down terraces past small clusters of farmhouses and the odd communal spring.

Longer walks

If that circuit whets your appetite for **longer walks**, there are two main options. The high road through Hanuman Bhanjyang descends gently for about an hour and a half to ALI BHANJYANG (shops), then ascends along a ridge with fabulous mountain views, reaching KHANCHOK BHANJYANG two-and-a-half hours later. This would be about the limit for a day hike, but you could continue down to the subtropical banks of the Budhi Gandaki at ARUGHAT, 20km from Gorkha, and find basic lodging there – at this point you'd be a third of the way to Trisuli. Other, less distinct trails from Upallokot and the Ram Shah monument take roundabout routes to Ali Bhanjyang. Alternatively, follow the main trail west out of Gorkha village, which descends to the untrammelled Daraundi Khola Valley (1hr 30min) to join the main Pokhara–Trisuli trail. You could continue on for another three or four hours to AMPIPAL, a pleasant hill town with a hospital and lodging. Both routes can be combined into a **two-day loop**: Gorkha–Khanchok Bhanjyang–Daraundi crossing–Gorkha. For trekking from here, see Chapter Seven.

POKHARA

The Himalaya form the highest, sheerest rise from subtropical base to icy peaks of any mountain range on earth, and nowhere is the contrast more marked than at **POKHARA** (pronounced *Poke*-rhuh). Sited at just 800m above sea level, it boasts a nearly unobstructed view of the 8000m-plus Annapurna and Manaslu himals, 25km north; completely dominating the skyline, in beauty if not in height, is the double-finned summit of Machhapuchhre – "Fish Tail" – only one of whose peaks is visible from Pokhara. Basking in the view, Nepal's main "resort" area (a word with humbler connotations than you'd expect) lolls beside the shore of **Phewa Tal** (Phewa Lake), well outside the actual town of Pokhara. This is Nepal's little budget paradise: carefree and culturally undemanding, though highly commercialised, with a steaks-and-cakes scene second only to that in Kathmandu.

If you're spending more than a week in Nepal, chances are you'll touch down in Pokhara at some point – as the only city served by "tourist" buses, it's usually the first place that travellers venture to outside the Kathmandu Valley. For trekkers, Pokhara is the gateway to Nepal's most popular trails; for everyone else, it's the most beautiful place in Nepal that's accessible by public transport. Daytrips around the Pokhara Valley beckon, and if the area is short on temples and twisting old alleys, you might find that a relief after Kathmandu's profusion. Despite its shallow hedonism – which definitely gets cloying after a while – Pokhara is an ideal place to recharge your batteries, especially after a trek: in comparison, Kathmandu seems downright claustrophobic.

Because it's 500m lower than the capital, Pokhara is a better place to be in winter, but rather hot from May onwards. With lower foothills to the south, it's also less protected from the monsoon – if it's raining in Kathmandu, it'll be pouring in Pokhara. Touring the valley, you'll be struck by the active, shaping presence of water everywhere: lakes and rivers are conspicuous features here, and even the paddies are traced by canals of milky mountain water.

The **telephone code** for Pokhara is ☎061.

Orientation

Pokhara's layout requires some explanation if you plan to do any sightseeing (an activity which, admittedly, isn't a top priority for most visitors here). To get your bearings, start with the tourist areas of **Lakeside** and **Damside**, set 1km apart on the eastern and southeastern edges of **Phewa Tal**, where you'll find all the good **budget lodgings** and **restaurants**.

Northeast of the lake, **Pokhara Bazaar** (in Nepal, *bazaar* refers to any commercial centre) is maddeningly diffuse, sprawling a good 5km along two north–south roads and a ladder of cross streets – the map doesn't begin to suggest how interminably far it is to cycle the entire length of it. Roughly 1km east of Damside are Pokhara's **airport, tourist office** and several of the **upmarket hotels**, with the **bus park** 1km north of the airport. A further 1.5km northwards, the bustling **Mahendra Pul** area forms the heart of the new, southern end of town, while the subdued **old bazaar** occupies the highest ground further north. At the extreme northern end, the parking area of the former **Shining Hospital** serves as the departure point for most treks from Pokhara.

Arriving and getting around

A half-dozen **tourist buses** (variously billed as "Swiss", "Deluxe" and "2X2 Minibuses") shuttle between Kathmandu and Pokhara daily. Although twice as expensive (Rs110) as the more numerous (and crowded) local buses, they're more comfortable and an hour or two quicker; just be sure to book at least a day ahead. Due to a typically inscrutable dispute, tourist buses refuse to drive on to Lakeside/Damside, and instead deliver passengers into the hands of the hotel touts at the **main bus park**, 2–3km away. After the jarring ride, you'll want to spend as little time as possible here – unless you're on a skeletal budget, a taxi is the only sensible way to reach the lake. If you're entering from the south along the Siddhartha Highway, ask to be let off at **Pardi** (the local name for Damside) and take a short walk west to get to lodgings.

Flying from Kathmandu to Pokhara ($61) cuts out some of the hardships of the journey, but be prepared, as always, for Kafkaesque scenes at the airport. The mountain views from aloft are stupendous; take the first flight of the day, before clouds obscure the peaks, and book early for a seat on the right side of the plane. From the **airport** it's a one- or two-kilometre walk to Damside and Lakeside.

Poor local transport makes **getting around** time-consuming, widening the divide between lake and bazaar and making it that much harder to tear yourself away from the tourist fleshpots. Pokhara's single **local bus** route makes a long and painfully slow anti-clockwise loop from Lakeside to Damside, up past the airport to Shining Hospital and then back down to Lakeside; a crosstown journey takes the better part of an hour.

Taxis are seldom to be found around the Lakeside and Damside guest houses, but innkeepers will book one for you given a couple hours' notice. The nearest taxi hangout – it's not formal enough to be called a rank – is the roundabout at the beginning of the Baidam (Lakeside) road, and they can also usually be found near the bus park, the Shining Hospital carpark and the airport. Taxis are unmetered: Lakeside to the bus park should cost Rs30, to Shining Hospital Rs40. To keep the price down, tell the driver you're willing to share.

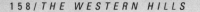

FOR FOOD
GERMAN BAKERY ——— NR
                                T

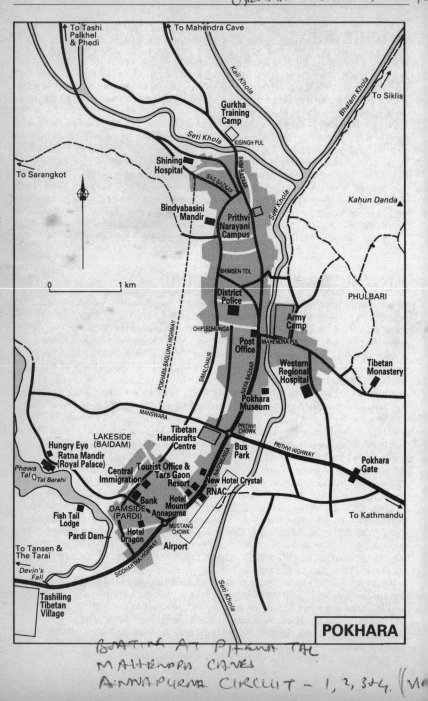

To Tashi Palkhel & Phedi

To Mahendra Cave

Kali Khola

To Siklis

Bhalam Khola

Gurkha Training Camp

Seti Khola

KISINGH PUL

To Sarangkot

Shining Hospital

BAG BAZAAR

BHIM BAZAAR

Seti Khola

Kahun Danda

Bindyabasini Mandir

Prithvi Narayani Campus

BHIMSEN TOL

PHULBARI

District Police

Army Camp

CHIPLEDHUNGA

POKHARA-BAGLUNG HIGHWAY

SIMALCHAUR

Post Office

MAHENDRA PUL

Western Regional Hospital

Tibetan Monastery

NAYA BAZAAR

Pokhara Museum

MANSWARA

Tibetan Handicrafts Centre

PRITHVI CHOWK

Bus Park

PRITHVI HIGHWAY

LAKESIDE (BAIDAM)

Hungry Eye

Ratna Mandir (Royal Palace)

Phewa Tal

Tal Barahi

Central Immigration

Tourist Office & Tara Gaon Resort

MAHENDRAPUL

New Hotel Crystal

RNAC

Pokhara Gate

To Kathmandu

Fish Tail Lodge

Bank

DAMSIDE (PARDI)

Hotel Mount Annapurna

Pardi Dam

Hotel Dragon

MUSTANG CHOWK

Airport

To Tansen & The Tarai

Devin's Fall

SIDDHARTHA HIGHWAY

Seti Khola

Tashiling Tibetan Village

POKHARA

BOATING AT PHEWA TAL
MAHENDRA CAVES
ANNAPURNA CIRCUIT - 1, 2, 3+4. (VI

A **bicycle**, rentable all over Lakeside and Damside for Rs15 a day, multiplies your mobility and flexibility enormously – it's the cheapest, most practical (and in some instances the only) way to explore the valley. At the time of writing, only a handful of mountain bikes were available for hire, but this should change rapidly. Pokhara has no tempos, autorikshas or pedal rikshas.

Accommodation

Pokhara is glutted with cheap and moderately priced **accommodation**, and even during the manic months of October and November you'll never have any problem getting a room. Scores of small lodges have been built in recent years by ex-Gurkhas and Thakalis (the enterprising innkeepers of the trekking region north of Pokhara): reminiscent of farmhouse bed-and-breakfasts, these homely establishments offer the cheapest hot-water lodgings in Nepal, although rooms with attached baths are generally overpriced. Prices quoted here are high-season rates – needless to say, everything is negotiable in the off-season, when lodges may discount their rooms by fifty percent or more. Prices are given in dollars where payment is required in hard currency.

Most independent travellers stay in **Lakeside** or **Damside**, and with good reason. Far removed from the din of the bazaar, overlooking the lake and peaks and awash with western food and comforts, both areas offer a numbingly easy existence. Pokhara's best and most expensive hotel, *Fish Tail Lodge*, is also located here (many of the other upmarket places are less happily situated near the airport).

The only official **campsite** is a dreary affair near *Hotel Fewa* (Rs20 per tent). If you're desperate to pitch a tent, though, a few of the secluded Lakeside lodges can provide nicer, if not cheaper, campsites.

Lakeside (Baidam) – cheap and moderate places

With its strip of bamboo restaurants, corrugated-tin curio shacks and breeze-block guest houses, **Lakeside** is like Robinson Crusoe meets Las Vegas. Self-consciously hip, it sometimes comes close to parodying itself (Bob Marley drones endlessly from restaurant sound systems), but for all that, it's laid-back and essentially rural: walk a couple of minutes away from the lake and you're in farmland. Some of Pokhara's most attractive guest houses are hidden away in this neighbourhood, also known as **Baidam**.

Lakeside covers a large area – the further north you stay, the further you'll have to walk or pedal to get anywhere. Also bear in mind that mountain views are better to the south and east.

Baba Lodge (☎20981). Rough-and-ready rooms, but popular for its restaurant. Rooms from Rs50 (single or double occupancy); with bath, Rs200.

French Cottage. The cheapest of several pleasant guest houses along this lane. Singles Rs25, doubles Rs30.

Full Moon Lodge. The last word in seclusion, set on a hilltop with a magnificent view of the lake – but it's a longish hike for food or drink. Singles Rs35, doubles Rs50.

Future Way Guest House. Quiet, with clean rooms and friendly management. Singles Rs40, doubles Rs50 and up.

Gurkha Lodge. Gardening buffs will love this place, tucked down a long Baidam lane. Singles with attached bath Rs200, doubles Rs220.

Himalayan Country Lodge. Rather out of the way, but well-appointed bungalow-style rooms with attached baths. Singles Rs100, doubles Rs200.

Hotel Fewa (☎20151). The only budget lodge right on the lake, with boats for hire and a nice lawn. Singles Rs45, doubles Rs75; Rs165/220 and up for rooms with bath. For those who really want to get away from it all, they have rooms across the lake for Rs30 and up.

Hotel Hungry Eye (☎20908). Overpriced but popular: centrally located, it's the nearest thing to a *Kathmandu Guest House* in Pokhara. Singles $12, doubles $15.

Hotel Monal (☎20879). Good facilities in a prime location on the strip. Singles start at Rs150, doubles Rs175; Rs300/325 with bath.

Hotel Snowland (☎20384). Trendy location, rooftop restaurant. Singles Rs65, doubles Rs75; Rs175/200 with bath.

Oriental Restaurant. Has a couple of pleasant rooms with balconies overlooking the lake. Singles Rs80, doubles Rs150 with bath.

Sarowar. Quiet, and featuring an old thatched farmhouse in the grounds. Singles from Rs75, doubles Rs100; Rs150/175 with bath.

Shangri La Lodge. Wonderfully secluded, and deviously well-hidden: follow the sign up a dirt lane until it veers left, then climb over a stile and walk another 100m along a trail. Singles Rs25, doubles RS50.

Damside (Pardi) – cheap and moderate places

If Lakeside is a rural Thamel, **Damside** is a suburban one. The social scene is less affected, its focus shifted from cafés to guest-house compounds, making the streets quieter and the neighbourhood more residential (the clientele is perhaps a tad older, too). The mountain views are better here than in Lakeside, but the lack of greenery's a pity. The choice of restaurants and handicraft shops is more limited, and if you're planning to hire trekking equipment you'll have to traipse over to Lakeside; on the other hand, Damside is more centrally placed for the bank, Central Immigration and sightseeing around the valley.

Hotel Garden (☎20870). Spacious, with helpful staff and a fair restaurant. Singles from Rs60, doubles Rs90; Rs125/250 and up for rooms with attached bath.

Hotel Yak & Yuppie (☎21709). Clean and bright, with well laid-out grounds and a competent patio restaurant. Singles Rs50, doubles Rs75 and up; Rs175/250 and up with bath.

Jeevan Guest House. A rustic stone-and-thatch cottage, whitewashed inside and out like a French farmhouse – the only lodge of its kind in Pokhara. Singles Rs25, doubles Rs40.

Super Lodge (☎21861). Clean and efficiently managed. Singles Rs40, doubles Rs60; Rs100/150 and up with attached bath. Next door, the *New Hotel Anzuk*, run by a Gurkha captain, is similarly good value for money.

In the bazaar – more cheap and moderate places

Pokhara Bazaar has little going for it, and it's hard to think of any good reason for staying here; its lodgings, catering mainly to Nepali and Indian businessmen, charge more for less (none have gardens, for a start). Most are in the **Mahendra Pul** area, west and south of the post office, together with a few untempting restaurants. The better (and pricier) choices are in Chipledhunga, west of the post office – try *Hotel Sun Koshi* (singles Rs100, doubles Rs150 with bath) or *Hotel Deurali* (singles Rs50, doubles Rs80; Rs180/240 with bath). The situation around the **bus park** is truly dire; if you're stuck, a couple of dives here charge Rs20/40 a night.

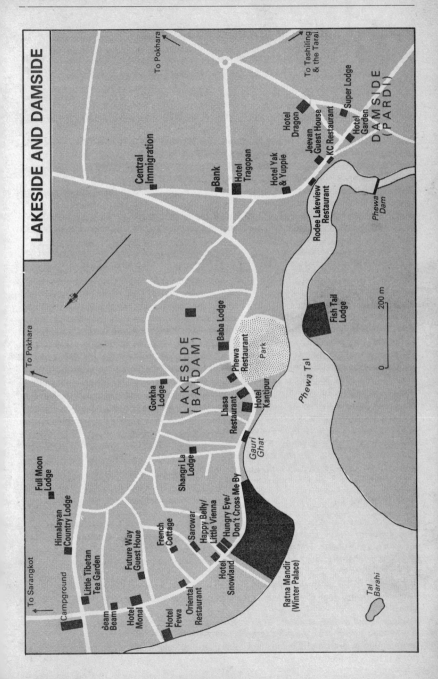

LAKESIDE AND DAMSIDE

To Pokhara

To Tashiling & the Tarai

Super Lodge

Hotel Dragon

Jeevan Guest House

KC Restaurant

Hotel Garden

DAMSIDE (PARDI)

Hotel Yak & Yuppie

Central Immigration

Bank

Hotel Tragopan

Rodee Lakeview Restaurant

Phewa Dam

To Pokhara

Baba Lodge

Phewa Restaurant

Park

L A K E S I D E (B A I D A M)

Gorkha Lodge

Lhasa Restaurant

Hotel Kantipur

Fish Tail Lodge

200 m

0

Phewa Tal

Gauri Ghat

Shangri La Lodge

Full Moon Lodge

Himalayan Country Lodge

Little Tibetan Tea Garden

Future Way Guest Houe

French Cottage

Sarowar

Happy Belly/ Little Vienna

Hungry Eye/ Don't Cross Me By

Hotel Snowland

Oriental Restaurant

Hotel Fewa

Hotel Monal

Beam Beam

Campground

To Sarangkot

Ratna Mandir (Winter Palace)

Tal Barahi

Pokhara's upmarket accommodation

It's advisable to book hotel rooms in advance, especially during the high season; where hotels have a Kathmandu booking office, the relevant phone numbers are given.

Fish Tail Lodge, Lakeside (Kathmandu: ☎01/221711). Two stars. Set amidst fabulous land-scaping, the only hotel on the west side of Phewa Tal enjoys an unrivalled view of the lake and the classic profile of the mountains behind. Access is by rope ferry. Singles $40, doubles $55.

Hotel Dragon, Damside (☎20052). Pretty garden with good views. Two stars. Air-conditioned rooms with Tibetan furnishings are $25 single, $35 double.

Hotel Mount Annapurna, opposite the airport (☎20027). Two stars. Disappointing rooms, though the lawn is worthy of the Raj. Singles $18, doubles $25.

Hotel Tragopan, Damside (Kathmandu: ☎01/225898). One star. New, good value for money. Singles $18, doubles $23.

New Hotel Crystal, opposite the airport (Kathmandu: ☎01/227932). Three stars. Pokhara's biggest hotel, with a pool and tennis court. Single rooms cost $18, doubles $23, or $32/47 with A/C.

Tara Gaon Resort, opposite the airport (Kathmandu: ☎01/410409). Two stars. Part of the government-run chain, with tidy bungalows but forlorn grounds. Singles $12, doubles $15.

Eating

Restaurants are everywhere in Pokhara and food is a major preoccupation. Lakeside, in particular, is one long trough of feeding opportunities. Eating also sets the social agenda: there are no bars or nightlife after around 11pm, but the congenial restaurants and cafés around the lake are easy places to make friends and find trekking partners. Take the implausibly international menus with a pinch of salt, and don't be fooled by the fanciful cake and pie displays – you might not get what you thought you'd ordered, but it'll probably taste pretty good anyway (especially after three weeks on the trail). Prices are generally comparable to Kathmandu's Thamel area – around Rs75–100 for a dinner. If pseudo-western food gets you down, many restaurants do set **Nepali meals**. For cheap and cheerful meals, try the myriad **momo shacks**, whose chatty proprietors play your choice of music on beat-up ghetto blasters.

Lakeside

Baba's Restaurant. A longstanding favourite, serving reliable western and Indian food.

Beam Beam. An especially cozy bamboo café-hangout, featuring backgammon boards and an open fire in winter.

Don't Cross Me By. Next-door neighbour of the *Hungry Eye* (below), almost as trendy and similarly overpriced.

Happy Belly Vegetarian Restaurant. Somewhat lacking in conviction, but dirt cheap.

Hotel Kantipur. Pricey, but good for meat dishes, including suprisingly palatable "cordon bleu".

Hungry Eye. Firmly established as the epicentre of Lakeside eating, offering decent pasta, steaks and sometimes inspired desserts – although its prices reflect its reputation.

Lhasa Restaurant. Good Tibetan and Chinese fare, notable mainly for its *tongba* (hot millet beer).

Little Tibetan Tea Garden. Run by friendly and devout Tibetans, a pleasant place for a light snack on the lawn.

Little Vienna Coffee House. Predictably strong on rostis, and good for a daytime sprawl in the wicker chairs.

Phewa Restaurant. Claiming to be "Supervised by a French Chef", its semi-convincing specialties include French onion soup and chocolate mousse.

Damside

Damside's hotels tend to have their own restaurants, so there are fewer separate eating places.

Hotel Yak & Yuppie. Probably the best of the in-house restaurants, with pleasant indoor and outdoor dining areas and an impressive, if unauthentic, Japanese menu.

KC Restaurant. One of two restaurants in Pokhara directly overlooking the lake; barbecue meats a speciality. No relation to the Kathmandu restaurant of the same name.

Rodee Lakeview Restaurant. The only other restaurant with patio seating beside the lake, and the home of Damside's premier cake display; cheap, and excellent for breakfast.

Phewa Tal

According to a local legend, **PHEWA TAL** covers the area of a once-prosperous valley, whose inhabitants one day scorned a wandering beggar. Finding only one sympathetic woman, the beggar warned her of an impending flood: as the woman and her family fled to higher ground, a torrent roared down from the mountains and submerged the town – the "beggar" having been none other than the goddess Barahi. The woman's descendants settled beside the new lake and erected the island shrine of **Tal Barahi**; for local innkeepers and restauranteurs, who've done rather well out of the lake, a few alms at her shrine still don't go amiss.

The other, geological explanation is that the entire Pokhara Valley, like the Kathmandu Valley, was submerged about 200,000 years ago when the fast-rising Mahabharat Lekh dammed up the Seti River. Over time, the Seti eroded an ever-deeper outlet, lowering the water level and leaving Phewa Tal and several smaller lakes as remnants. However, the legend might contain a grain of truth, as submerged tree stumps at the lake's northern end indicate that the water level rose in the not-too-distant past, perhaps because an earthquake blocked the outlet. Phewa was further enlarged by the installation of Pardi Dam in 1967, which brought electricity and irrigation to the valley – and gave Damside its name.

Filling the days – and evenings

Next to eating, promenading along **Lakeside** is the favourite pastime in Pokhara: the main drag never strays far from the shore, and with its pipal-shaded *chautaaras* (rest stops) it makes for pleasant strolling. A pretty spot – it would be prettier if there weren't so much rubbish – is **Gauri Ghat**, just up from *Hotel Kantipur*. Screened by a leafy *chautaara*, a set of steps leads steeply down to the lake and a *lingam* shrine set atop a rocky outcrop. Midway along the Lakeside strip is Ratna Mandir, the winter **Royal Palace**, a definite no-go area during the king's resi-

NAUTICAL PURSUITS

Boating (or just floating) on Phewa Tal is the easiest way to get away from the business of getting away from it all. Oversized rowing boats – they'll hold six easily – are for hire all along the eastern shore; after bargaining, the rate should settle at Rs20 per hour or Rs75 for the day. Dinghy sailboats, available from *Tal Barahi Boating Service* and *Fewa Hotel*, cost Rs40/hour or Rs200/day and hold up to four people. Keep an eye on the **weather**, especially if sailing – wind squalls are common in late spring, and it's easy to be becalmed at other times of the year. The shore around the Royal Palace is off-limits, and if you see gesticulating security guards you're too close. **Swimming** is best done from a boat: the shore is often muddy or littered, and the bacteria count doesn't bear thinking about.

An obvious first destination is **Tal Barahi**, the island shrine located a few hundred metres offshore from the palace. While the temple itself is modern and not much to look at, it's a busy spot on Saturdays, when the lake goddess exacts a steady tribute of blood sacrifices. If that doesn't put you off your lunch, the island makes a fine place for a picnic. During the wedding months in spring you may find yourself caught up in a flotilla of merrymakers headed for the island, where music, dancing and *raksi*-drinking go on until all hours.

From the island it's about the same distance again to the far shore which, with dense jungle, manic monkeys and few places to put ashore, is probably best observed from the water. Much further west along the shore – it's a fair old row – the jungle gives way to the terraced fields of **ANADU**, a Gurung village that gets few visitors despite being directly opposite Lakeside.

dence each February*. For rural scenes, follow the shambling water buffalo along any of the dirt paths from the lake and you'll immediately enter the lush farming area of **BAIDAM**, with oval thatched cottages, sugar-loaf haystacks, vegetable plots and banana-palm borders. At the northern end of Lakeside, the road narrows to a trail which can be followed along the unspoiled **northern shore**; side trails lead up to Sarangkot (p.167) from here. **Pardi Dam** is of no intrinsic interest, and unfortunately you can't walk across it, but a footbridge just downstream crosses the Pardi Khola, and trails from there lead west up the ridge, or south to Devin's Fall (p.173).

Shopping is a mainly outdoor activity in Lakeside and Damside, where laid-back curio stalls make a welcome change from the hard-driving salesmen of Kathmandu, even if their prices and selection don't quite compare. Specialities include batiks, wooden flasks (variously termed *pung*, *kere* and *teki*) and fossil-bearing *shaligram* stones from the Kali Gandaki (see p.178). *Mangal Bamboo Craft Centre*, south of the *Hungry Eye*, carries an unusual selection of handmade dolls and doll houses – for a hoot, ask the proprietor to demonstrate his erotic figures. Extremely persuasive Tibetans peddle their wares in Lakeside's cafe's, but these aren't produced locally, and carpets are best purchased at the Tibetan villages (see below). Pokhara is a good place to **sell things**, too – it's surprising what you can get for an old shirt, although most shops are more eager to trade.

---

*Despite the obligatory banners of loyalty displayed during royal visits, the king has made few friends in Lakeside. Apparently to improve HM's holiday view, all buildings within 200ft of the road up to the palace entrance were for several years under threat of demolition, but the idea now seems to have been quietly dropped.

While nightlife around Pokhara usually just means a second helping of pie, a good way to break the routine is to catch a **culture show**. Of the two held near the lake area, the one-and-a-half-hour programme in Damside's *Dragon Hotel* (nightly during the high season, usually at 7pm, but check – times vary; Rs50) is the more entertainingly amateur. The show at the *Fish Tail Lodge* (nightly at 6pm or 6.30pm; Rs80) only lasts an hour and the musicians are kept offstage for most of the performance.

Pokhara Bazaar

Most of **Pokhara Bazaar** was destroyed in a fire in 1949, leaving little of interest. The active, southern end of town around **Mahendra Pul** is new since the fire, while the remnants of the original Newar quarter begin 1km further northwest, running from the Bhimsen Mandir up to Bhim Bazaar. Perched on a hillock in the middle of this area you'll find the **Bindyabasini Mandir**, Pokhara's main cultural attraction, a quiet temple complex more noteworthy for its sweeping mountain views than its collection of shrines. The featured deity, Bindyabasini, is an incarnation of Kali, the mother goddess in her bloodthirsty aspect; animal sacrifices are common here, particularly on Saturdays and the ninth day of *Dasain* in October. Bindyabasini has a reputation as bit of a prima donna: in one celebrated incident, her stone image began to sweat mysteriously, causing such a panic that the late King Tribhuvan had to step in and order special rites to pacify the goddess.

The **Pokhara Museum** (Wed–Mon 10am–5pm; Rs5), located south of Mahendra Pul, contains a small exhibit of photos and artifacts of Nepalese ethnic groups, haphazardly arranged and with minimal English commentary. Tucked away in one corner of the Prithvi Narayan Campus at the northeastern part of town, the **Annapurna Regional Museum** (daily 10am–5pm; free), gives a similarly slapdash treatment of Nepal's natural history, the prize exhibit being a collection of Himalayan butterflies.

Immediately east of town lies the mossy, almost invisibly narrow **Seti River gorge**, where the abrasive torrent has cut like acid though the valley's soft sediments. It can easily be seen from the bridge east of Mahendra Pul (*pul* means bridge) – there's something remarkable about witnessing natural forces at work so close to the bazaar – but the footbridge east of the airstrip, and K. I. Singh Pul at the northern end of town on the way to Mahendra Cave (p.169), provide less rubbish-strewn vantage-points.

Traditional *Gurung* house

Listings

Banks *Nepal Rastra Bank*'s foreign-exchange counter, a short distance north of Damside, is open daily 7am–7pm.

Black market The rate is always better in Kathmandu. Far from approaching you, Pokhara shopkeepers and hoteliers have to be persuaded to change money unofficially, and few touts work the streets.

Books Though the stalls around the lake are small, collectively they can muster a good selection of new and second-hand books.

Car hire About Rs100 an hour with driver, available through travel agents. For journeys outside the Pokhara Valley, figure on Rs1700 per day.

Central Immigration A short walk north of the bank, it only issues trekking permits for the Annapurna region and 15-day visa extensions. Application hours are Sun–Thurs 10am–4pm, Fri 10am–1pm; permits and visas are ready in about an hour. For most trekking permits, an additional Rs200 Annapurna Conservation Area fee is payable. Passport photos are available in half an hour from studios near the office (Rs40).

Dope is available, but sold more discreetly than in Kathmandu. If you're going trekking, you'll find it much cheaper on the trail.

Film and processing Films are available at roughly Kathmandu prices, the best-stocked shops being west of the bank. A couple of places near Mahendra Pul do processing, and one or two shops around the lake can arrange it for a small surcharge.

Health The *Western Regional Hospital* (☎20066), with western and Nepali staff, handles emergencies and does stool tests. *Green Peace Medical Corner* ("Self-shining medicine for trekking"), near the driveway to *Hotel Fewa*, will forward stool samples to the hospital. Lakeside, Damside and the bazaar all have *pharmas*.

Laundry Most lodges take laundry for a few rupees per item; the places calling themselves "dry cleaners" return your clothes dry, but wash as wet as the others.

Massage Rs50 per half-hour at several Lakeside shacks. What the barbers call "massage" looks extremely painful and is probably best avoided.

Newspapers and magazines *International Herald Tribune*, *Time* and *Newsweek* are available in bookshops, usually several days late.

Post Office The main office, in Mahendra Pul, is open Sun–Thurs 10am–4pm, Fri 10am–3pm. A few tourist bookshops sell stamps and take letters to the post office for franking.

Provisions Chocolate, dried fruit, muesli and other trekking goodies are sold in shops around the lake. Pokhara can't match Kathmandu for brown bread, but the croissants aren't bad. Cheese, yoghurt and little cartons of ice cream can be had from the *Dairy Development Corporation*, 200m north of the *Hungry Eye* in Lakeside.

RNAC The typically shambolic cubbyhole at the airport (☎21021) sells tickets for flights out of Pokhara only. Open daily 10am–1.30pm & 2–3pm.

Telephone calls Many guest houses and shops have international dialling facilities, although at the time of writing it wasn't possible to call North America direct (this is expected to change soon). International calls are charged at Rs125 per minute, trunk calls to Kathmandu Rs15 per minute (minimum 3 min).

Ticket agents are everywhere. They sell tourist bus tickets for no extra charge, and will book seats on other buses for a fee of Rs20 or so – well worth it to avoid a special trip to the bus park. Some offer to make international flight bookings for a 10-percent fee. See "On from Kathmandu" in Chapter One for general advice on ticket agencies.

Trekking agencies As in Kathmandu, recommendations are risky. Guides and porters can be hired through almost any guest house or equipment-hire stall. See Chapter Seven for full details on trekking.

Trekking equipment The selection of stuff for hire isn't as good as in Kathmandu, but you'll pay for fewer days by hiring locally. Sleeping bags, packs and parkas are no problem (around Rs10 per day).

Tourist info The sleepy office opposite the airstrip can answer simple, specific questions. Open Sun–Thurs 10am–5pm (10am–4pm in winter) and Fri 10am–3pm.

BEYOND POKHARA: EXPLORING THE VALLEY

Daytrips around the Pokhara Valley make excellent training for a trek, and are an effective antidote to lakeside idleness. Excursions generally entail a healthy amount of cycling or hiking, often both. Start early to make the most of the views before the clouds move in, and bring lunch and a full water bottle.

Many of the **ethnic groups** that make treks north of Pokhara so popular – Gurungs, Magars, and Brahman and Chhetri Hindu castes – are equally well represented around the valley, and less touched by tourism. In addition, three **Tibetan villages** in the area are less commercial, and more instructive about Tibetan culture, than Patan's Jaulakhel settlement.

Mountain views: Sarangkot and Kahun Danda

For the classic, full-length spectacle of the Himalaya – featuring Dhaulagiri, the Annapurnas, Manaslu and the graceful pyramid of Machhapuchhre – hike up one of the hilltops north and east of Pokhara. **SARANGKOT**, a high point (1590m) on the ridge north of Phewa Tal, is the more popular and well-developed of the two. Any number of obscure woodcutters' paths ascend the ridge, but to avoid getting lost take the wide trail starting just south of the Bindyabasini Temple in the bazaar. Follow the signposted turn-off for about five minutes until a fork, where you bear right, and more steeply uphill; from here on it's a steady two-hour hike along the spine of the ridge, with tea, soft drinks and basic food available en route.

The scenery grows progressively more stunning as you ascend: the white peaks seem to levitate above their blue flanks, the gathering clouds add a quality of raw grandeur, while to the south, Phewa Tal shimmers in the hazy arc of the valley. If you hadn't been planning on trekking, this is where you might change your mind. At the summit, low stone walls are all that remain of Sarangkot, a fort (*kot*) of the Kaski kings that fell to the Gorkhalis without a fight in 1781. KASKI, seat of the kingdom that once ruled the Pokhara Valley, lives on as an insignificant hamlet an easy half-hour's walk further west below the ridge. From the village you can march up a long stone staircase to **Kaskikot**, where a plain Bhagwati temple and remnants of the Kaski citadel preside over an excellent view of the peaks.

Continuing west along the ridge for about two hours, the trail joins the main Jomosom trekking route at **NAGDANDA** (or NAUDANDA), a busy trekking bazaar and the first place from which Machhapuchhre's true fishtail profile can be seen. Though you can't continue further west without a trekking permit, you can spend the night here, or drop down to Phedi (see below) in under an hour, from which frequent jeeps run back to Shining Hospital – a long day's outing.

THE GURKHAS

As I write these last words, my thoughts return to you who were my comrades: the stubborn and indomitable peasants of Nepal. Once more I hear the laughter with which you greeted every hardship. Once more I see you in your bivouacs or about your fires, on forced march or in the trenches, now shivering with wet and cold, now scorched by a pitiless and burning sun. Uncomplaining, you endure hunger and thirst and wounds; and at the last, your unwavering lines disappear into the smoke and wrath of battle. Bravest of the brave, most generous of the generous, never had a country more faithful friends than you.

Ralph Lilley Turner *Dictionary of the Nepali Language* (1931)

Comprising an elite Nepalese corps within the British and Indian armies for over 175 years, the **Gurkha regiments** have been rated among the finest fighting units in the world. Ironically, the regiments were born out of the 1814-16 war between Nepal and Britain's East India Company: so impressed were the British by the men of "Goorkha" (Gorkha, the ancestral home of Nepal's rulers) that they began recruiting Nepalis into the Indian Army before the peace was even signed.

In the century that followed, Gurkhas fought in every major British military operation, including the 1857 **Indian Mutiny** and campaigns in Afghanistan, the North-West Frontier and Somaliland. More than 200,000 Gurkhas served in the world wars, and, despite being earmarked for "high-wastage roles", earned universal

To return directly from Sarangkot, follow any of the steep, southward-bound paths, which descend to Phewa Tal in an hour or so. A trail along the shore leads easily back to Lakeside or, if you've still got time, further up the lake.

Kahun Danda

If the view from **KAHUN DANDA**, the hill east of Pokhara, is a shade less magnificent than Sarangkot's, a lookout tower near the top gives you a better crack at it. The trail up the ridge is totally uncommercialised and consequently hard to find (the tourist map's depiction of trails is wildly misleading). Although it's furthest from Lakeside/Damside, the easiest and most interesting starting point is the **Tibetan monastery**, 2km east of Mahendra Pul. Standing at the top of a breathless couple of hundred steps at the southern base of Kahun Danda, the Karma Dhubgyu Chhokhorling Nyeshang Korti Monastery occupies a breezy spot – always good for keeping the prayer flags flapping – with valley views east and west. Around thirty monks and monklets man the monastery, which is modern and contains all the usual tantric paraphernalia (chanting daily around 4pm).

The trail to the lookout tower starts at the bottom of the steps, hugs the western base of the ridge for about 1km, and then climbs through several lazy settlements collectively known as PHULBARI. Keep heading towards the blocky tower (1460m), which is visible most of the way, and can be reached in about an hour and a half from the monastery. From the half-finished concrete platform, you can contemplate the tremendous force of the Seti River and its tributaries, which tumble out of the Annapurna Himal clouded with glacial debris (*seti* means white) and, merging at the foot of the Kahun Danda, split the valley floor with a bleached chasm.

respect for their bravery: ten of the one hundred **Victoria Crosses** awarded in World War II went to Gurkhas. Following India's independence after the war, Britain took four of the ten Gurkha regiments and India retained the rest. More recently, Gurkhas have distinguished themselves in Sarawak, Cyprus and the 1982 **Falklands War**, and are currently stationed in Hong Kong, Brunei, Belize and the UK.

Gurkhas are **recruited** mainly from the Magar, Gurung, Rai and Limbu hill tribes (growing up in the Nepalese hills is ideal preparation for the army). Most boys from these groups dream of making it into the Gurkhas, not only for the money – the salary of £5000 is about fifty times the Nepalese average – but also for a rare chance to see the world and return with prestige and a comfortable pension. Thousands compete each year for just 225 places, enduring a week of exhausting physical and mental tests. Those who are rejected are given their bus fare home, but many, too proud to return to their villages, head south to enlist in the less well-paid Indian regiments.

With Hong Kong to be handed over to China in 1997, Britain's need for military forces in Asia is expected to decline, and the Brigade of Gurkhas' Hong Kong head-quarters will soon be shifted, probably to Germany. New duties will have to be found for the Gurkhas – there's speculation that they would make excellent tank drivers, given their small size – but at the same time their **numbers are to be halved**, from 8000 to 4000. Anticipating this, Britain wound down its main recruiting and training centre in Dharan at the end of 1989, and all operations are now carried out at the smaller facility in Pokhara.

Descending back to the monastery, paths bearing to the left may suggest a **longer circuit** via the valley and villages on the east side of the ridge. Also eminently worth exploring is the tidily terraced side valley of the Bhalam Khola, immediately north of Kahun Danda. To get there directly from the tower involves some nasty bushwacking, so it's better to backtrack towards the monastery until you pick up the first main northbound trail. It's also accessible by a rough (mountain-bikable) track heading northwards on the east side of the Seti River.

Two roads north of Pokhara: to Mahendra Cave and Phedi

While it just about scrapes a description as a geological wonder, **MAHENDRA CAVE** (MAHENDRA GUPHA) is probably best thought of as a base from which to explore the snug hills and side valleys north of Pokhara, even though it's a long nine-kilometre haul from Lakeside/Damside. To get there, cross K. I. Singh* Pul (Bridge) at the top end of Pokhara and head north past the Gurkha Training Camp, turn right up a paved road 600m beyond the bridge, and follow it for about 3km to the end. The climb is relentless and if you're on a one-speed bike you'll have to push much of the way (the reward comes on the way back).

*A cross between Robin Hood and Che Guevara, **K. I. Singh** led the western insurgents in the 1951 overthrow of the Rana regime and restoration of Nepal's monarchy. Although on the winning side, his radical socialism kept him from office and eventually landed him in jail.

Water percolating down from the limestone hills above has etched away at the valley's alluvial sediments, creating a honeycomb of caves. Mahendra Cave used to be well-known for its limestone stalactites, but these have unfortunately been ransacked by vandals; a few surviving **stalagmites** are worshipped as Shiva *lingams* and daubed with red *sindur* because of their resemblance to phalluses.

Admission to the caves is Rs3 plus another Rs10 for the local kid who won't leave you alone until you hire him as a guide. Though the cave is neither dangerous nor vast – the accessible part takes about 10–15 minutes to tour – a guide is still useful, if only to show you which way to point your torch (a fairly essential item, since the electric generator rarely works and guides make do with feeble candles). They'll probably try to sell you a tour of **another cave** about ten minutes' walk away, promising a bigger chamber and better stalactites. It is, surprisingly, as advertised, but it's a hell of a scramble, and once inside it may strike you that, were it not for Nepalis' innate honesty, you could be rolled for everything you've got. For serious spelunkers only.

A *gaine*

Eastwards from Mahendra Cave, a trail beckons up the Kali Khola, a minor tributary of the Seti, to the village of MACHHUA. Horseshoe-shaped and stepped with perfect terraces, the valley looks like a sprouting Roman amphitheatre. Adventurous types might want to forge on. By traversing the ridge to the south, you should theoretically be able to return to Pokhara the same day via the Bhalam Khola. One or two hours' scramble to the top of the ridge to the north brings you onto one of the long southern spurs of Annapurna IV, suddenly and tantalisingly close to Machhapuchhre.

About 1km south of Mahendra Cave, the road from Pokhara passes through **BATULECHAUR**, a village locally famous for its **gaines**. Wandering minstrels of the old school, *gaines* are still found throughout the hills, earning their crust by singing ballads to the accompaniment of the *saranghi*, a four-stringed, hand-hewn violin: "I have no rice to eat/let the strings of the *saranghi* set to," runs the *gaine*'s traditional opening couplet. These days, many find they can make better money down at Lakeside serenading tourists.

The Pokhara–Baglung Highway

A second road heads northwest from Pokhara to **PHEDI**, currently the main starting point for treks in the Annapurna region (see Chapter Seven). Jeeps regularly shuttle up to Phedi from the Shining Hospital field, at the north end of Pokhara (Rs35), but there's little point coming here unless you're trekking or paying a visit to the Tibetan village of Tashi Palkhel (Hyangja) en route (see below). However, the road is being extended, and by 1991 it should be possible to drive to the lovely riverside village of Birethanti; construction of a $20-a-night hotel is already under way there. Eventually the road will reach Baglung, the zonal headquarters of the intensely populated hill area west of Pokhara, and someday it may go all the way to Jomosom.

When a bus service is introduced along this route (already provisionally called the **Pokhara–Baglung Highway**), it will open up a prime new area for travel, but also bring enormous changes to the local social order – not all for the good. As has happened elsewhere, the new road will bring wealth and prosperity to a few (mostly outside developers) and lure young people away to the cities. The old walking route will fall into disuse to the detriment of the villages along it, since trekkers and locals alike seldom walk when they can ride a bus. (See "Development Dilemmas" in *Contexts*.)

The Tibetan villages

If Tibet were free tomorrow, we'd drop our hammers and go. We wouldn't even think about it.

A Tibetan working on a building project at Tashi Palkhel

Twenty-five years ago, Dervla Murphy worked as a volunteer among Tibetan refugees in Pokhara, and called the account she wrote about her experiences *The Waiting Land* (see "Books" in *Contexts*). Pokhara's Tibetans are still waiting: three former refugee camps, now self-governing and largely self-sufficient, have settled into a pattern of permanent transience. Because Pokhara (unlike Kathmandu) has no Buddhist holy places, most Tibetans have remained in the camps, regarding them as havens where they can keep their culture and language alive. Many plainly don't see the point of moving out and setting up permanent homes in Nepal when all they really want is to return to their former homes in Tibet.

Located northwest, southwest and near the centre of Pokhara, the settlements are open to the public, and a wander around one is an experience of workaday reality that contrasts with the otherworldliness of, say, Baudha or Swayambhu. You'll get a lot more out of a visit if you can get someone to show you around – and if the tour inevitably finishes with a sales pitch back at your guide's one-room home, so much the better.

Tibetans in Nepal

At the time of the **Chinese invasion** of Tibet in 1950 and the **Dalai Lama's flight** in 1959, the refugees now living in Pokhara were mainly peasants and nomads inhabiting the border areas of western Tibet. The political changes in farway Lhasa left them initially unaffected, but as the Chinese occupation turned genocidal, thousands streamed south through the Himalaya to safety. They gathered first at Jomosom, where the terrain and climate were at least reminiscent of Tibet, but within months the area became overcrowded and conditions desperate. Under the direction of the Swiss Red Cross, three **transit camps** were established around low-lying Pokhara and about 2000 refugees were moved down. Thirty years on, the subtropical heat still heightens Tibetans' sense of displacement.

The **first five years** were hard times in the camps, marked by food rationing, chronic sickness and general unemployment. Relief came in the late 1960s, when the construction of Pardi Dam and the Prithvi and Siddhartha highways provided welcome work. Since then, the Tibetans' fortunes have risen with Pokhara's tourism industry, and carpet-weaving and other handicrafts have become the main source of income, especially for women. Many of the men work seasonally as trekking porters or guides, where they can make better money than in the camps. A small but visible minority have become smooth-talking curio salespeople, plying the cafés of Lakeside and Damside, but whereas Tibetans have by now set up substantial businesses in Kathmandu, opportunities are fewer in Pokhara, and prosperity has come more slowly.

Given Nepal's reliance on **Chinese aid**, the Tibetans are a source of some discomfort for the government. China regards the camps as potential counter-revolutionary hotbeds, and exerts pressure on Nepal to suppress any political activities there. While the "Free Tibet" movement is much bigger in India, where the Dalai Lama and the Tibetan government-in-exile are based, a shadowy **Tibetan underground** does exist in Nepal, chiefly among the disaffected youth of the camps. Don't expect anyone to discuss it openly, however, as Tibetan leaders have been warned that any "political" remarks could be grounds for prompt eviction. In 1989, HMG detained dozens of Tibetans during a state visit by the Chinese prime minister to pre-empt any embarrassing protests, and specifically banned any celebrations when the Dalai Lama was awarded the Nobel Peace Prize. See *Contexts* for more on the lives of Tibetan exiles.

Tashi Palkhel (Hyangja)

With 900 residents – 60 of them monks – **TASHI PALKHEL** (commonly known as **HYANGJA**, after the village at the top of the hill) is the largest of the three settlements. The entrance is clearly marked, about 5km northwest of Shining Hospital on the Pokhara–Baglung Highway; get there by bike (preferably one with gears) or jeep from Shining Hospital (ideally, on the way to or from a trek).

Most of what there is to see is on your left as you enter. The large weaving hall is the focal point of the camp's **carpet industry**, and surrounding it are wool dyeing and drying areas. Beyond this is a village of whitewashed stone houses, which you shouldn't barge into without an escort. The community also has a brand-new *gompa*, school and, the latest project, an old people's home – many of the original refugees are now getting on in years. Prices are negotiable at a couple of **handicrafts shops** near the entrance, though not so much as in private homes. If you decide to **stay overnight**, the guest house at Tashi Palkhel can supply beds (Rs15) and Tibetan food. Based here, it's reportedly possible to make a rewarding day hike through HYANGJA, across the bridge over the Mardi Khola and up the increasingly beautiful Seti Valley to GHACHOK, which has a basic inn.

Tashiling and Devin's Fall

Much easier to reach, yet still far from commercial, **TASHILING** lies about 2km west of Damside beside the main highway to India. On a bicycle you can be there in ten minutes. With some 550 residents, Tashiling is smaller than Tashi Palkhel, but laid out on much the same lines. It's best to make straight for the weaving hall and wool-dyeing shed, a good 400m down the main drive at the far end of the camp. A short walk from here to the camp's southern edge brings you to an abrupt drop and a glorious panorama of the valley of the Phusre Khola, a Seti tributary. On the way back to the entrance are a *gompa*, a primary school, several

ABOUT CARPET MAKING

At least ninety percent of the weaving of Tibetan carpets is done by **women**, since weaving can be carried out by mothers with small children. Perhaps a more important factor, though, is language – for a variety of reasons, Tibetan women have generally learned less Nepali and English than men, and so are less employable outside the camps. All this doesn't explain why at Tashiling, for example, where virtually all 115 of the weavers are women, the carpet masters, who choose patterns and oversee the weaving, are both men. It is, after all, a traditional society: while Tibetan women play a nearly equal role in finances and household affairs, there are certain categories of "women's work" and weaving is one of them.

Two weavers working as a team can complete a standard 3'x6' carpet in about a week, working from 7am to 5.30pm, six days a week. Based on an average of 60 knots per square inch, they will tie more than 150,000 knots. The pay for this tedious work is Rs20 a day. The **low wages** aren't the doing of exploitative managers (the camps are run as cooperatives) but are dictated by a free market awash with underemployed women. To make more money, many spin wool at home in the evenings.

Tibetan carpets are normally made from a blend of New Zealand sheep and Himalayan yak wools. After carding and **hand-spinning**, the yarn is dipped in large vats of boiling **dye** (mostly chemical dyes are used – good quality vegetable dyes, producing softer earth tones, are more expensive). Dyeing is done in the early morning so that the yarn can be hung out to dry in the sun before being rolled into 200-gramme balls, coded for colour and batch, and stored in a warehouse; weavers can then order up their colours by number, as instructed by a pattern or their carpet master.

As throughout Asia, **weavers** sit on benches in front of tall looms, deftly tying rows of woollen knots across hundreds of vertical cotton warp threads, beating each row down tight with a wooden mallet. Carpets are rated according to the number of knots per square inch (usually 60, 80 or 100) but an unseen element of quality is the consistency of the knotting and beating. The weaving done, carpets are taken off the looms and trimmed with shears to give an even finish. Embossing, an optional stage, subtly separates the colours to highlight the design.

Marketing is more sophisticated than it might at first appear. The carpets so haphazardly displayed in the shops of Pokhara and Kathmandu represent only a fraction of the total – most are in fact made to order for the export market, the majority being shipped to a few big wholesalers in London. A handful of export traders, led by the Carpet Trading Company, founded in 1966 with help from the Swiss Association for Technical Assistance (SATA), handle international distribution.

rows of distinctly Tibetan barracks-style stone houses (the windows trimmed with characteristic orange and white skirts) and, in a separate compound, a "children's village" for Tibetan orphans from all over Nepal. The **shops** near the entrance sell the usual trinkets, but with a smaller mark-up than stalls and peddlers around the lake; if you're planning to make any purchases while in Pokhara, it's worth coming here first to establish the going rate.

Just before Tashiling, on the opposite side of the highway, **Devin's Fall** marks the spot where the Pardi Khola (the stream that drains Phewa Tal) enters a grottoed channel and sinks underground in a sudden rush of foam and fury. In the autumn, with a good monsoon run-off, the effect can be quite impressive; in the spring it's a washout. The spot is perhaps more interesting as a source of pop mythology: known to locals as Patle Chhango, the sinkhole is said to have acquired its Western-sounding nickname when a "female European" was drowned while skinny-dipping with her boyfriend. An alternate spelling, David Fall, suggests it may have been the boyfriend who perished. The sign at the entrance reads "Devi's Fall", illustrating the Nepalese propensity to deify everything that moves (*devi* means goddess). The whole story sounds like a fabrication to warn local youths to shun promiscuous western ways. Entrance fee is Rs3.

The Tibetan Handicrafts Centre (Paljorling)

The smallest of Pokhara's Tibetan settlements, the **Tibetan Handicrafts Centre** (officially named **PALJORLING**) is now not so much a community as a factory with on-site housing; little wonder then that it rarely goes by its original name these days. Located just west of the bus park, it's like a rustic version of one of those edge-of-town factory showrooms, where the carpet-making operation is viewable but the emphasis is on retail sales. The Tibetans here are among Pokhara's most irrepressible salespeople. To its credit, the camp is much smaller and easier to suss out than the other two, so given its location it can be easily fitted in as a side trip on the way to town.

Rupa Tal and Begnas Tal

Lakeside might have almost as easily sprung up along the shores of **RUPA TAL**, 10km east of Pokhara; happily, this two-kilometre-long lake remains pristinely hidden in a bushy, steep-sided valley. Close by lies **BEGNAS TAL**, Rupa's bigger and better-known sister, framed by meticulously engineered paddy terraces that march right down to the shore. A walk along the top of the narrow ridge that separates the two lakes is one of Pokhara's great unsung attractions.

Don't let the distance on the map put you off: **getting there** is easier than it looks and an outing needn't take the whole day. Buses, departing every hour or so from New Road just south of Chipledhunga, take forty-five minutes and tend to be crowded. Cycling is more scenic, and usually quicker: the first 10km out along the Prithvi Highway is mostly downhill; turn left onto an unmistakeably broad, straight, unpaved (and unmarked) road, and from there it's a jangling 3km to the end of the line at **SISUWA** (aka BEGNAS TAL). You'd never guess it, but Begnas Tal is right around the corner from here. Sisuwa itself is a cipher – typical of so many roadhead towns, it seems to exist only

Harvesting rice

as a conduit for corrugated roofing, bags of cement and other tools of progress for the surrounding hills – but basic **food and lodging** are available if needed.

The **quick approach** to Begnas – not to be confused with the scenic one – is the dirt road to the left immediately before the cul-de-sac where the bus waits. It's not even five minutes' walk to the dam (ignore the "No Entry" signs and go through the gate), where Phewa-style **canoes** are hired out (Rs20 per hour). From here you could walk the length of the dam and make a tour of the wooded north shore.

A better introduction to the lakes, although it involves a fair amount of up and down, is the trail along **Panchbhaiya Danda**. Passing through upper Sisuwa, the busy thoroughfare ascends steadily to the ridge dividing the two lakes. Begnas is visible first, on the left, and then Rupa comes into view after the highest point of the ridge is passed, about 45 minutes from Sisuwa. What appear to be fences peeping above the water of both lakes are fish farms, installed with Japanese aid. In another ten minutes or so the trail forks at a cluster of shops: from here on, it's follow-your-nose time. The left fork, signposted "Syaklung", leads to another village called BEGNAS, and from there down to the lake. The "Karputar" fork heading to the right descends to the north end of Rupa Tal and TALBESI, with the possibility of a steep side trip to the hilltop fortress of **RUPAKOT**. This trail makes an attractive alternative way in to the Annapurna Circuit (see Chapter Seven).

SOUTH OF POKHARA

Sticking to roads, the only way to continue beyond Pokhara is to go south: a slow, uncomfortable, but occasionally rewarding journey along the **Siddhartha Highway** to the Tarai. In 160km the highway traverses four major river drainages, negotiates countless twists and turns, and usually claims a tyre or an axle; eight hours would be a fast run. Although it's the most direct route between Pokhara and the Indian border, give some thought to going via Chitwan if you're travelling by bus. Cyclists, however, will enjoy the variety, light traffic and relatively easy gradients.

From Pokhara, the road labours for an hour and a half to a high point at NAUDANDA, a little-used alternative starting point for treks into the Kali Gandaki/Annapurna region; minibuses from Chipledhunga in Pokhara shuttle up here every half-hour or so. An old Kaski fortress guards the pass from the hill just to the east. Entering the **Amdhi Khola** watershed, the highway wiggles tortuously across the valley side, purposely avoiding the flat, straight valley floor – in a country so reliant on agriculture, you don't put a road through the best farmland. After the dumpy bazaar of SYANGJA, the valley draws in and the hills rear up spectacularly in places, although you can't help noticing how badly overworked and eroded the land is in settled areas. Lunch is invariably at WALING, a nondescript wayside that owes its existence to busloads of hungry travellers. The road drops down to cross the rugged canyon of the **Kali Gandaki** at RAMDI GHAT, where cremations are sometimes conducted, before climbing almost 1000m to its highest point. A few kilometres beyond is the turning for Tansen, the only town of note in this area, situated some 3km off the highway. From the Tansen turning, it's an hour-and-a-half descent to Butwal (covered in Chapter Five).

Tansen

TANSEN is thoroughly second-rate, but endearingly so if given half a chance. Once the seat of a powerful kingdom, it's now a lowly district headquarters, slightly seedy and somehow left behind – shopkeepers still display black-and-white portraits of the king and queen. Yet slowly, almost reluctantly, Tansen yields its secrets: clacking *dhaka* cloth looms glimpsed though doorways; the potters of Ghorabanda; the view from Srinagar Hill, and superb hill-walking beyond. As such it's probably chiefly of interest to connoisseurs of the offbeat, although travellers coming up from India might consider breaking the journey here, for Tansen makes a more authentic introduction to Nepal than Pokhara.

Tansen's **history** goes back to the early sixteenth century, when the Sen clan of princes, already established at Butwal, chose it as a safer base from which to expand family holdings that soon covered the length of the lower hills, almost to Sikkim. Makunda Sen, Palpa's legendary second king, allegedly raided Kathmandu and carried off two sacred Bhairab masks, only to be cut down by a plague sent by the Pashupatinath *lingam*. Chastened by Makunda Sen's death, his successors settled for forming a strategic alliance with Gorkha, which bought them breathing space when the latter began conquering territory in the mid-eighteenth century. Aided by a friendly Indian rajah, Palpa staved off the inevitable until 1806, when it became the last territory to be annexed to modern Nepal. Tansen remains the headquarters of Palpa District, and many still nostalgically refer to it as *Palpa*. You might also hear it called Tansing, which was its original Magar name – the hills here are Magar country, although the town is now predominantly Newar.

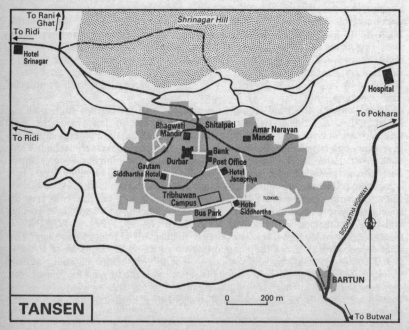

Practicalities: arriving, sleeping and eating

Try to get on a bus that's going directly to Tansen: buses bound for Pokhara or the Tarai don't leave the Siddhartha Highway, and instead drop you off at BARTUN, the village at the start of the three-kilometre Tansen spur road. If you're lucky there may be a shuttle bus from Bartun to the Tansen bus park, otherwise it's a steep one-kilometre hike up the cobbled path that starts immediately north of the intersection (there are no taxis or rikshas in Tansen). The town spills down the flank of Srinagar Hill, with the **bus park** occupying the lowest, newest level, surrounded by a tacky bazaar area.

As you'll soon discover, Tansen prepares a number of frustrations for the traveller, the first being a marked lack of cheerful **budget accommodation**. Most lodges are ranged around the bus park, which is terrifically noisy and a long slog from the centre. The only one that seems to be familiar with western travellers is *Hotel Siddhartha*; it's as dreary as the rest but at least some English is spoken (Rs35 for doubles with common bath). Quiet and more central, *Hotel Janapriya*, near the top of the pedestrian shortcut to town, is a recommended alternative (Rs35 double, Rs77 with bath). Power cuts are common and water in constant short supply, as there's not enough electricity to drive the town water pump – the government has been trying for years to coax the town to shift down to the valley where water is plentiful.

All this needn't concern you if you're on a bigger budget. *Hotel Srinagar* (☎075/20045), on the ridge above town, has all mod cons, though it's rather poky for the price (dorm beds $6, singles $16, doubles $24; rupees accepted).

Don't expect much of the **food** and you won't be disappointed. Loads of nameless diners around the bus park serve *daal bhaat* and sweets, and most of the guest-house restaurants can do eggs and a sort of toast in the morning. If you're passing through before or after hill-walking, *Hotel Srinagar* can help break the monotony: breakfast comes with a splendid view, and they also do hearty packed lunches (Rs95).

The town

Things improve once you've escaped the bus park and found your way to the **upper town**. The direct footpath past the *Hotel Janapriya* emerges at what English-speakers call Bank Street, home of a modest bazaar and a *Nepal Bank* branch; across the street is the prosaic twentieth-century Durbar. Bank Street ends at Shitalpati, where you'll find the only visible reminder of Tansen's grand past – **Baggi Dhoka** (Chariot Gate), tall enough for elephants and their riders to pass through, and supposedly the biggest of its kind in Nepal. West of here are Tansen's oldest neighbourhoods, whose cobbled alleys and brick houses could pass for parts of Kathmandu without the crowds. The lane going east from Shitalpati leads down to the nineteenth-century **Amar Narayan Mandir**, a pagoda-style temple; and stopping place for *sadhus* on their way to *Janai Purnima* festivities at Muktinath in late July or early August.

Wherever you wander, keep an eye out for **dhaka weavers**, who work at wooden treadle looms shaped like upright pianos. Woven in many hill areas, *dhaka* fabric is created by shuttling coloured threads back and forth across a constant vertical background to form repeating, geometric patterns. "Palpa" *dhaka*'s trademark is the use of brightly dyed *pashmina*, a fine goat's wool, against a white cotton background – it's famous throughout Nepal, and many *topis* (Nepali caps) are made from it. The simplicity of *dhaka* designs allows for almost infinite improvisation: each weaver decides without chart or counting threads where to lay the colours to form the patterns; many know a hundred or more basic designs and invent new ones all the time. The process is labour-intensive and the fabric doesn't come cheap: a good-quality Palpa weave will set you back about Rs200 a metre.

Getting out: Shrinagar Hill and beyond

The best thing about Tansen is getting out of it and exploring the outlying hill country and unaffected Magar villages. People on the trail will likely greet you with delighted smiles and the full palms-together *namaaste*. They might also ask for medicine – the few westerners who frequent these parts are usually doctors from the United Mission Hospital, 1km east of Tansen.

First stop on most excursions is **Shrinagar Hill** (1525m), north of town. The most direct route, which takes about half an hour, starts from a small Ganesh temple above Shitalpati, but you have to zigzag a bit to get to the temple; from *Hotel Srinagar* it's an easy 20-minute walk east along the ridge. The top is planted with thick pine forest – there's no special place to catch the view, but the soft needles are great for picnicking. To the north, the Dhaulagiri and Annapurna *himals* hover on the skyline; from this distance Machhapuchhre, so prominent from the perspective of Pokhara, takes a back seat. On the other side, beyond Tansen, lies the luxuriant Madi Valley, which in autumn and on winter mornings is filled with a silver fog.

To Ridi and Rani Ghat

For walks beyond Shrinagar there are at least two strong options, the more eventful being a thirteen-kilometre hike to **RIDI BAZAAR**. From *Hotel Srinagar*, walk west to a fork at a guard shack, bear right and in half an hour you'll reach CHANDI BHANJYANG; turn left and descend through a handsome canyon before rejoining the unpaved road for the last 7km. Set on the banks of the Kali Gandaki, Ridi is considered sacred because of the wealth of *shaligrams* – fossil-bearing stones associated with Vishnu – found in the river here. It used to be said that if a person were cremated at Ridi and his ashes sprinkled into the river, they would congeal to form a *shaligram*, and if the stone were then made into a likeness of Vishnu, the devotee would be one with his god. Ridi has declined in importance over the years, but remains an occasional cremation ground and, in October and January, a pilgrimage site for ritual bathing.

The colourful commercial end of town lies across a stream that joins the Kali Gandaki here, while the magical eighteenth-century **Rishikesh Mandir** is south of the stream, just above the bus stop. According to legend, the idol inside the squat temple, a form of Vishnu, was fished out of the river and originally bore the likeness of a young boy, but over the course of years matured into adult form.

Six **buses** a day head back to Tansen, taking two hours. The return journey can be combined with a visit to **Palpa Bhairab**, up a short path off the road 8km before Tansen. The Bhairab image here is supposed to be so scary that not even the priest is allowed to look at it (a bit of quaint hocus-pocus, given that it's a replica of Kathmandu's easily viewable Kalo Bhairab), and the gilded *trisul* is claimed to be the biggest in Asia. Dakshin Kali-style animal sacrifices are performed on Saturday and Tuesday.

A shorter hike begins 200m east of *Hotel Srinagar* and descends 7km to **RANI GHAT**, another holy bathing and dying spot along the Kali Gandaki. Following a stream through a narrow gorge, the trail passes through an immensely satisfying landscape of streams, forest, terraced fields and trailside hamlets. Rani Ghat itself is incongruously dominated by an enormous derelict palace, built in the late nineteenth century by a former government minister who, according to the custom of the day, was exiled to Palpa after a failed palace coup.

Ghorabanda

The most fascinating of the villages east of Tansen, **GHORABANDA** is locally famous for its **potters**. It's just off the Siddhartha Highway, 3km north of the Tansen turning, but the only feasible way to get there is to walk. Take the dirt road from the Amar Narayan temple towards the United Mission Hospital, bear right on a trail after about 500m, descend and then contour through extensive paddy – if you've done it right, you'll drop down to the highway after about 2km, with Ghorabanda another 1km further along the road. Ghorabanda's potters, members of the Kumal caste, throw their almost spherical water jugs on heavy clay flywheels, shaping them and adding a stipple pattern with a wooden paddle, then sun-drying and finally kiln-firing them. The farmhouses and potteries of Ghorabanda spread down the hill from the *Palpa Pottery Industry* shop. The arrival of a westerner here is a major diplomatic event; it may be a good idea to enlist the help of the shop's proprietor, Bagh Bir Mukhiya, who speaks excellent English.

festivals

Besides the national holidays of *Dasain, Tihar, Shiva Raatri* and *Holi*, a few other festivals are specially celebrated in the western hills:

Magh Sankranti A day of ritual bathing in the Kali Gandaki River at Ridi and elsewhere, held on the first day of the month of *Magh* (Jan 14 or 15).

Chaitra Dasain The "small *Dasain*", celebrated at Gorkha Kalika with processions and animal sacrifices (April).

Janai Purnima The annual changing of the sacred thread worn by high-caste Hindu men is conducted at many river confluences, and brings *sadhus* to Tansen and Pokhara (late July or early August).

Bhagwati Jaatra Processions in Tansen commemorate the goddess Bhagwati and an 1814 battle in which Nepal routed British troops near here (mid-August).

travel details

Buses

From Pokhara at least five companies operate **tourist buses to Kathmandu**: *Memorie, Paradise, Shikhar Nepal, Student* and *Swiss Travels & Tours*; each has one or two coaches a day, journey time 6-7hr, Rs110. Tickets bought from Lake/Damside agents generally won't cost more. Never mind the snapshots of shiny new buses, just take the one that stops closest to your guest house. **Night buses to Kathmandu** depart from Lake/Damside (8hr).

All other long-distance buses leave **from the main bus park**: to Birganj (stopping at Tadi Bazaar for Chitwan, 6 daily; 10hr); Butwal (10 daily; 7hr); Gorkha (7 daily; 5hr); Janakpur (1 nightly; 12hr); Kakarbitta (2 nightly; 20hr); Kathmandu (8 daily; 8-9hr); Narayanghat (5 daily; 4hr); Nepalganj (3 nightly; 14hr); and Sunauli (7 daily; 8hr). Minibuses **from Chipledhunga** to Naudanda (infrequent; 1hr) and Sisuwa (hourly; 45min).

From Gorkha to Abu Khaireini (infrequent; 1-2hr); Birganj (2 daily; 7hr); Kathmandu (2 daily; 7hr) and Narayanghat (2 daily; 3hr).

From Tansen to Butwal (7 daily; 1-2hr); Kathmandu (1 night bus; 12hr) and Ridi (6 daily; 2hr).

Planes

From Pokhara to Jomosom (1-2 daily; 50min) and Kathmandu (4 daily; 40min).

Connections to India

It's possible to book **bus/train packages to India** through Pokhara ticket agents – but see caveats in the "On from Kathmandu" section in Chapter One.

CHAPTER FIVE

THE WESTERN TARAI

n a country best known for its mountains, the lowland **Tarai** often gets short shrift. A narrow strip of land stretching the entire length of Nepal's southern border – including several *dun* (inner Tarai) valleys north of the first range of hills – the Tarai was originally covered in thick, malarial jungle. In the 1950s, however, the government identified the southern plains as a major growth area to relieve population pressure in the hills, and, with the help of liberal quantities of DDT, brought malaria under control. Since then the jungle has been methodically cleared and the Tarai has emerged as Nepal's most productive agricultural and industrial region.

Fortunately, the government has set aside sizeable chunks of the **Western Tarai** as national parks and reserves, which remain as some of the finest **wildlife** and bird havens on the subcontinent: dense riverine forest provides cover for predators like tigers and leopards, swampy grasslands make the perfect habitat for rhinoceros, and vast, tall stands of *sal*, the Tarai's most common tree, throng with what at times seems to be the entire cast of *Bambi*. You'll probably only have the time to visit one national park; **Chitwan**, the richest in game and the most accessible, is deservedly popular, but if crowds bother you and you're willing to invest some extra effort (or money), check out **Bardia** and **Sukla Phanta**.

The region's other claim to fame is historical: Buddha was born 2500 years ago at **Lumbini**, and his birthplace – one of the four most important pilgrimage sites for Buddhists – is an appropriately serene place.

Travel to the western Tarai is straightforward, though exhausting as ever. **Bus** connections from Kathmandu and Pokhara are well-developed via Narayanghat or Butwal; the two most common destinations are Tadi Bazaar for Chitwan and Sunauli for the **Indian border**. The Tarai itself is traversed by a single main road, the **Mahendra Highway**, which when it's good is very good, but when it's bad it's horrid. The far western section of the highway is not only unfinished, it's also a dead end . . . maybe someday, when Nepal and India end their political posturing, the Mahendranagar border crossing will be reopened, reviving an adventurous back-door route from Kathmandu to Delhi. In the meantime, all journeys west of Sunauli require backtracking; internal **flights** can help.

Early spring is the **best time** for wildlife-viewing in the Tarai: in February and March, after the tall grass has been burned off, animals are at their most visible, temperatures are mild and *palash* ("flame of the forest") trees ignite into tongues of brilliant red. Autumn, for its part, brings unforgettable sunset views of the Himalaya. Winter's a good time to come down out of the hills, although even in the Tarai, mornings are misty and cold.

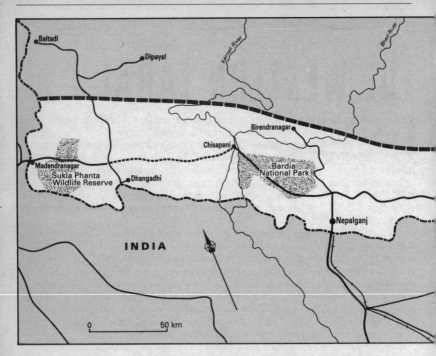

CHITWAN AND AROUND

Whatever your itinerary, **Chitwan National Park** is likely to be your first destination in the Tarai. The park is just a short detour off the Prithvi (Kathmandu–Pokhara) Highway, and if you're travelling to or from India it can be visited on the way to save backtracking.

Chitwan is the name not only of the park but also of the surrounding *dun* valley and administrative district. The name means "heart of the jungle" – a description that, sadly, now holds true only for the lands protected within the park, yet the rest of the **valley**, though it's been reduced to a flat, furrowed plain, still provides fascinating vignettes of a rural lifestyle that's different again from the hill-clinging existence of upland Nepal. Really ugly development is confined to the wayside conurbation of **Narayanghat/Bharatpur** – and even this has left the nearby holy site of **Devghat** unscathed.

Chitwan National Park

The best and worst aspects of **CHITWAN NATIONAL PARK** are that it can be done on the cheap and it's relatively easy to get to. In recent years the park has risen meteorically on the list of Things to Do in Nepal, so that these days, unless you go during the steamy season, you'll have to share your experience with a lot of other people.

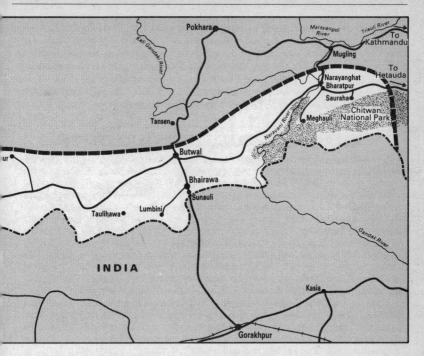

Doing the park **on a budget** means staying in SAURAHA, the instant safari village that's sprung up outside the eastern park entrance. Package trips and fixed prices have taken a lot of the spontaneity out of Sauraha, and in autumn it can get uncomfortably crowded, yet the thirty-odd lodges are remarkably intimate and the village retains an unhurried, almost soporific character (when electricity arrives in a couple of years, it may become a very different sort of resort). If you've got the money – at least $100 a night, all in – you can go for pampered seclusion at any one of a half-dozen **luxury** lodges and tented camps inside the park.

Chitwan has perhaps been oversold in recent years, often with misleading promises of "safari adventure". While its **wildlife** is astoundingly concentrated, remember that the dense vegetation doesn't allow the easy sightings you get in the savannahs of Africa. But go with realistic expectations, don't buy into the package-tour mentality, and it's still possible to enjoy yourself. **Elephant rides**, **jeep tours**, **canoe trips** and just plain **walks** each give a different slant on the luxuriant, teeming forest.

Getting there

Avoid **budget packages**. The reasons are many, but suffice to say that a three-day "safari" only gives you a day and a half in the park, doesn't save you any hassles, limits your flexibility, and invariably costs more than doing Chitwan on your own. Instead, **make your own way** to SAURAHA (pronounced *So*-ruh-hah). Buses bound for Birganj or points east let you off at TADI BAZAAR, where touts will have prepared the usual ambush for you; Sauraha is a dusty 6km south from Tadi, at the park boundary on the banks of the Rapti River, and getting there is a choice between ox cart, jeep, bicycle and shoeleather. **Ox carts** (aka "jungle helicopters", "Chitwan taxis") are ubiquitous, cost Rs20 (the price is fixed) and take at least as long as walking: you only fall for it once. **Jeeps**, when available and assuming full occupancy, charge a fixed Rs30. **Bikes** are for rent at Tadi for

TARAI CULTURE: THARUS AND NEWCOMERS

Two mysteries still surround Nepal's second-biggest ethnic minority, the **Tharus**: where they came from, and how they came to be resistant to malaria. According to their own oral history, Tharus are descended from high-caste Rajput women who were sent north by their husbands during the Muslim invasions and, when the men never returned for them, married their servants. There's some circumstantial evidence to support this: among the Rana Tharus of the far west, for example, traces of a matriarchy are still in evidence; the Tharu name could derive from the Thar Desert of Rajasthan in India, and Tharu women's preference for carrying objects on their heads is characteristically Rajasthani. Anthropologists dismiss this theory – it doesn't explain Tharus' Hindu-animist beliefs and somewhat Mongoloid features – and suggest that the tribe migrated from India's eastern hills, filtering across the Tarai over the course of millennia. Firm evidence is lacking either way.

As to the matter of **malaria resistance**, red blood cells seem to play a role – the fact that Tharus are susceptible to sickle-cell anaemia might be significant – but very little research has been done. At least as important, Tharus boost their natural resistance with a few common-sense precautions, such as building houses with tiny windows to keep smoke in and mosquitoes out.

Tharus are farmers and livestock raisers, clearing patches in the forest and warding off wild animals from flimsy watchtowers called *machaans*. Their whirling **stick dance** evokes their uneasy but respectful relationship with the spirits of the forest, as do the raised animal emblems that decorate their doorways. Fishing is an important activity – given the Tarai's high water table, it's easy enough to scoop out a pond and stock it – and you're likely to see fisherwomen wielding hand-held nets.

Tharu houses are made of mud and dung plastered over wood-and-reed frames, giving them a distinctive ribbed effect. Traditionally, western Tharus built communal **longhouses**, big enough for a half a dozen families or more and partitioned by huge vial-shaped grain urns, but most have now moved up to detached models. While **clothing** varies tremendously by area, Tharu women often wear thick silver bracelets above the elbow; tattooing of the forearms and lower legs is common among older women but is falling out of fashion with the younger generation.

The Tarai has long been viewed as Nepal's frontier and the Tharus dismissed as primitive aboriginals, and since the turn of the century – when, as a preliminary step to abolishing slavery, the government encouraged **slaves** to homestead the Tarai – it's been seen as a place where a settler can clear the land and start a new life. The government's malaria-control programme accelerated the process, and several million gung-ho **immigrants** have now cleared, tamed and transformed the Tarai into the breadbasket of Nepal, felling much of the valuable *sal* in the process. The migration is far from over – the Tarai's population is doubling every seventeen years (urban areas are doubling every ten years). In one generation, the Tharus have been outflanked, outfarmed and in many cases bought out. Traditional culture is still strong in the far west, but in other areas it's been all but drowned by a tide of hill, Indian and western tendencies.

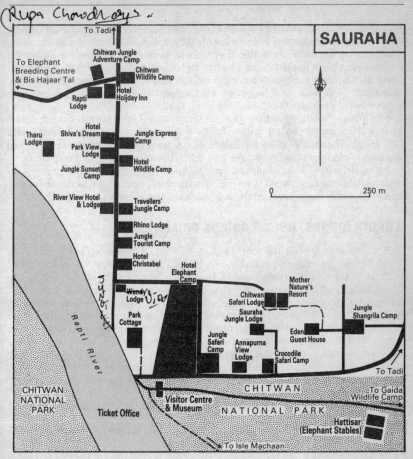

Rs15 a day – an option worth considering if you think you can pedal with a pack on. **Walking** takes less than two hours. When it's time for **moving on**, have your lodge book the bus ticket for you (preferably with *Sajha*) to be sure of a seat.

A visit to Chitwan can also be combined with a **raft trip** on the Trisuli River, bookable through rafting operators in Kathmandu (see "Onwards" in Chapter One). This can cut out some of the long drive, but no matter what the salesman says, the raft won't take you all the way to the park: Narayanghat is the end of the line.

Sleeping and eating: cheap options in Sauraha

All the **cheap places** in Sauraha have clubbed together and formed a sort of cartel, setting minimum prices for rooms and all guided activities. Singles are currently Rs35, doubles Rs60; the base rate for doubles with bath is Rs120, but since there are fewer of these the price tends to drift higher. The lodges all follow a formula: rustic mud-and-thatch huts, separate shower/toilet block, airy dining pavilion and shady garden or open lawn – they're like little budget country clubs. The ones on the east side of the village are generally more secluded. By far the biggest variable is the staff – turnover is high – so heed word-of-mouth referrals. Two that can be recommended are *Eden Guest House*, for its friendly atmosphere, and *River View Hotel and Lodge*, with the coldest (kerosene-powered) fridge in town. See the map for full details.

For **rooms with attached baths**, *Rhino Lodge* and *Jungle Tourist Camp* charge the statutory Rs120, while slightly posher rooms at *Jungle Express Camp* and *Jungle Tourist Camp* go for Rs200. If you want better than this, you're into packages – and the benefits of paying so much more are highly debatable.

Food is limited to variations on cutlets, macaroni, chop suey and trusty *daal bhaat* – lodge menus haven't been officially standardised, but in practice there's no discernible difference between them. Shacks sell bottled water and biscuits .

Luxury lodges, tented camps and hotels

Accommodation **inside the park** includes the most expensive hotels in Nepal. They pay the government massive fees to stake out exclusive concession areas, with the result that you really feel like you've got the park all to yourself. Some are lavish **lodges** with permanent facilities, others are more remote **tented camps** – camping in the softest possible sense, with fluffy mattresses, solar-heated showers and fully stocked bars – and some are both. All activities are included in the price .

You have to **book ahead** for these places. They arrange your transfer by private vehicle, plane or raft, which in most cases costs extra.

Chitwan Jungle Lodge (Kathmandu: ☎01/228918). The biggest operator in the park, with 32 rooms. $240 per person for 2 night/3 day package (includes transport).

Gaida Wildlife Camp (Kathmandu: ☎01/220940). Lodge situated close to Sauraha, $219 for 2 nights; jungle camp 8km south at base of hills, $221 for 2 nights.

Island Jungle Resort (Kathmandu: ☎01/216319). Tented camp on an island in the middle of the Narayani River. $233 for 2 nights.

Machan Wildlife Resort (Kathmandu: ☎01/225001P). Lodge has the only swimming pool in park, $246 for 2 nights; tented camp $124 for 2 nights.

Temple Tiger Wildlife Camp (Kathmandu: ☎01/221585). Tented camp at the west end of the park. $323 for 2 nights.

Tiger Tops (Kathmandu: ☎01/222706). The first and still the most fashionable – though tiger-baiting, once a key attraction, has been stopped. Perched on stilts, the lodge is pure jungle Gothic, $527 for 2 nights; tented camp is $190 per night; *Tharu Village*, Tiger Tops' culture camp, is $120 per night.

Less expensive compromises exist in Sauraha – they're more luxurious than the budget lodges, but they still share the same over-used patch of jungle. *Hotel Elephant Camp* (Kathmandu: ☎01/222823) offers two-night packages for $180; *Jungle Safari Camp* (Kathmandu :☎01/225615) charges $185 for two nights. See also *Hotel Narayani Safari*, p.193.

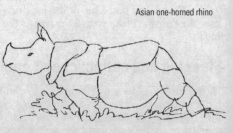
Asian one-horned rhino

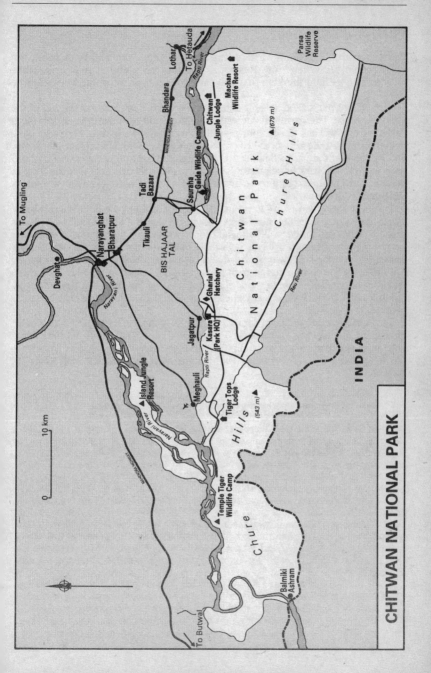

CHITWAN NATIONAL PARK

Park practicalities

Entry permits (Rs250) are valid for two days at a time, which tends to dictate the length of most travellers' stay. Rushed as it is, this can work out quite reasonably, but don't be led into thinking that you can "do" Chitwan in two nights and three days.

Permits are purchased at the ranger's office (daily 6am–5pm) to the left of the visitors' centre. The permit queue can be slow around opening time, so get there early. No one will ask to see your permit as you enter the park – there's no gate; you enter by wading across the river. Park **hours** are 6am to 6pm, but in practice you can stay in the park till sunset. **Camping** is by written permission only: you have to go to the park headquarters at Kasara, show the warden your itinerary in person, and give him 24 hours to alert the army squadron responsible for guarding that part of the park.

The best **safety tip** is not to go into the jungle without a guide. You probably won't even see a tiger, let alone be attacked by one, but rhinos and sloth bears present very real dangers. It's unusual for a year to go by without at least one tourist mauling, and a few locals invariably get gored during the January thatch-gathering. A rhino will lower its head and take a step back if it's about to charge; if it does, try to run in a zigzag path and throw off a piece of clothing (the rhino will stop to smell it) or better yet, climb the nearest big tree. If a bear charges, climb a *small* tree. Don't get anywhere near a mother with young ones of either species.

The **visitor centre** (daily 8am–5/6pm) has a modest but fairly informative display on the ecology of the park. The **maps** on the wall are useful for getting your bearings; park maps are completely unobtainable in Sauraha, so it's advisable to get one before you leave Kathmandu (see "Information and Maps" in *Basics*).

MAN VERSUS NATURE

It's an open question whether Chitwan has been blessed or cursed by its own riches. Its big game couldn't escape the notice of trigger-happy maharajas for long: when Jung Bahadur Rana overthrew the Shah dynasty in 1846, one of his first actions was to make Chitwan a private hunting preserve for rulers and visiting dignitaries. The following century saw some truly **hideous hunts** – King George V, during an eleven-day shoot in 1911, killed 39 tigers and 18 rhinos. In those days the technique, if you could call it that, was to send *shikaris* (trackers) into the forest to locate a tiger and set out a buffalo calf as bait. The sahibs were then alerted, loaded onto elephants and, joined by other huntsmen, the whole party of as many as 600 elephants and riders would approach the spot from all directions. As the circle closed, helpers would spread white sheets between the advancing elephants to keep the tiger from breaking through. High up in their *howdahs*, the sahibs could get off shots at point-blank range.

Still, the Ranas' patronage afforded Chitwan a certain degree of protection, as did malaria. That all changed in the early 1950s: the Ranas were thrown out, the monarchy restored, and the new government launched its malaria-control programme. Settlers poured in and **poaching** went unpoliced – rhinos, whose horns were (and still are) valued for Chinese medicine and Yemeni knife handles, were especially hard-hit. By 1960, the human population of the valley had trebled to 100,000, and

Activities in the park

Most activities take place in early morning or late afternoon, when wildlife-viewing is best. All of the following can, and in most cases should, be arranged through your lodge. It's essential to book the night before, or even earlier during the cut-throat months of October and November. All prices are fixed by the lodge association and are in addition to the Rs250 park entry fee.

Guided walks

Every lodge has its own **guides** – lads in their teens, they're some of the most keen, personable characters you'll meet in Nepal, on and off the job. English usually isn't a problem, although bear in mind that if your guide yells *look*, that means "hide" in Nepali! Guides' knowledge of species, especially birds, can be encyclopedic (much of it lifted from K. K. Gurung's *Heart of the Jungle* and Flemings' *Birds of Nepal* – see "Books" in *Contexts*). There are three levels of guide certification, the highest being "senior naturalist".

Walking is the best way to observe the park's prolific **bird life**. The region is an important stopover spot for migratory species in December and March, as well as home to many year-round residents – bring binoculars and look for parakeets, Indian rollers, paradise flycatchers, kingfishers, hornbills and ospreys. Walking is also a way to appreciate the **smaller attractions** of the jungle at your own pace: orchids, strangler figs, six-foot-high termite mounds, tiger scratchings, rhino droppings piled up like cannon balls. Experienced jungle-walkers say they get their best **animal sightings** on foot, but that can't apply when they've got four or five flat-footed neophytes in tow. Throw away that shopping list of animals; you have to be content with what's on offer. You *are* virtually guaranteed a rhino (probably several), and deer and monkeys are easy to spot, but tiger sightings are rare – maybe one or two a week.

the number of rhinos had been slashed from 800 to 200. With the Asian one-horned rhino on the verge of extinction, Nepal emerged as an unlikely hero in one of conservation's finest hours. Chitwan was set aside in 1964 as a **rhino sanctuary** (it became Nepal's first national park in 1973) and, despite the endless hype about tigers, it's rhinos that are Chitwan's biggest attraction and its greatest triumph.

Chitwan now boasts 400 one-horned rhinos – a quarter of the world population – and numbers are growing healthily. Thanks no doubt to the deployment of an entire army batallion in the park, poaching, which is such an intractable problem in Africa, is almost nil. About 60 **tigers** have been counted in the park; they, too, are on the rebound, and the establishment in 1984 of Parsa Wildlife Reserve, along Chitwan's western edge, secured a vital secondary habitat for them. Altogether, **51 species of mammals** are found in Chitwan, including four kinds of deer, langur, guar, sloth bear, leopard, the rare gangetic dolphin, and an elusive herd of wild elephants that stomp around the southeastern corner. Chitwan is also an important sanctuary for **birds**, with more than 400 species recorded, as well as two varieties of **crocodile**.

But Chitwan's see-saw battle for survival continues. As the population of the valley swells, conservationists are worried that the park will eventually fall as an obstacle to progress. Tourism has undoubtedly helped to stave off the siege by making animals and trees worth more alive than dead, but cynics argue that the price of victory might be turning Chitwan into a theme park.

For more detail on Tarai wildlife, see "Natural History" in Contexts.

Walks **cost** Rs60 per person for a morning and Rs150 for a full day with lunch, plus a few rupees for the guide's nominal entry fee. An all-day walk doesn't necessarily increase your chances of seeing game – most of the rhinos hang out close to Sauraha – but it gets you further into the park where you aren't running into other parties every two minutes. There's also the possibility of turning this into an entertaining **overnight** trip: walk 18km to KASARA (the park headquarters), exit the park to spend the night at JAGATPUR, and return the next day through the park via a different route.

One short walk you could probably chance **unguided** is to Isle Machaan, a hide overlooking a rhino wallow. The trail sets off from the visitor centre and runs parallel to the river southeastwards for half an hour.

Elephant rides

In terms of cost per hour the jeep's a better deal, but how often do you get to ride an elephant? The park keeps a dozen ridable animals and sends them out on one-hour trips at around 8am and 4pm; the **cost** is Rs200, plus an extra Rs25 for your lodge to arrange the trip for you. During slack times you can sign yourself up at the ranger's office at 6am for one of that day's rides, but normally the queue starts forming in the wee hours. A word of warning: the king has been known to spirit Chitwan's elephants away for months at a time for royal hunting expeditions.

The elephant's stately gait takes you back to a time, as recently as the early 1950s, when this was the way foreign delegations entered Nepal. The *phanit* (driver) sits astride the animal's neck, giving it commands with his toes and peri-

---

ASIAN ELEPHANTS

In Nepal and throughout southern Asia, elephants have been used as ceremonial transportation and beasts of burden for thousands of years, earning them a cherished place in the culture – witness the popularity of elephant-headed Ganesh, the darling of the Hindu pantheon. Thanks to this **symbiosis** with man, Asian elephants (unlike their African cousins) aren't seriously endangered, even though their native habitat has all but vanished.

With brains four times the size of humans', elephants are reckoned to be as **intelligent** as dolphins; recent research suggests they may communicate subsonically. What we see as a herd is in fact a complex social structure, consisting of bonded pairs and a fluid heirarchy, usually headed by a female. Though they appear docile, elephants have strongly individual personalities and moods. They can learn dozens of commands, but they won't obey just anyone – and as any handler will tell you, you can't make an elephant do what it doesn't want to do; that they submit to such cruel head-thumping by drivers seems to have more to do with thick skulls than obedience.

Asian elephants are smaller than those of the African species, but their statistics are still formidable. A bull can grow up to ten feet high and weigh four tons, although larger individuals are known to exist (see "Sukla Phanta Wildlife Reserve" for an account of the biggest elephant in Asia). An average day's intake is **50 gallons of water and 200kg of fodder** – and if you think that's impressive, wait till you see it come back out again. Life expectancy is seventy to eighty years and, much the same as with humans, an elephant's working life can be expected to run from its mid-teens to its mid-50s; since adolescence lasts so long, it's generally cheaper to capture wild elephants and train them rather than breed from females. One of the only elephant **breeding farms** in Nepal is located 4km west of Sauraha.

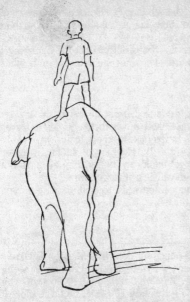

odically walloping its huge skull, and attentively fending branches out of passengers' way. An elephant is the only safe way to get around in the grasslands – especially in autumn, when the grass towers 8m high – and it's the best way to observe **rhinos** and possibly wild boar or sloth bear. Rhinos have terrible eyesight and rely on their keen sense of smell, but since the elephant's scent masks your own it's possible to approach quite close and without fear of attack. From the height of an elephant's back you get a clear view of these prehistoric tanks, with their armour-plated skin, twitching ears and highly coveted horns.

You can visit the government **hattisar** (elephant stables), a short walk from Sauraha. The best time to catch the elephants is mid-afternoon, when they're sure to be around for feeding time. In hot weather they're taken down to the river for a bath at midday – immensely photogenic.

Jeep rides . . . and gharial crocodiles

For some reason, vehicles don't seem to worry the animals much, although you're limited to the game you can see from dusty four-wheel-drive trucks, which pretty much means **deer**. A jeep ride is the closest thing to a tour of Chitwan, as it also takes in the park's two permanent sights, the gharial crocodile breeding project and Kasara Durbar, both about 20km west of Sauraha; nearby is Lami Tal, a prime spot for **birds**. The whole trip takes three or four hours and **costs** Rs200, plus Rs15 to see the gharials. Most lodges have their own jeep; the park only allows four or five in at a time, but as long as you book early enough your lodge will get you a seat on whichever jeep is going.

The longest of the world's crocodiles – adults can grow to more than 6m from nose to tail – the **gharial** is an awesome fishing machine. Its distended snout, about the size of a cricket bat and bristling with a fine mesh of teeth, snaps shut on its prey like a spring-loaded trap. Unfortunately for the gharial, its eggs are regarded as a delicacy, and males are hunted for their bulb-like snouts (*gharial* means bulb), which are believed to have medicinal powers.

In 1978, the world suddenly realised there were only 200 gharials left. Chitwan's **breeding project** was set up in 1980 to incubate eggs under controlled conditions, upping the survival rate, which is only one percent in the wild, to 35 percent. More than 300 hatchlings have been released, mainly into the Narayani River along the west side of the park, but it won't be possible to gauge success until females raised at the hatchery start laying eggs themselves, normally in their eighth year. As if the gharials didn't already have the deck stacked against them, they now face a new threat: in a classic case of one hand of the government not knowing what the other is doing, HMG has allowed the construction of two Chinese-sponsored **paper mills** on the Narayani upstream of Chitwan – with little or no effluent control. Biologists fear that chemicals released into the river from these mills, which started operating in 1989, will be the final nail in the gharials' coffin. So see them while you still can.

Kasara Durbar, now the park headquarters, was built in 1911 for George V's infamous hunt. Nearby is a meagre **museum**, with not much on offer besides animal skulls and pickled crocodiles.

River trips

Wooden canoes are moored at the end of the lane in front of the visitor centre. The set itinerary is to depart after breakfast, float down the Rapti River for 45 minutes and then walk back in time for lunch. It's mainly an opportunity for more **bird-watching**, but during the winter months the chances of seeing **mugger crocodiles** sunning themselves on the gravel banks are better than even. In hot weather the outing is less rewarding, and the walk's a sticky chore.

The canoe ride only **costs** Rs25, but the guided walk back is Rs50, plus you have to pitch in for the guide's boat ticket.

Activities outside the park

The so-called Rhino Patrol, the army's anti-poaching detachment, has effectively put a stop to off-road **walks** outside the park west of Sauraha. Eastwards, along the park boundary in the direction of *Gaida Wildlife Camp*, guides can show you an early-morning bird-watching route passing through BACHHAULI, the closest Tharu village to Sauraha.

Other day trips can be made by bike, rentable from a couple of shacks in Sauraha. **Bis Hajaar Tal** ("Twenty-Thousand Lakes"), 14km from Sauraha by road, is excellent for bird-watching in spring and autumn and a likely spot to see mugger crocs in winter. The name refers to the maze of oxbow lakes sprinkled in an untouristed enclave of *sal* forest. To get there, cycle to Tadi Bazaar, follow the highway 3km west to TIKAULI where it crosses a canal, then go southwest on a gravel road beside the canal for 5km. With a guide, you could take a more direct route to the lakes on foot, and there's also the option of continuing on to Kasara (see "Guided walks", above). More distant and completely out of the way are the waterfalls on the **Lothar Khola**, a contemplative spot with a healthy measure of birdlife; cycle or flag down a bus to LOTHAR, 30km east of Tadi, and from the bus stop walk ten minutes upstream. Halfway to Lothar, a jeep track just west of BHANDARA leads north to **BAIRENI**, a particularly well-preserved Tharu village.

Impromptu dance evenings are popular in Sauraha, and if possible be sure to catch a **Tharu stick dance**. A mock battle in which participants parry each other's sticks with graceful, split-second timing, the dance symbolises the drama of the hunter and his quarry. Performances are by prior arrangement, but in the high season one of the lodges will lay one on for a package group nearly every night.

Narayanghat, Bharatpur and Devghat

It's hard to travel very far in Nepal without at least passing through NARAYANGHAT: the construction of the Mugling–Narayanghat highway has made it the gateway to the Tarai and the busiest crossroads in the country. What was, a decade ago, a far-flung intersection is now a quarter-mile-long strip of diesel and *daal bhaat*, and it's said that real estate changes hands here for higher stakes than in Kathmandu. While the gods of progress smile on Narayanghat, **BHARATPUR**, its sister city to the east, though still the headquarters of Chitwan District, is fast becoming a ghost town. Unflattering as all that may sound, you may have occasion to stay, or at least eat, in the area; the side trip to Devghat should provide an incentive.

Buses to Pokhara and Devghat have their own bus park, at the north end of town on the road to Mugling. All others stop at the fast-food parade just east of Pulchowk (the intersection of the Mugling and Mahendra highways), except for minibuses to Tadi Bazaar, which start from Sanghamchowk (the next major intersection to the east). **Rikshas** will take you anywhere within the two towns for Rs5 or less.

For **lodging**, the most palatable budget option is *Hotel River View*, behind the Pokhara bus park, which really does have a river view (Rs40 single, Rs60 double; Rs80 double with bath). Near Sanghamchowk, *New Bisauni Guest House* charges Rs66 for a room with bath. Higher-class accommodation is available in Bharatpur at *Hotel Narayani Safari* (☎056/20130), which has air-conditioning, a pool and tennis courts (single $30, double $40). **Food**, plentiful but not wildly exciting, can be found around Pulchowk. Standing out slightly from the greasy spoons and whisky shacks are *Abhinandan Cafeteria* and *Fishtail Lodge and Restaurant*, with English menus and Indian/Chinese/"Continental" (ie everything with chips) food. *Hotel Narayani Safari*'s dining room does astonishingly good meals that run to about Rs150 a head.

Around Narayanghat: Devghat and the Kali Temple

DEVGHAT (or DEOGHAT), 5km northwest of Narayanghat, is a lot of people's idea of a great place to die. An astonishingly tranquil spot, it stands where the wooded hills meet the shimmering plains, and the blue-green Trisuli and the black Kali Gandaki merge to form the Narayani, one of the major tributaries of the Ganga (Ganges). The ashes of King Mahendra, the present king's father, were sprinkled at this sacred *tribeni* (a confluence of three rivers: wherever two rivers meet, a third, spiritual one is believed to join them), and scores of orthodox Hindus patiently live out their last days here hoping to achieve an equally auspicious death and rebirth. It's a sort of Hindu hospice – shady, contemplative but not at all morbid.

Buses shuttle between Narayanghat and Devghat hourly, taking about twenty minutes, but the more pleasant **footpath** that parallels the river through the woods doesn't take much longer. In either case, you come to the Trisuli and cross it by a footbridge, then bear left to the village. You can also cross the river further downsteam by **dugout canoe** – for the return to Narayanghat, the ferryman, if he thinks he can be spared from his duties, might consent to take you back for Rs25 or so.

Though dozens of small shrines lie dotted around the village, none is big or particularly interesting: you come here more for the atmosphere than the sights. Devghat is home of a well-known guru, the one-armed **Gauri Baba**, who gives audiences to serious seekers; a statue of his more famous predecessor, Galeswar Baba, is usually surrounded by a congregation of devotees. A huge **fair**, the *Tribeni Mela*, is held here on the new-moon day of January–February. At other times, *sadhus* and pilgrims do *puja* at the point where the rivers meet – cremations are also held here – and old-timers meditate outside their huts in the sun. Be sensitive to the residents, and don't disturb them or touch anything that might be holy: many are orthodox Brahmans and your touch would be polluting. There's **no lodging** at Devghat, but it probably wouldn't be appropriate to stay overnight anyway.

Given the right weather – cool and with good visibility – the **Kali Temple** on the hill west of Narayanghat could detain you for half a day or so. From Pulchowk, cross the bridge over the Narayani River to the village of GAINDAKOT, and a trail from there reaches the temple in 30–45 minutes. Animal sacrifices are held on Saturday, but the main attraction is the commanding **view** of Chitwan, Devghat and the Kali Gandaki surging through its final barrier before reaching the Tarai.

LUMBINI TARAI

Hordes of travellers hurry through this ancient part of the Tarai, west of Chitwan; few take the time to look around. It's best known, unfairly, for **Sunauli**, the main overland corridor to and from India. Yet only 20km away, seldom visited and utterly unhyped, is **Lumbini**, birthplace of Buddha and the site of ruins going back almost 3000 years.

Getting there isn't too difficult: two main highways – the Siddhartha and the Mahendra – connect the region with Pokhara and the rest of the Tarai, and buses to Sunauli, the border crossing here, are frequent. The journey to Lumbini is a bit fiddly, but well worth the extra effort. Accommodation and food here, as in most other parts of the Tarai, are readily available but usually very basic.

Butwal

Westwards from Narayanghat the Mahendra Highway runs across a washboard of cultivated fields, skirts the occasional cemetery of charred stumps and briefly climbs over a jungle-cloaked spur of the Chure Hills. The road is good and it's a relatively painless, if dull, three hours to **BUTWAL**. Crouching uninvitingly at the mouth of a canyon, Butwal is the hub of the Lumbini administrative zone: north lies Pokhara; south is Sunauli and the Indian border; and to the west, the Mahendra Highway barrels along to Nepalganj and, someday maybe, Nepal's far-western border.

Placed at the start of an important trade route to Tibet, as well as the pilgrim trail to Muktinath, the **tax post** at Butwal was for centuries a tidy little earner for Palpa (Tansen) and, later, Kathmandu. Later, it came to be an important staging post for Nepal's most lucrative export: Gurkha soldiers, bound for the recruiting office at Gorakhpur in India. In the early nineteenth century, Nepal and the East India Company fell into a dispute over the territory around Butwal, and the murder of some British police here touched off a two-year **war with Britain**. Nepal scored several improbable early victories here and elsewhere, but, outnumbered four to one, was eventually forced to surrender. Under the terms of the resulting treaty, the Tarai territories from Butwal west had to be ceded to the British (Nepal struck a deal to get the disputed land around Butwal back the same year). Any reminders of the past are, however, conspicuously absent in modern Butwal.

Practicalities

The **bus park** is at the west end of town, a few hundred metres south of the bridge over the Tinau River. However, buses that aren't starting or finishing at Butwal stop at "Traphik Chowk", a bazaar area on the Siddhartha Highway as it skirts the east side of town. If you need a **cheap room**, walk past *Hotel Sandeep* (where rooms are airless and overpriced) and make for *Butwal Guest House* at the big roundabout two blocks south of Traphik Chowk (Rs35 without bath, Rs50 with), or failing that, try *Santosh Guest House*, two blocks west of Traphik Chowk (Rs40/60). Butwal has a **posh hotel**, the *Sindoor* (✆073/20189), which, though stranded in an industrial wasteland just south of the bus park, has river views and a decent restaurant serving food at Kathmandu prices; rooms are $16 single, $24 double.

Bhairawa, Sunauli and the border

Half an hour south by bus, **BHAIRAWA** (officially, the name has been changed to SIDDHARTHANAGAR, but it's not catching on) is a virtual rerun of Butwal. The bazaar, located west of the main roundabout on the Siddhartha Highway, supports a sizeable minority of Muslim traders and, like so many border towns, exists mainly to peddle mundane western goods to acquisitive Indians.

As a base camp for Lumbini, though, it does the job, especially if the where's-the-party atmosphere of Sunauli isn't your style. The most pleasant way to **get to Lumbini** is **by bicycle**, which you should be able to rent informally at one of the repair shops in town. **Minibuses** start across the street to the north of *Hotel Yeti*.

For **lodging**, try – in descending order of price and hygiene – *Hotel Yeti* (✆071/20551) on the Siddhartha Highway (single with bath Rs220, double Rs275), *City Guest House* (Rs65/75 with bath, Rs35/45 without) or *Ratna Guest House* (Rs30/50 with bath, or Rs10 for a dorm bed), the latter two located in the bazaar. For **onward bus tickets** there are two competent agents near *Hotel Yeti*; all long-distance buses originate in Sunauli, but getting a seat from Bhairawa is no problem as long as you book it the day before.

Sunauli and the border

Four kilometres south of Bhairawa – Rs1.50 by tempo, Rs10 by slower riksha – **SUNAULI** (Soo-*no*-li) is the most convenient **border crossing** between Nepal and most parts of India. Bus/train package deals to or from India usually involve an overnight here (see the "On from Kathmandu" section in Chapter One for more on these). It's a good place to glean information from travellers coming the other way or meet up with people going the same way, but when the bus leaves the next morning you'll want to be on it.

For **accommodation**, *Hotel Jay Vijay* (Rs40 for rooms with bath, Rs70 with hot shower) is the best of a motley selection. *Hotel Mamta* (Rs75 with cold shower, Rs50 without), coasting on package business from Kathmandu and Pokhara, is awful. Lodging on the India side is even worse. The **food** in Sunauli isn't bad – whichever way you're heading, the menus give a taste of what's in store further on – and you can choose from the hotel restaurants or the so-so *Gorkha Restaurant*.

As a funnel for traffic from India, Sunauli is well served by **buses**, but be sure to book ahead, since an empty seat in Sunauli might be spoken for in Bhairawa. For onward tickets or general advice, *Hotel Mamta* has its own travel agent.

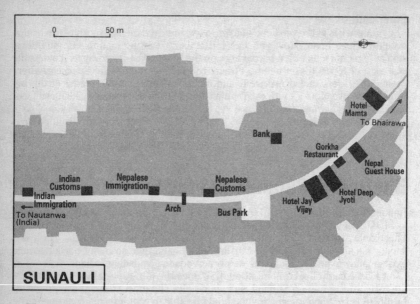

SUNAULI

The **bank** on the Nepal side is open daily from 7.30am to 6pm, but the one on the Indian side doesn't open till 10am, after most buses have left. The **money-changers** in Sunauli don't give a speck over the official rate, so if you're entering Nepal wait till Kathmandu to do any serious changing (but if you're leaving Nepal, see *Basics* for advice on changing money back); Indian rupees are readily accepted in Sunauli but not beyond. Figure on half an hour to get through Nepalese and Indian **border formalities**, and remember that Nepal **time** is fifteen minutes ahead of India. The offers of riksha rides aren't to be taken seriously, since from start to finish it's only a distance of about 200m.

Lumbini

After I am no more, Ananda! Men of belief will visit with faithful curiosity and devotion to the four places – where I was born . . . attained enlightenment . . . gave the first sermons . . . and passed into Nirvana.

Buddha (c. 543–463 BC)

For the world's 300 million Buddhists, **LUMBINI** is where it all began. **Buddha's birthplace** is arguably the single most important historical site in Nepal, and not only the source of one of the world's great religions but also the centre of Nepal's most significant **archaeological finds**, dating from the third century BC. Little-visited and positively oozing with serenity, it's the kind of place you could whizz round in two hours or soak up for days.

Buddha has long been a prophet without much honour in his own country: the area around Lumbini is now predominantly Muslim, while the main local **festival** is a Hindu one, commemorating Buddha as the ninth incarnation of Vishnu – it's held on the full moon of the Nepalese month of *Baisakh* (April–May). Celebrations of **Buddha Jayanti** (Buddha's birthday) are comparatively meagre because, the local monks will tell you with visible disgust, Buddhists from the hills think Lumbini is too hot in May. But big changes may be in store. The government has set aside a huge tract of land for a wildly ambitious **pilgrimage centre** consisting of monasteries, cultural facilities, gardens, fountains and a tourist village. Far-fetched as it sounds, the project has the backing of the United Nations and has raised piles of cash from Japan and Korea; two buildings and acres of landscaping have already been completed. If the remaining plans come off, Lumbini will be a radically different place in a few years' time. Should we be cynical? With Nepal, you never know . . .

Practicalities

Dust off your Buddhist tolerance (or fork out Rs300 for a taxi), because **connections** to Lumbini are slow. Twice-hourly minibuses from Bhairawa take an interminable two hours and leave you to walk the last 1km; last bus back is 5.30pm and you have to meet it on the main road where it dropped you off. Rikshas are more expensive (Rs40) and no faster, though less crowded. If possible – and if it's not too hot – **go by bike**: head west out of Bhairawa and keep your eyes peeled for the little blue signs, bearing left at a fork after 20km and turning right on a dirt track about 2km later.

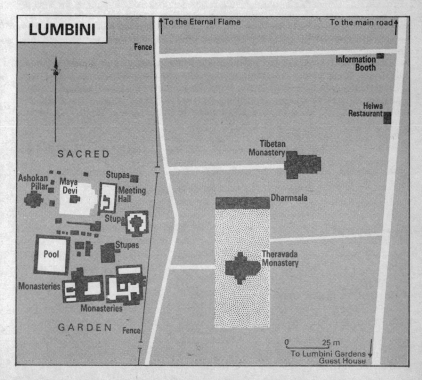

The sight that greeted visitors in 1990 – blame the Lumbini Development Trust if it's different when you get there – was a billboard map of the "Lumbini Master Plan", a vestigial **tourist information** booth, the primitive *Heiwa Restaurant* and the rear of one of Lumbini's two monasteries. The *Heiwa* is the only source of hot **food** around the ruins, and its Nep-Jap menu reflects the usual clientele. The **lodging** situation is equally thin, but for a cheap stay try the *dharmsala* (pilgrims' lodging), tranquilly set in a mango garden between the two monasteries but sorely lacking in things like clean toilets or washing facilities (price is a donation: they seem happy with Rs25 per person). Literally the only other option is the almost-posh *Lumbini Gardens Guest House* (Kathmandu: ☎01/215322), hidden a good kilometre up the lane past the "master plan" map and correspondingly further from the birthplace grounds ($14 single, $20 double). If you don't mind the walk, their restaurant beats the *Heiwa* for taste, if not atmosphere.

BUDDHA: A LIFE

The year of Buddha's **birth** is disputed – it was probably 543 BC – but it's generally agreed that it happened at Lumbini while his mother, Maya Devi, was on her way to her maternal home for the delivery. He was born Gautama Siddhartha ("he who has accomplished his aim"), the son of a king and a member of the Sakya clan, who ruled the central Tarai from their capital at Kapilvastu (see "Tilaurakot", below). Brought up in his father's palace, Gautama lived a sheltered life until, at the age of 29, he made a fateful trip into town where, according to legend, he encountered an old man, a sick man, a corpse and a hermit: old age, sickness and death were the end of life, he realised, and contemplation seemed the only way to understand the nature of suffering.

Gautama fled the palace and spent five years as an ascetic before concluding that self-denial brought him no closer to the truth than self-indulgence. Under the famous *bodhi* tree of Bodh Gaya in India, he vowed to keep meditating until he attained **enlightenment**. It took 49 days, and Gautama became the Buddha, released from the cycle of birth and death. He made his way to Sarnath (near modern Varanasi in India) and preached his **first sermon**, setting in motion, Buddhists believe, *dharma*, the wheel of the truth. Although he's said to have returned to Kapilvastu to convert his family, and according to some stories he put in an appearance in the Kathmandu Valley, Buddha spent most of the rest of his life preaching in northern India. He **died** at the age of 80 in Kasia (Kushinagar), about 100km southeast of Lumbini. For a full explanation of Buddhism, see "Religion" in *Contexts*.

The Sacred Garden

A stone's throw west of the information booth, the **"Sacred Garden"** where Buddha was born contains all of Lumbini's treasures in an area no bigger than a football pitch. By all accounts a well-tended grove in Buddha's day, the spot was consecrated soon after his death, and at least one monastery was attached to it by the third century BC when Ashoka, the great north Indian emperor and Buddhist evangelist, made a well-documented pilgrimage to the spot. Ashoka's patronage established a thriving religious community, but by the time the intrepid Chinese traveller Hiuen Tsang visited in the seventh century it was limping, and must have died out after the ninth century.

The garden was lost for 600 years and its **rediscovery**, in 1895, was one of the greatest (and luckiest) finds of the century. Armed with ancient and often contradictory accounts, the German archaeologist R. A. Führer had managed in the previous year to unearth some separate but related relics near Taulihawa. Believing he was on the Buddha's trail, he arranged to return to the same spot, but at the last minute his Nepali escort requested a more convenient meeting place about 25km to the east. By sheer coincidence, the party made camp practically on top of the garden; while Führer slept, a porter – no doubt answering the call of nature – stumbled upon the ruins, which had been obscured by thick jungle.

The centrepiece of the site is the slab-featured, and frankly unattractive, **Maya Devi Mandir**. Yet the temple's appearance belies great antiquity: the ornate brickwork on the west side dates the building to the Indian Gupta period (fourth to seventh centuries), and it's likely that it was built on the site of an even earlier structure. Tragically, the gigantic pipal (*bodhi*) tree arching over the entrance is due to be cut down because its roots are interfering with the monuments. Inside is a bas-relief sculpture of Buddha's birth that may be as old as the third century BC – so worn are the features, from centuries of *puja*, that Führer at first dismissed the temple as Hindu because locals were worshipping the image as Tathagata, a fertility goddess. A recent replica reconstructs the tableau: Maya Devi, Buddha's mother, grasping a tree branch for support, a tiny Buddha standing fully formed at her feet, and (ecumenical, this)

Buddha's birth

the Hindu gods Indra and Brahma looking on. The sculpture illustrates an elaborate Buddhist nativity story, according to which the baby Buddha leapt out of the womb, took seven steps and proclaimed his world-saving destiny. The square, brick-sided **pool** beside the temple is supposed to be where Maya Devi bathed after the delivery.

West of the temple, the **Ashokan Pillar** is the oldest monument in Nepal. Again, it's not much to look at – fenced in and capped with concrete, it looks like chimney – but the inscription (also Nepal's oldest), recording Ashoka's visit in 249 BC, is the best evidence available that Buddha was born here. Pillars were a sort of trademark of Ashoka, serving the dual purpose of spreading the faith and marking the boundaries of his empire: this one announces that Ashoka granted Lumbini tax-free status in honour of Buddha's birth. The heavily restored brick **foundations** of buildings and stupas around the site, dating from the second century BC to the ninth century AD, chart the rise and fall of Lumbini's early monastic community.

Two active **monasteries** face the Sacred Garden and are open to the public; neither is very old, and like all the modern buildings in the area they're slated for demolition to make way for the master plan (their monks are promised bigger and better premises in the new Lumbini). The soaring **Tibetan monastery** displays a typical array of prematurely-aged frescos and gilded Buddhas and *bodhisattvas* in glass cabinets; a handful of monks chant in early morning and mid-afternoon. The more austere **Theravada** establishment attached to the *dharmsala* offers less to look at, but one of its two gold-robed monks speaks good English.

A walk northwards from the Maya Devi temple, pleasant for its own sake, hits the highlights of the slowly unfurling master plan. The elevated path passes through what will be a reflecting pool encircling the Sacred Garden, and beyond is an **eternal flame**, a fitting remembrance of the "Light of Asia". From here you can follow the kilometre-long central canal past the future locations of the East and West Monastic Centres: no sign of them yet, but the canal is alive with bird-life – around sunset, flocks of parakeets whistle past with a sound like boome-rangs. Work is further along on **"Lumbini Village"** at the north end of the canal; at the time of writing, the Korean-built museum and library were in place (but forlornly vacant), while the auditorium, hotels, restaurants and shops remained stubbornly on paper.

Tilaurakot

A dusty 24km west of Lumbini, **TILAURAKOT** is believed to have been the capi-tal of ancient Kapilvastu, Buddha's childhood home. Although it's yielded up far more ruins and relics than Lumbini, due to its back-of-beyond location it's recom-mended only for die-hard archaeology buffs. On a bicycle you could get there from Lumbini in not much more than an hour, going west at the fork north of Lumbini and north at TAULIHAWA; going by public transport, however, you're stuck with the twice-daily minibus from Bhairawa to Taulihawa, which takes a good four hours and leaves you with a 2km walk from there. Food and lodging is available only at Taulihawa, and it's very basic.

The Tilaurakot **excavations** have unearthed the remains of a palace, consist-ing of thick fortress walls, four gates, a moat and a couple of giant stupa bases. At least thirteen layers of human habitation have been found, going back to the ninth century BC. A small **museum** displays some of the 3000 coins found in the area (including one bearing the Sakya name), together with pottery and toys.

THE FAR WEST

If the far west has anything to offer, it's adventure. Beyond Butwal you get the immediate sensation of leaving the beaten track; west of Nepalganj, unless you go with a tour, you're practically bushwhacking.

For travellers, the remoteness of the region has actually increased in recent years due to the closing of the far-western border crossing: Mahendranagar, once only six hours from Delhi, can now be reached only by an horrendous two-day judder from Kathmandu. Construction work on the final far-western section of the **Mahendra Highway** hasn't helped, turning a 200-kilometre stretch of tolerably bad road into a nightmare. The worst of the job was supposed to have been finished by 1991, but delays appear inevitable and it looks like overlanders can expect hellish journeys west of **Nepalganj** for a few years yet. Over the long term, a fast link with the rest of the country will bring enormous changes to the far west – mostly positive ones, it appears, although it's impossible to say whether it will have been worth the vast cost.

In the meantime, if you're willing to brave it, the far west offers two remote and unspoiled wildlife parks, **Bardia National Park** and **Sukla Phanta Wildlife Reserve**. So far they've only been developed by a couple of Chitwan-style luxury safari operators, but with proper preparation they can be done on a shoestring.

Nepalganj and Birendranagar

The Mahendra Highway, new and admirably smooth in this section, makes good time to Nepalganj, crossing a spur of the Chure Hills and following the pleasingly rural Rapti Valley (no relation to the river of the same name in Chitwan). North of here lies Dang, home of the white-clad Dangaura Tharus and, by the look of it, fine cycling country. Nearing Nepalganj on the main highway, the hills to the south peter out and the bleached vastness of the Indian plains flattens the spirit.

Nepalganj

Trade and transport hub of the far west – for what little trade and transport there *is* in the far west – **NEPALGANJ** is, more interestingly, Nepal's most **Muslim city**. The presence of Muslims in the Tarai is hardly surprising, of course, since the border with India, where Muslims comprise a large minority, was only determined in the nineteenth century. Until just prior to the 1814–16 war with the British, this part of the Tarai belonged to the Nawab of Oudh, one of India's biggest landowners; after Nepal's defeat it was ceded to the East India Company and only returned to Nepal as a goodwill gesture for services rendered during the Indian Mutiny of 1857. A fair few Muslims fled to Nepalganj during the mutiny – Lucknow, where the most violent incidents occurred, is due south of here – and others filtered in during the Rana years, seeing opportunities for cross-border trade. The result is a permanent Muslim community, self-contained but maintaining business and family links with India – indeed, the entire city feels overwhelmingly Indian, with its cheap neo-Mughal architecture and frenetically mundane bazaar. Imperious warnings against trade in Indian rupees ("by order of the Nepal Rastra Bank") are a further reminder that India is just 6km down the road.

Nepalganj sprawls more than a city of 50,000 should; lately its numbers have been swollen by labourers and project managers working on the Mahendra Highway. Its heart is **Tribhuwan Chowk**, the lively but dilapidated intersection of the city's two main shopping thoroughfares, south of which rikshas wait beneath an Indian-style Hindu temple that sits in the middle of the road like a toll booth. The **Muslim quarter** lies northeast of Tribhuwan Chowk – "picturesque" is probably too strong a word, but one canopy-shaded section is almost like a souk, with bearded traders done up in crocheted caps and pyjama-like clothes, and transactions conducted on wooden benches in the street. The mosques in this area are disappointingly modern, and at any rate out of bounds to nonbelievers. Hindu worship and trade is centred around the nondescript **Bageshwari Mandir**; behind the temple is a large pool with a jaunty statue of Mahadev (Shiva) in the middle – marvellously kitsch.

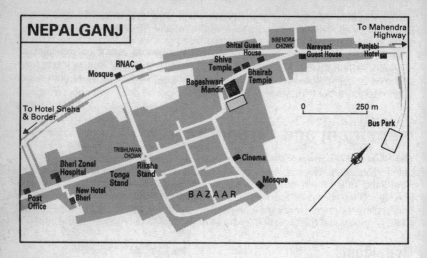

Practicalities

Hardly anybody sets out to see Nepalganj, but a few people heading further west end up spending an unintended night here – if you're flying to any of the far-western airstrips there'll be a change in Nepalganj and, all too often, some problem or other with the onward flight. Nepalganj's **airport** (see below for details), the country's second-busiest, is a six-kilometre plod north of town by *tonga* (horse-drawn cart) or riksha. The **bus park** has been inconveniently banished to the extreme north end of the city, and it might be a good idea to buy an onward ticket when you arrive to avoid the extra trip later on.

Nepalganj has a surprisingly good selection of **accommodation**, though there's nothing fancy. Top of the line is *Hotel Sneha* (☎081/20119), a favourite with Western project workers (Rs125 single, Rs175 double, all with bath; Rs25 to camp on the lawn), while *New Hotel Bheri* runs a distant second in this price range (Rs200 for a double with bath). Closer to town but correspondingly noisier, several cheap lodges are grouped between the Bageshwari temple and Birendra Chowk. Best of these are *Shital Guest House* (Rs35 for a double without bath) and *Narayani Guest House* (Rs60); the proprietor at the latter may be able to fix you up with a bicycle.

If you don't speak Nepali, **eating** in Nepalganj is pretty much a smile-and-point operation at roadside carts or *daal bhaat pasaals*. North of the Bageshwari temple, a couple of holes in the wall run by displaced Sherpas and Humla Bhotiyas do terrific *momos*, but that's all they do. Near the bus park, the popular and efficient *Punjabi Hotel* – there's no English sign, but it's next door to Bageshwari Motors – specialises in "daal-fried-roti" and fish curry. The *Sneha*'s restaurant serves decent Western food, but it's not worth a special trip if you're not staying there.

Onwards: flights

If you're moving any further west, consider **flying**: western Nepal is where *RNAC's* domestic service really comes into its own, and Nepalganj is the hub for all flights in the region. The $77 Mahendranagar flight is worth every penny to avoid an appalling 20-hour bus journey, and if you're planning to trek around Jumla ($77) or Simikot ($88), flying from Nepalganj saves a good deal of money over flying from Kathmandu. (The Kathmandu–Nepalganj fare is $99.) **RNAC's office** (☎081/21205; Sun–Fri 8am–4pm, Sat 8am–noon) is out on the highway that bypasses town, west of Tribhuwan Chowk. The queue for tickets starts forming before 8am; *RNAC* makes more money filling planes with shop wares than passengers, so be prepared to fight for a ticket.

Birendranagar (Surkhet)

Ninety kilometres northwest of Nepalganj – too far off the beaten track for most – **BIRENDRANAGAR** (as often as not called by its old name, **SURKHET**) comes as a pleasant surprise. Placed in the middle of an undulating *dun* valley, it's neither as hot, flat nor Indian as towns closer to the border. It's also managed to escape the usual shabby fate of Tarai boomtowns, thanks, surprisingly, to government planning – HMG is in the process of transferring the western regional headquarters from Nepalganj to here, a move that's creating plenty of jobs and trade. A good deal of development effort is going into the valley, too, led by a big Canadian IRDP (integrated rural development project) and a gaggle of Peace Corps, VSO and other volunteers.

You might find yourself in Birendranagar for the start of a trek – from here it's a week to Rara Lake – or to raft in the Bheri River, which is half an hour south of town. By **bus**, it's a rugged six-hour trip from Nepalganj, but the road is being improved all the time. It doesn't seem to have been tried yet, but the trip would make an excellent one-day ride on a **mountain bike** – and once here, the bike would come in handy for getting around the valley. A trekking permit is required for travel north of the valley.

The must-see of the area is 2km out of town on a wooded knoll in the middle of the valley: **Karki Bihar** houses the remains of an ancient Buddhist temple, and the surrounding forest contains deer and (supposedly) leopards. In town, the only real attraction is **Bulbule Tal**, a new but agreeably cool and shady park that's good for bird-watching. **Food and lodging** is of the most basic sort here, with only one hotel, the *Rada*. For help, the best tactic might be to latch onto one of the many Western aid workers.

Bardia National Park

With Chitwan becoming increasingly mass-market, **BARDIA NATIONAL PARK**, northwest of Nepalganj, beckons as an unspoiled alternative. In many ways, it's what Chitwan used to be: hard to get to and still barely developed, it's the largest area of undisturbed wilderness left in the Tarai; only one tented camp operates inside the park, with a sister lodge outside, both charging upscale rates. Sauraha-style budget accommodation is absent, but camping is allowed.

A wildlife reserve since the 1970s, Bardia was upgraded in 1988 to a national park – Nepal's newest. Ecologically, it spans the same subtropical habitats as Chitwan, from dry hills and *sal* stands to thick riverine forest and grassland. Nepal's biggest river, the awesome **Karnali**, forms the park's western boundary and major watering hole, and the density of wildlife and birds along this western edge is second only to Chitwan.

Bardia's star species is the **blackbuck**, an uncommonly graceful antelope with corkscrew horns, found in greater numbers here than anywhere else. Langurs, wild boar and deer are seen everywhere, and at least twenty **tigers*** live in the park – as in Chitwan, the chances of seeing one are slim – along with leopards, sloth bears and assorted other nocturnal creatures. **Rhinos**, hunted to extinction in Bardia in this century, were reintroduced in 1986 and appear to be flourishing; a small herd of **wild elephants** often crashes around the western side of the park. The Karnali River is probably the best place in Nepal to get a peep at rare **gangetic dolphins**, which favour the river's deep channels, and **mahseer**, a sporting fish that can weigh up to 40kg; mugger (and with a lot of luck, gharial) crocodiles might also be spotted in winter. The commonest sight of all around Bardia are **termite mounds**, looking like sand-coloured volcanoes, which reach their greatest height – up to eight feet – here.

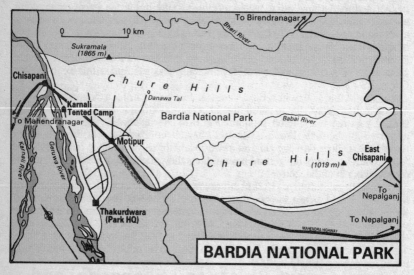

BARDIA NATIONAL PARK

Bardia on $110 a day

The easy way to do Bardia is to book a **luxury package** at *Karnali Tented Camp* or *Karnali Lodge* (Kathmandu: ☎01/222706), both run by the same company that owns *Tiger Tops* in Chitwan. A fraction of the price (but still a hefty $110 a night, plus $50 for the transfer to and from Nepalganj), the *Karnali* outfits are strong on nature interpretation and geared for genuine enthusiasts. The lodge does elephant rides and sightseeing tours to a nearby Tharu village, while the tented camp, overlooking the mighty Karnali, serves as the base for jeep rides, bird walks and raft trips. It's the only wildlife camp in Nepal that still **baits tigers** by tying a buffalo calf to a stake each evening; if a tiger takes the bait, guests rush to

---

* Though protected by international agreement as an endangered species, tigers aren't always safe: the king of Nepal still uses Bardia for private hunts, and in 1989 he bagged a tiger here.

a nearby blind to watch the kill by spotlight. The practice is now discouraged by the Nepalese government.

Bardia on a budget

Doing Bardia independently would be a challenge – at the time of writing, no foreigners had ever tried it, although the park warden has a fee structure all worked out just in case. If you give it a go, let us know.

As with so many remote parts of the Tarai, a **mountain bike** would spare you a lot of hassles: in this case, it could turn a ratty four-hour bus ride and a dangerous walk through jungle into an exciting full-day ride. Head north on the paved road from Nepalganj towards Birendranagar, make a left at EAST CHISAPANI (about 8km north of the Mahendra Highway roundabout, where the forest starts), and from there it's a matter of following the track for 60km or so along the park boundary – passing a couple of unmodernised Tharu villages en route – to the headquarters at **THAKURDWARA**.

Without wheels, you'll have to board a westbound **bus** from Nepalganj and ask to be let off at the MOTIPUR guard post, from which it's a two- or three-hour walk on a dirt track to Thakurdwara. (The park HQ is supposed to be moved to Motipur when this section of the Mahendra Highway is completed, possibly as early as 1991.)

Thakurdwara isn't even remotely set up for visitors, so you'll have to be self-sufficient for the entire time you're there. Check in with the warden, who'll assign you a campsite nearby. Park **admission** is Rs250 and the **camping fee** is another Rs100 per person per night – a high price to pay for zero facilities, but it probably reflects the true environmental cost of using the park more accurately than the room charges at Chitwan's Sauraha village. Located in a game-rich corner of the park near the Karnali River, Thakurdwara is well-placed as a base from which to see the park, but **getting around** may be a problem: ask about **elephant rides** which, when available, are supposed to cost Rs60. **Guides** can be hired through the warden's office, and although none speak English they can at least lead you to wildlife and keep you out of harm's way.

The wild west: Chisapani, Dhangadhi and Mahendranagar

While it's under construction, the Mahendra Highway from Nepalganj west to Dhangadhi is the **worst bus ride in Nepal**. It takes sixteen hours to cover 200km, most of the time spent bucking along beside the half-finished highway and sloshing past half-finished bridges. Countless streams – trickles in winter, impassable torrents in the monsoon – dice the route, and the misery of fording each one makes you realise that the challenge of the Mahendra Highway is mainly one of bridge-building.

The halfway point is **CHISAPANI**, where the road veers north to cross the Karnali River, surging out of a gap in the rugged foothills, at its narrowest point. A state-of-the-art, single-span suspension **bridge**, the longest of its kind in the world, is under construction here with World Bank money (completion 1991 at the earliest). A lot is riding on the project: the first fixed link with the rest of the country, it will open up the often neglected far west to development, but while most agree that development here is a Good Thing, some are questioning why the government and aid agencies are building a Rolls Royce of a bridge for a Mini of a road. In the meantime, a decidedly low-tech cable **ferry** makes the crossing, two vehicles at a time, between 10am and 6pm.

The World Bank has its hand in another, even bigger project 1km upstream – the **Karnali Dam**, surveyed in detail but shelved for the moment, would (if fully configured) be the biggest hydroelectric dam in the world. Environmentalists argue that the project would destroy one of the last remaining habitats of the gharial crocodile; if you take a walk north of town you stand a good chance of seeing one (for more on gharials, see the Chitwan section). Another, longer walk starts from the east bank of the river, heading north and then east up to the crest of the ridge that forms the northern boundary of Bardia National Park.

Overlooking the forested west bank of the river, Chisapani's polyglot little **bazaar** does a steady trade with shoppers from the hills, some of whom walk a week or more to buy basic provisions here. If you're stuck or you just can't hack the bus anymore, there are a few makeshift **bunkhouses** at the west end of the bazaar.

Another 100km west and back out of the trees, **DHANGADHI** is a flatter, duller and altogether more conventional border town sitting 12km south of the highway, off a paved spur road to India – unless you're catching a bus from here, there's little reason to go. The **bus park** is about 400m east of the main roundabout on the India road, and the breezeblock bazaar about 1km east of that. The **airstrip** ($149 to Kathmandu) lies 10km north of town on the way back to the highway – rikshas are plentiful – and the **RNAC office** (☎091/21205; Sun–Fri 8am–4pm, Sat 8am–noon) stands by the main roundabout. **Lodgings** are pretty grim, the most palatable being *Hotel Taruan & Lodge* in the bazaar (just opposite the *Jesus Bookstore*!), where a double room is Rs40.

Westwards from the Dhangadhi turn-off, the highway is paved and the bus is once again a bearable option. At the end of the line is **MAHENDRANAGAR**, another tawdry border town but with a good deal of spark, thanks to daytripping shoppers who stream in on the good road from India. The town is laid out in an unusually logical grid south of the highway; with the **bus park** at the northwest end and the **airstrip** a long, clattering riksha ride to the southwest, almost at the entrance to Sukla Phanta Wildlife Reserve (see below). **Lodging** is clustered along the street one block east of the road into town: *Samjhana Hotel & Lodge* is Mahendranagar's finest (Rs75 double, Rs20 dorm bed), while *Gauri Hotel* and *Mahakali Hotel & Lodge* (both Rs40 double) are less clean but tolerable. The **RNAC office** (☎20196; erratic hours) is on the same street. **Eateries** around the hotels and along the main east–west drag do a fair range of Nepali meals, snacks and Indian sweets.

Mahendranagar's bustle is only a border aberration, though, and the outlying region is one of the most traditional parts of the Tarai. Tharu sharecroppers work the fields, maintaining an apparently happy symbiosis with their old-money landlords, and their **villages**, scattered along dirt tracks north of the Mahendra Highway, still consist of traditional communal longhouses. Villagers go completely over the top for visitors and positively preen for the camera – a Polaroid would be a *big* hit – but it's bad manners to breeze in without at least enough Nepali to repay them with thanks and a little conversation.

Sukla Phanta Wildlife Reserve

In Nepal's extreme southwest, a different feature appears on the land: *phantas*, great swathes of natural grassland that could almost be mistaken, albeit on a smaller scale, for the savannahs of East Africa. **SUKLA PHANTA WILDLIFE RESERVE**, south of Mahendranagar, is dotted with them, and touring it is, for once, really like being on safari. The reserve is home to the world's largest population of **swamp deer** – sightings of 1000 at a time are common – and a herd of **wild elephants**.

Practicalities

The reserve entrance is within sight of Mahendranagar's airstrip; **RNAC flies** once a week from Kathmandu ($160) and up to three times a week from Nepalganj ($77). Alternatively, fly to Dhangadhi (twice a week from Kathmandu, $149) and take the bus the rest of the way. From Mahendranagar, the reserve entrance is reached by riksha and is 1km beyond the airstrip.

As with Bardia, there's an easy way and a hard way to visit Sukla Phanta, and the easy way involves more money – still, even if you hate the idea of a **luxury safari**, this might be the place to do one. An unpretentious family outfit, *Silent Safari* (Kathmandu: ☎01/418755) runs customised trips for much less than the cost of most Chitwan group packages (about $65 a night). *Silent Safari* is a man – Col. Hikmat Bisht, former hunter, retired military attaché, patrician landowner and self-styled man of the forest – and a trip with him is one of the most delightfully idiosyncratic experiences in Nepal. His **tented camp** is pitched next to a waterhole in deep jungle – real Tarzan country – and there's also the unique opportunity to spend a night or two in a *machaan* (tree-top blind) for nocturnal sights and sounds.

Doing Sukla Phanta **on the cheap** isn't impossible, but you have to be pretty resourceful. The stumbling block is **transport** within the reserve, since pedestrians and cyclists aren't allowed (the guards don't want a mauling on their hands; well, it *is* a jungle out there). Elephants, which are theoretically for hire, would in any case only be good for short forays. You really need a vehicle, preferably a jeep – which is the only feasible way to track game across the *phantas* – but there aren't even any taxis in Mahendranagar, and your chances of hitching a ride are as slim as the visitor's book. You could try offering money around town, or you might be lucky and meet up with an expat engineer going for a weekend break; if you manage to crack it, the **entry fee** is Rs250 and **camping** is Rs100 per person per night. Sleeping in the open isn't recommended, but the towers at Rani Tal and Sukla Phanta would make superb shelters. The nearest **food** is in Mahendranagar.

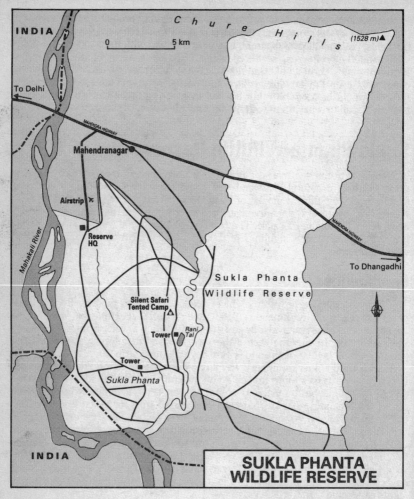

INDIA

C h u r e   *H i l l s*   (1528 m)▲

To Delhi

MAHENDRA HIGHWAY

Mahendranagar ●

Airstrip ✈

Mahakali River

Reserve HQ

MAHENDRA HIGHWAY

To Dhangadhi

S u k l a   P h a n t a
W i l d l i f e   R e s e r v e

Silent Safari Tented Camp △

Tower ■   *Rani Tal*

Tower ■

Sukla Phanta

INDIA

**SUKLA PHANTA
WILDLIFE RESERVE**

The reserve

Several four-wheel drive tracks crisscross the reserve, making itineraries flexible, but first stop is bound to be *the* **Sukla Phanta** at the southwestern end, a rippling sea of grass which turns silvery-white in October (*sukila* means white in the local Tharu dialect). You're guaranteed **swamp deer** here, and in quantity – make for the view tower in the middle and scan for them with binoculars. As *barasingha* ("twelve points"), the swamp deer was one of Kipling's beloved *Jungle Book* animals – "that big deer which is like our red deer, but stronger" – and common throughout the plains and hills; today it's an endangered species, finding safety in numbers in the *phantas* and particularly the boggy parts where seasonal fires don't burn off the grasses. **Tigers** make occasional kills, but **poachers** present the greatest threat: the reserve has a chronic poaching problem, and the sound of gunshots coming from the southern (Indian) end is distressingly frequent. Although guards have orders to shoot poachers on sight, they're pretty toothless without a vehicle . . .

Having seen your obligatory *phanta*, make a beeline for **Rani Tal** (Queen's Lake), near the centre of the reserve. Surrounded by riotous, screeching forest, the lake – really, a lagoon – is like a prehistoric time capsule, with trees leaning out over the shore, deer wading shoulder-deep around the edges and crocodiles occasionally peering out of the lotus-littered water. The **bird life** is like nothing you've ever seen, a dazzling display of cranes, cormorants, eagles and scores of others. You can watch all the comings and goings from a tower by the western shore. Nearby is an overgrown **brick circle**, a mile in circumference, which locals say was the fort of Singpal, an ancient Tharu king (Rani Tal is said to have been his queen's favourite spot); the fact that the remains have never been excavated shows how little historical research has been done in western Nepal.

Though you'd think they'd be hard to miss, chances are Sukla Phanta's **elephant herd** will give you the slip – they spend winters south of the border, feasting on sugar cane. Evidence of their passage is abundant, however, especially along the road south from the entrance, where in places the forest looks like it's been hit by a tornado. The dominant male, dubbed **Thulo Hatti** ("Big Elephant"), leaves footprints nearly two feet in diameter; based on what few sightings have been made, he's estimated to stand eleven feet tall at the shoulder, weigh over five tons, and have tusks a metre long, making him the biggest Asian elephant alive.

festivals

In addition to the following local festivals, *Dasain* (known as *Dashera* near India), *Tihar* (*Diwali*), *Shiva Raatri* and *Holi* are celebrated in most Tarai areas.

Tribeni Mela Pilgrimage to Devghat on the day of the first new moon in January–February.

Vishnu Jaatra Celebration of Buddha as an incarnation of Vishnu at Lumbini on the full moon of April–May.

Buddha Jayanti Anniversary of Buddha's birth, enlightenment and death, held at Lumbini (May).

Jithiya Similar to *Tij* (see "Festivals" in Chapter Two), a festival for women celebrated in Tharu villages on the full moon during October–November.

travel details

Buses

From Narayanghat to Bhairawa (daily; 4hr); Devghat (hourly; 20min); Gorkha (2 daily; 4hr); Pokhara (5 daily; 4hr) and Tadi Bazaar (frequent; 45min). These buses all originate in Narayanghat, though countless others stop on their way through.

From Butwal to Kathmandu (7 daily; 8hr); Nepalganj (9 daily; 6hr); Pokhara (10 daily; 7hr); Sunauli (frequent; 1hr) and Tansen (7 daily; 2hr).

From Bhairawa to Kathmandu (*Sajha*: 2 daily; 9hr); Lumbini (every half hour; 2hr) and Taulihawa (2 daily; 4hr).

From Sunauli to Kathmandu (8 daily; 10hr) and Pokhara (7 daily; 8hr).

From Nepalganj to Birendranagar (hourly; 6hr); Birganj (3 daily; 14hr); Dhangadhi (3 daily; 16hr); Kathmandu (6 daily; 15hr) and Pokhara (3 nightly; 14hr).

From Dhangadhi to Baitadi (daily; 16hr+); Dadeldhura (daily; 8hr+); Dipayal (daily; 14hr+) and Mahendranagar (hourly; 3hr).

Planes

From Nepalganj to Jumla (daily; 45min); Kathmandu (daily; 1hr 30min); Mahendranagar (weekly; 25min); Sanfebagar (4 weekly; 35min); Silgadhi Doti (4 weekly; 40min) and Simikot (seasonal; 1hr).

From Dhangadhi to Jumla (seasonal; 1hr); Kathmandu (2 weekly; 2hr); Sanfebagar (3 weekly; 25min); Silgadhi Doti (4 weekly; 20min) and Simikot (seasonal; 1hr).

From Mahendranagar to Kathmandu (weekly; 2hr 45min) and Sanfebagar (3 weekly; 30min).

Connections to India

Buses from Sunauli (India side) to Gorakhpur (hourly; 3hr); Varanasi (3 daily; 8hr) and Delhi (5 daily; 22hr). From Gorakhpur you can make broad-guage **train** connections throughout India.

CHAPTER SIX

THE EASTERN TARAI AND HILLS

As with the west, the **eastern Tarai** – the portion east of Chitwan – is where Nepal dovetails with India, and in many ways it offers the best of both worlds. Overwhelmingly rural, the plains have a timeless, almost genteel quality: thatched houses perch on stilts, clumps of bamboo and palms erupt in green explosions, and the foothills, if not the Himalaya, are always within sight. Most travellers only flit through here on their way to the border crossings of **Birganj** (for Patna) and **Kakarbitta** (for Darjeeling), and outside these places you won't find a speck of commercialism. The cities are admittedly awful, but with one outstanding exception: **Janakpur**, a pilgrimage centre that's immensely famous among Hindus but seldom visited by westerners, which provides all the exoticism of India without the attendant hassles. Although large tracts of jungle are less common east of Chitwan, bird-watchers can check out **Koshi Tappu Wildlife Reserve**, straddling the alluvial fan of the mighty Sapt Koshi River.

What few visitors the **eastern hills** get tend to be trekkers bound for the Everest or Kanchenjunga massifs, which rear up like goalposts on the northern horizon – but while the prospect of travelling 20-plus hours by bus from Kathmandu puts most people off, this isn't a problem if you're already in the eastern Tarai. By turns riotously forested and fastidiously terraced, the hills are great for day-hiking, even if you've vowed not to trek (but get a permit anyway, just in case you change your mind). At least two towns here are worth visiting in their own right: **Hile**, a rowdy frontier bazaar with a Tibetan ambience, and **Ilam**, Nepal's tea-growing capital.

Both the eastern Tarai and hills are noticeably better off than the non-touristed parts of the west; **travel connections** are (by Nepalese standards) comprehensive, and even in remote places you should be able to **eat** well, if not western. A phenomenon unique to eastern Nepal is the **haat bazaar**, or weekly market, and it's well worth trying to coincide with one or two of these pan-cultural extravaganzas.

THE EASTERN TARAI

For travellers coming by road from other parts of Nepal, Hetauda is the gateway to the eastern Tarai: from Tadi Bazaar (Chitwan) it's an easy two-hour bus ride to Hetauda along the **Mahendra Highway**, hugging the hills as it follows the attractive *dun* (inner Tarai) valley of the Rapti River; the **Rajpath** (see Chapter Three) enters the town from the north and continues south to the Indian border at Birganj.

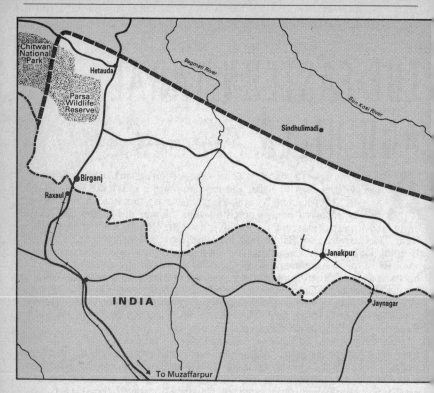

Both west and east of Hetauda, **buses** along the Mahendra Highway are frequent and relatively fast. If you're **cycling**, many of the small bazaars en route can provide basic food and, at a pinch, lodging.

The Rajpath: Hetauda to the border

There is something peculiarly sinister and ominous about the jungle of the Tarai. You have that feeling that danger in one form or another lurks around every corner . . . Over everything a strange, oppressive silence broods . . . A big gray ape chatters at us maliciously from his perch on an overhanging rock. A leopard, camouflaged almost to invisibility by his spotted hide, steals on stealthy feet across the road. There is a sudden crash of underbrush behind the jungle wall – an elephant or a tiger perhaps.

E. Alexander Powell, *The Last Home of Mystery* (1929).

For centuries the only developed corridor through the Tarai, this route was, before air travel, every foreigner's introduction to Nepal. A narrow-gauge railway used to run from Raxaul, the last Indian station, as far as Amlekhganj; dignitaries were transported from there by elephant over the first band of hills to Hetauda,

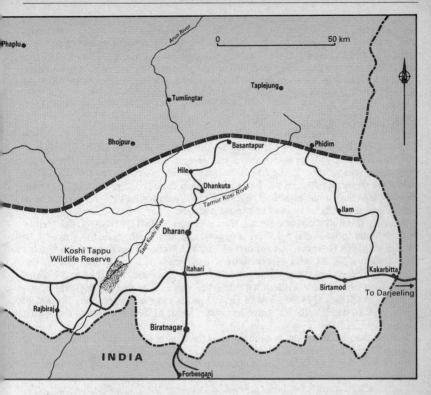

before being carried the rest of the way to Kathmandu by donkey or sedan chair. Those few who made the journey during Nepal's isolation years before 1951, such as the bombastic Mr Powell, did so only by invitation of the prime minister or king. The construction of the **Rajpath** in the 1950s eliminated the need for elephants and sedan chairs, but the railway wasn't decommissioned until the 1970s (the tracks are still in place).

Hetauda

Clumped around the junction of the Mahendra Highway and the Rajpath, **HETAUDA** (HETAURA) is still a staging-post on the India–Kathmandu route, but whatever romance it may once have had has long gone. Dilapidated Indian trucks rumble through on their way up the Rajpath with fuel for Kathmandu, while buses stop here at all hours: it's a restless, transient place. If you're trying to get from here to Daman or Kathmandu, trucks take on passengers at the north end of town, where you'll also find a number of tea stalls and a couple of serviceable *sekuwa* restaurants. The bus park is located southwest of the main intersection.

Cyclists will probably **spend the night here**, as there are no other worthwhile places to stay between Daman and the border or Chitwan. Fortunately, *Motel Avocado* (☎20429) more than compensates for Hetauda's shortcomings (singles with attached bath Rs175, doubles Rs200 and up): located in a quiet compound well north of the bazaar, the grounds are shaded by a small grove of avocado trees (planted by displaced Californians when this was the US AID guest house), and in late autumn practically everything on the menu has avocado in it. Running a distant second is *Hotel Rapti*, at the south end of town (rooms with attached bath Rs100); lodges in the bazaar are apt to be very noisy.

South to Birganj

Heading south over the low **Chure Hills**, the Rajpath enters a strange landscape of stunted trees, wide gravel washes and steeply eroded pinnacles. These hills are the newest wrinkle in the the Himalayan chain, heaved up as the 30-million-year-long collision between the Indian and Asian continental plates ripples southwards – less than a half a million years old, they're so young that the surface sediments haven't yet been eroded to expose bedrock.

Leaving the hills once and for all, the road passes AMLEKHGANJ, the former rail terminus (now Nepal's main fuel depot), and 4km further on, the entrance to **Parsa Wildlife Reserve**. An annexe of Chitwan National Park, providing secondary habitats for its wild elephant herd and many of its sub-adult tigers, the reserve isn't developed for visitors; no food or lodging are available, and visitors aren't allowed in on foot without a guide (who may also be unavailable). However, camping is supposed to be allowed (Rs100 per person per night, plus the Rs250 entry fee), so a self-sufficient traveller would stand to have the run of the whole place.

The Mahendra Highway branches off to the east at PHATLAYA, 3km south of the Parsa entrance, and SIMARA, another 3km south, heralds a dreary succession of factories and fields that continues all the way to Birganj. For obscure reasons of national security, Nepal passed a law in the mid-1980s requiring that all new factories must be built at least 10km from the Indian border, which is causing the major border cities to flare northwards.

Birganj and the border

Nepal's busiest port of entry, **BIRGANJ** is a thoroughly disagreeable place – an unflattering introduction to Nepal if you're just arriving and a rude send-off if you're leaving. The latest census (1981) puts Birganj's population at 43,000, but like most of the Tarai's urban centres it's probably doubled in size since then. All traffic to and from the border has to pass straight through the city – a planned highway bypass has yet to materialise – reducing the main street to an uncrossable torrent of lurching trucks, buses and bullock carts. The bus park, which is the busiest in the country after Kathmandu's, is dusty and dire (except in wet weather, when it becomes a fetid quagmire).

Nevertheless, some travellers may have to pass this way: Birganj is the only border point where you can bring a private vehicle or motorcycle across, and if you're touring India and Nepal by bicycle you might want to cross here once to avoid backtracking. **The border** is 4km south of the city centre, and RAXAUL, the first Indian town, a further 4km on. If you don't have your own wheels, rikshas charge about Rs40 from Birganj to Raxaul (make sure the price quoted is in Nepalese rupees); *tongas* (horse-drawn carts) are cheaper, but they won't wait while you go through customs and immigration.

There are no facilities at the border, but you can manage quite comfortably for **food and lodging** in Birganj. The best bets are *Hotel Kailas* (singles Rs35, doubles Rs70; with bath, Rs65/95 and up) and *Hotel Diyalo* (singles with bath Rs90, doubles Rs125 and up), side by side near the bus park – both have excellent Indian restaurants, while *Kanchha Sweets*, nearby, serves up an astounding assortment of *barphi* and other Indian goodies. You'll also find *sekuwa*, fried fish and other street food in stalls around the bus park. The **bank** is open for exchanging money Sunday to Thursday 10am to 3pm and Friday 10am to noon; Birganj has no black market. **Buses** connect Birganj with Kathmandu, Pokhara and most Tarai cities (ticket booths are all around the bus park).

If you're stranded in Birganj, you could probably kill a couple of hours in the old-ish market area around **Maisthan**, a mother-goddess temple northeast of the bus park. Beyond that, though, the city has little to offer: **Adarsh Nagar** is a fairly humdrum market area that's unlikely to appeal to anyone except daytripping Indian shoppers, and the new (and as yet unfinished) west side of town is utterly devoid of interest.

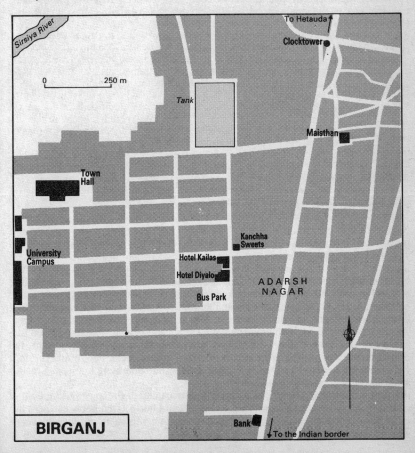

THE ETHNIC SCENE

There seems to be an unwritten rule in Nepal that all migrations have to be from west to east, with the result that contingents of almost every Nepalese ethnic group now jostle together in the eastern quarter of the country.

The original inhabitants of the eastern hills were the **Kirantis** (or Kiratas), a warlike tribe mentioned in the *Mahabharata* who may well have been the same Kiratas who ruled the Kathmandu Valley in semi-mythological times. The Kiranti nation long ago fragmented into several tribes, the most important ones being the **Rais** and **Limbus**. Like the Magars and Gurungs of the west, members of these dauntless hill groups make up a significant portion of the Gurkha regiments; similarly, they follow their own form of shamanism, but increasingly embrace Hindu or Buddhist practices, depending on their location. Unusually, the Kiranti clans bury their dead – cremation is the usual practice throughout the subcontinent – and Limbus erect distinctive rectangular, whitewashed grave markers: three tiers high for women, four for men. Rais, who have a reputation as a staunchly independent people, traditionally occupy the middle-elevation hills west of the Arun River, while Limbuwan, as the Limbu homeland is sometimes still called, is centred around the lower slopes of the Tamur Kosi Valley, further east.

Rais and Limbus had the hills virtually to themselves until a spate of migrations, beginning in the late eighteenth century, completely transformed the ethnic map of eastern Nepal. The Gorkhali army marched in and annexed the region in 1776; in their wake, **Brahmans** and **Chhetris** began infiltrating the Arun Basin and **Newars** took over the trading crossroads. At about the same time, **Sherpas** and **Tamangs** were steadily elbowing the Rais out of Solu, and more recently, **Magars** and **Gurungs** have hopped across from their traditional homelands in the west. Little wonder, then, that when the Rais and Limbus were recruited by the British in the last century to pluck tea in Darjeeling, they, too, headed east (pick up any packet of Darjeeling tea and chances are there'll be a Limbu girl on it).

Even more than in western Nepal, the clearing of the eastern Tarai during the past three decades has spurred a new, feverish land rush, as hill people in turn displace the native **Tharus** and other minorities; meanwhile, **Biharis** and **Bengalis** keep arriving in droves from India. Bouncing along the Mahendra Highway, where housing and dress styles change from one village to the next, you almost feel as if you're watching the migration in motion.

Janakpur

JANAKPUR, 165km east of Birganj, is indisputably the Tarai's most fascinating city. Often called Janakpurdham (*dham* denoting a sacred place), it's a holy site of the first order, and its central temple, the ornate **Janaki Mandir**, is an obligatory stop on the Hindu pilgrimage circuit. Although Indian in every respect except politically, the city is, by Indian standards, small and manageable: motorised traffic is all but banned from the centre, tourist hustle is completely absent, the poverty isn't oppressive and the surrounding countryside is delightful. To top it all, Janakpur's **steam railway** – the only railway still operating in Nepal – makes an entertaining excursion in itself.

Hindu mythology identifies Janakpur as the capital of the ancient kingdom of **Mithila**, which probably controlled a large part of north India between the tenth and third centuries BC, and the city features prominently in the *Ramayana*: it was in Janakpur that **Rama** – the god Vishnu in mortal form – strung a magic bow to win the hand of **Sita**, the Mithila princess. Recounting the divine couple's separation and heroic reunion, the *Ramayana* holds Rama and Sita up as models of the virtuous husband and chaste wife; in Janakpur, where the two command almost cult status, the chant of "Sita Ram, Sita Ram" is repeated like a Hindu Hail Mary and *sadhus* commonly wear the tuning-fork-shaped *tika* of Vishnu.

Despite the absence of ancient monuments to confirm its mythic past – no building is much more than a century old – Janakpur remains a strangely attractive city. Religious fervour seems to lend an aura to everything; the skyline leaves a lasting impression of palm trees and the onion domes and pyramid roofs of local shrines. Most of these distinctively shaped shrines are associated with **kutis** – self-contained pilgrimage centres and hostels for *sadhus* – some 500 of which are scattered throughout the Janakpur area. Janakpur's other distinguishing feature is its **sacred ponds** – there are dozens of them – which here take the place of river ghats for ritual bathing and *dhobi*-ing. Clearly man-made, the rectangular tanks might (as locals claim) go back to Rama's day, although it's more likely that they've been dredged over the centuries by wealthy merit-seekers.

Janakpur runs a full and varied **festival calendar**, the highlight being *Viveh Panchami*, the re-enactment of Rama's and Sita's wedding which draws at least 100,000 pilgrims in late November or early December. *Rama Navami* (Rama's birthday), celebrated in March or April, attracts nearly as many, while some 10,000 people join the annual one-day *parikrama* (circumambulation) of the city in the first week of March, many performing prostrations along the entire eight-kilometre route. But at any time of the year, Janakpur's atmosphere is charged with an intense devotional zeal – new shrines are forever being inaugurated and idols installed, while *kuti* loudspeakers broadcast religious discourses and the mesmerising drone of the harmonium.

Arriving and getting settled in

Janakpur lies 30km south of the Mahendra Highway; direct **buses** connect it with Kathmandu (*Sajha* service) and Kakarbitta and the station is an easy riksha ride from the city centre. You could conceivably **fly** here from Kathmandu (three flights a week; $55), in which case you'll land at the airstrip 2km south of town. *RNAC*'s office (☎041/20185), located at the northeast end of town, is open daily from 10am to 4pm. The typically uninformative **tourist office** (Sun–Thurs 10am–4pm, Fri 10am–3pm) is across the street.

While Janakpur's scarcity of **accommodation** normally doesn't present a problem, you need to book well ahead during the big festival times. *Hotel Welcome* (☎041/20224), though nothing fancy, is fairly central and is at least used to dealing with foreigners (singles Rs35, doubles Rs60 with common bath; rooms with attached hot-water shower Rs125 and up). *Hotel Rama* (☎041/20059) is a quieter but more out-of-the-way alternative (singles Rs44, doubles Rs55 with attached bath), while *Shree Janak Lodge* – along with a few other nearby places without English signs – offers cheaper, dingier rooms. If you're prepared to **camp**, you could probably pitch a tent in one of the pilgrims' groves just north of the bank or south of Ratnasagar Kuti.

Food is plentiful, and if you like Indian sweets or *chiura dahi* (beaten rice and curd) you can take your pick from a host of nameless places around the Janaki and Ram temples. For curries and such, try *Amber Restaurant* or its vegetarian neighbour, the *Sagar* – although their menus aren't in English, unfortunately – or

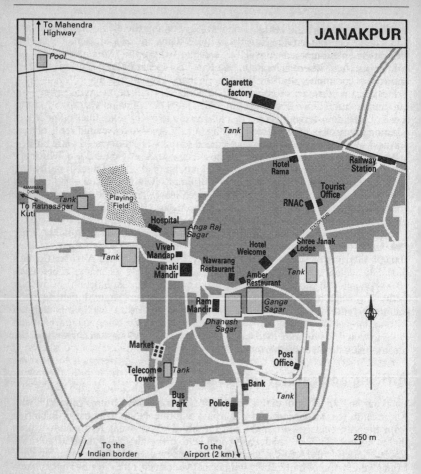

the nearby *Nawarang Hotel*, a popular, no-frills canteen. To sample the local brew, ask for *sophi* or *dudhiya*, aniseed-flavoured spirits that are just about drinkable when mixed with Sprite.

Though the city is easy enough to **get around** on foot, rikshas are a terrific deal – they wait in efficient ranks all over town and don't bump up their rates for foreign customers. You might be able to hire a bicycle informally through *Hotel Welcome*.

The city

A palatial confection of a building in the Mughal style, the **Janaki Mandir** (pronounced *Jaa*-nuh-ki) is supposed to mark the spot where a golden image of Sita was discovered in 1657 and, presumably, where the virtuous princess actually lived. The present marble structure, erected in 1911 by an Indian queen, is already looking a little worse for wear. The outer building encloses a courtyard and inner sanctum, where at least twice a day (generally 8am and 4pm) priests draw back a curtain to reveal an intricate silver shrine and perform various rituals for attending worshippers; non-Hindus are allowed to watch, and the priests even seem willing to bestow blessings on unbelievers – upon payment of the appropriate fee, of course. It's an enchanting place at night and early in the morning, when the devout gather in lamplit huddles and murmur haunting hymns. The temple

The Janaki Mandir

is also a traditional place for boys to get their first haircuts, and male dancers in drag (*natuwa* in Nepali), who are often hired to perform at the hair-cutting ceremony, can sometimes be seen here.

Climb the stairs to the roof of the outer building for a view of the central courtyard and the dense, brick-laned **Muslim village** butting right up against the temple's rear wall: one of Janakpur's most extraordinary aspects is the way rural life can be seen almost in the heart of the city. North of the temple, the new and rather sterile **Ram Janaki Viveh Mandap** ("Rama Sita Wedding Pavilion") houses a turgid tableau of the celebrated event. The squat, pagoda-style building looks like it cost a pretty penny to build, which is probably why they charge Rs5 to look at it.

Walk westwards from here to the highway and you reach **Ramanand Chowk**, the nucleus of many of Janakpur's *kutis* and a major *sadhu* gathering place during festivals. In an alcove at the southwest corner of the intersection, devotees have been chanting the names of Rama and Sita continuously since 1986 (the vigil, sponsored by wealthy individuals, is to last a total of twelve years). Two wealthy and well-known establishments, Ramanand Ashram and Ratnasagar Kuti – the latter, rising grandly in the midst of farmland, looking uncannily like a Russian Orthodox church – are located in this area, but are closed to the public.

The city's oldest, closest quarter lies to the south and east of the Janaki Mandir – making your way through this area, with its sweet shops, *puja* stalls and quick-photo studios, you begin to appreciate that Janakpur is as geared up for Indian tourists as Kathmandu is for western ones. The main landmark here, the Nepalese pagoda-style **Ram Mandir**, isn't wildly exciting except when it serves as the venue for *Rama Navami* festivities. Immediately to the east, **Dhanush Sagar** and **Ganga Sagar** are considered the holiest of Janakpur's ponds: the sight of Hindus performing ritual ablutions in the fog at sunrise here is profoundly moving, and during festivals the scene is on a par with Varanasi's famed ghats in India.

The railway

If you've already had dealings with Indian trains, Janakpur's **railway** will be less of a thrill, but it's still an excellent way to get out into the countryside – this part of the Tarai features some of the most meticulously kept farmland you'll see anywhere, and on a misty winter's morning the ride past sleepy villages and minor temples is nothing short of magical. Built in the 1940s to transport timber to India from the now-depleted forest west of Janakpur, the narrow-gauge line these days operates primarily as a passenger service. The dilapidated locomotives and carriages are undoubtedly original, and may well be even older than the railway, since Nepal tends to acquire much of its machinery as hand-me-downs from India.

Janakpur is the terminus for two separate lines, each about 30km long: one eastbound to JAYNAGAR, just over the border in India, and the other westbound to BIJALPUR. **Trains for Jaynagar** depart at 7.30am and 3.30pm, and trains coming the opposite way are supposed to leave Jaynagar at the same time (but check: times may vary). You'll doubtless be stopped by Nepalese customs at KHAJURI, about two hours from Janakpur (if not, you could have trouble re-entering Nepal). For a shorter trip, get off at BAIDEHI, about an hour from Janakpur, and catch the train coming the other way about half an hour later – or walk back: it's only 12km. The **Bijalpur service** runs only once a day each way, departing at 4pm at either end, so you'll have to alight at KHUNTA or LOHARPATI in order to return to Janakpur the same day; alternatively, you can walk to Khunta by way of Ramanand Chowk and return by train.

The **fare** to Jaynagar is Rs8 in second class or Rs15 in first, the latter being far from luxurious but perhaps a shade less crowded. Arrive early for a seat; on the way back you'll almost certainly end up sitting astride a consignment of mustard-oil tins on the roof.

MITHILA PAINTING

For 3000 years, Brahman women of the region once known as Mithila have maintained an unbroken tradition of **painting**, following techniques and ritual motifs passed down from mother to daughter. The colourful, almost psychedelic images can be viewed as fertility charms, meditation aids or a form of story-telling, but on a deeper level they represent, in the words of one critic, "the manifestation of a collective mind, embodying milennia of traditional knowledge".

From an early age girls practice drawing complex symbols derived from Hindu myths and folk tales, which over the course of generations have been reduced to *mandala*-like abstractions. By the time she is in her teens, a girl will be presenting simple paintings to her arranged fiancé, perhaps using them to wrap gifts; more complicated papier mâché versions may follow, and the courtship culminates with the painting of a **kohbar**, a sort of marriage proposal in the form of an elaborate fresco on the wall of the couple's future bedroom. Based on the *lingam* and *yoni* symbols, the *kohbar* is a powerful celebration of life, creation and everything; other motifs include footprints and fishes (both representing Vishnu), the *swastika* (an auspicious symbol in Hinduism), Rama and Sita, and Surabhi, "the Cow of Plenty, who inflames the desire of those who milk her".

The usual technique is first to outline the intended design in black, embellishing it with fantastic detail until it fills the entire surface, and finally illuminating it with brilliant primary **colours** (though garish, the natural dyes used somehow reflect the

Koshi Tappu Wildlife Reserve

East of the Janakpur turn-off, the Mahendra Highway rolls along uneventfully all the way to the Sapt Koshi River. The latter half of this section barrels across long stretches of farmland punctuated by bamboo thickets and idyllic little villages – the kind of places you can't imagine anyone would ever leave – which probably explains why cyclists passing though here sometimes complain of being stared at by locals.

The landscape changes markedly at the Sapt Koshi, eastern Nepal's biggest river. Crossing the **Koshi Barrage** – not a dam, but a series of flood-control gates – you can look in amazement at the immense body of water that squeezes through here before fanning out again into the shimmering haze of India. Reaching the far side, the highway bends north and runs parallel to a disused railway: keep an eye out for the rusty old steam engines which, until the railway tracks were severed in the 1988 Dharan earthquake, hauled rubble to build up the ten-metre embankments that keep the Sapt Koshi in check during the monsoon.

Straddling a vast floodplain of shifting grassland and sandbanks north of the barrage, **KOSHI TAPPU WILDLIFE RESERVE** is the most low-keyed and do-it-yourself-able of the Tarai's parks. It's not bound to appeal to most travellers – there are no tigers or rhinos, nor even any jungle – but bird-watchers can have a field day here, for Koshi Tappu is one of Asia's most important stopping places for migratory **birds**; though Chitwan boasts more species, the number of individuals here is greater, and you're bound to tick off several varieties you haven't seen anywhere else. The reserve was established to protect one of the subcontinent's last surviving herds of **wild buffalo** (*arna*), now 160 strong and

---

intensity of the local landscape). Perhaps the most striking aspect of Mithila art is that, almost by definition, it's ephemeral: paintings are intended to be thrown away like wrapping paper, and even the most amazing mural will be washed off within a week or two. Painting is considered a form of prayer or meditation; once completed, the work has achieved its end.

Although Mithila paintings are much more common across the border in India's Bihar state, where they're often sold, murals can occasionally be seen in village temples outside Janakpur. For caste reasons, you're unlikely to be invited into a Brahman home, but if you're interested in arranging a private **tour** of artists' houses contact Swami Dharmajyoti at the *Hotel Vajra* in Kathmandu.

Detail from a mithila painting

recovering healthily after a devastating 1985 flood.* Also resident in the reserve
are blue bull (*nilgai*), wild boar, langur, spotted deer (*chital*), and a semi-wild bull
elephant dubbed Ganesh Maharaj by locals, who consider him sacred and set out
food for him; passengers on the Kathmandu–Kakarbitta night bus have reported
seeing Ganesh Maharaj lumbering across the Mahendra Highway around dawn.
In addition, gharial crocodiles from the Chitwan hatchery have been introduced
here – it's too early to say if they'll survive – and a small number of gangetic
dolphins are reportedly trapped upstream of the barrage

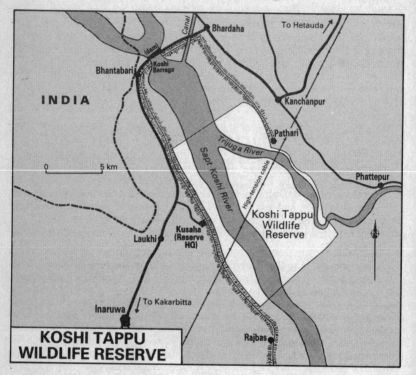

Doing Koshi Tappu

The reserve is marked by a yellow sign beside the Mahendra Highway about
12km east of the barrage – or if you're coming from the other direction, 3km west
of LAUKHI – where an access road leads 3km north to the reserve headquarters
(generally known as the *warden ophis*). The warden maintains a mud-walled
"lodge" that sleeps eight (Rs10 per person) and a hand pump for washing, and

---

*However, wildlife experts are concerned about the number of domestic buffalo getting
into the reserve and mating with the wild ones: if this is allowed to continue, the result
could be a semi-domestic herd whose continued protection would be hard to justify.

you can get *daal bhaat* and tea at the miniscule hamlet of KUSAHA, just to the east of the office. The Rs250 **entry permit** is valid for one day, or as long as you stay at the warden's lodge. **Elephants** are allegedly for hire (Rs200 per hour), but they're kept clear on the other side of the river at PHATTEPUR (theoretically reachable by local bus from KANCHANPUR). Vehicles aren't allowed in the park, although you could cycle for miles along the eastern embankment. The reserve has no guides, English-speaking or otherwise.

With no rhinos or large carnivores, Koshi Tappu is comparatively safe for wandering around **on your own**. Generally speaking, the area east of the Sapt Koshi is boring and you're better off making for the opposite shore, where the game- and bird-watching is best: from the reserve headquarters, follow the dirt road onto the embankment, turn left and then make a right at the second man-made breakwater (just after the 13km marker). In 1990, dugout canoes were ferrying passengers across the Sapt Koshi from a point about 1km west of here, but enquire locally about the current situation, as the river changes course every monsoon. Once across the river you're on *the* Koshi Tappu, an isthmus between the Sapt Koshi and Trijuga rivers (*tappu* in Nepali means "island", which is what this is during the wet months), and the scrub forest here is the main stomping ground of buffalo and blue bull (actually an antelope). Stalking the wild cousins of common water buffalo is sometimes hard to take seriously – especially when they moo – yet these are big animals and can make a thunderous noise when frightened; and while they normally run away at the first scent of humans, you have to make sure not to block their escape.

Biratnagar

BIRATNAGAR (pop. 180,000) is Nepal's second-biggest city, and at its present galloping growth rate it will overtake Kathmandu by the turn of the century. Though the city is prospering as a magnet for industry and trade – it's on a direct line to the port of Calcutta – foreign observers foresee major growth-related problems in the coming years: jute is in decline, Birganj is muscling in on trade with Calcutta, and government offices have been shifted north to Dhankuta, yet immigrants from the hills and India keep pouring in looking for work. You still see bullock carts hauling raw jute to the mills near the border, but modern Biratnagar is probably best exemplified by the prosaic zipper factory north of town. The city's one other claim to fame is as a political hotbed: thanks to its proximity to India's West Bengal state, Biratnagar has long been a sort of safe house for many of Nepal's communist parties, which until recently were banned; how these parties will fare in the 1991 elections is anyone's guess, but they're unlikely to give up the struggle as long as West Bengal is controlled by Marxists.

More Indian than Nepalese, Biratnagar's streets are lined with a depressing array of concrete buildings and border-bazaar shops. That said, the city centre is relatively laid-back and traffic-free (out on the main road, though, it's pretty squalid). There are few sights, but if you're here on a Wednesday don't miss Biratnagar's **haat bazaar**, held in a field east of town, where you can count on a colourful assembly of Tharus, Rais, Limbus and various Indian castes. In the countryside surrounding Biratnagar, Tharus and Danuwars (a related group, whose women wear their homespun saris like togas) are indigenous: to sample **village life**, head out on the road towards RANGALI, east of town, or visit the

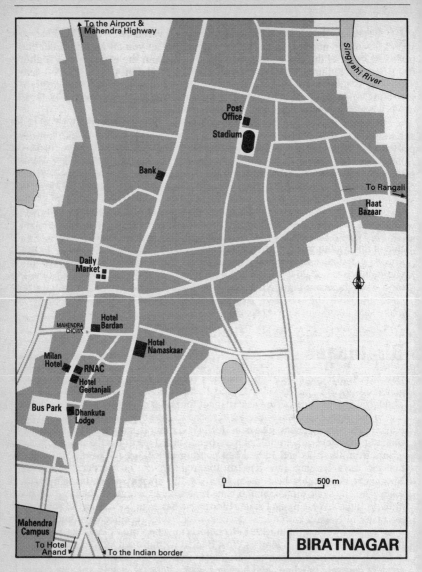

To the Airport &
Mahendra Highway

Singyrahi River

Post
Office

Stadium

Bank

To Rangali

Haat
Bazaar

Daily
Market

Hotel
Bardan

MAHENDRA
CHOWK

Hotel
Namaskaar

Milan
Hotel

RNAC

Hotel
Geetanjali

Bus Park

Dhankuta
Lodge

0   500 m

Mahendra
Campus

To Hotel
Anand

To the Indian border

BIRATNAGAR

area around DUHUBI, off the main road about halfway between Biratnagar and
the Mahendra Highway. The JOGBANI border crossing, 5km south of town, is
open only to Nepalis and Indians.

Practicalities

Kathmandu–Kakarbitta **buses** don't go through Biratnagar, but stop at ITAHARI,
an unpleasant crossroads bazaar on the Mahendra Highway (basic lodgings avail-

able); Biratnagar is 23km south, and Dharan, covered later in "The Eastern Hills", lies to the north. Direct buses to Biratnagar let you off at the dismal bus park southwest of the city centre. Travelling to or from the eastern hills, **flights** from here to Kathmandu (daily, $77), Tumlingtar (4 times a week, $44) and Taplejung (3 times a week, $50) might prove useful. The airport is 4km north of town (Rs20 by riksha) and the *RNAC* office (☎021/22576), near the bus park, is open daily from 10am to 3pm.

Biratnagar's newest and best **accommodation**, *Hotel Anand* (☎021/23712), sits well south of town – the rooms are expensive (singles start at Rs150) but the place has a pleasant lawn and serviceable restaurant. Closer to the city centre, *Hotel Namaskaar* is popular with businessmen, despite being noisy and overpriced (singles from Rs90). Of the cheap lodges out on the main road, *Hotel Geetanjali* is the brightest and least smelly (singles Rs50, doubles Rs100). Be sure to request mosquito netting.

For **food**, make for the rough-and-ready eateries north of Mahendra Chowk, which do tasty *sekuwa* and *maachhaa masaala* (local carp fried in a spicy tomato sauce); try also *chiura badhmas* (a snack of beaten rice, toasted soyabeans, spring onions, ginger and oil) and *dudhiya*, the local aniseed-flavoured *raksi*. For Indian curries, visit *Hotel Bardan* at Mahendra Chowk, and for breakfast the *Namaskaar*. The main shopping street north of the *Namaskaar* contains a few unexceptional sweet shops (*mithaai pasaal*).

To Kakarbitta and the border

From Itahari, the Mahendra Highway's final 100-kilometre leg crosses the frontier districts of **Morang** and **Jhapa**. Once renowned for its virulent malaria, Morang remains untamed in parts, but hill settlers, encouraged by the government, are steadily moving in, and logging companies are whittling away at the jungle. Jhapa, further east, is now largely cultivated and dotted with monotonously similar villages, each containing a wide, dusty bazaar full of people selling delicious oranges and cheap bangles; half-timbered houses on stilts are the work of transplanted Limbus. Jhapa's tea plantations, though flat and not much to look at, are a reminder that Darjeeling is barely 50km away as the crow flies, and Ilam, Nepal's prize region, sits in the hills just north of here.

A border crossing with a real backwoods flavour, **KAKARBITTA** feels like one of those all-night shantytowns that Indian buses always seem to stop at, where you wake up to men selling peanuts and *bidis* by candlelight and ask "where the hell are we?" Unlike other border towns, it's too far out in the sticks to be much of a trading centre, and the only apparent link with the rest of the world is the fleet of night buses that roars in from Kathmandu every morning and roars out again every afternoon. You don't want to stay here any longer than necessary.

If you need to **spend the night**, *ABC Lodge* is Kakarbitta's finest (rooms Rs80, dormitory beds Rs30), with *Apsara Lodge* running a slightly more rustic second place (singles Rs30, doubles Rs40–50). Places around the bus park serve snacks and *daal bhaat*, but *Hotel Shere Punjab*, which does a few passable Indian dishes, is the only one that could properly be called a **restaurant** – it's also something of a nightspot, although the electricity never seems to stay on long enough to make the drinks cold. There's no black market in Kakarbitta: lodges and restaurants will swap Nepalese and Indian rupees at the market rate, but to change hard currency you'll have to use the **bank** (*Nepal Rastra Bank*, a pink building sign-posted only in Nepali; daily 7am–5pm). The tourist office is useless.

The wide Mechi River forms **the border**, about 500m east of town, and as it's a 15-minute walk between Kakarbitta and RANIGANJ, the first Indian village, you might as well take a riksha (not that you'll be able to fend them off anyway). Taxis and buses to SILIGURI, the rail station for Darjeeling and Calcutta, depart from the junction just east of Raniganj; touts offer to "guide" travellers to Darjeeling for Rs60, but you can easily do it yourself for half that. Remember that you need a **Darjeeling permit** from the Indian Embassy to enter India here. If you're coming from India and planning to catch one of the night buses to Kathmandu, they all leave Kakarbitta at 5pm, but you need to arrive at least a couple of hours early to be sure of a good seat; most other routes are plied by day buses.

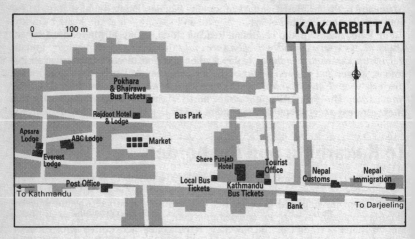

THE EASTERN HILLS

Two roads link the Tarai with the hills east of the Sapt Koshi – the **Dhankuta road**, leaving the Mahendra Highway at Itahari, and the **Ilam road**, beginning at Charali. Bus services are more fickle here than along the Mahendra Highway, so it's always wise to make an early start. Either road would make a superb jaunt on a mountain bike. While this section describes short hikes in the area, remember that you're officially supposed to have a trekking permit to go more than a day's walk off a road.

The Dhankuta road

Call it development or call it colonialism by another name, but the big donor nations have staked out distinct spheres of influence in Nepal, and nowhere is this more apparent than in the British bailiwick around Dhankuta. Britain's interest in this area has not been without ulterior motives: half the Gurkha regiments are filled by recruits from the eastern hills, and the biggest Gurkha training camp was, until recently, in Dharan. In the 1970s, no doubt pricked by a sense of obligation to the people of the area, Britain initiated a series of projects based in Dhankuta under the banner of the **Koshi Hills Development Programme** – agriculture, forestry, health and cottage industries have all been funded by British aid through this programme, but the biggest and most obvious undertaking has been the road to Dharan, Dhankuta, Hile and Basantapur.

From the Mahendra Highway, the road winds languidly through forest as it ascends the Bhabar, the sloping alluvial zone between the Tarai and the foothills. Dharan, 16km north of the highway, sits a slightly cooler 300m above the plain.

Dharan

Noisy and tawdry, **DHARAN** isn't much of a place to linger – not, that is, unless you're a member of the development elite and staying out at the former Gurkha Camp, the closest thing in Nepal to Club Med – but if you're heading for Dhankuta or Hile you'll have to stop here.

Dharan hit world headlines in 1988 when a powerful **earthquake** killed 700 people and flattened most of the town – the main bazaar has been hastily rebuilt, but bricks and rubble are still piled everywhere and things look decidedly ramshackle. Disaster struck a second time at the end of 1989 when the **British Army**, forseeing force reductions, pulled out of Dharan and handed the Gurkha Camp back to HMG. The withdrawal dealt a blow to would-be recruits here, who must now travel all the way to Pokhara to compete for even fewer places in the regiments (for more on the Gurkhas, see p.168); most of Dharan's *khukuri* smiths disappeared overnight, and shopkeepers still bemoan the loss of Gurkha trade.

Yet **the bazaar** still does a bustling business, since for people throughout the eastern hills Dharan is the proverbial Bright Lights where they come to sell oranges by the sackload and spend their profits on kitchen utensils, provisions and bottles of *Urvashi* from the bazaar's well-stocked spirits stalls. In the area northeast of the central Bhanu Chowk you'll see hill women investing the family fortune in gold ornaments – the age-old safe haven – and shops selling fantastic Raj-era silver coins to be strung into necklaces. If you're in the market for a cauldron, check out the brass-workers' quarter further east.

The most amazing thing about Dharan is the sheer contrast between the bazaar and the **Gurkha Camp** (as it's still called), a Rs10 riksha ride west of the bus stand. You can wander freely around the grounds now, which you wouldn't have been allowed to do when the Gurkhas occupied it, and although there's not much to see, the long, tree-lined lanes are blessedly quiet – it's like a university campus during summer break. The camp has been placed under the Ministry of Health, which now runs the hospital but doesn't seem to have a clue what to do with the rest of the facilities. Rather than watch the best golf course in Nepal go to seed, the British transition team has leased it from the government and renamed it the **Dharan Club**: for about Rs200 you can rent clubs, hire a caddy and play eighteen holes, and the swimming pool and tennis and squash courts can be used for Rs100 per day.

CHATARA, the finishing point for rafting trips on the Sun Kosi, lies 15km west of Dharan; Land Rovers make the trip starting from west of Chatta Chowk (Rs13). Walk an hour north of Chatara and you reach the sacred confluence of **Barahachhetra**, site of a temple to Vishnu incarnated as a boar (Barahi) and an annual pilgrimage on the day of the full moon of October–November.

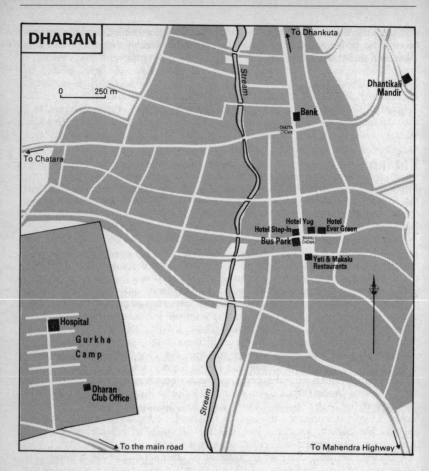

DHARAN

To Dhankuta

0   250 m

Stream

Dhantikali
Mandir

Bank

CHATTA
CHOWK

To Chatara

Hotel Yug   Hotel
Hotel Step-In   Ever Green
Bus Park   BHANU
CHOWK
Yeti & Makalu
Restaurants

Hospital

Gurkha
Camp

Stream

Dharan
Club Office

To the main road   To Mahendra Highway

Practicalities

All **buses** terminate in Dharan. Services from here to Biratnagar and Kakarbitta
are fairly frequent, and up to six (night) buses ply between Dharan and
Kathmandu – to reach other Tarai destinations, change at Itahari or Biratnagar.
Buses to Dhankuta and points north are always chronically overcrowded, and it
can be a real ordeal getting a seat; enquire about road conditions, as landslides
sometimes turn the journey into two separate rides.

By the time you read this, a **tourist bungalow** may have been set up within
the Gurkha Camp – enquire at the *Dharan Club* – and if so it might be worth
paying quite a bit extra to avoid staying in the bazaar. Otherwise, *Hotel Ever
Green* seems to be the best bet if you can get in (rooms with bath Rs65), otherwise you'll have to settle for *Yug Hotel* (rooms Rs65 with bath, Rs45 without) or
Hotel Step-In (singles Rs25, doubles Rs50, all without bath), both grotty and
noisy. Service at the *Yug*'s and *Ever Green*'s **restaurants** is neither swift nor

enthusiastic, but the food isn't bad, whereas the *Yeti* and *Makalu* restaurants are maddeningly inept; street vendors around Bhanu Chowk sell some weird and wonderful fried morsels.

North to Dhankuta

From Dharan the road switchbacks abruptly over a 1400-metre saddle with dramatic views, then descends to cross the Tamur Kosi at MULGHAT (280m) before again climbing to **DHANKUTA**, stretched out on a ridge at 1150m. Some buses carry on to Hile and Basantapur, but you might have to change here.

Though you'd never guess it by looking at it, Dhankuta is the administrative headquarters for eastern Nepal; the logic of this choice is unclear – perhaps Kathmandu mistrusted leftist Biratnagar and Dharan. Unfortunately, the road that was supposed to consolidate Dhankuta's position has, if anything, undermined it by siphoning off trade to Dharan and Hile, and the only thing that seems to be holding the place together is British aid: the Koshi Hills project is based here (you see their shiny Land Rovers everywhere), as are Save the Children, Britain Nepal Medical Trust and assorted VSO and Peace Corps volunteers. But for travellers who make it this far, it's an easygoing, predominantly Newar town, with pedestrian-only streets, smartly whitewashed houses and shady *chautaaras*. The outlying area is populated by Rais, Magars and Hindu castes, who make Dhankuta's **haat bazaar** (Thursday) a tremendously photogenic affair.

Although you can't see the Himalaya from here, the area also makes fine **walking** country, and you're bound to run into chatty aid workers or ex-Gurkhas on the trail. In **SANTANG**, a Rai village about 45 minutes southeast of town, women can be seen embroidering beautiful shawls and weaving *dhaka*, which is as much a speciality of the eastern hills as it is in the west (see "Tansen" in Chapter Four). You can walk to Hile in about two hours by taking shortcuts off the main road: stick to the ridge and within sight of the electric power line.

Dhankuta practicialities

Project workers get first priority at the *Koshi Hills Development Programme Rest House*, Dhankuta's most salubrious **place to stay**, but it doesn't hurt to ask at the *KHDP* office (☎353) at the north end of the bazaar just off the road to Hile; the spanking-clean rest house, which is located *south* of the bus park, features a garden, solar hot water and dining room (Rs150 per person). Cheapies in the bazaar – *Maino Lodge* and *Hotel Parichaya*, to name two – are cold-water, trekking-standard outfits. Try the nameless Sherpa **restaurant** about 100m downhill from the *Parichaya* for excellent *momos* and *tongba*, *Lodge Sangalo* for snacks, or the *KHDP Rest House* for stodgy western fare.

Hile

HILE (pronounced *Hee*-lay) is one of the most exciting places a traveller can visit in Nepal without a trekking permit. That's a deliberately barbed compliment: if you're here to start (or finish) a trek – and you'd be crazy to come all this way and *not* trek – Hile might seem anticlimactic, yet this spirited little pioneer settlement would merit a stay even if it weren't a trailhead.

Seemingly teetering over the deep, often fog-shrouded Arun Valley, Hile huddles along the main road, 10km beyond Dhankuta and 750m higher up along the same ridge (the road is scheduled to be paved by 1991 – expect an erratic bus service in the meantime). A straggling strip of temporary-looking shops, a few hotels and a couple of one-room *gompas* just about sums up **the bazaar**; you can walk the length of it in five minutes. The shops bristle with commodities like plastic containers, ready-made clothes, metal pots and salt, all bound for the hinterland: **porters** gather in Hile by the hundreds, and the trail to Tumlingtar, three days up the Arun Valley, is like a *doko* highway.

A *jhankri* (shaman) of the hills

Local Rais, Newar merchants and Indian entrepreneurs are all dicing for a piece of Hile's action, but its most visible minority are Bhotiyas (see Chapter Seven), who appear to have relocated en masse from the highlands near Kanchenjunga. Undoubtedly one of the most exotic things you can do in Nepal is to spend an evening in a flickering Bhotiya kitchen sipping hot millet grog from an authentic **tongba**: unique to this area, these miniature wooden casks with brass hoops and fitted tops look like they were designed for Genghis Khan (innkeepers might agree to sell one for Rs200–300). Hile's **haat bazaar** (Thursday) is lively, but not as big as Dhankuta's.

Magnificent **views** (even by trekking standards) are just a half-hour's hike from Hile. Walk to the north end of the bazaar, bear left up a dirt lane and after 150m turn left again up a set of steps to join the HATTIKHARKA trail, which contours around the hill, skirts an army base and finally reaches a grassy plateau. The panorama spreads out before you like a trekking map: to the northwest, Cho Oyu and Makalu float above the awesome canyon of the Arun (though Everest is hidden behind the crest, you can see its characteristic plume); the ridges of the Milke Danda zigzag to the north; and part of the Kanchenjunga massif pokes up in the northeast. It's heaven – pity about the army base, though*. A quicker, truncated view can be had from the top of the ridge south of Hile. The trail to Tumlingtar angles to the left near the north end of the bazaar, passing the British-funded agricultural research station at PAKHRIBAS en route.

Practical details

Hile's Bhotiya **lodges** are pretty savvy about catering to foreigners, though innkeepers don't speak much English. *Hotel Gajur*'s rooms are clean (singles

---

*The military presence here suggests that – as is so often the case – the Dhankuta–Hile road has been built more for reasons of security than development; and given the base's location, one suspects its purpose is to deter domestic unrest, not foreign invasions.

Rs25, doubles Rs45) and its kitchen is legendary for *momos*, *sokuti* (fried meat) and *tongba*. The rooms are somewhat bigger at *Hotel Himali* (Rs35, single or double), though the dining area isn't so cozy. Lodges and shops are surprisingly well-stocked with tinned food, chocolate, instant coffee and other trekking provisions. To return to Kathmandu from here, several **buses** a day go as far as Dharan, where you can try for a seat on the nightly bus to the capital or continue on to Itahari and intercept one of the night buses coming from Biratnagar.

Beyond Hile

About six buses a day rumble on to the end of the road – which for the moment is Basantapur, a dusty hour and a half from Hile – but this is the kind of country where you just hitch a ride with any vehicle that's going. You get tremendous views of the Makalu massif for most of the way, and Everest manages to pop into view near the end. If the World Bank has its way, this road will be extended to NUM, 30km from the Tibet border beside the Arun River, where the controversial **Arun III** hydroelectric diversion is planned to go. Opponents fear the road would cause even more damage to the environment than the diversion; fortunately, the massive project has been put on hold by the recent political upheavals and not even the normally bullish World Bank seems willing to invest $700m in Nepal at the moment.

Very much a rerun of Hile, **BASANTAPUR**'s lively, muddy bazaar sits in a saddle at 2400m. Besides being the main supply line for the entire northeast corner of Nepal, Basantapur has begun to play host to trekking groups bound for Kanchenjunga and several **lodges** have sprung up, the most aggressive being *Hotel Yak* (singles Rs20, doubles Rs30), which even sports a "Today's Menu" board. The hills around here are a delight for **walking**: mixed pasture and dense mossy forest, rhododendrons, orchids, jasmine, and very friendly villages. Likely targets are CHAUKI, a pleasant village a couple of hours north of Basantapur, and Kopha Pokhri, a lake with great views two or three hours further on. Anything after that is a trek.

The Ilam road

Like the Dhankuta road, the Ilam road keeps getting longer: originally engineered by the Koreans to connect the tea estates of Kanyam and Ilam with the Tarai, it now reaches Phidim and is in the process of being extended to Taplejung.

Buses to Ilam start at BIRTAMOD, located on the Mahendra Highway 8km west of the actual start of the road at CHARALI – they tend to be very crowded, and the last one leaves at 10am or 11am. The journey takes about six hours by bus; by bike it would probably be a two-day trip. After traversing lush lowlands, the road begins a laborious 1600-metre ascent to KANYAM and its undulating monoculture of tea. At PHIKAL, a few kilometres further on, a side road on the right takes a shortcut to Darjeeling; the PASHUPATI border crossing isn't open to westerners, unfortunately. Beyond Phikal the road descends 1000m in a series of tight switchbacks – where it hasn't been cleared, the forest here is magnificent – to cross the Mai Khola before climbing another 500m to Ilam (1200m).

Ilam

To Nepalis, **ILAM** (Ee-*laam*) means tea: cool and moist for much of the year, the hills of Ilam district (like those of Darjeeling, just across the border) are perfect for it. Ilam town, headquarters of the district, is a tidy little bazaar whose colourfully painted wooden houses, featuring prim balconies and decorated eaves, give it an unmistakeably alpine air – it looks a lot like Darjeeling, in fact, without all the hype and new construction, and if it only had better food and mountain views Ilam would make a terrific alternative hill resort.

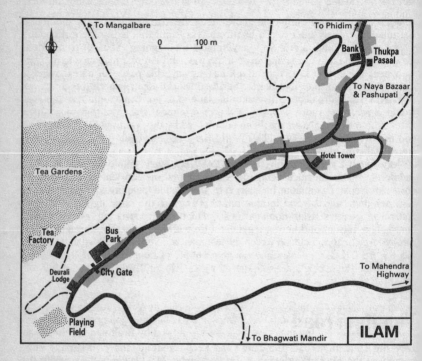

Settled by Newars, Rais and Marwaris (a business-minded Indian group with interests in tea), Ilam was at one time eastern Nepal's main centre of commerce. While hill towns like Ilam have lost much of their trading importance to the Tarai in recent years, its exuberant **haat bazaar** (held on a Thursday) still draws shoppers from a wide radius, and of course tea cultivation keeps the local economy stable. Unaccustomed to dealing with foreign travellers, **accommodation** here is on the spartan side, but the proprietor of *Deurali Lodge* (dorm beds Rs20, double rooms Rs35) at least speaks some English. Simple **meals** are possible at the *Deurali* and in several nameless eateries along the main drag – mostly it's just *daal bhaat* and packaged noodles, but you can get tasty *thukpa* at a place opposite the bank near the top of the bazaar.

The tea gardens and factory

The most pleasant thing to do in Ilam is stroll around the **tea gardens** which carpet the ridge above town and tumble down its steep far side; between April and December you can watch the pluckers at work, and at other times it's just a relaxing place to be. Nepal's first tea estate, it was established in 1864 by a relative of the prime minister after a visit to Darjeeling, where tea cultivation was just becoming big business. Marwaris, who had already cornered the cardamom trade here, soon assumed control of the plantation on a contract basis, an arrangement that lasted until the 1960s, when the government nationalised the industry under the *Nepal Tea Development Corporation. NTDC* now runs seven hill estates (some, like the one at Kanyam, much bigger than Ilam's), all of which are allowed to label their tea "Ilam"; Tarai plantations, which are privately run, call their product "Tarai" or "Jhapa".

You can visit the **tea factory** to see how the world's most popular beverage is produced. The process begins with the plucked leaves being loaded into "withering chutes", upstairs, where fans remove about half their moisture content. They're then transferred to big rolling machines to break the cell walls and release their juices, and placed on fermentation beds to bring out their characteristic flavour and colour. Finally, most of the remaining moisture is removed in a wood-fired drying machine and the leaves are sorted into grades ranging from the coveted TGFOP (Tippy Golden Flower Orange Pekoe, "tippy" referring to the tenderest new leaves) to the lowly PD (Pekoe Dust). Ilam's TGFOP compares favourably with the best of Darjeeling, and indeed most of it is exported to Germany to be blended into "Darjeeling" teas. A 500g bag costs about Rs80 here – much less than the comparable grade in Darjeeling. Tarai tea, incidentally, is processed by the more mechanised CTC (Curling, Tearing and Crushing) method, which produces the cheaper drink served just about everywhere in Nepal.

Beyond Ilam: walks and the road to Phidim

The Ilam area is noted for its greenness – higher up, the jungle is profuse and exuberant, and even the terraced slopes are teemingly fertile. Keep an eye out for cardamom, which grows in moist ravines and has become an important cash crop here. Rais make up the majority of villagers, followed by Brahmans, Chhetris and Limbus.

Rewarding **walks** set off in at least three directions. From the tea gardens, you can countour westwards and cross the Puwamai Khola, ascending the other side to MANGALBARE, site of a Wednesday **haat bazaar** even bigger than Ilam's (there are supposed to be views of Kanchenjunga further south along this ridge). A trail heading east from Ilam descends to cross the Mai Khola, where the annual **Beni Mela** attracts thousands of Hindus on *Magh Sankranti* (January 14 or 15), and continues on to NAYA BAZAAR. A sacred pond atop a wooded ridge north of Ilam, **Mai Pokhri** can be reached by walking or hitching along the road towards Phidim and making a right at BIBLIARTI, from which it's another two or three hours' ascent; SANDAKPUR, a superb viewpoint on the Indian border, is a day's walk further on, which suggests an illicit trek from here to Darjeeling. Finally, if you're looking for a quick leg-stretch, check out the small but attractively sited **Bhagwati Mandir** about 1km down the main road from *Deurali Lodge*.

Buses ply the road north of Ilam as far as **PHIDIM**, a run-of-the-mill district headquarters deep in Limbu territory, six hours further on. Although there's no checkpost, you're supposed to have a trekking permit to go there, and the local authorities are sensitive about having foreigners in the area ever since an awkward incident in 1989 in which two fundamentalist Christians were arrested for proselytising (they got off on a technicality).

festivals

Major holidays such as *Holi, Dasain* (known as *Dashera* in the Tarai) and *Tihar* (*Diwali*) are celebrated everywhere, and *Shiva Raatri* is popular in Hindu areas. In addition, look for these local festivals:

Beni Mela A celebration of the first day of *Magh* (January 14 or 15) with ritual bathing in the Mai Khola, near Ilam.

Losar Tibetan New Year, observed at Hile, Basantapur and other Buddhist places in the hills (February).

Barahachhetra Mela A pilgrimage to the Sapt Koshi River at Barahachhetra, near Dharan (late October or early November).

Rama Navami Rama's birthday, celebrated at Janakpur's Ram Mandir (late March or early April).

Viveh Panchami Janakpur's biggest festival, lasting five days and attracting 100,000 pilgrims to watch the wedding of Rama and Sita re-enacted at the Janaki Mandir (November or early December).

travel details

Buses

From Hetauda to Kathmandu (4 night buses, 1 *Sajha*; 8-9hr); many other buses pass through.

From Birganj to Janakpur (7 daily; 4 hr); Kathmandu (4 regular and 2 *Sajha*; 10hr) and Pokhara (6 daily; 10hr); for Tadi (Chitwan), take any Kathmandu or Pokhara bus.

From Janakpur to Biratnagar (3 nightly; 8hr); Birganj (7 daily; 4hr); Kakarbitta (2 daily; 9hr); Kathmandu (6 night buses, 1 *Sajha*; 10-12hr) and Pokhara (1 night bus; 12hr).

From Biratnagar to Dharan (frequent; 2hr); Janakpur (3 nightly; 8hr); Kakarbitta (hourly; 4hr) and Kathmandu (7 nightly; 16hr).

From Kakarbitta to Biratnagar (hourly; 4hr); Birtamod (frequent; 30min); Dharan (6 daily; 4hr); Janakpur (2 daily, 9hr); Kathmandu (8 nightly; 20hr) and Pokhara (2 nightly; 20hr).

From Dharan to Basantapur (2 daily; 5-6hr); Biratnagar (frequent; 1-2hr); Dhankuta (6 daily; 3hr); Hile (2 daily; 4hr); Kakarbitta (6 daily; 4hr) and Kathmandu (6 nightly; 16hr).

From Dhankuta to Hile (4 daily; 1hr) and Basantapur (same bus; 2-3hr).

From Birtamod to Ilam (5 daily; 6hr) and Phidim (2 daily; 12hr).

Planes

From Janakpur to Kathmandu (3 weekly; 40min).

From Biratnagar to Kathmandu (daily; 1hr 30min); Phaplu (weekly; 45min); Taplejung (3 weekly; 35min) and Tumlingtar (4 weekly; 1hr).

Connections to India

From Raxaul (Birganj), buses operate frequently to Patna (4hr), where you can catch broad-gauge trains to most parts of northern India.

From Raniganj (Kakarbitta), buses run approximately hourly to Siliguri and New Jalpaiguri (2hr), termini for Calcutta and the "toy train" to Darjeeling.

CHAPTER SEVEN

THE HIMALAYAN TREKKING REGIONS

A hundred divine epochs would not suffice to describe all the marvels of the Himalaya.

Hindu proverb

Rearing up over the subcontinent like an immense, whitecapped tidal wave, the **Himalaya** (Hi-*maal*-ya) is, to many travellers' minds, the whole reason for visiting Nepal. Containing eight of the world's ten highest peaks – including, of course, Everest – Nepal's 800-kilometre link in the Himalayan chain puts all other attractions in the shade. More than just majestic scenery, though, the "Abode of Snow" is also the home of Sherpas, yaks, yetis and snow leopards, and has always exerted a powerful spiritual presence: in Hindu mythology the mountains are where gods meditate and make sacrifices, while the Sherpas hold certain peaks to be the very embodiment of deities; mountaineers are often hardly less mystical.

Nepal's **trekking regions**, as defined by the government, take in all parts of the country more than about a day's walk from a paved road – a huge area covering nearly the entire northern half of Nepal, including not only the Himalaya but also large sections of the hills. These regions span an incredible diversity of terrain and culture, but one thing they all have in common is that you need a **trekking permit** to travel in them.

Trekking needn't be expensive nor agonisingly difficult. Most treks follow established routes where you can eat and sleep in simple inns for less money than you'd spend in Kathmandu; trails are often steep, to be sure, but you walk at your own pace, and no trek goes higher than about 5500m (the *starting* elevation for most climbing expeditions). That said, trekking is not for everybody – it's demanding, sometimes uncomfortable, and it does involve an element of risk. This chapter is organised to help you decide if you want to trek, and if so, how and where you might like to do it: the first section covers things you need to know about trekking in general, and the second gives overviews of the most popular treks.

Where you go will depend to a great extent on the **time of year**. In general, October and November are good for all mid- and high-elevation treks; December–February is a time to stay low; in spring you want to go high to get above the haze, especially from April on; and the monsoon (mid-June to late September or early October) is a washout nearly everywhere. More specific tips are given in the relevant trek descriptions.

TREKKING BASICS

This section runs through the different **styles** of trekking, **preparations** you'll have to make before setting off, **health** matters to be mindful of, and other factors of **life on the trail**. It's designed to complement the information given in standard trekking guides (see "Information, maps and books", below), with particular emphasis on the nuts and bolts of budget trekking.

Trekking styles

How you choose to trek will depend on your budget, time frame, and what sort of experience you're after. Trekking independently saves money and gives you a more individualised experience, but involves more preparations. Joining an agency trek minimises hassles and enables you to reach remote backcountry areas, but you pay dearly for it.

Trekking independently

Trekking independently means making all your own arrangements instead of going through a trekking agency – most budget travellers trek this way simply because it's cheaper. By carrying your own pack and staying in teahouses, a trek should **cost** no more than $7 a day – often as little as $3 a day – not including

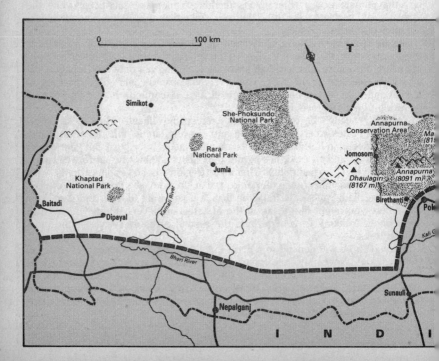

trekking permit and national park fees. Hiring a porter to carry your stuff will add about $4 a day, a guide $7 a day.

Doing it yourself gives you **more control** over many aspects of the trek: you can go at your own pace, stop when and where you like, choose your travelling companions and take rest days or side trips as you please. The downside is that you have to spend two or three days lining up trekking permits and bus tickets, renting equipment, buying supplies and perhaps tracking down a porter or guide. A further drawback is that you're effectively **confined to teahouse routes**; trekking to remote areas is difficult unless you speak Nepali or you're prepared to deal with considerable porter logistics.

Life on the trail is described later, but suffice to say that an independent trek is **less comfortable** than one arranged through an agency. Lodges can be noisy and lacking in privacy, while the food is sometimes very basic. The active teahouse **social scene** goes some way to compensating for this, however – even if you start out alone, you'll quickly meet up with potential trekking companions.

By not being part of a group you cause **less cultural disruption**, and are better placed to learn from Nepalese ways rather than forcing Nepalis to adapt to yours. Equally important, all the money you spend goes directly to the local economy (most of the money paid to trekking agencies goes no further than Kathmandu, and often finds its way overseas).

However, independent trekking **contributes to deforestation** – there's no way around it. If you stay in teahouses and order meals cooked over wood fires you encourage innkeepers to cut down more trees, and if you bring along a guide or porter, so do they. The hideous streamers of pink toilet paper seen on popular

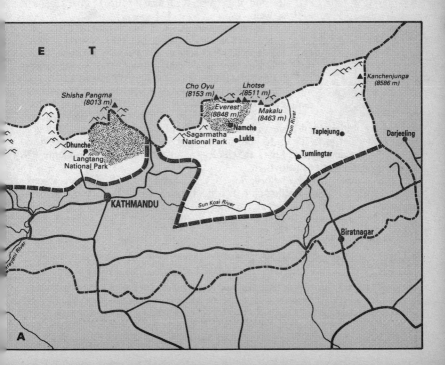

trails are usually the work of teahouse trekkers, since groups usually dig toilet pits and bury their waste. There are, however, ways to minimise your environmental impact – see the conservation tips below.

Hiring porters/guides

Porters are an important part of the Himalayan economy and there's no shame in hiring one. With a porter taking most of your gear, you only need to carry a small pack containing the things you need during the day; this can be a great relief at high elevations, and it's essential when trekking off established routes, where tents, food and cooking equipment have to be brought in. As porters rarely speak much English, you might want to pay more for a **guide** who does – although a guide is really only necessary if you're planning an esoteric trek. An increasing number of them are willing to carry gear as well, but this isn't always the case: ask.

Hiring a porter is simple – just ask your innkeeper, or try any trekking agency or equipment-rental shop. If you're not sure you need a porter, or you think you'll only need one for a few tough days of a trek, you can usually hire someone on the spot at Namche, Jomosom and many of the remote airstrips. The business is very informal and not always reputable, so shop around and interview more than one candidate if necessary. Make sure the agreed wage includes food – a porter can run up a huge bill if you're paying – and expect to pay a couple hundred rupees' tip at the end of the trek. It's a nice gesture to give a T-shirt as well.

The **responsibilities** of employing a porter or guide can't be overstressed, however. Several porters die needlessly each year, typically because their sahib (pronounced "sahb") thought they were superhuman and didn't mind sleeping outside in a blizzard. You *must* make sure your employees are adequately clothed for the journey – on high-altitude treks, that will mean buying or renting them shoes, a parka, sunglasses, mittens and a sleeping bag; establish beforehand if something is a loan. If they get sick, it's up to you to look after them, and since most porters hired in Kathmandu and Pokhara are clueless about altitude-related problems, it's your responsibility to educate them.

If you've never trekked before, don't try to organise a trek off the teahouse routes. Finding a guide familiar with a particular area will be hard, and transporting him with a crew of porters and supplies to the trailhead a major (and expensive) logistical exercise. Getting a trekking agency to do it might not cost much more.

Trekking with an agency

Treks organised through an **agency** are for people who haven't got the time or inclination to make their own arrangements. They **cost** anything from $15 to $150 a day, depending on the standard of service, size of the group, remoteness of the route, and whether you book the trip in your home country or in Kathmandu. The price should always include a guide, porters, food and shelter, although cheap outfits often charge extra for trekking permits, national park fees and transport, and may cut other corners as well. The cheaper the price, the more wary you need to be.

A trek is hard work however you do it, but a good agency will help you along with a few **creature comforts**: you can expect good food, "bed tea" and hot "washing water" on cold mornings, camp chairs, and a latrine tent with toilet paper. Depending on the size of your party, a guide, *sardaar* (guide foreman) or "Western trek leader" (native-English-speaking guide) will be able to answer questions and cope with problems. Trekking groups usually sleep in **tents**, which, while quieter than teahouses, are generally colder and more cramped. The daily routine of eating in a mess tent can get monotonous, and gives you **less contact** with local people. There's something to be said for safety in numbers, but trekking with a group imposes an **inflexible itinerary** on you, and if you don't like the people in your group, you're stuck.

In theory, agency treks are more **environmentally sound**, at least in the Everest and Annapurna areas, where trekkers' meals are required to be cooked with kerosene. In practice, however, cooks use wood whenever possible so they can sell the kerosene at the end of the trek – and, worse still, for each trekker eating a kerosene-cooked meal, two or three porters and other staff are cooking their *bhaat* over a wood fire.

The main advantage in trekking with an agency is it enables you to get **off the beaten track**: there's little point in using an agency to do a teahouse trek.

Budget agencies

Small "walk-in" outfits in Kathmandu and Pokhara, charging $15–25 a day (or rupee equivalent), are notoriously hard to recommend: most are fly-by-night operations offering mainly customised treks, though they're rarely competent to handle anything off the mass-market routes. Names change and standards rise and fall – if you hear of a good one through word of mouth, try it. A few of the more established agencies run scheduled treks, but again, usually only to the most popular areas; one exception is *Mountain Adventure Trekking* (☎414910), located in front of the *Kathmandu Guest House*, which does a few unorthodox trips for $25 a day.

Upmarket agencies

Kathmandu's **big operators** mainly package treks on behalf of overseas companies, but some offer scheduled treks for the local market, which are of the same "export" quality but at a lower price (typically $30–60 a day). Write for brochures to make sure your schedule coincides with theirs; for customised treks to exotic areas, write several months in advance, or be prepared to wait a week in Kathmandu while arrangements are being made. If you pay in foreign currency, be sure to get an official exchange receipt. The following list should get you started:

Asian Trekking, Keshar Mahal (off Tridevi Marg), Kathmandu (☎01/412821; PO Box 3022).

Journeys Mountaineering & Trekking , Kantipath, Kathmandu (☎01/225969; PO Box 2034).

Rover Treks & Expeditions, Naksal, Kathmandu (☎01/414373; PO Box 1081).

Sherpa Co-operative Trekking, Durbar Marg, Kathmandu (☎01/224068, PO Box 1338).

Yangrima Trekking & Mountaineering, Kantipath, Kathmandu (☎01/225608; PO Box 2951). Probably the most environmentally aware agency in Nepal.

Agencies in the UK

Booking through a **British company** lets you arrange everything before you leave home – but expect to pay £30–60 per day. The following are merely overseas agents – all their treks are sub-contracted to operators in Kathmandu like those mentioned above.

Art of Travel, 268 Lavender Hill, London SW11 1LJ (☎071/738 2038).

Classic Nepal, 33 Metro Avenue, Newton, Derbyshire DE55 5UF (☎0773/873497).

Exodus Expeditions, 9 Weir Road, London SW12 0LT (☎081/675 5550).

ExplorAsia, 13 Chapter Street, London SW1P 4NY (☎071/630 7102).

Himalayan Kingdoms, 20 The Mall, Clifton, Bristol BS8 4DR (☎0272/237163).

Himalayan Quest, 30 Hamilton Terrace, Leamington Spa, Warwickshire CV32 4LY (☎0926/450835).

Sherpa Expeditions, 131a Heston Road, Hounslow, Middlesex TW5 0RD (☎081/577 2717).

Preparations

Arranging a trek is like anything else in Nepal: complications arise, things inevitably take longer than planned, but it's unquestionably worth it in the end. How you trek will have a bearing on this – trekking independently involves more preparation than joining an organised group. The remainder of this chapter is geared specifically to independent trekkers, although most of the information will apply to groups as well.

Trekking permits

A **trekking permit** is required to enter any of the areas described in this chapter. Apply at the *Central Immigration* offices in Kathmandu or Pokhara (addresses on p.72 and p166); Pokhara is generally easier to deal with than Kathmandu, but both are frantic during October – especially just before and after the weeklong *Dasain* holiday. Permits cost Rs90 per week during the first month of your stay in Nepal and Rs112.50 per week thereafter (for Annapurna permits, there's an extra Rs200 conservation fee); they can sometimes be extended at checkposts along the trail, but don't count on it. When applying, bring your passport, two passport photos, and official receipts showing you've changed **$10 a day** for the duration of the permit. Be sure to fill in the correct

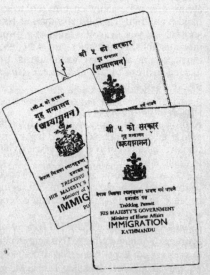

form: blue for Helambu/Langtang, yellow for Annapurna, pink for Everest and white for all other regions or treks in more than one region. Permits are usually ready later the same day. A separate stamp in your passport extends your visa up till the expiry date of the trekking permit.

A trekking permit still doesn't give you free run of the country – most border areas are closed, and peaks are restricted. Eighteen summits between 5500m and 6500m, designated **trekking peaks**, can be climbed only with an additional permit ($200–300 per party) obtainable from the *Nepal Mountaineering Association*, Ram Shah Path, Kathmandu.

Before setting off, **register with your embassy** in Kathmandu, as this will speed things up should you need rescuing. You can have the *Himalayan Rescue Association* (see below) forward the details to your embassy. It's also advisable to be **insured** for trekking; most travel-insurance companies double their rates to cover "hazardous sports" such as trekking.

Information, maps and books

The best source of current trekking **information** is the *Himalayan Rescue Association* (☎418755), located in the forecourt of the *Kathmandu Guest House*, which keeps a logbook full of comments from returning trekkers – invaluable for tips on routes and trekking agencies – and can advise on recent trail conditions, altitude sickness, first aid and equipment. You can also check out the HRA's noticeboard to find **trekking partners**,.

Nepal's trekking regions are fairly well **mapped**, although the rule, as always, is you get what you pay for. The inexpensive *Mandala* dyelines cover all the major routes, but are often misleading – much better, and pricier, are the *Schneider* maps of the Everest and Langtang/Helambu areas and the *ACAP* map of Annapurna, all of which are available in the bigger Kathmandu bookshops. Specific titles are recommended in the area descriptions given later in this chapter.

General **books** on the Himalaya are deitailed in *Contexts*, but trekking guides are listed below; all can be bought in Kathmandu.

Stephen Bezruchka *A Guide to Trekking in Nepal* (The Mountaineers £8.95). The most thorough, even-handed and sensitive book on trekking, containing background pieces on Nepalese culture and natural history.

Stan Armington *Trekking in the Nepal Himalaya* (Lonely Planet £4.95). A less perceptive, but more portable, alternative. Some people prefer its "Day 1-Day 2" route descriptions.

Hugh Swift *Trekking in Nepal, West Tibet and Bhutan* (Hodder & Stoughton £9.95). Gives vivid area accounts instead of detailed hour-by-hour route descriptions; good for obscure treks.

Bill O'Connor *The Trekking Peaks of Nepal* (Crowood £14.95). Describes climbing routes and trek approaches for all eighteen trekking peaks.

John L. Hayes *Trekking North of Pokhara* (Roger Lascelles £3.95). Short on context, but a lightweight option if you only intend to trek in this region.

Stephen Martin *Kathmandu and the Everest Trek* (Roger Lascelles £5.95). A similar treatment of a single region.

Alton C. Byers III *Treks on the Kathmandu Valley Rim* (Sahayogi Rs50). Mainly day hikes and overnights.

What to bring

Having the right **equipment** on a trek is obviously important, but when you see how little porters get by with you'll realise that high-tech gear isn't essential – bring what you need to be comfortable, but keep weight to a minimum. The equipment list given here is intended mainly for independent trekkers staying in teahouses; if you're planning to camp, you'll need quite a few more things, and if you're trekking with an agency you won't need so much.

By **renting** bulky or specialised items in Nepal, you'll avoid having to lug them around during the rest of your travels. Kathmandu has dozens of hire shops, while Pokhara's selection is somewhat more limited; if you're trekking in the Everest region, you can rent high-altitude gear in Namche. You'll be expected to leave a hefty deposit, typically $50-plus or an international air ticket. Inspect sleeping bags and parkas carefully for fleas (or worse) – if there's time before setting off, have them cleaned. Don't rent boots, as you're unlikely to get a good fit. You can often buy equipment from travellers leaving Nepal: check the restaurant notice boards in Kathmandu.

Clothes must be lightweight and versatile, especially on long treks where conditions vary from subtropical to arctic. What you bring will depend on the trek and time of year, but in most cases you should be prepared for sun, rain and snow. As explained in "Cultural Hints" in *Basics*, Nepalis have innately conservative attitudes about dress: in warm areas, women should wear calf-length dresses

---

EQUIPMENT CHECKLIST

Items marked (*) can be purchased in Nepal and those marked (**) can also be rented.

ESSENTIALS
Backpack** One with an internal frame and hip belt is best.
Sleeping bag** A three-season bag is adequate for hill treks; above 4000m, or in winter, you'll need a four-season bag and possibly a liner.
Medical kit See "Health".
Water bottle*
Toiletries
Toilet paper* See "Conservation Tips".
Towel
Torch* Remember that batteries run down faster in the cold.
Pocket knife
Sunglasses* A good UV-protective pair, ideally with side shields.
Sunscreen/lip balm At altitude, you'll need a high protection factor or zinc oxide.

FOOTWEAR
Hiking boots** Usually only necessary for treks over 4000m.
Trainers Okay for most trails, handy for evenings.
Flipflops* May be useful for evenings at low elevations.

CLOTHES
Shirts/T-shirts*
Trousers* Baggy (to leave room for thermal underwear) and with plenty of pockets.

or skirts with demure tops; men should wear a shirt and long pants wherever possible, and both sexes should wear at least a swim suit when bathing.

Bringing **camera** equipment involves a trade-off between weight and performance – a pocket 35mm model may be a good compromise. An SLR body with long and short zoom lenses will produce much better results, especially with a tripod and polarising filters, although it's heavy and obtrusive.

Health and emergencies

Guidebook writers tend to go overboard about the health hazards of trekking, but don't be put off – the vast majority of trekkers never experience anything worse than a mild headache. That said, health is of paramount concern when doing any strenuous physical activity, and all the more so when trekking, which routinely takes you a week or more from the nearest medical facilities. Stomach troubles can spoil a trek, while injuries or altitude sickness, if untreated, could prove fatal. It's best to err on the side of caution.

Children, old-age pensioners and disabled people have all trekked successfully, but a minimum **fitness** level is required. Needless to say, the better prepared you are physically, the more you'll enjoy the trek. If you're in any doubt about your ability to cope with strenuous walking, see your doctor; it's also worth knowing if you have any allergies, especially to antibiotics.

Skirt/dress* Mid-calf length is best.
Shorts Useful for lower elevations (men only).
Sweat pants Can be worn over shorts in morning; also good for evenings.
Socks Several thin cotton/blend and thick woollen* pairs.
Underwear
Sun hat Helpful at low elevations.
Wool sweater* Or a synthetic fleece jacket.
Thermal underwear Not necessary at low elevations.
Bandana To use as a handkerchief, sweatband or scarf.
Parka** Preferably down or a lightweight fibre.
Wool hat* One that covers the ears is best.
Wool mittens* Ski gloves are warmer, but bulkier.
Rain shell/poncho Breathable waterproof material (eg, Gore-Tex) is best. An umbrella* will probably suffice, and can also function as a parasol.

HIGH-ALTITUDE GEAR – OPTIONAL
Gaiters** Worth having for passes where snow is likely.
Down pants** A welcome luxury on cold evenings.
Ski poles** May be useful for keeping your balance in snow.
Ice axe** Rarely needed on teahouse treks.
Crampons** Ditto.

OTHER USEFUL ITEMS
Day pack
Camera equipment
Foam mat**
Sewing kit
Stuff sacks Handy for separating things in your pack.

Stomach troubles

The risk of **stomach troubles** is particularly high while trekking, and water is the usual culprit: you need to drink lots of fluids on the trail. Innkeepers normally boil water and tea, but not always for the statutory ten minutes, and at high altitudes the boiling point of water is so low that germs might not be killed. All running water should be assumed to be contaminated – wherever you go, there will be people, or at least animals, upstream.

Treating the water is not only the best line of defence against illness, it also reduces your reliance on boiled water. Iodine is the safest method, either in tablet form or, more commonly, as a two-percent liquid solution: use two to five drops per litre, depending on the cloudiness of the water, and wait at least twenty minutes before drinking; you might want to cover up the taste with powdered fruit drink. Chlorine-based tablets may not be effective against amoebas and giardia. Ceramic filter pumps produce pure water without the aftertaste, although they're expensive and take up space.

See "Health and Insurance" in *Basics* for tips on treating stomach upsets.

Diet and minor injuries

Nutrition in the Himalaya isn't great, but the food served in teahouses is generally adequate and well-balanced. On less-travelled routes, however, where *daal bhaat* and potatoes are often the only food available, you'll have to force yourself to eat large amounts to get enough calories and protein; you might also want to bring vitamin tablets.

Most minor injuries occur while walking downhill; **knee strains** are common, especially among trekkers carrying their own packs. If you know your knees are weak, bind them up with ace bandages as a preventative measure, and think about hiring a porter. Good, supportive boots reduce the risk of **ankle sprains** or twists. It's hard to avoid getting **blisters**, but make sure your boots are well broken-in, and change socks regularly, especially if they get wet. Apply moleskin to hotspots as soon as they develop, making sure to clean and cover blisters so they can heal as quickly as possible.

Coping with altitude

Barraged by medical advice and horror stories, trekkers all too often develop altitude paranoia. The fact is that just about everyone who treks over 4000m experiences some symptoms of **acute mountain sickness (AMS)**, but serious cases are very rare, and the simple cure – descent – almost always brings immediate recovery.

Causes

At high elevations there is not only less oxygen but also lower pressure, which can have all sorts of weird effects on the body: it can swell the brain, cause the lungs to fill with fluid, and even bring on uncontrollable farting. The syndrome varies from one person to the next, and fitness isn't a factor – in fact, young people seem to be more susceptible, possibly because they're more hung up about admitting they feel rotten. Most people are capable of acclimatising to very high elevations, but the process takes time and must be done in stages. The golden rule is **don't go too high too fast**: above 3000m, the daily net elevation gain should be no more than 500m; take mandatory acclimatisation days at around 3500m and 4500m – more if you're feeling unwell – and try to spend these days hiking higher. These are only guidelines, and you'll have to regulate your ascent according to how you feel. Trekkers who fly directly to high airstrips have to be especially careful to acclimatise.

Symptoms

AMS usually gives plenty of warning before it becomes life-threatening. Mild **symptoms** include headaches, dizziness, insomnia, nausea, loss of appetite, shortness of breath and swelling of the hands and feet; one or two of these shouldn't be cause for panic, but they're a sign that your body hasn't yet acclimatised to the elevation. You shouldn't ascend further until you start feeling better, or, if you do keep going, you should be prepared to beat a hasty retreat if the condition gets worse. Serious symptoms – persistent vomiting, delirium, loss of coordination, bubbly breathing and bloody sputum, rapid heart rate or breathlessness at rest, blueness of face and lips – can develop within hours, and if ignored can result in death.

Cure

The only effective cure for advanced AMS is **descent**. Anyone showing serious symptoms should be taken down immediately, regardless of the time of day or night – hire a porter or pack animal to carry the sufferer if necessary. Recovery is usually dramatic, often after a descent of only a few hundred metres.

Drink plenty of liquids at altitude – the body tends to retain water, and the air is incredibly dry; the usual adage is that you're not drinking enough unless you pee clear. Keeping warm, eating well, getting plenty of sleep and avoiding alcohol will also help reduce the chances of getting AMS. Some doctors recommend **Diamox**, a diuretic, to relieve mild AMS symptoms, although it has to be stressed that Diamox does nothing to treat the underlying cause of AMS; the dose is 250mg twice a day. For further advice on AMS, visit the *Himalayan Rescue Association*'s aid posts at Manang (on the Annapurna Circuit) and Pheriche (on the Everest trek).

Other altitude-related dangers such as **hypothermia** and **frostbite** are encountered less often by trekkers, but can pose real threats on high, exposed passes and in bad weather. Common-sense precautions bear repeating: wear or carry adequate clothing; keep dry; cover exposed extremities in severe weather; eat lots and carry emergency snacks; and make for shelter if conditions get bad. **Snowblindness** isn't a worry as long as you're equipped with a good pair of sunglasses.

Emergencies

Ninety-nine percent of the time, trekking in Nepal is a piece of cake and it's hard to imagine something going wrong. Though few trekkers ever have to deal with **emergencies** – illness, AMS, storms, missteps, landslides and avalanches are the main causes – they can happen to anyone.

Bezruchka's *A Guide to Trekking in Nepal* (see "Information, maps and books") gives full advice on emergency **procedures** and a rundown of hospitals, aid posts, airstrips and radio transmitters found near the main trekking routes. In non-urgent cases, your best bet is to be carried by porter or pack animal to the nearest **airstrip** or **hospital**, although bear in mind that medical facilities outside Kathmandu and a few other major cities are very rudimentary. Where the situation is more serious, send word to the nearest village with a radio requesting a **helicopter rescue**. A typical rescue costs $1200–2000, and they won't come for you until they're satisfied you'll be able to pay; being registered with your embassy will speed the process of contacting relatives who can vouch for you.

FIRST-AID CHECKLIST

Most of the following items can be purchased in Kathmandu or Pokhara for much less then they cost back home. This is a minimum first-aid kit – trekking guidebooks usually give much longer lists. See "Health and Insurance" in *Basics* for tips on self-diagnosis, and use antibiotics advisedly.

FOR INJURIES
Band-Aids Large and small sizes.
Gauze pads
Sterile dressing
Surgical tape
Moleskin Synthetic adhesive padding for blisters.
Elastic support bandages For knee strains, ankle sprains.
Antiseptic cream For scrapes, blisters, insect bites.
Tweezers
Scissors
Thermometer A low-reading one, for cases of hypothermia.

FOR ILLNESSES
Aspirin/Paracetamol
Cold medicine
Throat lozenges Sore throats are common at high elevations.
Diarrhoea tablets
Jeevan Jal Rehydration formula for diarrhoea.
Tiniba For giardia, amoebic dysentery.
Nalidixic Acid An antibiotic for diarrhoea (*Bactrim* is an alternative).
Diamox For treatment of mild AMS symptoms.
Mycostatin Vaginal tablets for yeast infections.

Trekking life

A trek, it's often said, is not a wilderness experience. Unlike other mountain ranges, the Himalaya are comparatively well settled, farmed and grazed – much of their beauty, in fact, is man-made – and the trails support a steady stream of local traffic. If you're trekking independently, you'll be sleeping and eating in teahouses and making equal contact with locals and other foreigners – you'll need a good deal of adaptability to different living situations, but the payback comes in cultural insights, unforgettable encounters, and of course breathtaking scenery.

Trailheads are typically at the end of a long, bumpy bus ride, and **getting there** is an integral part of the experience. This is also a big factor in deciding where to trek, as the going and returning can eat up two days (or more) and, in the case of far-flung treks reached by plane, can represent the single biggest expense. See *Basics* for general information on bus and air travel, and the "Flying to Lukla" box later in the Everest section of this chapter for more specific advice on mountain flights.

Trails

The **walking** slays everyone at first, but you find your own rhythm after a few days; most people take it in easy stages, from one glass of *chiya* to the next – there's no race to the top. It's best to set off early each morning to make the most of the clear weather, as clouds usually roll in around midday. Pad your schedule for rest days, weather and contingencies, and make time for at least one unusual side trip – that's when things get really interesting.

Trails are often steep and rough, and bridges precarious, but getting lost is seldom a worry. Stopping to chat and ask directions is part of the fun, and a good opportunity to learn some Nepali. **Trekking alone** is safe, but try to stay within sight of other people, as there have been a few mysterious disappearances over the years. Nepalis think all lone travellers are a bit odd, so you might find it worthwhile teaming up with others just to avoid the constant question, *Eklai?* ("Alone?"). Be sure to read "Cultural Hints" in *Basics*; again, *don't* give pens or rupees to children, whether they ask or not – if you do, every trekker that comes after you will be hounded for handouts.

CONSERVATION TIPS

The main environmental problem in the Himalaya is **deforestation**, and trekking puts an additional strain on local wood supplies; in addition, trekkers leave litter, tax local sanitation systems and contribute to water pollution. The following are suggestions on how to minimise your impact on the fragile Himalayan environment.

• Where the choice exists, eat at teahouses that cook with kerosene or electricity instead of ones that use wood.
• Try to time your meals and coordinate your orders with other trekkers; cooking food in big batches is a more efficient use of fuel.
• If trekking with an agency, see that all meals are cooked with kerosene, and complain if they aren't.
• Try not to take hot showers, except in inns where the water is heated by electricity.
• Treat water with iodine instead of asking innkeepers to fill your canteen with boiled water.
• Use latrines wherever possible. Where there's no facility, encourage the innkeeper to build one; go well away from water sources, and bury your faeces.
• Burn your toilet paper – there's nothing worse than the sight of pink toilet paper littering a beautiful mountain scene, and it can also spread disease.
• Use biodegradable soap and shampoo, and don't rinse directly in streams.
• Carry all non-burnable litter back out – that includes tins and batteries.

Teahouses

Teahouses along the routes are efficient little operations, with English signs, menus and usually an English-speaking manager. Although they cater exclusively to trekkers and their porters, these *bhattis* (as they're called in the Annapurna region; *chiya pasaal* elsewhere) follow the Nepalesetradition of providing practically free lodging – usually Rs2–5 a night – to dinner customers. Unfortunately for couples, dormitory accommodation is the rule, although separate rooms are available at the most popular stopping places. The beds may or may not come with padding; a sleeping bag is obligatory and a foam mat comes in handy. Some places even have wood stoves or electricity.

You'll find fewer comforts **on less-trekked trails**, however, where lodgings are likely to be private kitchens and meals are eaten by the fire in eye-watering smoke. Such places rarely advertise themselves, but once you've spent a little time off the beaten track you'll start realising that almost every trailside house with an open front is potential shelter.

Food and drink

Trekking cuisine is a world unto itself. Teahouses' plastic-coated cardboard menus promise tempting international delicacies, although you'll notice that the "spring roll" wrappings, "enchilada" tortillas, "pizza" crusts and "pancakes" all bear more than a passing resemblance to chapatis – but at any rate, eggs, porridge, custard and even (sometimes) apple pie are all reassuringly familiar, and goodies like chocolate and muesli are often available.

However, many trekkers order "Western" food simply because it's there, not because it's good, and indeed it costs much more than **local food**. In highland areas you'll be able to eat such Tibetan dishes as *momo*, *thukpa* and *riki kur*, and instead of porridge you might be served *tsampa* (see "Eating and Drinking" in *Basics*); at lower elevations, *daal bhaat* and packet noodles are the standard offerings. A further advantage of eating local fare is that it's often quicker: there are usually unlimited quantities of *daal bhaat* steaming away on the back burner, whereas foreign food has to be made specially.

When **ordering**, bear in mind that the cook can only make one or two things at a time, and there may be many others ahead of you: simplify the process by coordinating your order with other trekkers. Most innkeepers expect dinner orders to be placed several hours in advance, and there's usually a dog-eared notepad floating around on which you're meant to keep a tally of everything you've eaten. Pay when you leave, and be sure to bring plenty of small money on the trek, since innkeepers often have trouble changing anything over Rs50.

Tea and "hot lemon" are the main **drinks** on the trail. Bottled soft drinks and even beer are common along the popular routes, but the price of each bottle rises by about Rs5 for each extra day it has to be portered from the nearest road. Don't miss trying *chhang*, *raksi* and *tongba* – again, see *Basics* for fuller explanations of these alcoholic specialities.

Sanitation

Washing and toilet facilites, where they exist, are basic. You'll generally have to bathe and do laundry under makeshift outdoor taps in freezing cold water, which explains why hot springs are such major attractions. A few teahouses in the Annapurna and Everest regions provide hot water for washing, and some even rig up primitive shower cubicles. An increasing number of teahouses are installing outdoor latrines (*chaarpi*), but don't be surprised if you're pointed to a half-covered privy hanging over a stream, or simply to a paddock.

THE TREKS

Nepal's mountains can be divided into five regions, the first three being most suitable for first-time trekkers. The sections below give overviews of the areas and describe the major trekking possibilities within them, but if you want a step-by-step route description you'll need a full-blown trekking guidebook.

In choosing a trek, you have to take into account a number of factors. On a limited budget and schedule, you'll be restricted to the **Annapurna** and **Helambu/Langtang** regions north of Pokhara and Kathmandu. Given more time or money, you'll be able to tackle **Everest** or some of the longer Annapurna routes. With experience, or a sense of adventure, you should consider treks in the more remote regions of **eastern** and **far western Nepal**. The box below summarises the major teahouse treks.

Annapurna

About three-quarters of all trekking permits are issued for the **Annapurna** region north of Pokhara. The popularity is well deserved, since nowhere else do you get such a rich feast of spectacular scenery and varied hill culture. Compared to most other regions, **logistics** are simple: treks all start or finish close to Pokhara, and transportation to trailheads is well developed; with great views just three days up the trail, short treks are particularly feasible. Pokhara is the only place outside Kathmandu with a Central Immigration office that issues **trekking permits**, and the Pokhara office is, if anything, saner than Kathmandu's (see "Pokhara Listings" in Chapter Four for details). If your trek starts and ends in Pokhara, you'll be able to store excess luggage and **hire equipment** there as well.

The popular treks in the Annapurna region have become **highly commercialised** and culturally rather tame – this is the Costa del Trekking. To be fair, most trekkers regard familiar food, mattresses, English signs and western company as pluses, but if you're looking to get away from it all, look elsewhere.

Annapurna Himal faces Pokhara like an enormous settee, 40km across and numbering nine peaks over 7000m, with Annapurna I above all at 8091m. It's an area of stunning diversity, ranging from the sodden bamboo forests of the southern slopes (Lumle, northwest of Pokhara, is the wettest place in Nepal) to windswept desert (Jomosom, in the northern rain shadow, is the driest). The *himal* and adjacent hill areas are protected within the **Annapurna Conservation Area Project** (ACAP), for which you have to pay a Rs200 **entry fee** when applying for your trekking permit. A quasi-park administered by a non-governmental trust, ACAP has to walk a fine line between environmental protection and economic development – tourism is big business here. The project has set up kerosene depots to wean innkeepers away from wood fuel, while latrines and rubbish pits are being constructed to cope with the strain trekkers put on local sanitation.

Meanwhile, ACAP is training lodge owners in the basics of hygiene and hotel management; to their credit, lodges with ACAP certificates are usually run to high standards.

Autumn is the **best season** for treks around Annapurna, but winter is fine for the shorter, lower treks; spring can be disappointingly hazy, and quite hot at the lower elevations from mid-April on. The region is adequately covered by the *Mandala* "Pokhara to Jomosom Manang" **map** (1:125,000); better, but more expensive, is *ACAP*'s "Annapurna" (1:125,000).

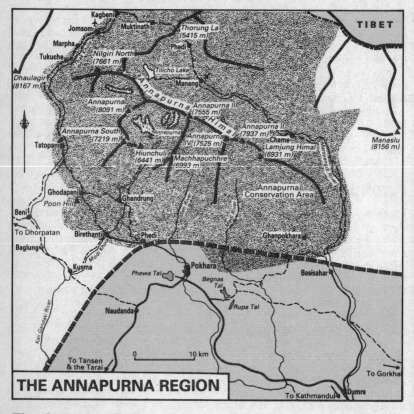

THE ANNAPURNA REGION

The Jomosom Trek

The **JOMOSOM TREK** is an acknowledged classic: an ideal sampler of Himalayan scenery and culture, and, not surprisingly, the most commercialised stretch of trail in Nepal. A guide definitely isn't necessary. **Food and lodging** are of a relatively high standard, and many lodges have electricity and hot showers; all have English menus and outdo each other with the Westernness of their cuisine. For this they charge **higher prices** than on any other trek: for basic food, drink and lodging you need to budget about Rs200 per day.

TREKS AT A GLANCE

Trek	Days	Best Months	Elevation	Difficulty	Comments
Helambu	3–10	Oct–April	800–3600	Moderate	Easy access, uncrowded, varied; only modest views.
Gosainkund	5–7	Oct–Dec, Feb–May	1950–4380	Strenuous	Sacred lakes; festival in July–August.
Khaptad	5–7	Oct–April	1100–3000	Moderate	Fly in; only marginally teahousable; sacred area.
Poon Hill	5–8	Oct–April	1100–3200	Moderate	Easy access, excellent views; very commercial.
Rara	6–8	Oct–Nov, April–June	2400–3500	Moderate	Fly in; must be prepared to camp; pristine lake and forest.
Pokhara – Kathmandu	7–10	Nov–March	400–1450	Easy	Pleasant hill walk, snow-free in winter; basic teahouses.
Langtang	8–12	Oct–May	1700–3750	Moderate	Beautiful alpine valley close to Kathmandu.
Lower Kali – Gandaki	8–12	Nov–March	900–3200	Moderate	Longer version of Poon Hill, returning a less commercial way.
Annapurna Sanctuary	9–12	Oct–Dec, Feb–April	1100–4130	Moderate/ Strenuous	Spectacular scenery, easy access; acclimatisation necessary.
Dhorpatan circuit	10–14	Oct–April	470–3400	Moderate	May need guide, shelter and food.
Jomosom/ Muktinath	12–16	Oct–April	1100–3800	Easy/ Moderate	Spectacular, varied; very commercial.
Everest (Lukla fly-in)	14–18	Oct–Nov, March–May	2800–5550	Strenuous	Superb scenery; flights a problem; acclimatisation necessary.
Annapurna circuit	16–21	Oct–Dec, March–April	450–5380	Strenuous	Incredible diversity and scenery; high pass requires care and acclimatisation.
Everest (Jiri walk-in)	26+	Oct–Nov, March–April	1500–5550	Very strenuous	Wonderful mix of hill and high-elevation walking, but with a lot of up and down.
Everest (eastern approach)	30+	Nov, March	300–5550	Very Strenuous	Similar, but with an even greater net vertical gain.

The full Jomosom trek takes about two weeks, but the trail network is extensive, so shorter and longer variations are possible; the first half of the trek, which can be done on its own, is described first. The usual **starting point** is moving slowly uphill: at the time of writing, the procedure was to take a jeep (45min, Rs35) from Shining Hospital in Pokhara to PHEDI, but the road has been extended to Lumle and is bound eventually for Birethanti, Baglung and Beni (see p.170). By 1991 there should be a bus service along the road and Birethanti will be the trailhead, which will chop two or three days off treks in this area. It's also possible to start from Lakeside in Pokhara, going by way of Sarangkot, though few people do.

To Poon Hill

If you haven't time to do the full Jomosom trek, you can get a taster of it by turning the first half into a one-week circuit. The route ambles through steep, lush hill country, taking in some lovely Gurung villages and, weather permitting, rewarding you with outstanding views of the Annapurnas and Machhapuchhre. The **trails** are wide and well maintained, though steep in places, and unfortunately the first couple of days are spent rather too close to the new road. The highest point reached is 3200m, which shouldn't present any altitude problems, but it's high enough that you'll need **warm clothes** at night; rain gear is also advisable.

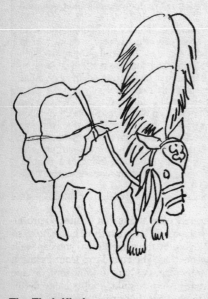

Several trails make for Poon Hill, all generally heading east of Pokhara. Most people start up the more southerly route, calling at NAGDANDA (or NAUDANDA), KAARE and the picturesque stream-side village of **BIRETHANTI**. A day and a half northwest of Birethanti, and 2000m higher, is **POON HILL**: watching the mountains at sunrise from here is probably the single most done thing in the trekking universe; if clouds block your view, as they often do, it's well worth hanging on for an extra day. From Poon Hill, you can return through magnificent stands of giant **rhododendrons** and **orchids** to the pretty Gurung town of **GHANDRUNG**, where the Annapurna Sanctuary trail heads north, and on back to Pokhara.

The Thak Khola

North of Poon Hill, the trail drops into the valley of the Kali Gandaki (locally called the **Thak Khola**) and the fun really begins: as you follow the course of the world's deepest gorge – the 8000-metre hulks of Dhaulagiri and Annapurna tower on either side – the scenery changes by the mile; the valley is also famous for its **ethnic diversity**, Thakalis being the dominant group.

The walking actually gets easier after Poon Hill (and by this time you should be in better shape), and the trail stays below 3000m until the last day's climb to

BHOTIYAS AND THAKALIS

Bhotiya is the Nepali term for all northern border peoples of Tibetan descent. Unfortunately, Bhotiyas themselves have tended to resent the label ever since an 1854 government edict, intended to find places for all minority groups in the Hindu caste system, placed them in the lowly category of "enslavable alcohol-drinkers" because they ate yak meat (which Hindus regarded as being almost as bad as eating beef). Most prefer to identify with a specific regional group, of which there are at least a dozen in Nepal; Sherpas, the best-known Bhotiya group, are highlighted in the Everest section later in this chapter.

In most ways, Bhotiyas are indistinguishable from Tibetans. Except in certain areas in the far west, where some have been influenced by Hinduism, they are exclusively **Buddhist**, and their *chortens* (stupa-like cremation monuments), *mani* walls (consisting of slates inscribed with the mantra *Om mani padme hum*), *gompas* (monasteries) and prayer flags (*lung ta*: literally, "wind horse") are the most memorable man-made features of the Himalaya. Farmers, herders and trans-Himalayan traders, they always settle higher and further north than other ethnic groups. Bhotiya villages vary in appearance, but those in the Annapurna region are strongly Tibetan, with houses stacked up slopes so that the flat roof of one serves as the grain-drying terrace of the next. Like Tibetans, they like their tea flavoured with salt and yak butter, and women wear trademark rainbow aprons (*pangden*) and wrap-around dresses (*chuba*).

Unencumbered by caste, Bhotiyas are noticeably less tradition-bound than Hindus, and **women** are better off for it: they play a more nearly equal role in household affairs, speak their minds openly, are able to tease and mingle with men publicly, and can divorce without stigma. Having said that, even Bhotiyas tend to consider a female birth to be the result of bad karma, and during death rites lamas customarily urge the deceased to be reincarnated as a male.

A hill group with influence far beyond their small numbers, the **Thakalis** are the ingenious traders, innkeepers and pony-handlers of the Thak Khola, the valley followed by the Jomosom Trek. Their entrepreneurial flair goes back at least to the mid-nineteenth century, when the government awarded them a regional monopoly on the salt trade; since then, many have branched out into more exotic forms of commerce – importing electronics from Singapore and Hong Kong is a popular wheeze – while others have set up efficient inns (*bhatti*) in many parts of the western hills.

Muktinath at 3800m – make way for the jingling pony trains that feature so prominently in this area. There's essentially only one route through the Thak Khola, so unless you fly, **backtracking** is unavoidable; but by the same token, you can walk as far as you like and head back when you need to. The round-trip from Pokhara to Muktinath takes about two weeks. If you **fly** from Pokhara to Jomosom, or vice versa, you cut the time in half; *RNAC* averages two scheduled flights a day ($40), but they're often delayed or cancelled due to poor weather or bad visibility.

The towns of the Thak Khola are worthy destinations in their own right. **TATOPANI** is renowned for its western food, citrus gardens and **hot springs**. Further up, the trail passes through thick, monkey-infested forest to **TUKCHE**, once the main Thakali trading centre, and **MARPHA**, a tidy, stone-clad village surrounded by apple and apricot orchards. **Day hikes** and overnight trips up from the valley floor are the best way to appreciate the incredible dimensions of the Thak Khola and the peaks around it: little-trekked trails lead to North

Annapurna Base Camp, the Dhaulagiri Icefall and Dhampus Pass. Above Tukche, the vegetation dies out as you begin to enter the Himalayan rain shadow, and a savage, sand-blasting wind from the south makes it unpleasant to trek after midday. **JOMOSOM**, though it gives its name to the trek, is no place to linger unless you've got business at the airstrip – far more romantic is the fortress town of **KAGBENI**, only a couple of hours further on, with its medieval ruins and terra-cotta Buddhist figures. Geographically speaking, you're on the edge of the Tibetan plateau here, with the main Himalaya chain looming magnificently to the south.

Finally, it's a 1000-metre climb up a side valley – out of the wind, thankfully – to poplar-lined **MUKTINATH**, one of the most important religious sites in the Nepal Himalaya. The *Mahabharata* mentions Muktinath as the source of mystic *shaligram* fossils (see "Natural History" in *Contexts*); a priest will show you around the Newar-style temple and its wall of 108 water spouts, while further down the trail is a Buddhist shrine that shelters two miraculous perpetual flames. *Yartung*, a madly exotic **festival** of horse-riding, is held at Muktinath around the full moon of August–September.

The lower Kali Gandaki

On the return journey, if you don't feel like slogging back up to Poon Hill, you can keep following the Kali Gandaki River south from Tatopani, a low-key **valley walk** with occasionally impressive views; since there's little up and down, it's possible to make good time. This route sees far fewer trekkers than the main Jomosom trail, so **accommodation** and **food** are cheap but rudimentary. At this low elevation the weather is balmy in winter, but in spring and early autumn the heat and mosquitoes are unpleasant. The trail passes through cultivated land and villages, where Magars and Gurungs are the dominant **ethnic groups**, as well as the big Newar bazaars of BENI, BAGLUNG and KUSMA.. When the road from Pokhara is finished, this is bound to become a more popular escape route from the Jomosom area, but for the time being, starting/finishing points are Phedi (north of Pokhara), Naudanda (on the Siddhartha Highway) or Tansen (see Chapter Four).

The Annapurna Sanctuary

The aptly named **ANNAPURNA SANCTUARY** is the most intensely scenic short trek in Nepal. From Ghandrung on the Jomosom route, the trail bears singlemindedly north into the very heart of the Annapurna range: following the short, steep Modi Khola Valley, it soon leaves all permanent settlements behind, climbs through dense bamboo jungle and finally, rising above the vegetation line, makes for a narrow notch between the sheer lower flanks of Machhapuchhre and Hiunchuli. Once past this sanctuary "gate", it stumbles across moraines to a cluster of huts (sometimes still called "Machhapuchhre Base Camp") and, further on, to the so-called **Annapurna Base Camp**. Wherever you stand in the sanctuary, the 360-degree views are unspeakably beautiful, and although clouds roll in early, the curtain often parts at sunset to reveal radiant, molten peaks. The altitude is 3800m: bring warm gear.

The sanctuary can be treated as a week-long side trip from the Jomosom trek, or a ten- to twelve-day round trip from Pokhara. The actual distance covered isn't great, but **altitude**, **weather** and **trail conditions** all tend to slow you down – the trail gains almost 2000m from Ghandrung to the sanctuary, so unless you're already well acclimatised you'd be wise to spread the climb over four days. Frequent precipitation makes the trail extremely slippery at the best of times, and in winter it can be impassable due to snow or avalanche danger. The many **lodges** above CHOMRONG are seasonal, but getting more comfortable all the time, though **food** hasn't been one of their strong points ever since ACAP instituted a standard menu and removed all creative competition.

Two **other "sanctuaries"** east of here are getting quite popular with organised parties: the upper valleys of the Seti and Madi rivers offer similar scenery, but to explore them fully you'll need all your own supplies and a competent guide.

The Annapurna Circuit

The **ANNAPURNA CIRCUIT** is a challenging but rewarding three-week trek with excellent views, plenty of cultural contact and the greatest net vertical gain of all the popular routes. Starting in subtropical paddy at about 500m the trail ascends steadily to the 5415-metre **Thorung La** (Pass) before returning along the Jomosom route; a minimum of sixteen days is required, but a few extra days should be set aside for digressions, acclimatisation and other contingencies. The trek is strenuous, and you'll need boots, gloves and very warm clothes for the pass, and a good four-season bag for a night spent at 4400m. Although the eastern half of the circuit is much less developed for trekkers than the Jomosom side, **food and lodging** are always available, and somewhat cheaper (Rs150 per day should be plenty). A guide isn't necessary. The full circuit is best done between mid-October and mid-December – crossing the Thorung La is risky from January till March, though not out of the question, while the lower parts of the trek are uncomfortably warm from April on. Snow can block the pass at any time of year, so be prepared to wait it out or go back down the way you came. You can **fly** in or out of Manang ($88 from Kathmandu), saving a week of walking, but *RNAC* runs only a limited and seasonal schedule.

Nearly everyone goes around the circuit anticlockwise, the only reason being that the Thorung La makes a longer climb from the Jomosom side, requiring an extra acclimatisation day above Muktinath: the upshot of this is that if you go anticlockwise you'll be in step with the same people

In the upper Marsyangdi Valley

for the entire trek, whereas if you go clockwise you'll be constantly passing people coming the other way. The usual **starting point** is Dumre (see Chapter Four). In dry weather, jeeps shuttle from there along a primitive track to BESISAHAR (4 hours, Rs75), cutting out the first day and a half of the trek – if all goes well, you can leave Kathmandu in the morning and be in Besisahar that night, but the jeep ride is so ghastly that many people prefer to walk. If you're coming from Pokhara, you can avoid Dumre and instead follow the Pokhara–Trisuli trek (see below) to Besisahar in two days.

The route follows the Marsyangdi valley north and then west all the way to the pass. The first few days are a long preamble through terraced farmland and frequent villages, with only fleeting views to whet your appetite, but then, in the course of two days, the valley constricts and the trail climbs steeply, leaving the paddy behind and passing through **successive climatic zones**: temperate forest, coniferous forest, alpine meadows and finally the arid steppes of the rain shadow. The walk from CHAME to **MANANG** is spectacular and shouldn't be rushed: the sight of the huge, glacier-dolloped Annapurnas towering almost 5000m above the valley will stay with you forever. Manang is the largest town of the **Manangis**, the Bhotiya clan that has settled the upper Marsyangdi, and its architecture, like that of all the older villages here, is strongly Tibetan; *gompas* at Manang and BRAGA are well worth visiting. Manang also has an airstrip and a **Himalayan Rescue Association post**, where they do a daily talk on AMS. If you're going for the Thorung La, the next night will probably be spent at **PHEDI**, a grotty place where you'll be woken up at 4am by trekkers who've been told (wrongly) that they have to clear the pass by 8am. The climb up the pass, and the knee-killing 1600-metre descent down the other side to Muktinath, is a tough but exhilarating day. The remainder of the circuit follows the Jomosom trek (see above).

Hill treks: Pokhara–Trisuli and Dhorpatan

Geographically these treks belong in the *Western Hills* (Chapter Four), but it makes more sense to describe them along with the Annapurna treks since they share some of the same trails. They're not heavily trekked or at all commercial, but they pass through well-settled hill country and cheap, basic food and lodging can usually be found. It would be a good idea to have a guide, however. Apply for a white "mixed area" trekking **permit** (not available at the Pokhara Central Immigration office). **Maps** of these treks are available in the *Mandala* series.

Pokhara–Trisuli

The old **POKHARA–TRISULI** trail is little trekked now that it's been super-ceded by the Prithvi Highway, and that's its chief recommendation. A gentle, low-altitude trek, it wanders though typical hill country and dozens of laid-back ethnic villages, with Annapurna, Manaslu and Ganesh Himal popping up often enough to keep things ticking over scenically. This is the only serious trek that's snow-free all year, making it a good choice for winter.

The trek can be done in six days, but allow a minimum of a week; many trek-kers start or finish at Gorkha, the midway point, for an easy outing of three to five days. There are any number of ways to get started from Pokhara, but to bypass a lot of road-walking, take a bus to SISUWA (BEGNAS TAL) and take any trail heading east and north towards Besisahar on the Annapurna Circuit – try to go by way of **GHANPOKHARA**, a lovely Gurung village – finally reaching Gorkha (see Chapter Four) in a minimum of three days. From there it's another three days or so to Trisuli (see Chapter Three), as the trail undulates between subtropical valleys and scenic ridges.

The Dhorpatan Circuit

The **DHORPATAN CIRCUIT** breaks away from the Jomosom trek at BENI (see above) and wanders westwards up into high, open hill country with commanding views of Dhaulagiri Himal. The trail climbs steadily up a tributary of the Kali Gandaki, crossing a tough but beautiful 3400-metre pass and reaching the broad Dhorpatan valley in about four days, where the attraction isn't the valley itself but the opportunities for exploring the huge **Dhorpatan Hunting Reserve** north of it. In a day, you can get up onto the 4100-metre summit immediately north of the valley for dynamite views; if you're prepared for a few nights out you can continue into the rugged Dhaulagiri area, check out mountaineering base camps and maybe even see some **blue sheep**. Leaving Dhorpatan, two lower, less dramatic routes complete the circuit, one returning to Pokhara via BAGLUNG and the other finishing at Tansen (see Chapter Four).

Two weeks would be a realistic time frame for Dhorpatan. The circuit is fairly demanding, taking you much higher than the Pokhara–Trisuli trek, and much further from roads and telephones should something go wrong. It sees very few trekkers; a **guide** is worth having. Lodging is available throughout, but you'll have greater flexibility if you **bring your own equipment**. Anytime between October and April is fine for Dhorpatan, although in winter the high route may be blocked by snow.

Helambu, Langtang and Gosainkund

Trekking **north of Kathmandu** is strangely underrated and uncrowded. The most accessible of all the trekking regions, it's well suited to one- or two-week itineraries, which is handy if you're trying to cram a trek into a short stay in Nepal or you don't want to stray far from Kathmandu. What it lacks in superlatives – there are no 8000-metre peaks in the vicinity (unless you count Shisha Pangma, across the border in Tibet) – it makes up for in base-to-peak rises that are as dramatic as anywhere: Langtang, in particular, delivers more amazing views in a short time than any other walk-in trek in Nepal, with the possible exception of the Annapurna Sanctuary.

Two distinct basins and an intervening highland lend their names to the major treks here; each stands on its own, but given enough time and good weather you can mix and match them. **Helambu** is closest to Kathmandu, comprising the rugged north–south valleys and ridges that lie just beyond the northeast rim of the Kathmandu Valley. North of Helambu, running east–west and tantalisingly close to the Tibet border, lies the high, alpine **Langtang** valley, which in its upper reaches burrows spectacularly between Langtang and Jugal Himals. Northeast of Helambu, and highest of all, is **Gosainkund**, a series of sacred lakes set on a treeless plateau. One practical inconvenience is that the connections between these three treks aren't reliable – snow often blocks the passes between Helambu and the other two – and done on their own, the Langtang and Gosainkund treks require you to retrace your steps for most of the return journey.

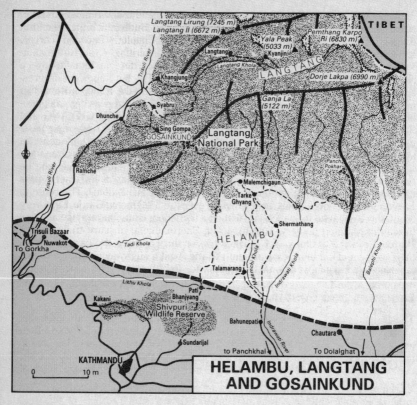

Langtang Lirung (7245 m)
Langtang II (6672 m)
TIBET
Yala Peak (5033 m)
Pemthang Karpo Ri (6830 m)
Langtang
Kyanjin
Langtang Khola
LANGTANG
Khangjung
Trisuli River
Dorje Lakpa (6990 m)
Syabru
Dhunche
Ganja La (5122 m)
Sing Gompa
Langtang National Park
GOSAINKUND
Panch Pokhari
Ramche
Trisuli River
Malemchigaun
Tarke Ghyang
Trisuli Bazaar
Shermathang
Nuwakot
To Gorkha
Tadi Khola
HELAMBU
Malemchi Khola
Indrawati Khola
Balephi Khola
Talamarang
Likhu Khola
Pati Bhanjyang
Kakani
Shivpuri Wildlife Reserve
Bahunepati
Indrawati River
Chautara
Sundarijal
KATHMANDU
to Panchkhal
To Dolalghat
0   10 m

HELAMBU, LANGTANG AND GOSAINKUND

    Food and lodging here is patchy, but never a problem on the usual routes, and isn't expensive – Rs150 a day should suffice. The area is covered by the *Mandala* (1:150,000) and *Schneider* (1:100,000) **maps**, both titled "Helambu–Langtang".

Helambu

HELAMBU (or HELMU) is great for short treks: access from Kathmandu is easy, and an extensive trail network enables you to tailor a circuit to your schedule. The area spans a wide elevation range – there's a lot of up and down – but you need not go higher than about 2700m, so acclimatisation is rarely a consideration. Winter treks are particularly feasible. The peaks of Langtang Himal are often visible, but the views aren't as dramatic as those in other areas. Helambu was once considered a hidden, sacred domain, and its misty ridges and fertile valleys are still comparatively isolated; relatively few people trek here, and with so many trails to choose from, they tend to spread themselves out. The food is generally limited to *daal bhaat*. Helambu's Bhotiyas call themselves **Sherpa**, although they're only distant cousins of the Solu-Khumbu stock: their ancestors probably migrated from Kyirong, the area just north of the Kodari border crossing. Tamangs are also numerous, while the valley bottoms are farmed mainly by Hindu castes.

SUNDARIJAL, a local bus or taxi ride from Kathmandu, is the most common **starting point**, but alternative trailheads include Budhanilkantha, Sankhu, Kakani, Nagarkot and Panchkhal (all described in Chapters Two and Three). However you go, first impressions are somewhat dispiriting – the Kathmandu Valley approaches are heavily populated, and the route from Panchkhal follows a road for several hours (buses ply at least to SIPA GHAT) – but things get progressively better as you move northwards. Most trekkers make a loop around two main ridges and the valley of the Malemchi Khola, trying to stay as high as possible and taking in the villages of **MALEMCHIGAUN**, **TARKE GHYANG** and **SHERMATHANG**. The walk between the latter two is especially rewarding, passing picturesqe monasteries and contouring through forests of oak, rhododendron and *daphne*, whose bark is used to make paper. The bird life here is also abundant.

Other variations on Helambu are more challenging. Gosainkund can be reached by a long day's walk from Malemchigaun, crossing a 4600-metre pass and requiring an overnight stop to acclimatise at GOPTE (3430m). The route to Langtang heads north from Tarke Ghyang over the 5122-metre **Ganja La**, a very tough three-day hike for which you'll need a tent, food, crampons and ice axe (it's usually impassable January–March). From Shermathang, obscure trails lead to **Panch Pokhri** (3800m), a set of lakes two or three days to the east, and from there you could continue east or south to the Arniko Highway. All these routes take you into Langtang National Park (entry fee Rs250).

Langtang and Gosainkund

The Langtang and Gosainkund treks couldn't be more different from Helambu. They make straight for specific destinations, gaining elevation quickly and then leaving you to explore at your own pace; to return, a certain amount of backtracking is unavoidable, unless you cross into Helambu. Culture is not a big part of either, except during *Janai Purnima*, a massive Hindu **pilgrimage** held at Gosainkund during the full moon of July–August.

Both treks **start** at DHUNCHE, about eight hours by bus from Kathmandu (change at Trisuli: the connection is automatic but might not leave time for lunch, so bring food). Above Trisuli the road is unpaved and slow, taking four hours to reach Dhunche, even though it's only 20km as the crow flies; the road has replaced what used to be the first two days of these treks, and Dhunche, an unmemorable administrative centre, has boomed since its completion.

Both treks fall within **Langtang National Park**; the **entry fee** of Rs250 is collected at RAMCHE, about halfway between Trisuli and Dhunche.

Langtang

The **LANGTANG TREK** can be done in as little as a week, but day hikes in the upper valley are sure to detain you for another two or three days. It takes about a day to get interesting, first following the continuation of the Dhunche road (a spectacularly destructive feat of engineering, built to reach a lead and zinc mine in the Ganesh Himal, north and west of here) up the unpromising valley of the Trisuli river before leaving the road and rounding a bend to SYABRU in the Langtang Valley. The next two days are spent climbing briskly up the gorge-like lower valley, where oaks and rhododendron give way to peaceful hemlock and larch forest; after ascending an old moraine, snowy peaks suddenly loom ahead and the gorge opens into a U-shaped glacial valley. Springtime is excellent for flowers here, and in autumn the berberis bushes turn a deep rust colour.

Two Bhotiya villages occupy the upper valley: **LANGTANG** (3300m), the bigger of the two, makes a good place to spend a night and acclimatise, while **KYANGJIN** (3750m) boasts a small *gompa*, a cheese factory (fabulous curd) and an attractive chalet-lodge. Other lodges operate seasonally between Kyangjin and the Langtang Glacier, a full day's walk further up the valley. You'll want to spend at least a couple of nights in the upper valley to explore the glaciers and ascend the 5033-metre **Yala Peak** (Tsergo Ri), from which you can view an awesome white wilderness of peaks, including 8013-metre Shisha Pangma.

You can **return** by crossing into Helambu over the Ganja La (see above), but most people go back down the valley, varying the trip by going via KHANGJUNG, high up on the grassy northern side, and SYABRUBENSI, site of a Tibetan resettlement project. To link up with Gosainkund, you have to backtrack to Syabru.

Gosainkund

GOSAINKUND can be trekked on its own in as little as five days, but because of its high elevation – 4380m – it's perhaps best done after acclimatising in Langtang or Helambu. Combined with either of these, it adds three or four days; a grand tour of all three areas takes sixteen or more days.

From either Dhunche or Syabru, trails lead up through rhododendron forest to the monastery and cheese factory of SING GOMPA (3250m). Above here, the trail climbs through more forest before emerging above the tree line for great

Pilgrims walking to Gosainkund

views of Manaslu, Ganesh and and finally reaching a high, barren plateau. At least two rough-and-ready lodges sit by the shore of Gosainkund, the most sacred of the half-dozen **lakes** here that Hindus associate with various gods. A famous legend recounts how Shiva, having saved the world by drinking a dangerous poison, struck this mountainside with his *trisul* to create the lake and cool his burning throat. In good weather you can climb a nearby summit (5144m) for superb views.

Everest (Solu-Khumbu)

Everest – or to give it its proper Nepali name, **Sagarmatha** ("Brow of the Ocean"), or its even more proper Sherpa name, **Chomolungma** ("Mother Goddess of the World") – is more a pilgrimage than a trek. As with all pilgrimages, it is a tough personal challenge with a clear goal at the end. Lasting images, however, are of the revelations along the way: remote monasteries, irrepressible Sherpas, and peaks with almost human moods and personalities. Prior experience isn't strictly necessary, but treks in this region require extra effort.

The Everest region is the main trekking destination east of Kathmandu, and in terms of popularity it runs a rather distant second to Annapurna. It divides into two distinct areas: the lower, greener and more populous country to the south is **Solu** – if you're not flying in, you'll probably begin at Jiri and spend the first week of your trek walking eastwards across Solu's deep canyons and tall ridges – while **Khumbu**, wedged between Solu and the Tibetan border, comprises the spectacular, harsh landscape of Everest and the surrounding peaks and glaciated valleys.

The dilemma of **getting there** puts many people off. The choice is between **flying** into Lukla, at 2800m on the doorstep of Khumbu (costing $83 each way, *if* you can get a seat), and **taking the bus** to Jiri in Solu (which adds 5–7 days' walking each way). In an ideal world, you would walk in from Jiri to get acclimatised, and fly out of Lukla to avoid backtracking, but it seldom works out that way: flights often get cancelled, and at any rate most seats in and out of Lukla are block-booked by organised trekking parties. Largely for this reason, more than half the people who trek Everest go with a group.

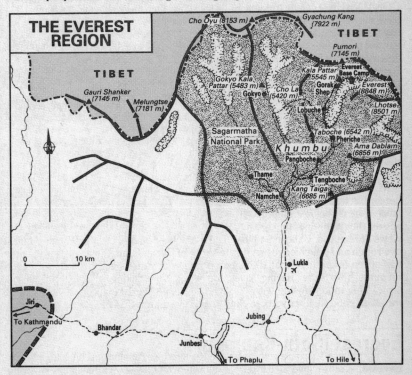

The walking in Solu is very strenuous, while in Khumbu, **altitude** is the overriding factor – to get a good look at Everest, you'll have to spend at least four nights above 4000m and at least one at around 5000m. There is a risk of developing acute mountain sickness (AMS) and you must know the signs. Not only is this the highest of the standard treks, it's also the **coldest**, so you'll need a good four-season bag, several layers of warm clothes, and sturdy boots that will keep out mud and snow. A great help on this front are the well-stocked **rental shops** of Namche, in Khumbu, where you can stock up on high-altitude gear and return it on the way back down. Because of weather, the trekking "window" is especially short in Khumbu – early October to mid-November, and late March to late April – and this, in turn, creates a seasonal stampede on the trails and at the Lukla airstrip. Winter isn't out of the question, but it's just that much colder.

FLYING: THE LUKLA LOTTERY

Lukla's bumpy gravel airstrip is the bottleneck of the Everest region. If you're trekking independently and planning to fly in or out, you need to know how to work the system.

During peak times, all seats are booked months ahead by trekking agencies, who always overbook to be on the safe side and only release unused tickets on the day of departure. One trick, then, is to see if you can buy a **returned ticket** from *RNAC* in Kathmandu on the day; if that's cutting it too fine, you could try approaching the big trekking agencies and offering them $10–20 over face value for one of their spares.

A better strategy is to **go against the flow**. Taking advantage of optimum weather, agencies all tend to fly their groups in and out of Lukla at the same peak times – at those times you can often get a seat going the *other* direction. The heaviest times for agency bookings to Lukla are approximately the third week in October and the first week in April, returning to Kathmandu 17–21 days later.

Unfortunately, getting a ticket is only half the battle. During the high season *RNAC* schedules five flights a day to Kathmandu, but often the clouds move in before they can all get in and out – thus many get **cancelled or postponed**. The problem is mainly a concern at the Lukla end, where the demand for seats is greatest and tension runs high among stranded trekkers. If your flight is cancelled, you go to the bottom of a waiting list and it can take days to get to the top; a "postponed" flight, on the other hand, generally means a delay of only one day. What's the difference between a cancelled flight and a postponed one? *Bakshish*. The Kathmandu airport controllers hold an informal auction, and trekking agencies will bid as much as $1000 to buy their restless clients' early return – this is one of the many behind-the-scenes expenses that drive up the cost of organised trekking. If you're on a tight schedule, however, it's worth going with an agency that's big enough to pull strings for you back in Kathmandu.

Passenger lists are made up in Kathmandu, and the Lukla *RNAC* office can't take advance bookings; they do, however, keep a **waiting list**, and if you arrive in Lukla without a return ticket it can't hurt to put yourself on it. Even if you do have a return ticket, getting on the list for a later flight may serve as a back-up in case your original flight is cancelled. Neither will be to any avail unless you pay your hotel keeper something to make sure your name isn't lost in the shuffle.

While Everest isn't nearly as heavily trekked as Annapurna, its high-altitude **environment** is even more fragile. Khumbu, with only 3000 inhabitants, receives more than 5000 trekkers a year (plus probably twice as many porters); even some trek leaders privately admit that the best thing for the area would be to give it a rest from trekking for a few years. Most of Khumbu is protected within **Sagarmatha National Park** – soon to be expanded further to the east, as well as into Tibet – which is helping to preserve the remaining forest, but it can't be said often enough: have as little to do with wood-burning as possible.

The popular trails through Solu-Khumbu are all **teahousable**. The main Jiri–Lukla–Namche–Base Camp route is very straightforward, but a **guide** is advisable if you're planning to do anything unusual. Solu-Khumbu is the easiest area in Nepal to hire a **woman** porter – a Sherpani – although few speak enough English to serve as guides.

Solu: the Jiri walk-in

The **JIRI WALK-IN** is the most popular Everest approach, as Jiri is connected by bus to Kathmandu, and innkeepers along the trail are reasonably accustomed to serving westerners (other approaches are described in the "Eastern Nepal" section). The **bus** is no picnic, though, taking anywhere from nine to thirteen hours – experienced climbers often joke that they'd scale Everest tomorrow but they'll never take the bus to Jiri again. It's also possible to catch one of the twice-weekly **flights** to PHAPLU, four days east of Jiri, though it's not much cheaper ($77) than flying all the way to Lukla, three days further on.

Cutting across the lay of the land, the trail bobs between valleys as low as 1500m and passes as high as 3500m: the ups and downs can be disheartening, but the fitness and acclimatisation gained come in handy later on. A few glimpses of peaks – notably Gauri Shankar (7145m) – urge you along during the first five or six days, although Solu's lasting images are of tumbling gorges, rhododendron

THE SHERPAS

Nepal's most famous ethnic group, the **Sherpas** probably migrated to Solu-Khumbu four or five centuries ago from eastern Tibet; their name means "People from the East". They were originally nomads, driving their yaks to pasture in Tibet and wintering in Nepal, until change came from an unlikely quarter: the introduction of **the potato** in the 1830s is believed to have been the catalyst that caused Sherpas to settle in villages, and the extra wealth brought by this simple innovation financed the building of most monasteries visible today.

Sherpas maintain the **highest permanent settlements in the world** – up to 4700m – which accounts for their legendary hardiness at altitude. Their mountaineering talents were discovered as early as 1907, and by the 1920s hundreds of Sherpas were signing on as **porters** with expeditions to Everest and other Himalayan peaks – from the Tibet side, ironically, as Nepal was closed at the time. When mountaineering expeditions were finally allowed into Nepal in 1949, Sherpas took over the lion's share of the portering work, and four years later **Tenzing Norgay** reached the top of Everest, clinching Sherpas' worldwide fame. The break couldn't have come at a better time, for trans-Himalayan trade, once an important source of income, was cut short by the Chinese occupation of Tibet in 1959. Since then, Sherpas have deftly diversified into tourism, starting their own trekking and mountaineering agencies, opening lodges and selling souvenirs; conveniently, the trekking season doesn't conflict with summer farming duties.

Like Tibetans and other Bhotiya groups, Sherpas are devout Buddhists – most villages of note support a *gompa* and a few monks (or nuns) – but in a throwback to animism which is perfectly permissible in Lamaist Buddhism, they revere **Khumbila**, a sacred peak just north of Namche, as a sort of tribal totem, and regard fire as a deity (it's disrespectful to throw rubbish into a Sherpa hearth). Sherpas eat meat, of course, but in deference to *dharma* they draw the line at slaughtering it – they hire Tibetans to do that.

forests and terraced fields hewn out of steep hillsides. In the past thirty years Solu has benefitted from several projects funded by **Edmund Hillary's Himalayan Trust**; groups of children may accompany you on their way to one of the "Hillary" schools in the area.

The route passes through some important Sherpa villages, notably **BHANDAR** and **JUNBESI**, the latter with an active monastery. Most trekkers are understandably impatient to get up to Everest or back to Kathmandu, but **side trips** to the cheese "factory" at THODUNG and the Thubten Chholing *gompa* north of Junbesi are fascinating. From **JUBING**, a Rai (see Chapter Six) village five days in, the trail finally bends north towards Everest, following the valley of the Dudh Kosi. Two days later, it sidesteps LUKLA and joins the well-trodden route to Khumbu.

The bulk of traffic through Solu consists of porters humping in gear for trekking groups and expeditions flying into Lukla, and this is reflected in the no-frills **food and lodging** available. You'll have a hard time spending more than Rs100 a day here. Solu is covered by the *Mandala* "Lamosangu to Mount Everest" **map** (1:110,000); *Schneider's* "Tamba Kosi" and "Shorong/Hinku" (1:50,000) show the route in greater detail.

Khumbu

The trail north from Lukla is the trunk route of the **EVEREST TREK**: everyone walks it at least once, and all but a few backtrack along it as well. Most trekkers follow it to the end at Kala Pattar (the classic viewpoint of Everest) and Everest Base Camp, both about eight days northeast of Lukla; quite a few combine this with a trip to the beautiful Gokyo lakes, about the same distance north of Lukla.

Khumbu **lodges** are heavily geared for trekkers, and you should have no trouble getting a bunk and a good meal wherever you go along the busier trails (in Lukla and Namche you can even get hot showers and cinnamon rolls). **Prices** aren't unreasonable, considering the distance supplies have to be carried, and daily expenses should be less than Rs200 – that's if you don't drink too many Cokes, which cost as much as Rs40. An additional expense is the Rs250 **entry fee** for Sagarmatha National Park.

Khumbu is well **mapped**. By far the best for the area from Namche north is *Schneider's* "Khumbu Himal" (1:50,000), while *Mandala's* "Khumbu Himal" (1:50,000) covers the route from Lukla north.

Lukla to Everest Base Camp and Kala Pattar

From Lukla the trail meanders north along the Dudh Kosi before bounding up to **NAMCHE** (3450m), where Khumbu and the serious scenery start. Nestled handsomely in a horseshoe bowl, the Sherpa "capital" has done very well out of mountaineering and trekking over the years. Besides trekking equipment, Namche's shops sell print film, maps, batteries, postcards and souvenirs, albeit at inflated prices, and there's also a bank and post office. Most lodges have electricity (one even has a microwave oven). Try to make your trip coincide with the pan-cultural **Saturday market**, or visit the national-park **visitors' centre**, perched on the ridge east of town, which contains an informative museum. About two hours north of Namche stands the once-famous and soon-to-be-reopened *Everest View Hotel*, the only luxury hotel anywhere in the Nepal Himalaya.

Beyond Namche, the trail veers north-east into a tributary valley and climbs to **TENGBOCHE**, surrounded by protected juniper forest and commanding a show-stealing view of everybody's favourite peak, **Ama Dablam**. Tengboche's much-photographed monastery burned down in January 1989 and is currently being rebuilt at a cost of $800,000 (for astrological reasons, work wasn't allowed to start until April 1990). *Mani Rimdu*, the Sherpa

Namche bazaar

dance-drama **festival**, is held here on the full moon of November–December. The trail continues to **PANGBOCHE**, containing Khumbu's oldest *gompa*, where for a donation the *lama* will show you some *yeti* relics, and on to PHERICHE (4250m), site of a **Himalayan Rescue Association post** (AMS talks every afternoon during the trekking season). From here up settlements are strictly seasonal, and their stone enclosures and slate-roofed huts are reminiscent of Scottish crofts.

From Pheriche the route bends north again, ascending the moraine of the Khumbu Glacier and passing a series of monuments to Sherpas killed on Everest, to reach LOBUCHE (4930m). Another day's march along the glacier's lateral moraine brings you to GORAK SHEP (5180m), the last huddle of teahouses – and a cold, probably sleepless night. The payoff comes when you climb up the grassy mound of **Kala Pattar** (5554m): the extra height provides an unbelievable panorama, not only of **Everest** (8848m) but also of its neighbours Lhotse (Nepal's third-highest peak, at 8511m) and Nuptse (7861m), as well as the sugarloaf of Pumori (7165m). A separate day trip can be made across the amazing Khumbu Glacier to **Everest Base Camp**. You may encounter a half a dozen or more expedition parties here, constantly ferrying supplies up the dangerous Khumbu Icefall to higher camps; the climbers may be happy to have well-wishers, but if they seem wary of trekkers you can't blame them.

Gokyo Lakes

The scenery is every bit as good at **Gokyo Lakes**, in the next valley to the west, and other trekkers are noticeably fewer. If you're equipped to spend a night out and are good at route-finding (the *Schneider* map will help), you can be there in two days from Gorak Shep, crossing the strenuous 5420-metre **Cho La** (Pass) west of Lobuche and descending a treacherous scree slope. Without a tent, you'll have to backtrack almost to Tengboche, and then follow the Dudh Kosi north for two days to GOKYO, set beside the immense Ngozumba Glacier (Nepal's biggest). Several brilliant blue lakes, dammed up by the glacier's lateral moraine, dot the west side of the valley above and below Gokyo. The high point of Gokyo is an overlook called, again, **Kala Pattar**, surveying a clutter of blue teeth – Cho Oyu , Everest, Lhotse and Makalu are just the ones over 8000m – and the long grey tongue of the Ngozumba Glacier. You can also scramble north beside the glacier as far as Cho Oyu Base Camp.

EVEREST

The world's highest mountain was named after **Sir George Everest**, head of the Survey of India from 1823 to 1843. Politically off-limits until the early twentieth century, the climb to the summit was first attempted from the Tibetan side in 1922 by a British party that included **George Mallory**, who coined the famous "because it is there" phrase. Two years later, Mallory and Andrew Irvine reached at least 8500m – without oxygen – before disappearing into a cloud; their bodies were never found, and some believe that they reached the summit. Several more attempts were made until World War II suspended activities, and climbs were further hampered by the Chinese invasion of Tibet in 1950, which closed the northern approach to mountaineers.

With the opening of Nepal in 1951, however, attention turned to southern approaches and a race between the Swiss and the British was on. The mountain was finally scaled, using a route via the South Col, by New Zealander **Edmund Hillary** and Sherpa **Tenzing Norgay** in a British-led expedition in 1953. On the morning of May 29, Hillary planted the Union Jack, the Nepalese and United Nations flags on the summit; Tensing left an offering of sweets and biscuits to the mountain's gods.

Throughout the next two decades, increasingly big expeditions put men and women on the top by various routes, and sometimes got carried away in their bids for lucrative sponsorship – in 1970 a Japanese, Yuiichi Miura, *skied* most of the way down the mountain, breaking a number of bones in the process. Since the mid-1970s the trend has been away from large-scale assaults in favour of small, quick "alpine-style" ascents. Dominating the field for more than a decade, Austrian **Reinhold Messner** was one of two climbers to reach the summit without oxygen in 1978, and in 1980 he made the first successful solo ascent of Everest. The mountain continues to attract as many as thirty expeditions a year, mainly from the Nepal side – by mid-1990, 291 people (eleven of them women) had reached the summit and 103 had died in the attempt.

Eastern Nepal

Treks in **eastern Nepal** are hampered by a fundamental problem of access: Hile, the usual trailhead, is two days from Kathmandu by bus. However, it's possible to enter (or leave) this region by way of Everest, which cuts out the long ride in one direction. Flights are also good value for money here – the one from Kathmandu to Tumlingtar costs only $44. **Food and lodging** is patchy, though, and seldom geared for trekkers.

You're supposed to have a white "mixed-area" **permit** to trek in this region, but no one is going to hassle you if you've got an Everest permit and you're only passing through on your way down. The only trekking **map** of the area is the *Mandala* "Dhankuta to Kanchenjunga, Mt. Everest, Makalu & Arun Valley" (1:192,500).

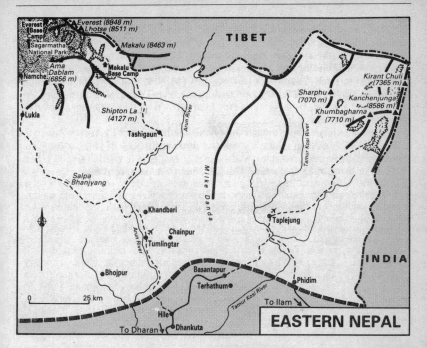

Ethnically, eastern Nepal is even more diverse than the Annapurna region: Rais and Limbus are dominant in the hills, Gurungs and Magars are found in smaller numbers, while Sherpas, Tamangs and other Bhotiyas inhabit the high country and Hindu castes the valleys. Everest, Makalu and Kanchenjunga provide stunning **views** from most high points. Flora and fauna are also of great interest to specialists, especially the **butterflies** and other insects of the upper Arun Valley, and the **rhododendrons** of the Milke Danda, a long ridge east of the Arun.

The Everest eastern approach

While still not nearly as developed as the Jiri walk-in, the **EASTERN APPROACH** to Everest is becoming more popular and facilities along it are expanding yearly. It's usually treated as an "escape route" from Everest by trekkers who want to avoid the long backtrack to Jiri; there's no reason why the itinerary can't be done in reverse, except perhaps that it's better to gain some confidence on the more developed Everest trails before tackling this less-trekked region. Another factor to consider is the **season**: try to do the lower section of the trek when it's cooler.

The **route** leaves the Jiri walk-in at KHARTE, about a day south of Lukla, and heads southeastwards to reach Tumlingtar five to seven days later. The first half of this stretch passes through tangled hills inhabited mainly by Rais; after reaching a high point at the lush and wild Salpa Bhanjyang (3350m), it descends steadily to the deep, hot and predominantly Hindu Arun Valley. TUMLINGTAR is a big and busy town overlooking the Arun; *RNAC* flies from there to Kathmandu about four times a week ($44), although the flights are often booked up. If you're returning to Kathmandu by bus, carry on to Hile (see Chapter Six), two days south and 1400m higher; alternatively, you could walk another week from Tumlingtar to Ilam (Chapter Six) by way of CHAINPUR, a tidy village renowned for its brassware. Both routes are **teahousable** and a guide isn't needed, but don't expect English signs or any fancy food – you'd be wise to bring a few days' worth of provisions just in case.

At least one **other route** aims roughly due south from the Everest region to the LAMINDANDA airstrip (twice a week to Kathmandu, $66). If you can't get on a flight there, trails continue south to the Tarai or east to Hile via BHOJPUR, a beautiful Newar town and Nepal's most famous *khukuri*-making centre.

THE YETI

The *yeti* ("man of the rocky places") has been a staple of Sherpa and Tibetan folklore for centuries, but stories of hairy, ape-like creatures roaming the snowy heights first came to the attention of the outside world during the early days of British rule in India. British explorers in Tibet reported seeing mysterious moving figures and large, unidentified footprints in the snow – captivated by the reports, an imaginative Fleet Street hack coined the term "abominable snowman" – but it wasn't until 1951, during the first British Everest expedition from the Nepal side, that climber Eric Shipton took clear photographs of *yeti* tracks. Since then, several highly publicised *yeti*-hunts, including one led by Sir Edmund Hillary in 1960, have brought back a wealth of circumstantial evidence but not one authenticated sighting.

Sceptics dismiss the *yeti* as a straightforward myth, of course, arguing that the hairy creatures in question are more likely bears, and oversized footprints probably bird tracks, melted and enlarged by the sun. Meanwhile, relics kept at the *gompas* of Pangboche and Khumjung have failed to provide scientific proof of the *yeti*'s existence – the "skulls" have been examined by experts and deemed to be made of serow (Himalayan wild goat) skins, while the skeletal hand at Pangboche is believed to be human. Yet yaks continue to be mauled, and Sherpas insist the *yeti* isn't a hoax. Perhaps the most significant aspect of the *yeti* is humans' reaction to it: we want it to exist, like the Loch Ness Monster – some secret part of the world that mankind hasn't yet discovered and explained – yet in our endless curiosity we want to find and dissect it. Thankfully, it has eluded us so far.

Makalu Base Camp and Kanchenjunga

Many other hill treks north of Hile and Ilam are probably feasible without supplies – development workers in the area rave about a circuit from PHIDIM to BASANTAPUR via TAPLEJUNG. BHOJPUR and CHAINPUR, beautiful Newar towns within two or three days' walk of Hile, would also make great targets. If the massive Arun III hydroelectric project is ever built on the Arun River, the access road will no doubt open the region up further.

For the moment, however, relying solely on teahouses, it isn't possible to trek into the Himalaya east of Everest. **Makalu Base Camp**, a three-week trek from Hile up the Arun Valley and over the Shipton La (4127m), requires a tent and food for ten days; the last tea house is at TASHI GAUN, less than a day from the Arun.

Reputedly the most incredible trek in this part of Nepal is to the foot of **Kanchenjunga**, at 8586m the third-highest peak in the world, but special permits for that area are issued only through trekking agencies. Because of its remote location in the extreme northeastern corner of the country, Kanchenjunga is a very expensive trek; most groups fly in and out of TAPLEJUNG (weekly from Kathmandu, $110).

Far western Nepal

West of Dhaulagiri, the Himalaya subside somewhat and retreat north into Tibet, and the band of foothills flares out to become an almost impenetrable jumble. The northern third of the region, left in the rain shadow of the foothills, receives little monsoon moisture – in every way but politically, this highland strip is part of Tibet. Jagged Himalayan grandeur isn't so much in evidence, but there's a wildness and a vastness here, and the feeling of isolation is thrilling.

The **far west** is the deep end of trekking in Nepal, and the treks here are well off the beaten track: they're a chore to get to, they require a lot of preparation and, with the exception of Rara Lake, you'll find that very few westerners have gone before you. All that might appeal if you're an experienced trekker looking for new challenges, but if you're a first-timer, forget it.

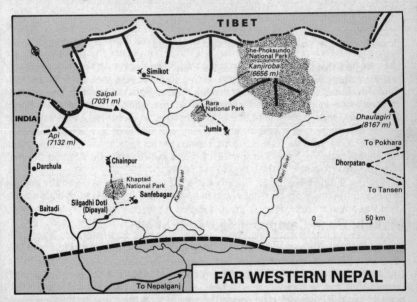

Logistics make or break a trek in the far west. Given the distances involved, you'll need to fly to the starting point, but **flights** from Kathmandu are few and often delayed; connections from Nepalganj are more frequent and considerably cheaper, though no more reliable, and Nepalganj isn't as nice a place to be stuck waiting for a flight. **Food and lodging** are in uncomfortably short supply, so you'll need to bring a tent, cooking utensils and at least some provisions. You should be prepared to carry it all yourself, because **porters** here are a fickle lot and often can't be spared from their farmwork. **Guides** are also scarce, so you shouldn't venture out without a reasonable command of Nepali. If you go on an **organised trek** you may not be entirely insulated from these inconveniences – and for this reason agencies will probably try to steer you to more easterly destinations.

As roads gradually penetrate into the far west, trekking might become easier. In the meantime, the four treks described below are the most realistic possibilities. Three require a white "mixed area" **permit** (the fourth, Dolpa, requires a special permit, issued only through trekking agencies). For **maps**, see the *Mandala* "Jumla to Api & Saipal Himal" and "Jomosom to Jumla & Surkhet" (both 1:250,000).

Rara National Park

RARA NATIONAL PARK is the best-known – and for the non-specialist, probably the least daunting – of the far western treks. The usual itinerary is a loop that starts and ends at JUMLA, 150km north of Nepalganj, and takes about a week. The country is wild but unspectacular: a sea of choppy, mostly forested hills, offering only glimpses of modest Himalayan peaks, but the highlight is pristine **Rara Lake**, Nepal's largest, surrounded by a wilderness area of meadows, forest and abundant wildlife.

In terms of practicalities, the Rara trek has always been a challenge. You want to **fly in and out**. In theory, *RNAC* flies to Jumla daily from Nepalganj ($44) and once or twice a week from Kathmandu ($127), but delays and cancellations are the rule and you can't get a confirmed booking for the return flight in advance – try to arrange this as soon as you arrive, but be prepared to walk back to BIRENDRANAGAR (SURKHET), a week's hike. **Food** is available in Jumla, at inflated prices, but beyond the bazaar is often unavailable at any price. There are **lodges** in Jumla and a bunkhouse at the lake; in between, there are a few teahouses where you might be able to stay, but camping is more pleasant and certainly more reliable. The orthodox Hindus of this area aren't at all keen about having outcaste westerners inside their homes, but may let you sleep on the roof. The **park fee**, payable at the lakeside hut, is Rs250.

Technical difficulties aside, Rara makes a fair compromise between the popular treks and the really obscure ones, and in a way combines the best of both worlds: like the popular treks, Rara is given detailed route descriptions in the trekking books so you can do it without an organised group or even a guide, yet it's remote enough to ensure that you'll see few if any other westerners. Starting at Jumla (2400m), the route crosses two 3500-metre ridges before reaching the lake at 3000m. The park is one of the best places in Nepal to see mountain **wildlife**, including Himalayan black bear, thar, goral, musk deer and the rare red (lesser) panda. Autumn and spring are the **best seasons**, and Rara is particularly worth considering in May and June, when the weather elsewhere is getting too hot or unpredictable. Winter flights are hopelessly unreliable – a pity, since the far northwest offers the best potential skiing in the country. A day and a half south of the lake is **SINJA**, where the ruins of the capital of the twelfth- to fourteenth-century Khasa dynasty (see "The Historical Framework" in *Contexts*) can be viewed across the river.

Humla

Tucked away in the extreme northwest corner of Nepal, **HUMLA** is high, dry and strongly Tibetan. Rounded, snowcapped peaks hem the district in on three sides and shut out most outside influences, including the monsoon. Trekking facilities are nonexistent, but the Buddhist highlanders are more accommodating to strangers than the caste-conscious Hindus further south.

The "Humla Trek", as performed by perhaps a dozen aid workers so far, is a walk of seven to nine days from SIMIKOT (Humla's district headquarters) to Jumla, stopping at Rara Lake along the way. Doing it vice versa – going towards the mountains – would seem more natural, but bear in mind that Jumla is easier to get out of than Simikot. *RNAC* flies from Nepalganj to Simikot up to three times a week (seasonal; $88); the airstrip is at nearly 3000m, so you may feel the altitude. You'll need to be **completely self-sufficient**, and if you don't speak Nepali you'll need a guide.

A *chorten*

The trail to Rara involves a good deal of up and down, but goes no higher than 3600m. In May–June, which is the **best time** to go, the wildflowers are out of this world. Most of the country north and east of the route is out of bounds to foreigners, which knocks out a few tempting side trips, but one allowable exception is **Raling Gompa** (4000m), a tough, full-day climb north of Simikot. Raling is the most sacred of Humla's many Buddhist monasteries; an hour and a half further on is an important pilgrimage spot where a **festival** is held on the full moon of May–June.

Khaptad National Park

Set on a plateau in the middle of the foothills, **KHAPTAD NATIONAL PARK** is, for lack of a better term, a *spiritual* park: a five-square-kilometre core area has been set aside for "meditation and tranquillity" – no alcohol, tobacco or killing of animals allowed – comprising a pilgrimage spot of Hindu shrines and sacred streams. The centrepiece of the park, literally, is the Khaptad Baba, a famous holy man in the grand old mountaintop-guru tradition.

Numerous tales surround the **Khaptad Baba**, all impossible to substantiate because he declines to answer questions about himself. His followers swear he's over 100 years old (he doesn't look it) and that he used to be a doctor in Kashmir before moving up to Khaptad forty years ago to meditate. He speaks excellent

English and, hardest to explain, always seems mysteriously well-informed about any subject, however esoteric. A surprising cross-section of the Nepalese intelligentsia follow the Baba, and even the king has been known to fly in for consultation; no doubt thanks to his pull with HM, the Baba won a long campaign to establish Khaptad as a national park in 1985.

The trek is still new and there's no established protocol for doing it, but it's nominally **teahousable** and (barring transport hitches) should take no more than a week. Two year-round **airstrips** – at SILGADHI DOTI ($66 from Nepalganj, $138 from Kathmandu) and SANFEBAGAR ($61 from Nepalganj) – are within one or two days' walk of the park (a third, CHAINPUR, is seasonal). The return flight will present difficulties, especially if you choose to finish at a different airstrip to avoid backtracking: it's wise to end up at Silgadhi Doti so that you have the fall-back option of **taking the bus back** to Dhangadhi in the Tarai – at a pinch you could even walk back in three or four days. **Food and lodging** are available at the airstrip towns, JHINGRANO (the southern park entrance) and the park HQ. The food is poor and you'll want to bring as much of your own as possible, but you should be able to get by without a porter; a **guide**, however, is necessary. The **park entry fee** is Rs250.

Hovering at about 3000m, the **central plateau** consists of rolling, open grassland and forest, with barking deer, monkeys and pheasants in good supply. **Views** are impressive, in places, of Saipal (7031m) and Api (7132m), the far west's tallest peaks. The main attractions of the plateau are a sacred confluence, site of the *Ganga Deshara* **festival** in May–June, and the **Baba's hut**. A trek to Khaptad wouldn't be complete without an audience with the Baba, but be sure to bring a gift (food is traditional).

Dolpa (She-Phoksundo National Park)

DOLPA is an enormous, isolated and mostly off-limits district northwest of Dhaulagiri and bordering Tibet, the western half of which has been set aside as **SHE-PHOKSUNDO NATIONAL PARK**, Nepal's biggest park. This was the setting of Peter Mattheisson's *The Snow Leopard* (see "Books" in *Contexts*), and the book is as close as most of us will ever get to it. Southern ("Inner") Dolpa, up to the fabled Lake Phoksundo and She Gompa, is open to **organised groups only**; the rest remains closed to foreigners. The park, established in 1984, protects what must be an awe-inspiring region of deep, luxuriant valleys, unclimbed peaks and rare fauna (including the snow leopard) – even if you can't go, it's reassuring to know it's there.

festivals

The festivals listed below are mainly high-altitude affairs; at mid- and lower elevations you'll also encounter the popular celebrations of *Holi, Dasain, Tihar, Magh Sankranti* and *Shiva Raatri*.

Losar Tibetan New Year, celebrated at *gompas* throughout the high country (February).

Ganga Deshara Thousands of pilgrims gather at Khaptad five days before the full moon of May–June.

Dalai Lama's birthday Observed in Tibetan areas with parades and prayers (July 6).

Janai Purnima The annual changing of the sacred thread worn by high-caste Hindu men draws pilgrims to Gosainkund and Muktinath (late July or early August).

Yartung A fair with horse-racing, dancing, drinking and gambling, held at Muktinath (late August or early September).

Mani Rimdu A traditional Sherpa dance-drama, held at Thami (May) and Tengboche (November or December).

travel details

Buses

From Kathmandu to Gorkha (2 daily; 7hr); Jiri (3 daily; 9-13hr); Sundarijal (4 daily; 1hr) and Trisuli (6 daily; 4hr).

From Trisuli to Dhunche (2 daily; 4hr).

From Pokhara to Naudanda (infrequent; 1hr) and Sisuwa (hourly; 45min).

Planes

From Kathmandu to Jumla (weekly; 1hr 40min); Lamidanda (2 weekly; 45min); Lukla (up to 5 daily; 45min); Manang (seasonal; 1hr); Phaplu (2 weekly; 40min); Silgadhi Doti (weekly; 2hr); Taplejung (weekly; 1hr 15min) and Tumlingtar (4 weekly; 1hr).

From Pokhara to Jomosom (1-2 daily; 50min).

From Biratnagar to Phaplu (weekly; 45min); Taplejung (3 weekly; 35min) and Tumlingtar (4 weekly; 25min).

From Nepalganj to Jumla (daily; 45min); Sanfebagar (4 weekly; 35min); Silgadhi Doti (4 weekly; 40min) and Simikot (seasonal; 1hr).

From Dhangadhi to Jumla (seasonal; 1hr); Sanfebagar (3 weekly; 25min); Silgadhi Doti (4 weekly; 20min) and Simikot (seasonal; 1hr).

From Mahendranagar to Sanfebagar (3 weekly; 30min).

PART THREE

THE
CONTEXTS

THE HISTORICAL FRAMEWORK

For a tiny Himalayan backwater, Nepal has played a surprisingly pivotal role in Asian history. In its early days it reared Buddha and hosted the great Indian emperor Ashoka; much later, its remarkable conquests led it into wars with Tibet and Britain, and during the past three decades it has come to be regarded as a vital buffer state by both India and China. Its name and recorded history go back nearly 3000 years, although it has existed as a nation for barely 200: before 1769, "Nepal" referred only to a kingdom based in the Kathmandu Valley.

BEGINNINGS

Neolithic tools found in the Kathmandu Valley indicate that humans have inhabited parts of Nepal for tens of thousands of years — and the fact that the shrines of Swayambhu and Changu Narayan are located on hill tops suggests that ancient animists may have lived and worshipped there as much as 200,000 years ago, while the valley floor was submerged under a primordial lake. The Newar creation myth, which tells of the *bodhisattva* Manjushri releasing the waters and establishing Swayambhu, perhaps preserves a dim racial memory of that prehistoric era.

Nepal's early semi-mythological geneologies aren't borne out by any archaeological evidence, but at some points they tally with other sources. The **Kirata** (or Kiranti) tribe pops up in several Hindu texts — and even in Ptolemy – although the term might well have applied to all hill people in the first millennium BC; significantly, the Kirata were often described as a warlike people known for carrying deadly knives. Whoever they were, by the sixth or seventh century BC the Kirata appear to have divided into two distinct groups, one controlling the eastern hills and the other the Kathmandu Valley.

Hindus were by this time encroaching on the less malarial parts of the Tarai and founding the city-states of **Mithila** (modern Janakpur), the scene of many of the events in the *Ramayana* epic, and **Kapilvastu** (now Tilaurakot), where Buddha spent his unenlightened years during the sixth or seventh century BC. North India was unified under the **Mauryan empire** (321–184 BC), whose most famous ruler, Ashoka, was responsible for spreading Buddhism throughout the subcontinent, including Nepal. Following the fall of Maurya, north India was again divided among a number of states and Hinduism began a slow but inexorable comeback in the Tarai.

EARLY DYNASTIES

Nepal's history comes into sharper focus with the arrival of the **Lichhavis**, a north-Indian clan who overthrew the Kiratas around 200 AD and established their capital at Deopatan, near modern Pashupatinath. Exploiting Nepal's position as a trading entrepôt between India and Tibet, the Lichhavis founded a strong, stable and culturally sophisticated dynasty. No buildings from the period survive, but contemporary accounts by Chinese travellers describe "multi-storied temples so tall one would take them for a crown of clouds" – perhaps a reference to the pagoda style that was to become a Nepalese trademark. Under Lichhavi sponsorship, artisans ushered in a classical age of stone sculpture and produced Nepal's most acclaimed pieces, many of which still casually litter the Kathmandu Valley. Although Hindus, the Lichhavis endowed both Hindu and Buddhist temples – Pashupatinath and Swayambhu were built, or at least expanded, during their rule – and established a policy of religious tolerance that has been maintained to the present day.

Much of what we know about the Lichhavis comes from a handful of stone inscriptions whose authors were probably more intent on self-praise than historical accuracy. The earliest inscription, dated 454 AD and still on view at Changu Narayan, extols **Mana Deva**, the legendary builder of the Baudha stupa. The greatest of the Lichhavi line, **Amsuvarman** (c. 600–620) is said to have composed the first Sanskrit grammar and struck the first Nepalese coins. "Down to the reign of this monarch the gods showed themselves plainly in bodily shape," intone the Nepalese chronicles, "but after this they became invisible." By this time Nepal had become a vassal of Tibet, and Amsuvarman's daughter Bhrikuti, who was carried off by the Tibetan king, is popularly credited with introducing Buddhism to Tibet.

The Lichhavi era came to a close in 879, and the three centuries that followed are sometimes referred to as Nepal's "Dark Ages". The Nepalese chronicles record a long list of **Thakuri kings**, although the title was probably a Hindu honorific and not the name of an hereditary dynasty; these kings may well have been puppets installed by one or more of the powers controlling the Tarai at the time. Nonetheless, learning and the arts continued to thrive, and from the eleventh century onwards the valley became an important centre of Tantric studies (see "Religion", p.286).

THE KHASAS AND MALLAS

While the Thakuris were ruling central Nepal, yet another Hindu clan, the **Khasas**, migrated up from the plains and carved out a small fiefdom in western Tibet. In the early twelfth century a Khasa king, Nagaraja, moved his capital down to Sinja in the Karnali basin and established a powerful dynasty which at its height controlled a broad sector of the Himalaya from Kashmir to present-day Pokhara. The history of the Khasas is little understood, for they left few written records and only minor ruins at Sinja (now Hatsinja) and Dullu, south of Jumla.

Nepal entered a new and much better documented period of its history when the Thakuri king of Bhaktapur, Ari Deva, took the title **Malla**, probably in the year 1200. Malla was, in fact, a popular royal form of address in India at the time – the Khasa kings also called themselves Mallas – but the name has come to be associated with at least three separate dynasties, lasting more than five centuries, that presided over the renaissance of Nepalese culture during which most of the temples and palaces still on display in the Kathmandu Valley were built.

The early Malla era was marked by great instability: the Khasas mounted several raids on the valley, although they were never able to gain a ruling foothold, and in 1349 Muslims swept up from Bengal and pillaged both Hindu and Buddhist holy sites in a brief spree of destruction and violence. Despite these disruptions, trade flourished, many of the valley's smaller cities were founded, and Arniko, the great Nepalese architect, was dispatched to the Ming court to instruct the Chinese in the art of building pagodas. In 1382 **Jayasthiti Malla** inaugurated a period of strong central rule from Bhaktapur, but his most lasting contribution was to dragoon his Buddhist subjects into the Hindu hierarchy by dividing them into 64 occupational castes – a system which remained enshrined in Nepalese law until 1964. Malla power reached its zenith under **Yaksha Malla** (1428–82), who extended his domain westwards to Gorkha and eastwards as far as present-day Biratnagar. Upon his death, the kingdom was divided between three sons, and for nearly three centuries the independent city-states of Kathmandu, Patan and Bhaktapur (and occasionally others) feuded over lucrative trade arrangements with Tibet. Judging by the opulent *durbars* built during this period, there must have been enough to go around, and the intense rivalry seems to have been good for both art and business.

The Khasa kings didn't fare so well, and by the late fourteenth century their empire had fragmented into a collection of petty provinces. The Muslim conquest of north India during the early part of the century figured indirectly in Khasa's downfall: a steady stream of princes from Rajasthan, which had borne the brunt of the invasion, limped into the Khasa hills in search of consolation prizes, and rapidly wheedled their way into positions of power. Those who took the reins of the Khasa provinces came to be known as the **Baisi Rajas** (Twenty-Two Princes), while others who subjugated Magar and Gurung states to the east became the **Chaubisi** (Twenty-Four).

UNIFICATION

For three centuries the *Chaubisi* and *Baisi* confederacies maintained an uneasy status quo, forming numerous defensive alliances to ensure that no one state could gain control over the rest. Divided, they were small, weak and culturally backward. **Gorkha**, the most easterly territory, was no different from the rest, except that it was that much closer to the Kathmandu Valley and that much more jealous of the Mallas' wealth. Under the inspired, obsessive leadership of **Prithvi Narayan Shah** (1722–75), Gorkha launched a campaign that was to take 27 years to conquer the valley, and as long again to unite all of modern Nepal.

At the time of Prithvi Shah's rise to the throne, in 1743, rivalry between the three Malla kings had reached an all-time high. Still, Gorkha wasn't nearly strong enough to invade Nepal outright; Prithvi Shah first captured Nuwakot, a day's march northwest of Kathmandu, and from there directed a ruthless twenty-year **war of attrition**. By 1764 he was able to enforce a total blockade, starving the valley and at the same time replenishing Gorkha's coffers with Tibetan trade. Kirtipur was targeted for the first major battle, and surrendered after a six-month siege. Answering a plea from the Kathmandu king, Jaya Prakash Malla, the East India Company sent in 2400 soldiers against the Gorkhalis, who proceeded to cut them to shreds; only 800 returned. On the eve of the *Indra Jaatra* festival of 1768, Jaya Prakash, by now rumoured to be insane, let down the city's defences and **Kathmandu fell** to the Gorkhalis without a fight. They took Patan two days later, and Bhaktapur the following year, and by 1774 had marched eastwards all the way to Sikkim.

Suspicious of Britain's growing influence in India, Prithvi Shah adopted a closed-door policy that was to remain in force until the 1950s. Missionaries were thrown out forthwith: "First the bible, then the trading station, then the cannon," he warned. The bloody **battle for succession** that followed Prithvi Shah's death set the pattern for Nepalese politics well into the twentieth century. Yet when they weren't stabbing each other in the back, his successors managed to subdue Gorkha's old *Chaubisi* and *Baisi* rivals in the west, so that by 1790 Nepal stretched far beyond its present eastern and western borders. Lured on by promises of land

grants – every hillman's dream – the Nepalese army became a seemingly unstoppable fighting machine, with Kashmir in its sights.

Westward progress was interrupted by a brief but chastening **war with Tibet**. Troubles had been brewing for some time over trade relations, and the Tibetans were growing alarmed by Nepal's encroachments on their ally, Sikkim. In 1788 and again in 1791, Nepal invaded, plundered a few monasteries and extracted tribute from Tibet, but in 1792 the Tibetans launched a counterattack, penetrating as far as Nuwakot and forcing Nepal to accept harsh terms.

Nepal's further adventures in the west brought it into increasing **conflict with Britain**'s East India Company, which by now controlled India, and open hostilities broke out in 1814 when Nepal annexed the Butwal sector of the Tarai. For the British, the dispute provided a perfect pretext to "open up" Nepal, which had been so tantalisingly closed to them, and thus to muscle in on trade with Tibet. Britain attacked with a force of 50,000 men against Nepal's 12,000, expecting an easy victory; in the event it took two years and heavy losses before finally bringing Nepal to heel. The **Treaty of Segauli** forced Nepal to accept its present eastern and western boundaries and surrender much of the Tarai, and worst of all, to admit a British government representative in Kathmandu. Yet so impressed were the British by "our valiant opponent" – as a plaque at an Indian battle site proclaims – that they began recruiting Nepalis into the Indian Army before the treaty had even been signed, and these companies formed the basis for the famed **Gurkha regiments** (see p.168). Britain restored Nepal's Tarai lands in return for its help in quelling the Indian Mutiny of 1857.

THE RANA YEARS

The Kathmandu court was practically paralysed by intrigue and assassinations during the first half of the nineteenth century, culminating in the ghastly **Kot Massacre** of 1846, in which fifty-five courtiers were butchered in a court-yard off Kathmandu's Durbar Square. In the ensuing upheaval, a shrewd young general, **Jang Bahadur**, seized power, took the title **Rana** and proclaimed himself prime minister for life, an office which he later made hereditary by establishing a complicated roll of succession. For the next century, the kings of Nepal were mere puppets, while Ranas ruled like shoguns and packed the palace with their ever-increasing offspring. Authoritarian and blatantly exploitative, they built grandiose palaces while putting virtually no money into development, suppressed education for fear it would awaken opposition, and remained firmly isolationist to avoid losing control to the British. Ironically, an impoverished Nepal suited Britain, since it assured a steady supply of willing Gurkha cannon fodder.

Jang Bahadur appreciated the value of staying on good terms with the British Raj, now at its zenith; in 1850 he broke with tradition and travelled to England, where he met Queen Victoria and by all accounts cut a dashing figure. He returned with a number of western affectations, including a fondness for neoclassical architecture and epaulets, and soon after, to his credit, abolished the practice of *sati*. Other Ranas continued in the same vein. **Chandra Shamsher Rana**, who came to power in 1901 by deposing his brother*, is best known for building the thousand-roomed Singha Durbar and (belatedly) abolishing slavery. By 1940, underground resistance against the regime was developing, and **Juddha Shamsher Rana** had four plotters executed; after the fall of the Ranas these men were declared martyrs and a monument near the Kathmandu GPO was erected in their honour.

THE MONARCHY RESTORED

The Ranas' anachronistic regime couldn't survive long after the World War II, from which over 200,000 soldiers returned with dangerous ideas of freedom and justice. In 1948 the British withdrew from India, and with them went the Ranas' chief support; the new Indian government mistrusted the Ranas, and became genuinely worried about Nepal's weakness as a buffer state after China's Communist takeover in 1949. Seeking stability, India signed a far-reaching **"peace and friendship" treaty** with

Nepal in 1950 which, despite the upheavals that were to follow, remains the basis for all relations between the two countries.

Later the same year the strategic balance shifted again, as the Chinese invaded Tibet and the **Nepali Congress Party**, recently formed in Calcutta, called for an armed struggle against the Ranas. Within a month, King Tribhuwan requested asylum at the Indian embassy and was smuggled away to Delhi; the next morning, the Nepali Congress Party launched simultaneous assaults on Birganj and Biratnagar. Sporadic fighting continued for two months until the Ranas, internationally discredited, reluctantly agreed to enter into negotiations. Brokered by India, the so-called **Delhi Compromise** arranged for Ranas and the Congress Party to share power under the king's rule.

The compromise was short-lived. **Tribhuwan**, a previously retiring figure, emerged as a "hero of the revolution" and an adroit politician, and before the end of 1951 he had dismissed the Rana prime minister. This ended the Rana regime, but not Rana influence: by an agreement that has never been made public, the Shah royal family continues to appoint Ranas to most key military posts, and the families are inseparably tied by marriage (the queen is a Rana). In his four years as king, Tribhuwan neither consolidated his power nor delivered the elections he promised. Unaccountable to the voters, the party bosses who controlled the interim government were hardly an improvement over the Ranas.

PANCHAAYAT POLITICS

Crowned in 1955, **King Mahendra** lost no time in offsetting the parties' power by developing his own grassroots network of village leaders, forcing the parties to do likewise. They demanded elections; the king stalled, but finally agreed to a vote in 1959. Amazingly, the Nepali Congress Party swept 70 percent of the seats, and under Prime Minister **B. P. Koirala** began bypassing palace control and creating a party machine very much like India's. Mahendra was none too pleased with this **"experiment with democracy"**, as it came to be called – the following year he sacked the cabinet, banned political parties and threw the leaders in jail; for the rest of his reign he relied on heavy police measures to quell dissent.

---

*Probably with British help: two months earlier, he had gone on a private hunting trip with Lord Curzon; two years later he helped the British invade Tibet, and in 1927, when Nepali dissidents in India were protesting Rana rule, the British obligingly suppressed them.

In place of democracy, Mahendra offered the **"partless" panchaayat system**, a uniquely Nepalese form of government that grew out of the king's old-boy village network. Village councils (*panchaayats*) were established to look after local affairs; these were to send one representative on to a district council, which in turn elected members to a national assembly. The king chose the prime minister and cabinet and appointed one fifth of the national assembly, which served as a rubber stamp for his policies. "Partylessness" meant, of course, one party – the king's. The *panchaayat* system conveniently preserved an illusion of democracy while silencing opposition and ensuring loyalty to the king: in other words, it was a new and improved version of absolute monarchy. Corruption was the same as before, only now more decentralised, as every village *panchaayat* wallah had a tiny piece of the pie.

India was unhappy with the changes, but Mahendra, unlike his father, didn't owe his crown to India, and sought wider international support. He threw open Nepal's doors to **foreign aid**, which endeared him to the major powers, enriched the state's coffers and swelled the bureaucracy, if nothing else (see "Development Dilemmas"). After the 1962 Sino-Indian border war, Mahendra was able to exploit Nepal's buffer position with particular skill, alternately playing off the two powers against each other to obtain economic and military aid; no sooner had India completed the Rajpath, Nepal's first highway from the plains to Kathmandu, for example, than Mahendra persuaded the Chinese to extend the road to Tibet, much to India's horror. The **"China card"** became an important unofficial strand of foreign policy, but ultimately it helped bring down the *panchaayat* system.

The present king, **Birendra**, assumed power after Mahendra's death in 1972, although for astrological reasons wasn't crowned until 1975. Educated at Eton and Harvard, the young king set out as an enlightened reformer, taking steps to curb the bureaucracy and cronyism that had flourished under his father. Tightening Mahendra's laissez-faire policies on tourism – which had become Nepal's major industry – he cracked down on the growing hippy population by tightening visa restrictions. In 1975 he made the shrewdest and most popular move of his career when he proposed making Nepal a **Zone of Peace**, a Swiss-style neutrality pledge that would at first glance appear to be completely unassailable. India, however, has consistently opposed the measure as a violation of the 1950 "peace and friendship" treaty, which provides for mutual defence, while cynics like to point out the irony of Nepal – home of the world's most formidable mercenary soldiers – declaring itself a zone of peace.

Birendra's domestic reforms soon ran out of steam, and discontent grew over corruption and the slow pace of development. Widespread uprisings broke out in 1979, forcing the king to promise a national **referendum** in which voters could choose between the *panchaayat* system and multiparty democracy. Democracy lost by a margin of 55 to 45 – many say the vote was rigged – and the *panchaayat* system was retained.

During the 1980s Birendra proved himself to be an earnest but weak leader, easily manipulated by advisers and the queen – forever chaperoned by minders with walkie-talkies, he simply fell out of touch with the people. Despite token tinkerings to the system, the gravy train got more crowded throughout the decade, and insiders, sensing that the regime's days were numbered, tried to grab everything they could in the time remaining. In 1988 the king's brother, Dhirendra, was forced to relinquish his title as prince to avoid wide-ranging corruption charges. The king himself was rumoured to have Swiss bank accounts and an island in the Maldives (or Greece). Diplomats insist Birendra was uninvolved with any shady dealings, but if he didn't know what was going on in his name he was incredibly naive. Political opponents were imprisoned, while freedom of speech and the press were nonexistent.

DEMOCRACY

The chickens started coming home to roost in March 1989, when India, outraged by (among other things) Nepal's purchase of anti-aircraft guns from China, retaliated with a crippling **trade embargo**. Indian Prime Minister Rajiv Gandhi – who had long professed a deep distaste for Birendra's antiquated monarchy – apparently believed shortages of fuel and medicines would touch off a popular uprising and topple the regime in a matter of weeks. Only his timing was off. The government rode out the immediate crisis by closing the universities, rationing fuel and whipping up traditional anti-Indian sentiment, until the Indian elections in December, when Gandhi's more conciliatory successor, V. P. Singh, eased the embargo.

But after eight months of hardship, inflation and police action, Nepalis were fed up, and India could no longer be cast as the villain. The previous year had witnessed China's failed prodemocracy movement at Tiananmen Square and the spectacularly successful revolutions in eastern Europe: Nepalis were enormously stirred by these examples. Seeing their chance, the banned opposition parties united in the **Movement to Restore Democracy**, demanding an end to the *panchayaat* system and the creation of a constitutional monarchy. They called for a national day of protest on February 18, 1990 – a date already designated by the government, with unintended irony, as Democracy Day. Hundreds of opposition members, including leaders Ganesh Man Singh and Krishna Prasad Bhattarai, were duly placed under house arrest, and the planned revolt got off to a shaky start. Yet *Falgun 7* (the Nepali date of Democracy Day) marked the true start of Nepal's democracy movement, which in subsequent weeks gathered strength, resulting in violent clashes and deaths in Bhaktapur, Narayanghat and Hetauda. Even while under detention, opposition leaders were able to call strikes and blackouts at will. The king, counselled by hardliners, kept silence.

On April 3, protesters overran Patan, and three days later an estimated 200,000 people marched up Kathmandu's Durbar Marg towards the Royal Palace. The army fired into the crowd, killing between twenty and five hundred people – the true number will never be known

– and an ominous shoot-on-sight curfew was imposed. Finally moved to action by the **massacre**, the king dissolved his cabinet, legalised political parties and invited the opposition to form an interim government with Bhattarai as prime minister. Further convulsions followed, as an impatient populace suspected the king of playing for time to avoid making real reforms (as one commentator observed, "Birendra's chief problem in turning himself into a constitutional monarch is that he believes he already is one"). Coming under increasing pressure from the major aid-giving nations, the king appointed a commission to draft a **new constitution** enshrining democracy, human rights and a constitutional monarchy. The *panchaayat* system was dead.

In the aftermath of the revolution, optimism is running high, and the country is pulling itself back together with admirable speed. **Elections** are due by May 1991. But in a country with little experience (or even understanding) of democracy and a 35-percent literacy rate, it will require no small effort to ensure a fair and meaningful outcome. The present interim government is an uneasy alliance of pragmatists and communists, united in opposition but not necessarily in their political agendas, and they face an uphill struggle to revive the economy. Many Nepalis cynically expect the new politicians to be just as self-serving as the old ones; the *panchaayat* cronies could well try to stage a comeback. Meanwhile, the fate of Birendra is still in the balance: his image has tarnished in the past year, and he may lack sufficient popular support to survive even as a **constitutional monarch**. Crown Prince Dipendra, who recently completed his A-levels at Eton, might step into his father's shoes soon, or never.

RELIGION: HINDUISM, BUDDHISM, SHAMANISM

To say that religion is an important part of Nepalese life is a considerable understatement: it *is* life. In the Nepali world view, just about every act has spiritual implications; the gods are assumed to have a hand in every success or misfortune and must be appeased continuously. Belief and ritual form the basis of the whole social order, governing the way husbands relate to wives, parents to children and even the king to his subjects.

Three religious strands intertwine in Nepal: Hinduism, Buddhism and shamanism. In theory, these faiths are philosophically incompatible, but Nepalis, being an exceptionally tolerant lot, tend to overlook the differences. As practised by the masses, each employs superstition and rites of passage to get followers through the present life and codes of behaviour to prepare them for the next; Hindu priests, Buddhist lamas and tribal shamans play similar roles in their respective communities. Indeed, it's really only outside observers who bother to distinguish between the religions and dwell on their outward differences — most Nepalis find such distinctions needlessly academic.

Hinduism is the state religion of Nepal, and the government claims that 90 percent of the population is Hindu. However, there are social advantages to professing Hinduism in Nepal, and official statistics don't reflect the fact that many Nepalis blithely combine Hinduism with Buddhist or shamanist beliefs. In general, Hinduism prevails at the lower elevations and Buddhism in the Himalaya, while shamanism is strongest among the ethnic minorities of the hills.

HINDUISM

Hinduism doesn't conform to western notions of what a religion should be, and indeed the word "religion" is totally inadequate to describe it. Hindus call it *dharma*, a much more sweeping term that conveys faith, duty, a way of life and the entire social order. Having no common church or institution, its many sects and cults preach different dogmas and emphasise different scriptures. On social matters, Hinduism can be tragically rigid — witness the caste system — and when it comes to rituals, rather petty. Yet it's a highly individualistic system, offering worshippers an almost limitless choice of deities and admitting many paths to enlightenment. By absorbing and neutralising opposing doctrines, rather than condemning them as heresies, it has flourished longer than any other major religion.

Hinduism has been evolving since approximately 1600 BC, when **Aryan** invaders swept down from central Asia and subjugated the native Dravidian peoples of the Indus and Ganges plains. They brought with them a pantheon of nature gods and goddesses, some of whom are still in circulation: Indra (sky and rain) is popular in Kathmandu, while Surya (sun), Agni (fire), Vayu (wind), and Yama (death) retain bit parts in contemporary mythology. These so-called Vedic gods were first immortalised in the *Vedas* ("Books of Wisdom"), which were probably written between the twelfth and eighth centuries BC, and it was during this period that most of the principles now identified with Hinduism were thrashed out.

To make sure they stayed on top of the conquered Dravidians, the Aryans banned intermarriage and codified the apartheid-like **caste system**; *varna*, the Sanskrit word for caste, means "colour", and to this day members of the higher castes generally have lighter skin. Initially, four castes were established: Brahmans (priests), Kshatriyas (warriors and rulers), Vaisyas (traders and farmers) and Sudras (artisans and menials); over time, the lower two divisions spawned innumerable occupational subcastes. The *Rig Veda*, Hinduism's oldest text, put a divine seal of approval on the arrangements by proclaiming that Brahmans had issued from the mouth of the supreme creator, Kshatriyas from his arms, Vaishyas from his thighs and Sudras from his feet.

Brahmans, entrusted with the brain work, proceeded to exploit their position by inventing preposterously complex rituals and sacrifices, and making themselves the indispensable guardians of these mysteries (cow-worship probably dates from this period). Despite this stagnation, the philosophical foundations of

Hinduism were laid during the late Vedic period and recorded in a series of discourses known as the ***Upanishads***. Ever since, Hinduism has run along two radically different tracks: the Brahmans' hocus-pocus popular religion, with its comic-book deities and bloody sacrifices, and the profound, intuitive insights of *gurus* and *rishis* (teachers).

The essense of Hinduism, unchanged since the *Upanishads* were written, is that the soul (*atman*) of each living thing is like a lost frag-ment of the universal soul – ***brahman***, the ulti-mate reality – while everything in the physical universe is mere illusion (*maya*). To reunite with *brahman*, the individual soul must go through a **cycle of rebirths** (*samsara*), ideally moving up the scale with each reincarnation. Determining the soul's progress is its ***karma*** – its accumulated "just desserts" – which is reck-oned by the degree to which the soul conformed to ***dharma***, or correct Hindu behav-iour, in its previous life. Thus a low-caste Hindu must accept his or her lot to atone for past sins, and follow *dharma* in the hopes of achiev-ing a higher rebirth. The theoretical goal of every Hindu is to cast off all illusion, achieve release (*moksha*) from the cycle of rebirths, and dissolve into *brahman*.

Hinduism has assembled a vast and rich body of mythology over the past three millen-nia, largely in an effort to personalise *brahman* for the masses. Early on, a few of the Vedic gods were renamed, relieved of their old nature associations and given personalities to illus-trate divine attributes. The concept of the **Hindu "trinity"** – Brahma the creator, Vishnu the preserver and Shiva the destroyer – was developed, and the process of god-creation was speeded by the invention of numerous ***avatars***, or manifestations of gods. Hinduism's best-loved epics, the *Mahabharata* and the *Ramayana*, portray two of Vishnu's *avatars*, Krishna and Rama, as models of human conduct (although as often as not Hindu gods, like their Greek counterparts, are made out to be vain and foolish).

The explosion of deities has given rise to a succession of **devotional cults** over the centu-ries, the most important of which nowadays are *Vaishnava* (followers of Vishnu), *Shaiva* (Shiva) and *Mahadevi* (the mother goddess); the latter often goes by the name *Shakti*, a tantric term explained below. Brahma is rarely

iconographically depicted and consequently not widely worshipped.

THE HINDU PANTHEON

If you're daunted by Hinduism's technicolour array of gods and goddesses, don't worry: your average Hindu would be hard pressed to name most of them. While Hinduism is said to boast of 300 million deities, they can all be thought of as representations of the one supreme god (this paradox isn't hard to deal with if you've been trained that everything is illusion anyway). The most important gods, described below, can easily be identified by certain trade-mark implements, postures and "vehicles" (animal carriers). As for gods' multiple arms and heads, these aren't meant to be taken liter-ally: they symbolise omnipotence, while severed heads and trampled corpses signify ignorance and evil.

VISHNU

Vishnu (often known as Narayan in Nepal) is the face of dignity and equanimity, typically shown standing erect holding a wheel (*chakra*), mace (*gada*), lotus (*padma*) and conch (*sankha*) in his four hands, or, as at Budhanilkantha, reclining on a serpent's coil. A statue of **Garuda**, Vishnu's bird-man vehicle, is always close by. Vishnu is also sometimes depicted in one or more of his ten incarnations (*das avatar*), which follow an evolutionary progres-sion from fish, turtle and boar to man-lion, dwarf, axe-wielding Brahman and the legen-dary heroes Rama and Krishna. Rama is asso-ciated with **Hanuman**, his loyal monkey-king ally in the *Ramayana*, while Krishna is most commonly seen on calendars as a chubby blue baby, flute-player or charioteer. Interestingly, Vishnu's ninth *avatar* is Buddha – this was a sixth-century attempt by *Vaishnavas* to bring Buddhists into their fold – and the tenth is Kalki, a messiah figure invented in the twelfth century when Hindus were being persecuted at the hands of Muslim invaders. Vishnu's consort is **Lakshmi**, the goddess of wealth, to whom lamps are lit during the festival of *Tihar*.

SHIVA

Shiva's incarnations are countless, ranging from the hideous Bhairab, who alone is said to take 64 different forms, to the benign

Pashupati ("Lord of the Animals") and Nataraj ("King of the Dance"). To many devotees he is simply Mahadev: Great God. The earliest and still the most widespread icon of Shiva is the **lingam**, a phallically shaped stone fertility symbol* commonly housed in a boxy stone *shivalaya* ("Shiva home"). Shiva temples can be identified by the presence of a *trisul* (trident) and the bull **Nandi**, Shiva's mount, who is himself something of a fertility symbol.

Many *sadhus* worship Shiva the *yogin* (one who practises yoga), the Hindu ascetic supreme, who is often depicted sitting in meditative repose on a Himalayan mountaintop, perhaps holding a chillum of *ganga*. Pashupatinath is the national shrine to Shiva as **Pashupati**, and is patronised by *Pashupata*, *Kaplika* and other *Shaiva* sects, who take it to be Shiva's winter home. Another popular image of Shiva is as the loving husband with his consort, Parvati: the two can be seen leaning from an upper window of a temple in Kathmandu's Durbar Square. Nearby stand two famous statues of **Bhairab**, the tantric (see below) interpretation of Shiva in his role as destroyer: according to Hindu philosophy, everything – not only evil – must be destroyed in its turn to make way for new things.

MAHADEVI

The mother goddess is similarly worshipped in many forms, both peaceful and wrathful, and indeed many of these are reckoned to be the consorts of corresponding Shiva forms. As **Kali** ("Black") she is the female counterpart of Bhairab, wearing a necklace of skulls and sticking out her tongue with bloodthirsty intent; as **Durga** ("Unapproachable") she is the demon-slayer honoured in the great *Dasain* festival. In Nepal she is widely worshipped as **Bhagwati** ("Powerful"), the embodiment of female creative power; in all these forms, the mother goddess is appeased by sacrifices of uncastrated male animals. On a more peaceful level,

she is also Parvati (daughter of Himalaya), Gauri ("Golden") or just **Mahadevi** ("Great Goddess").

GANESH

Several legends tell how **Ganesh**, Shiva's and Parvati's son, came to have an elephant's head: one states that Shiva accidently chopped the boy's head off, and owing to an obscure restriction on the god's restorative powers, was forced to replace it with that of the first creature he saw. The god of wisdom and remover of obstacles, Ganesh must be worshipped first to ensure offerings to other gods will be effective, and a Ganesh shrine or stone will invariably be found near other temples. Underscoring Hinduism's great sense of the mystical absurd, Ganesh's vehicle is a rat.

Of the other Hindu deities, only **Saraswati**, the goddess of learning and culture, receives much attention in Nepal. She is normally depicted holding a *vina*, a musical instrument something like a sitar.

BUDDHISM

Buddha was born in what is now Nepal (see "Lumbini" in Chapter Five) in the sixth or seventh century BC, and his teachings were in many ways a protest against the ritualism to which popular Hinduism had by then been reduced. Buddha rejected the caste system and the mystical aspects of Hinduism, while freely borrowing its doctrines of reincarnation and *karma*, along with many yogic practices; the result was an agnostic, pragmatic philosophy that placed a greater emphasis on the active pursuit of enlightenment.

Like Hindus, Buddhists strive for release from the cycle of rebirths, but whereas the Hindu ideal is to reunite with the creator, Buddhism's *nirvana* is a state of perfect and final peace reached upon enlightenment. Buddha taught that enlightenment could be attained by mastering the **four noble truths**: that suffering is part of existence; suffering is caused by desire; the taming of desire ends suffering; and desire can be tamed by following the **eightfold path**, a set of deceptively simple guidelines for achieving *dharma*. The whole prescription is called the **Middle Way** because it involves neither embracing nor renouncing the world, but essentially not being

---

* The phallic aspect of the *lingam* is perhaps overplayed by non-Hindus. Gandhi wrote: "It has remained for our Western visitors to acquaint us with the obscenity of many practices which we have hitherto innocently indulged in. It was in a missionary book that I first learned that the Shiva *lingam* had any obscene significance at all." Then again, Gandhi denied most things to do with sex.

attached to it. True **non-attachment**, by casting off the illusion of self, is enlightenment. "Self," said Buddha, "is a fever."

In its original form, Buddhism was for many followers a full-time monastic pursuit. But for most lay people, the lonely quest for enlightenment was too hard-core and impersonal; to compete with the more accessible Hindu gods and goddesses, Buddhism evolved a populist strand known as **Mahayana** ("Great Vehicle"). Reintroducing elements of worship and prayer, Mahayana Buddhism developed its own pantheon of *bodhisattvas* – enlightened intermediaries, something akin to Catholic saints, who have forgone *nirvana* until all humanity has been saved. Many of these were a repackaging of older Hindu deities, who were now given new names and roles as protectors of *dharma*.

Followers of the original teachings called their school **Theravada** ("Way of the Elders"), but to Mahayana Buddhists it came to be known, somewhat disparagingly, as **Hinayana** ("Lesser Vehicle"). This tradition remains active in Sri Lanka and much of southeast Asia. The Mahayana doctrine spread to China, Korea and Japan, adapting differently to each; on the Indian subcontinent, however, it gradually lost its distinct identity, and by the seventh century it had for all practical purposes been absorbed back into the ocean of Hinduism.

TANTRA AND VAJRAYANA

Even as Buddhism was on the wane in India, a new religious movement was developing in Bengal and Bihar that was to give a radically new bent to both Buddhism and Hinduism. *Tantra* erupted like the punk rock of religion, proclaiming that *everything* in life can be used to reach enlightenment: the five things normally shunned in orthodox Hinduism and Buddhism as poisons – meat, fish, parched grains, alcohol and sex – are embraced wholeheartedly on the tantric path. Sex, in particular, is regarded as the central metaphor for spiritual enlightenment, and it is this inversion of the sacred and profane that has given *tantra* its somewhat risqué reputation. *Tantra* abounds in esoteric imagery, *mantras* (verbal formulas) and *mandalas* (diagrams used to aid in meditation), which together make up a sort of mystic code intended only for initiates.

According to **Hindu *tantra***, the female principle (***shakti***) possesses the creative energy which is capable of activating the male force. The gods are powerless until joined with their female counterparts – in tantric art, Bhairab is often shown locked in a grim sexual embrace – and in many of her guises the mother goddess has become *Shakti*, one half of a tantric union of sexual opposites. The human psyche, too, is held to consist of male and female forces that must be harnessed: followers of Hindu *tantra* are trained to visualise the body's female energy rising like a snake from the level of the sexual organs, ascending the seven psychic centres (*chakras*) of the spinal column to reach the male principle at the top of the head, resulting in realisation.

Buddhist *tantra*, known as **Vajrayana** ("Way of the Thunderbolt"), reverses the symbolism of these two forces and makes the male principle of "skill in means" the active force and the female principle of "wisdom" passive. In tantric rituals, these forces are symbolised by the the hand-held "lightning-bolt sceptre" (*vajra*), which represents the male principle, and the bell (*ghanta*), representing the female. Expanding on Mahayana's all-male pantheon, Vajrayana introduces female counterparts to the transcendent Buddhas and some of the *bodhisattvas*, and sometimes depicts them engaged in sexual positions.

LAMAISM (TIBETAN BUDDHISM)

Vajrayana Buddhism found its greatest expression in Tibet, which it reached (by way of Nepal) in the eighth century. At the time, Tibet was under the sway of a native shamanic religion (see below) known as **Bon**; Vajrayana eventually overcame Bon*, but only by taking on board many of its symbols and rituals, thus creating the spectacularly distinct branch of Buddhism that outsiders call **Lamaism**.

Lamaism turned Bon's demons into fierce guardian deities (*dharmapalas*) – these can usually be seen flanking monastery (*gompa*) entrances – and incorporated elements of Bon magic into its meditational practices. Since blood sacrifices were out of the question, they

---

* Unrepentant Bon priests were banished to the Himalaya, and even today vestiges of the Bon tradition may be encountered while trekking: for example, a follower of Bon will circle a religious monument anti-clockwise, the opposite direction to a Buddhist.

were adapted into "vegetarian" offerings in the form of conical dough cakes called *torma*. The emphasis on the **lama** (Tibetan Buddhist priest) as spiritual guide no doubt derives from the ancient role of the Bon shaman, and the *Bardo Thödol* ("Tibetan Book of the Dead") is basically a shamanic guide to the after-death experience.

While its underlying principles aren't much different from that of Mahayana Buddhism, Lamaism has a tendency to express them in incredibly esoteric symbolism. The **Wheel of Life**, often depicted in *thankas* and on monastery walls, is an intricate exposition of *karma*, judgement and the various levels of rebirth that can be attained. The *stupa*, an ancient abstract representation of the Buddha, is developed into a complex statement of Buddhist cosmology, and Buddhahood is refracted into five aspects, symbolised by the five transcendent or *dhyani* **(meditating) Buddhas**, which can be seen in niches surrounding the Swayambhu *stupa*. Each of these is associated with an attribute of Buddhahood; by visualising one of the *dhyani* Buddhas in meditation, one is supposed to identify with its facet of Buddha nature. *Bodhisattvas* are reckoned to be emanations of the *dhyani* Buddhas. **Prayer wheels** and prayer flags – usually bearing the *mantra*, *Om mani padme hum* ("Oh hail to the jewel in the lotus") – are Tibetan innovations which probably grew out of the tantric view of the world as being in a constant state of motion.

Lamaism sets great store by the oral continuity of teachings, so the divergence of various sects over the centuries has had more to do with different lineages than major doctrinal differences. The leader of each sect, and indeed of each monastery, is held to be the reincarnation (*tolku*) of his or her predecessor, and is expected to carry on the same spiritual tradition. Of the **four main sects**, the oldest is the *Nyingma-pa* ("Red Hat"), founded in the eighth century by Guru Padma Sambhava, who, if all the stories told about him were true, meditated in every cave in Nepal. The *Sakya-pas* broke away in the eleventh century, tracing their lineage from the second-century Indian philosopher Nagarjuna. The *Kagyu-pa* order emerged in the eleventh and twelfth centuries, inspired by the Tibetan mystic Mapa and his disciple Milarepa, who also meditated his way around Nepal. The *Gelug-pa* ("Yellow Hat") sect, led by the **Dalai Lama**, is the only one

that takes a significantly different theological line; born out of a fifteenth-century reform movement to purge Lamaism of its wackier practices, it places greater emphasis on rational discourse.

THE NEWARI SYNTHESIS

Ask a Newar whether he's Hindu or Buddhist, the saying goes, and he'll answer "yes": after fifteen centuries of continuous exposure to both faiths, the Newars of the Kathmandu Valley have concocted a unique **synthesis** of the two. To religious scholars, the Newari religion is as exciting as a biologist's missing link, for some believe that it provides a picture of the way Mahayana and Vajrayana Buddhism functioned historically in India.

Until only the past two centuries, the Newars held fast to the original monastic form of tantric Buddhism – as the *bahals* of Kathmandu and Patan still bear witness – while their rulers pursued the Hindu tantric path. However, the Kathmandu Valley has become progressively "Hinduised" since the unification of Nepal in the eighteenth century: the monasteries have largely disappeared, their monks have married, and the title of **Vajracharya** (Buddhist priest) has become a hereditary caste like that of the Brahman priests. Today, Newari Buddhists are perhaps the only Buddhist culture that no longer maintains active communities of monks or nuns. Although the acceptance of caste and the decline of monasticism have shifted the balance in favour of Hinduism, at the popular level the synthesis remains as well-bonded as ever.

When Newars refer to themselves as **Buddha Margi** (Buddhist) or **Shiva Margi** (Hindu), they often do so only to indicate that they employ a Vajracharya or Brahman priest; even this doesn't always hold true, though, as many *jyapus* (farmers) call themselves "Hindu" and attend Hindu festivals, yet still use Vajracharyas. In any case, Newar rituals vary little from Hindu to Buddhist.

Puja (an act of worship) is performed to gain the favour of deities for material requests as often as for "spiritual" reasons. An integral part of all Newar rituals is the "*puja* of five offerings", consisting of flowers (usually marigolds), incense, light (in the form of butter lamps), *sindur* (coloured powder) and various kinds of purified food (usually rice, dairy products, sometimes sweets). Before **darshan** (audience with a deity), the devotee or the priest uses consecrated water to wash him or herself and to bathe the deity. After the deity has symbolically accepted and eaten some food, the remainder is taken back by the devotee as **prasad** (consecrated food). This, along with a **tika** made with the coloured powder, confers the deity's blessing and protection.

Priests are ordinarily engaged for the more important **life-cycle rites** (birth, marriage, death) or for larger seasonal festivals; wealthier Newars may also seek private consultations at times of illness or for astrological readings. Brahman priests don't perform animal **sacrifices**, but they do preside over the rituals that precede them. This brings up one of the rare differences between Hindu and Buddhist Newars: while Hindu Newars are enthusiastic sacrificers – they call the bloody ninth day of the *Dasain* festival *Syako Tyako* (roughly, "the more you kill, the more you gain") – Buddhists seldom participate. During *Dasain*, Tibetan monasteries in Nepal hold special services to pray for good rebirths of the sacrificed animals.

THE NEWARI PANTHEON

All the Hindu and Buddhist deities already discussed are fair game for Newars, along with a few additional characters of local invention. Some deities specialise in curing diseases, others bring good harvests – as far as Newars are concerned, it doesn't matter whether they're Hindu or Buddhist so long as they do the job. The following are some of the figures uniquely adapted by the Newars.

Machhendranath, honoured by Newars as a rainmaker par excellence, typifies the layering of religious motifs that so frequently takes place among the Newars. As Avalokiteshwara, the *bodhisattva* of compassion, he is widely invoked by the *mantra, Om mani padme hum*. Depending on his incarnation (he is said to have 108), he may be depicted as having anything up to a thousand arms and eleven heads. While it's unclear how Avalokiteshwara came to be associated with the historical Hindu figures of Machhendranath and Gorakhnath, it was certainly in part the result of a conscious attempt by Hindu rulers to establish religious and social bonds by grafting two Hindu saints on to a local Buddhist cult.

Kumari, the "Living Goddess", is another often-cited example of Newari syncretism (religious fusing): although acknowledged to be an incarnation of the Hindu goddess Durga, she is picked from a Buddhist-caste family. **Bhimsen**, a mortal hero in the Hindu *Mahabharata* who is rarely worshipped in India, has somehow been elevated to be the patron deity of Newar shopkeepers, both Hindu and Buddhist.

Manjushri, the *bodhisattva* of knowledge, has been pinched from the Buddhist pantheon to play the lead part in the Kathmandu Valley's creation myth (although he is often confused with Saraswati, the Hindu goddess of knowledge). He is always depicted with a sword, with which he cuts away ignorance and attachment, and sometimes also with a book, bow, bell and *vajra*. Likewise **Tara**, the embodiment of the female principle in Vajrayana Buddhism, assumes special meaning for Newars, who consider her the deification of an eighth-century Nepali princess.

Quintessentially tantric, the **Bajra Joginis** (or *Vajra Yoginis*) command their own cult at four temples around the Kathmandu Valley. These may be regarded as the wrathful aspect of Tara, although in practice they are worshipped in almost the same manner as Kali or Durga, which includes receiving blood sacrifices. Harati, the Buddhist protector of children, is zealously worshipped by Newars under the name **Ajima**.

Throughout Nepal, stones and trees marked with *sindur* may be seen: vestiges of older animist practices, these may mark the place where a nature goddess (generically known as **Mai**), local spirit or serpent (**naga**) is supposed to live. There are many types of these lesser spirit beings who require offerings to safeguard passage through their respective domains.

SHAMANISM

More ancient than Hinduism or Buddhism, **shamanism** is practiced in diverse ways throughout the world by peoples fortunate enough to have been overlooked by the institutional religions. Concerned with maintaining the correct balance between the physical and spiritual realms, shamans are employed to consecrate sacred ground, cure illnesses, exorcise demons and other mystical rituals. Shamans typically use magical incantations and fall into trances, during which they enter the spirit world to mediate with the forces of the cosmos on behalf of their flock.

Shamanism is the traditional religion of most of Nepal's native ethnic groups, and while many have adopted at least outward forms of Hinduism or Buddhism (depending on their location), it is still widely practised in the western and eastern hills. The generic Nepali word for shaman is *jhankri*, although each group has its own term. Forms and rituals also vary from one tribe to another, but a *jhankri* – usually wearing a headdress of peacock feathers and carrying a double-sided drum – is always unmistakeable.

Charles Leech

TIBETAN EXILES IN NEPAL

On October 7, 1950, the People's Republic of China, which had concluded its own communist revolution only a year earlier, invaded – or, as Beijing still insists, "liberated" – Tibet. The Tibetan Army was easily overpowered, and by May 1951 Tibet was forced to sign a treaty accepting Chinese rule, onthe understanding that China would not interfere with Tibetan government or culture.

During the following eight years, however, Chinese troops gathered in increasing numbers in Lhasa, the Tibetan capital; Tibetan monks were tortured, women raped and children taken from their homes for "re-education" in China. The Chinese imposed disastrous new agricultural methods on Tibetans, causing widespread famine. Tension mounted, fighting flared up in the east, and in March 1959 a full-scale **uprising** erupted in Lhasa. It was brutally crushed by the Chinese and thousands of Tibetans were executed or imprisoned, while Tibet was formally annexed to China. The **Dalai Lama**, Tibet's spiritual and political leader, fled to India; he still resides in Dharmsala, where the Tibetan government-in-exile is based. Tens of thousands of Tibetans followed, making their way into Nepal and India by various routes through the Himalaya.

For three decades, Tibet has endured outright **genocide** at the hands of the Chinese: the Dalai Lama's Bureau of Information calculates that 1.2m Tibetans have been executed, tortured, killed in battle, starved or died in Chinese labour camps; during the 1966–76 Cultural Revolution, virtually every monastery was deliberately destroyed. An organised **guerrilla movement**, supported by the CIA, fought the Chinese along the Nepalese border until the early 1970s, when the US-China thaw led to its dissolution. Until recently, Tibet's plight was largely ignored by the major powers, but China's **Tiananmen Square massacre** and the Dalai Lama's receipt of the 1989 Nobel Peace Prize have put discussion of Tibetan independence back on the agenda.

Today, 15,000 out of a total 110,000 **Tibetan exiles** live in Nepal, predominantly in the Kathmandu and Pokhara valleys. An encouraging number have by now achieved success in the carpet and handicrafts businesses, although many others continue to labour at carpet looms for very low wages. Still others are playing active roles in establishing Baudha as a centre of Buddhist study, thus sustaining Tibetan religion and culture until the Chinese occupation of Tibet is ended. The following profiles contrast the experiences of two Tibetans now living in Nepal.

CHOKYI NYIMA RINPOCHE: A LAMA

Chokyi Nyima Rinpoche ("Sun Lotus of the Precious One") was born in Kunying, a village about 150 miles north of Lhasa, in the year of the Iron-Hare, 1951, the son of a recognised *tulku* (reincarnate lama) and an aristocratic mother. At the age of one and a half, after successfully completing numerous tests prescribed by Tibetan Buddhist tradition, he was identified as the seventh incarnation of Gar Druchen, a spiritual emanation of Nagarjuna, the second-century Indian Buddhist philosopher. Soon after, the young *rinpoche* ("precious one", a title given to revered Tibetan Buddhist teachers) was enthroned at his predecessor's monastery, Drong Gon Thubten Dargyeling, in central Tibet.

Chokyi Nyima recalls how 35 of the monastery's 500 monks were involved in lifelong retreats, as opposed to the more common three- to nine-year retreats, living in caves with "no door, only a window to pass food through, and they would never come out for the rest of their life" – a testament to the extreme faith with which some 200,000 monks and nuns devoted their lives in over 6000 monasteries and nunneries prior to China's occupation of Tibet.

Following the failed Tibetan uprising and subsequent upheavals of 1959, Chokyi Nyima and his family were whisked into exile in Gangtok, Sikkim, where, along with 53 other young *rinpoches*, he studied briefly in an English boarding school. He soon resumed his traditional monastic education, however, and for the next fifteen years studied under a series of famous Buddhist teachers.

Chokyi Nyima relates how one day, when he was nineteen or twenty, he and another young *tulku* approached their tutor, Gyalwa Karmapa, head of the *Kagyu-pa* sect of Tibetan Buddhism, with the intention of entering a three-year retreat. "He scolded us, saying, 'You are foolish, you just want to go in a cave to sleep. You are *tulkus*, you need to save and help the sentient beings . . . why do you think you are being educated like this? Even though I am very happy that you have a willingness to go on a retreat at such a young age – on the one hand it is a good quality, but on the other hand it is not good *enough*!'" Finally sealing Chokyi Nyima's future, Gyalwa Karmapa said, "I think it is your *karma* to teach, especially to foreigners. You will go to Nepal and help your father (Urgyen Rinpoche) build a monastery." Chokyi Nyima still fondly recalls the wisdom of his teacher: "His mind was like the ocean, whereas our minds were but a drop in that ocean."

In 1974, Chokyi Nyima came to Baudha to help his father build the Ka Nying Shedrupling Monastery, and soon after, on the instructions of Gyalwa Karmapa, was made its abbot. Ka Nying Shedrupling today houses some 120 monks and lay people, who are dedicated to preserving and spreading Tibetan Buddhism through traditional wood-block printing of *pechha* (Tibetan liturgical texts), translating and publishing Buddhist books in English, and maintaining a large library of books on Buddhist topics.

Following the wish of his tutor, Chokyi Nyima began teaching not only the local community but also a growing number of foreigners. "I like to find out what kind of people they are, why they came here and what they are searching for," he says. In fact, one of his first Western *dharma* students has just begun a three-year retreat at a Buddhist centre in Scotland. Tibetan Buddhists aren't surprised by the spread of Buddhism in the West, for they regard it as the fulfilment of an eighth-century prophecy attributed to Guru Padma Sambhava, the legendary founder of Buddhism in Tibet: "When the iron bird flies and horses run on wheels, the Tibetan people will be scattered across the face of the earth, and the *dharma* will come to the land of the red men."

One morning during one of his daily public audiences, where there are invariably two or three westerners, Chokyi Nyima explains his thoughts on the increasing number of westerners interested in Tibetan Buddhism. Thoughout the informal talk he is occasionally interrupted by pilgrims and the faithful coming to receive his blessings and exchange *katas*, the white scarves Tibetans give as an offering of good luck. "I've found that the teachings are touching more and more people from different countries, because they ring true," he says. "Many westerners, especially the younger generation, are putting more faith in Western science only to discover that there are still many unexplained things. But because they have grown up with the idea of always searching for new answers to old phenomena, they usually have a very open mind. This is very much like what the Buddha said: 'Don't take my word for it, but find out the truth for yourself.'"

To this end, one of the aims of Ka Nying Shedrupling, as well as of many other monasteries, is to make Mahayana Buddhism readily available in the West. In Chokyi Nyima's words, "If peace comes to every individual, then there will be no conflicts, no problems, because nowadays too many people think often only of themselves. That's why we train more monks to be sent all over the world to help others to share their knowledge of the peace and caring message of the Buddha."

The often serious tone that Chokyi Nyima uses to make a point is never overshadowed by his humble and good-natured personality. As we leave the morning teaching, he gives us a mischievous look and says, "You must meditate! Don't be lazy and forget what I've said," throwing three oranges at us from a pile given as offerings.

Andy Balestracci

GEN TASHI: A KHAMPA

A boyishly trim man with a chiselled jaw is making the last stitches on a brown *chuba* (Tibetan wrap-around dress). "There! In time for *Losar**," he says to a Manang woman, who is wearing several raw-looking chunks of turquoise and coral strung around her neck.

* Tibetan New Year.

"Please, won't you –"

"No, I said *no*. Your aunt will just have to wear something else. It's two days to *Losar*, and you want me to stitch another *chuba*? It's *Losar*, woman; we Tibetans drop all work. You go home and get the altars prepared, and leave me to my preparations."

Gen Tashi takes off his thick glasses, revealing curiously brown-bluish eyes. He bought the round-cut glasses in Lhasa on his way back from his hometown a few years ago; folding them, he puts them away with great care.

In the same room sits a younger man, Karma, shaking out black snuff onto his thumb from an aspirin bottle. He inhales with gusto, then digs out a square piece of woollen cloth from under the rug on his bed to blow his nose. "Drop everything, do your *pujas*, and enjoy yourself at *Losar* – it's only once a year," he tells the woman.

"All right, all right. *Losar* is *Losar* I know," she says, laughing. "I won't bother you anymore. *Tashi delek** to you – but please, after *Losar* . . ." And with her new *chuba* wrapped in newspaper under her arm, she leaves Gen's workroom.

For a man of 66, Gen Tashi cuts a trim figure. He sits cross-legged, ramrod straight. When people comment about his lithe figure, he says he is light because of his daily *koras* (circumambulations) around the Swayambhu hill. "The *koras* make you feel you can walk on and on," he says.

Considering his present occupation and boyish good-nature, it's hard to believe that Gen spent more than a decade as a guerrilla fighter just south of the Tibetan border. He was born to a peasant family in the valley of Gyelthang, at the southeastern edge of the Tibetan plateau (the district is today part of the so-called Tibetan Autonomous Prefecture of Dechen). At the age of fourteen he became a monk at Gyelthang's Sumtseling Monastery, which at the time supported 2000 monks, and for the next eighteen years spent at least part of each year at the monastery observing special prayers and liturgies. For the rest of the year, when he was old enough, Gen went on family trading trips east to Dali and Lijiang in Yunnan (China), and west to Lhasa and southwest Kalimpong in Sikkim, where Chinese tea and Indian cotton and manufactured goods

were traded. The trade helped finance Gen's monastic exams and initiations.

Chinese troops marched into Gen's district in 1954 and began imposing exorbitant taxes on traders, though they held back from enforcing immediate political changes. At the time of the 1959 uprising, Gen – who had just turned 36, an age considered inauspicious by Tibetans – and his family were on a butter-buying trip near Lhasa, attempting to raise money for their lama's examinations. Joining other Khampas (people of Kham, a province in eastern Tibet) caught away from home by the uprising, Gen rushed to help guard the Norbu Lingka, the Dalai Lama's summer palace in Lhasa, until the Dalai Lama could escape. Anticipating reprisals from the Chinese after the uprising, Gen fled south to Gangtok, Sikkim, where he and many compatriots found work building mountain roads.

Later the same year, the news of a re-formed guerrilla movement known as the "Four Rivers and Six Ranges" reached Sikkim. Gen and a dozen fellow Gyelthangbas quickly joined up and were deployed to Mustang, the arid, rugged area north of Pokhara, where he participated in a variety of sabotage activities against the Chinese garrisoned across the border in Tibet. "I became good at hiding arms and ammunition underground," he says, not with bravado but with a sigh at being engaged in martial activities anathema to his vows as a Buddhist monk: several years have passed since he relinquished his vows.

But lacking in international support, the guerrilla operations in Nepal gradually petered out, and the military camps became semi-permanent settlements. Gen dropped out of the movement and took up tailoring, earning a living by sewing *chubas* for the camp. Finally, after twelve years in Mustang, he and Karma, a fellow Khampa, together with Karma's wife, decided to move down to Kathmandu: their lives and the struggle didn't seem to be leading anywhere.

What had it all been for? "Well, we carried the hope that we could return to our fatherland," says Gen, for the first time showing emotion.

For their new lives in the capital, they found themselves hopelessly handicapped. By then, the efforts of other Tibetans to turn the folk art of carpet-weaving into a commercially viable venture was paying off; most of them were no

* Good day.

longer refugees. In contrast, Gen, Karma and his wife had to adjust to a new environment, learn a new language and start from scratch. The only livelihood they could turn to was stitching *chubas*.

For years they were barely able to make ends meet, but recently Karma has started earning large commissions selling antique carpets. Now only Gen needs to stitch *chubas*, while Karma's wife manages the household. She and Karma have a twelve-year-old son, Dhendup, who attends a Tibetan school in the valley. Unlike Gen and his parents, Dhendup can write and speak in English, Tibetan and Nepali. He calls Gen grandfather.

Among the shrinking number of first-generation Tibetan exiles in Nepal, especially those of Kham, Gen's story is a common one. Many spent a large part of their adult lives fighting for their country. Now, with just as much hope, though perhaps with less urgency, they still look to the day when they can return to their homeland. Until then, they continue to circumambulate and pray and work for their younger ones.

K.T.G.

To get involved in the Tibetan cause, contact the Tibet Support Group UK, 100 Axminster Road , London N7 6BS.

DEVELOPMENT DILEMMAS

This is How a Nation Pretends to Survive

This is Machhapuchhre, Your Excellency!
And that's Annapurna.
And, beyond that are
The ranges of Dhaulagiri.
You can see them with your naked eyes.
I don't think you'll need any binocular, sir.
We want to open a three-star hotel, Your
  Excellency!
Will you give us some loan?

Your Excellency!
This is Koshi, that's Gandaki
And, that one, yes, that blue one, is
  Karnali.
You might have read in some newspapers
That rivers in Nepal are on sale.
But that's not true, sir.
In fact, we have named our zones
In the name of these rivers.
It's our plan to generate electricity from
  them.
Will you give us some loan?

This is Kathmandu Valley, Your Excellency!
I mean country's capital,
Which contains three cities –
Kathmandu, Lalitpur and Bhaktapur.
Please mind the smell!
You may use your handkerchief, if you like.
It's true we have not been able to build
Either the sewer or public lavatories.
But in the next five-year plan
We are definitely going to introduce
"Keep the City Clean" programme.
Will you give us some loan, Your
  Excellency!

Min Bahadur Bista (1989).

With a per-capita income of just $160, Nepal is one of the world's poorest nations. Its population is rising at an annual rate of 2.6 percent, and even in the most optimistic projections its population of 18 million is expected to triple by the middle of the next century. With agriculture unable to keep pace with population, Nepal's "food deficit" is widening yearly and the country has little hope of ever feeding three times as many people – indeed, because of erosion due to overuse and deforestation, productivity is actually declining. There are, however, silver linings to all these dark clouds.

Nepali schoolchildren are frequently asked to write essays on "What I Would Do if I Were King". There are, of course, no right answers. Nepal is sloshing with foreign experts, all clamouring to offer their suggestions – and money – yet despite the efforts of the past four decades the country remains (economically) poor. Some say the lack of coordination between donor agencies has hindered development. Others point to tangible improvements that have been made, such as increases in life expectancy and literacy. Still others claim that Nepal's problems have been vastly overstated by the government (to ensure continued aid) and development agencies (to justify their payrolls).

"Development" is a word like "progress": it means different things to different people, and all too often is assumed uncritically to be a desirable end in itself. Throughout the world – not only in Nepal – no one has yet worked out whether development is in fact a Good Thing, and if so what form it should take. But after spending time in the field, many aid workers conclude that Nepalis – who lead rich and elegantly simple lives, nearly self-sufficient and unencumbered by modern problems – have more to teach the "developed world" than it has to teach them .

Pragmatists usually argue that development is going to come anyway, and communities should at least be given a fair choice as to what kind of development they want, rather than being forced to choose between development and non-development. But while no one advocates withholding aid or denying Nepalis' aspirations to certain material improvements, many in the development world reckon that Nepali schoolchildren are probably better able to solve their own problems than foreign experts, and that Nepalis ought to be the ones who decide what is appropriate development for Nepal.

POVERTY

Most people agree that Nepal's overarching problem is **poverty**, which can be traced to a number of factors: steep terrain, which makes farming inefficient and communication difficult; landlocked borders; few natural resources; a rigid social structure that entrenches the rich against the poor; and a comparatively late start (the Nepalese government did essentially nothing for its people before 1951). Unable to do anything about these causes, most development organisations have devoted themselves to alleviating symptoms.

All too often, foreigners (and, it has to be said, some Nepalis) have tended to view Nepal's situation as a set of problems that could be identified, measured and **solved in isolation**. Better health and sanitation are obvious requirements, but providing them increases the rate of population growth, at least in the short term. Curbing population is no simple task, for it is rooted in poverty and the low

---

THE DEVELOPMENT INDUSTRY

Everyone loves to give aid to Nepal. Although tourism is officially listed as the country's number-one source of foreign exchange, the development industry is far, far bigger. Aid to Nepal has increased ten-fold in the past fifteen years, and now brings in about $350 million annually.

Foreign development projects in Nepal fall roughly into three categories. **Bilateral** (and multilateral) aid – that is, money given by foreign governments directly to Nepal – has built most of Nepal's infrastructure (roads, dams, airports), as well as the biggest IRDPs (see overleaf). Many smaller projects are carried out by some 200 foreign **non-governmental organisations (NGOs)**; some are well-known, such as Oxfam and Save the Children, while others consist of just one person doing field-work and raising sponsorship money in his or her home country. Christian organisations aren't allowed to operate independently and must work under an umbrella NGO, United Mission to Nepal, which is tightly controlled by the Nepalese government. Voluntary NGOs, such as Britain's Voluntary Service Overseas (VSO) and the US Peace Corps, don't run any of their own projects, but instead slot volunteers into existing HMG programmes. Finally, **international lending bodies** like the World Bank and Asian Development Bank act as brokers to arrange loans for big projects with commercial potential – usually irrigation and hydroelectric schemes.

Many of these organisations do excellent work; almost all are motivated by the best possible intentions. However, money cannot automatically solve Nepal's problems, as some of the biggest projects have learned to their cost. By paying their imported experts ten or twenty times more than Nepalis to do the same job, the big bilateral missions cause resentment or, worse, encourage Nepalis to gather round the aid trough instead of doing useful work. To the extent that they import experts and materials, they undermine Nepalis' ability to do things for themselves, fostering a crippling **aid dependency** which now permeates almost every level of society. In 1973, foreign handouts made up 40 percent of Nepal's development budget; now it's 74 percent, and some wags joke that the country can't *afford* to develop lest it jeopardise development funding.

At their worst, bilateral aid and international loans are often little more than pious fronts for **neocolonialism**. Organisations like the World Bank measure Nepal by narrow economic indices and invariably prescribe western-style technological fixes. Per-capita income, for example, is meaningless in a country where most people are self-sufficient farmers. In Nepal, **self-sufficiency** is a considerable virtue – encouraging farmers to irrigate and buy fertilisers to grow cash crops may raise their income, but not necessarily their quality of life. It will, however, give western banks a capital project to finance, western contractors an irrigation system to build, western chemical companies a new market for fertilisers, and western consumer-goods companies new consumers. Meanwhile, Nepalese cash crops will be exported (probably to India), even as Nepalis suffer malnutrition.

For bilateral donors – especially India and China – foreign aid is a handy way of buying **political influence**, and it's also a means of stimulating the donor country's own domestic economy: more than half of British aid to Nepal (which amounts to £10 million annually) is paid directly to British **contractors**. Some of these companies spend tens of thousands of pounds to prepare their bids for advertised contracts – it's a very lucrative business, aid.

status of women. Simultaneously, agriculture has to be improved to feed the growing population, deforestation reversed to stop the fuelwood crisis, and industry developed to provide jobs. Irrigation projects, roads, hydroelectric diversions are needed . . . you get the idea. Even if you resolve that development should be left to Nepalis, education, or at least "awareness-raising" programmes, will be required to get the ball rolling, and that means not so much building schools as addressing the poverty that keeps children from attending classes.

To take a more **holistic approach**, the big donor countries have come up with the idea of Integrated Rural Development Projects (IRDPs), in which various sub-projects are coordinated to complement each other. The Swiss IRDP at Jiri and the British one in Dhankuta are prominent examples. Unfortunately, projects like these violate the "**small is beautiful**" maxim: they're terribly expensive (and therefore unlikely ever to be successfully passed on to Nepali management), prone to corruption and, in the end, limited to tiny geographic areas. Again, there are no easy, pat answers – only dilemmas.

The issues set out below only scratch the surface of complex issues. Many simplifications have been made. Some dilemmas are unique to Nepal, but many – if not most – are common to the entire "**developing**" **world**. The vast majority of people in the "developed" world are dangerously ignorant of the terrible pressures building in the poorer nations; travelling in Nepal affords a chance to witness the inequities first-hand and grapple with some of the dilemmas, which cannot help but make you re-examine your own lifestyle.

HEALTH

People rarely starve to death – usually **malnutrition** weakens their systems to a point where simple infections prove fatal. It may seem hard to believe, but 80 percent of Nepal's cute little children are undernourished, and up to 15 percent are clinically malnourished. As a result, **child mortality** (ages 0-5) is estimated at 165 per 1000, although this is an improvement over 1960, when the figure was 300 per 1000 – almost one in three. The introduction of cheap oral rehydration packets, together with simple immunisation programmes, are largely responsible for saving these lives.

Nepal is one of the few countries in the world where men live longer than women: **life expectancy** is 54 for males, 51 for females. Females are the last in the family to eat (one study found that Nepali girls under the age of five suffer 50 percent higher malnutrution than boys) and are expected to work harder (another study estimated women do 57 percent of all farm work in Nepal).

Poor sanitation and crowded, smokey conditions contribute to Nepal's high incidence of **disease**. Up to 80 percent of the population are reckoned to be suffering from parasitic infections at any one time, and 15 percent have TB. On the bright side, mosquito spraying in the Tarai has reduced malaria cases to about 25,000 annually, compared with 2 million a year during the 1950s. Improved public **sanitation** is gradually being introduced, but in the booming Tarai cities covered sewers are barely keeping pace with growth, while village latrines are still rarely found off trekking trails. Communal taps have been built in some of the more accessible hill villages to provide safe **drinking water**.

Although the government, aided by United Mission to Nepal, has constructed over 80 hospitals to date, western-style facilities are neither affordable nor appropriate for most villages; a better measure of progress on this front has been the creation of some 800 primary health-care posts, where health assistants (often local people) are trained in traditional Ayurvedic practices.

POPULATION

Slowing **population growth** isn't just a matter of passing out a few condoms. In Nepal, as in other countries, children are an investment for old age, since there's no state pension to draw on; moreover, Nepalis tend to have large families because they can't be sure all their children will survive. Hindus, especially, keep trying until they've produced at least one son, who alone can perform the prescribed death rites for his parents to ensure a speedy rebirth.

While it's not the place of aid workers to contradict Hindu beliefs, population-control efforts can have little impact unless the **status of women** in Nepal is raised, which is a long and difficult matter of education – not so much of women, who already know they're repressed, but of the men who do the repressing. Many "womens' programmes" have failed because they've assumed that women only need to be provided with the awareness and skills to improve their situation – in fact they can do little if their husbands still hold the power.

The other reasons for **high fertility** can be removed by reducing poverty and child mortality. This, at least, is what has happened in many other countries and it should work in Nepal, but unfortunately it involves a period of rapid population growth until the birth rate settles down to match the lower death rate.

At the moment, Nepal's population picture looks pretty scary. Currently doubling every 27 years, the population has a momentum that is unlikely to be checked in the present generation, simply because of the number of girls already approaching child-bearing age. Meanwhile, the government's **family planning** efforts are still woefully inadequate: only 15 percent of Nepalis practice any form of contraception at all. The remoteness of villages makes it all the more difficult to get the message out.

If Nepal's population doubles or triples, where will all the extra people live? As it happens, this is not a brand-new situation, for large parts of the middle hills have probably been overpopulated for the past century. **Emigration** – to other hill areas and, more recently, to the Tarai – has always regulated the people pressure. Fortunately for Kathmandu, Nepal's terrain sweeps most rural refugees down to the Tarai and India, not the capital. It's estimated that the country's urban population will double during the 1990s, and most of this increase will be taken up by the Tarai cities – and perhaps India. However, the problem of where people will live isn't as thorny as what they'll eat.

AGRICULTURE

If the population doubles, **food production** must double – Nepal can't really afford to import food. Expanding the acreage under cultivation only adds to deforestation, so it's far preferable to find ways of increasing the **productivity** per acre.

Various methods have been tried in Nepal, as in other countries. Agriculture experiment stations, such as the British-funded facility at Pakhribas in the eastern hills, have achieved mixed results in showcasing **high-yielding**

seeds and **animal breeds**; where these have been appropriate, local farmers have readily embraced them, but often they have proved to be impractically expensive. The official **Agriculture Development Bank**, which was created to provide credit for poor farmers to make simple improvements, has proved so bureaucratic that only wealthier farmers can avail themselves of it. Because the government, controlled by vested interests, has failed to enforce **land reform**, 63 percent of cultivable land is owned by 16 percent of the population.

Irrigation is a high priority, since it permits an extra crop in the dry season, and small-scale community projects are being built with generally good results, but the government's inefficient and poorly maintained programme has benefited few farmers (usually the best-off ones). It's been estimated that a big government-built system costs at least eight times more per acre than a community-built one. The government has also tried to encourage the use of **chemical fertilisers** through subsidies, but this has only led to black-marketeering, with most of the fertiliser being resold to India. Sometimes the best technique is the simplest one – in some remote areas, the introduction of a few common garden vegetables is improving local diets and even extending growing seasons.

Most people agree that agriculture must receive the main thrust of development efforts in Nepal. With over 90 percent of Nepalis making their living from the land, it's unrealistic to look for miracles elsewhere.

DEFORESTATION AND EROSION

In the Nepal hills, population, agriculture and environmental damage combine in a worrying vicious cycle: the need for more food leads to more intensive use of the land, which degrades the environment and lowers productivity, which further increases pressure on the land. An expanding population needs not only more **firewood** (92 percent of Nepal's energy comes from wood and dung), but also more **fodder** for livestock, who provide manure to maintain soil fertility. Overuse of firewood and fodder results in **deforestation**, as does any expansion of farmland. Trees help anchor the fragile Himalayan topsoil – removing them causes **erosion** and landslides, which not only reduce the productivity of the land but also send silt down to the Bay of Bengal, resulting in disastrous **floods** in Bangladesh.

Or so goes the theory. In practice, emigration seems to stabilise the cycle, and studies give wildly differing estimates for the rate of deforestation. The most that can be said is that the situation is definitely bad in some areas, but not so bad in others. Experts still can't decide whether erosion is due to deforestation, or simply the natural sloughing and shifting of very young mountains.

Even the government now admits it got it wrong in the 1950s when it **nationalised the forests** to protect them. Before that, the forests had been competently managed by local communities; but when the trees were taken away from them, locals felt they had no stake in their preservation, and because government enforcement was weak they easily plundered them. HMG's new policy of **community forestry** is supposed to give the forests back to the people, recognising that villagers are in fact very ecologically minded and will manage their forests responsibly and sustainably so long as they don't fear re-nationalisation. While foreign development projects have concentrated mainly on **reforestation**, newly planted areas account for only about one percent of Nepal's forest cover.

Deforestation is a separate issue **in the Tarai**, where the trees have been felled as a matter of policy, to make way for settlers and earn money for the government through state-sanctioned timber sales (mostly to India). Although the vast majority of the Tarai's magnificent native forest has gone in the past four decades, the clearing continues – 1989 saw a temporary but ominous four-fold jump in firewood cutting due to India's blockade of Nepal's kerosene supply. Nepal has won praise abroad for setting aside large chunks of the Tarai's forests as **national parks** and wildlife reserves, but the government can expect mounting resistance from its own people, who question why such valuable land should be set aside for tourists and crop-destroying animals.

APPROPRIATE TECHNOLOGY

Nepal's steep, mountain-fed rivers are estimated to have enough **hydroelectric** potential to power the British Isles, and many believe this to be the perfect solution to the country's fuelwood crisis. Major diversions have been built at Khulekani (south of Kathmandu) and Marsyangdi (on the Prithvi Highway), and extremely large-scale projects have been proposed for the Arun and Karnali rivers. No one actually claims that these dams can directly substitute electricity for firewood in the average Nepalese home, but supporters argue that the power could stimulate industry and be sold to India, which would generate money so that Nepal could gradually extend its budding **rural-electrification** programme. Opponents point out that large-scale diversions are environmentally disruptive and ludicrously expensive to build in Nepal's inaccessible terrain. They also reject the assumption that a switch from "non-commercial" fuel to electricity would constitute economic growth.

There is considerably more support for **microhydro** projects, dozens of which have already been installed (both with foreign and private Nepalese funding) to supply electricity for a few hundred households each. Yet no matter how it's produced, electricity is of no use to the vast majority of Nepalis who can't afford it, and it can only play a limited role in offsetting deforestation: as far as most rural Nepalis are concerned, wood is free, whereas electricity costs rupees – and electric appliances cost dollars. Some observers reckon that providing electric lights only encourages people to stay up later and burn more wood to keep warm. In trekking villages like Namche and Tatopani, however, where innkeepers cook with electricity, the net wood savings is probably worthwhile.

Roads, like hydroelectric and irrigation projects, don't come out well in cost-benefit analyses in Nepal, though planners insist that they're necessary for development. They cost far more than Nepal could ever afford without aid, and are almost as expensive to maintain; many are hastily built for royal visits to remote district headquarters, only to wash away with the next monsoon. The wealthy – bus owners, truckers, merchants, building contractors – benefit from road-building, while porters and shopkeepers along the former walking route lose out.

At the household level, appropriate technology has to be something the average Nepali peasant can afford, which isn't much. Several groups have worked hard to introduce "**smoke-**

THE END OF THE ROAD

Anna Robinson worked for three years as a VSO volunteer in Doti District, in the far western hills, and is now field officer for VSO Nepal.

Gazing down from the hill, over terraces of paddy fields, we could see the first truck making its hesitant journey up the spiralling new dust road. Local people ran down the main street of the bazaar to meet the first iron monster to complete the ascent.

For them it was the excitement of seeing a machine that moved along the ground. For me it was the feeling that here, at last, was a link with the outside world. There was the weekly plane to Kathmandu, of course. But with only eighteen seats – and $30 a seat at that – it was hardly significant to most people.

Excitement about the road lasted quite a while. Then people became less frightened and awestruck, and the verges were no longer dotted with rapt, admiring observers. Those who could afford the fare became seasoned travellers and were no longer to be seen vomiting out of the windows as the truck lurched along. In fact it became an accepted part of daily life – rather like the plane: it came and went, affecting few people.

Goodies

But down by the airstrip, a shantytown of temporary shacks sprang up overnight with the coming of the road. Here was where all the goodies that came by truck from India were to be found: plastic snakes that wriggled, gilt hair-slides, iron buckets, saucepans and – best of all – fresh fruit and vegetables.

For us foreigners, and the paid office workers, accustomed to going for weeks with nothing but potatoes and rice in the shops, it seemed like paradise.

Every day more and more apples, oranges, onions, cabbages and tomatoes would make their way up the hill. There was even a rumour that ten bottles of Coca-Cola had been sighted in the bazaar.

One morning, as I was eyeing a big plastic bucket full of huge Indian tomatoes in a local shop, a woman pulled my arm. "Don't you want to buy mine?" she asked. And there, in her *doko*, were a few handfuls of the small green local tomatoes.

Just a fortnight earlier I would have followed her eagerly, begging to be allowed to buy some. Now the shopkeeper laughed at her: who would want to buy little sour green tomatoes when there were big sweet red ones to be had?

For women like her, trudging in for miles from one of the surrounding villages to sell her few vegetables, there was no longer a market. The influential bazaar shopkeepers negotiated deals with the Indian traders with their truckloads of vegetables. The new road meant new money for the shopkeepers – but less for the poor, whose livelihood was undermined and who had no way of buying the wonderful new merchandise.

Casualties

There were other casualties, too. Gaggles of poor women, who had made a living out of carrying people's baggage from the airstrip to the bazaar, were once a common sight, haggling in angry, spirited voices over the price of their services. But with the coming of the new road, people simple boarded one of the trucks – baggage and all. Ragged and downtrodden at the best of times, these women were reduced to silently and gratefully accepting any rate people were prepared to pay for their help.

I began to wonder about the road. But I needn't have worried. Soon the monsoon rains arrived and the swelling river took charge of things. Within days the bridge was completely washed away, leaving several trucks stranded on the wrong side of the river, never to return to India.

After the monsoon

The original truck continued to creak up and down the winding road between the airstrip and the bazaar, its fuel being hoisted across the river by rope-pulley, but became so overcrowded that one day it broke down halfway up the hill. As the road had been almost completely washed away by the rain, it was simply left there in the middle of the road.

When the monsoon ended, it was overgrown with creepers and made a very pleasant home for a local family.

By then the grand new road was little more than a memory. The women porters went back to climbing regularly up and down the hill; the shantytown vanished as quickly as it had appeared; and everyone went back to eating rice and potatoes as before.

Last I heard, a foreign-aid agency had decided to rebuild the road, with a proper bridge this time: in the interests of development.

Anna Robinson

Reproduced by permission of New Internationalist Publications.

less" *chulos* (stoves), which burn wood more efficiently and reduce unhealthy kitchen smoke. Yet even this simple innovation illustrates the dilemmas of tampering with traditional ways: Nepalis complain that the new stoves aren't as easy to regulate and don't emit enough light, while the lack of smoke allows insects to infest their thatched roofs; thus many Nepalis are converting from thatch to corrugated metal.

EDUCATION

Nepal's education system has come a long way in a short time. There were no state **schools** before 1951 – now there are primary schools within walking distance of most villages. However, primary-school enrolment is probably well below the official figure of 82 percent, and actual attendance may be less than 25 percent. Only 13 percent of boys – and just 3 percent of girls - finish secondary school. **Literacy** has also made great strides, although the gulf between males (52 percent) and females (18 percent) is telling.

Thus far government policy has stressed quantity over quality, budgeting plenty of money for buildings but leaving little for salaries, but this has probably been a necessary first step in starting an education system from scratch. Since the proportion of qualified **teachers** is very low, most aid programmes have focused on teacher training. Western workers believe education could be a powerful catalyst for change in Nepal, but many complain that the current curriculum is geared for churning out bureaucrats and should be made more vocational and relevant to a peasant population.

INDUSTRY

Nepal's great industrial achievement during the 1980s was to increase its production of beer by 400 percent. In development economics, this is known as **import substitution**: for a country short on foreign exchange, a penny saved is a penny earned. Soft drinks, cigarettes, biscuits and shoes are similarly produced for domestic consumption. The only **export** to speak of is Tibetan carpets, and this unfortunately relies on *imported* wool. Similarly, 80 percent of the foreign exchange earned from **tourism** goes right back out of the country to pay for imported materials.

When it comes to industry, Nepal finds itself in a classic Third World bind. It can't profitably produce most items because its domestic market is so small (and poor), so it must send all its hard-earned foreign exchange to the developed countries in return for a few vehicles and transistor radios. The **Indian border** only makes the situation worse: India, being a big country and self-sufficient in most things, protects its own industries with high import duties; if Nepal did the same it would never develop, yet if it charged much lower import duties, cheap Indian goods would undercut Nepali ones. By steering a middle course, Nepal suffers a little bit both ways, and makes cross-border **trade** and **smuggling** more attractive activities than manufacturing. The few factories that have set up in Nepal are licenced monopolies, which tend to concentrate wealth in the hands of a few Kathmandu fat cats. Past HMG policies have offered no prizes for doing the right thing, although the new government promises significant changes.

BUREAUCRACY, CORRUPTION AND APATHY

Many aid workers identify the root cause of Nepal's slow development as "institutional problems", a euphemism which covers a multitude of sins. They speak of management bottlenecks, where **bureaucrats** hoard power to such an extent that project managers have to spend most of their time in Kathmandu queueing for signatures instead of getting things done in the field. They complain that Nepali managers are overly fond of desk jobs in the capital, regarding remote hill postings as punishment and making no secret of their disdain for the local people they're supposed to be helping. Slogans and planning targets are more in evidence than action, while planners tend to favour rigid, "top-down" approaches without consulting experts in the field. These traits aren't unique to Nepal, of course, and indeed many aid organisations are even more centralised and top-down-oriented.

Unfortunately, though, there is little tradition of public service in Nepalese government, and the free-for-all of **corruption** was particularly bad during the 1980s. Development agencies routinely had to pad their budgets by as much as 30 percent to allow for "**leakage**"

– it's been estimated that $1 billion has gone missing during the past decade. The graft has been perpetuated by artificially low salaries and, no doubt, by the sight of apparently limitless piles of development loot. Government regulations seem to have been devised to streamline the process – most bilateral aid, for instance, is required to be disbursed by HMG "line agencies", and for some reason United Mission to Nepal's entire budget must pass through a committee chaired by HRH the Queen. A common victimless crime among project managers is to divert hard-currency funds to private bank accounts, change it on the black market, produce the official equivalent in rupees and pocket the difference.

PROSPECTS

The foregoing isn't intended to make it sound as if Nepal's situation is hopeless, nor that there is no way for outsiders to help. Newcomers to the field tend to be the gloomiest ones, while people with a longer perspective are able to cite many major improvements. The country probably lost some ground during the greedy 1980s, but since the **restoration of democracy** in 1990 the country appears more hopeful than at any time in the past three decades under the previous system. The interim government has pledged to fight corruption and be more discriminating about accepting foreign (especially bilateral) aid. The fact that the interim cabinet contains a woman suggests that real changes might be on the way.

Given the more open political climate, responsible aid agencies stand a much better chance of achieving the work they've set out to do. There are plenty of good causes you may feel inclined to donate money to when you get home, and with a little effort you should be able to see a few in action during your travels and judge them by their fruits.

NATURAL HISTORY

The Himalaya are not only the world's tallest mountains, they're also the youngest – and still growing. Because of them, most of Tibet and parts of northern Nepal are high-altitude deserts, hidden in the Himalayan rain shadow, while many southern slopes, which bear the full brunt of the monsoon, are rainforest: nowhere in the world is there a transition of flora and fauna so abrupt as the one between the Tarai and the Himalayan crest, a distance of as little as 60km. As a result, Nepal can boast an astounding diversity of life, from rhinos to snow leopards.

GEOLOGY

The Himalaya provide perhaps the most vivid evidence for the **plate tectonics** (formerly known as continental drift) theory of mountain-building. According to this theory, the earth's crust is divided into a dozen or so massive plates which collide, separate and grind against each other with unimaginable force. The Himalaya are the result of the Indian subcontinental plate ramming northwards with particular force into the Asian plate – something like a car smashing into the side of a truck. It has been estimated that a 2000-kilometre cross-section of land along the collision zone has been compressed into 1000km, doubling the thickness of the crust and produc-

ing not only the Himalaya but also the vast Tibetan Plateau.

The shallow **Tethys Sea**, which once covered the entire region, was the main casualty in the process; its sedimentary deposits, now contorted and metamorphosed, can be seen at all elevations of the Himalaya. The first phase of mountain-building began around 70 million years ago, as the edge of the Asian plate, buckling under pressure from the advancing Indian plate, rose out of the sea to a height of about 2000m. Although it has since been lifted much higher, this **Tibetan Marginal Range**, which parallels the main Himalayan chain to the north, still stands as the divide between the Ganges and Tsangpo/Brahmaputra rivers. Unique among the world's major mountain ranges, the Himalaya don't form a watershed: rivers like the Kali Gandaki, Bhote Kosi (there are several by that name) and Arun cut right through the Himalaya because their courses were established by this earlier Tibetan Marginal Range.

The next major uplift occurred between 10 and 15 million years ago, when great chunks of the Asian plate were thrust southwards on top of the Indian plate, creating a low-altitude fore-runner of the Himalayan range. Things appear to have remained more or less unchanged until just 600,000 years ago – practically yesterday, in geological time – when what is now the **Tibetan Plateau** was suddenly jacked up to an average elevation of 5000m, and the Tibetan Marginal Range to about 7000m. From this point on, monsoonal rains became an important erosive force on the south (Nepalese) side of the mountains, while the north, left in the rain shadow, turned into a high desert. Southward-flowing rivers, fuelled by phenomenal gradients of up to 6000m in 100km, further eroded the landscape.

Most of Nepal's present features were created at the geological last minute. Beginning around 500,000 years ago, the Tibetan rim lunged forward along numerous separate fronts to form the modern **Himalaya**; averaging 8000m, Nepal's *himals* (massifs) show a freeze-frame of the current state of play. But mountain-building produces downs as well as ups: around 200,000 years ago, a broad belt of foothills subsided, creating Nepal's **midland valleys**, while the southern edge of this zone curled up to form the **Mahabharat Lekh** and, still further south, the **Chure Hills** (called the Siwaliks in India). These ridges rose so rapidly that they forced many southbound rivers to make lengthy east–west detours, and permitted only three principal outlets to the Tarai; the Bagmati and Seti rivers were initially dammed up by the Mahabharat Lekh, flooding the Kathmandu and Pokhara valleys respectively.

The Himalaya are believed to be rising still, albeit at a slower rate than previously. Periodic and severe **earthquakes** demonstrate that the earth continues to rearrange itself – one in eastern Nepal in 1988 killed 700 people – while **hot springs**, sometimes found near streams along trekking trails, are indicators of tectonic faultlines. **Erosion** is a particular problem in the Himalaya, where the mountains are continually sloughing off their skins, and landslides occur regularly during the monsoon. While **glaciers** play a part in shaping the terrain above about 5000m, the Himalaya aren't highly glaciated due to their sheer slopes (which can't support glacier-breeding snowfields) and relatively low precipitation at high elevations. On the whole, Himalayan glaciers are in a retreating phase, as they are in most parts of the world, and old moraines (piles of rubble left behind by melting glaciers) are commonly seen.

Nepal's valleys are like vast cutaway diagrams of geologic history, and trekking or rafting in them you'll be able to imagine the forces that have shaped the Himalaya. Igneous intrusions (usually granite) are common, but most outcrops consist of metamorphic rocks (schist, gneiss, limestone and dolomite), deposited as underwater sediments and later mashed and contorted under tremendous pressure; the wavy light and dark bands of the Lhotse-Nuptse Wall, in the Everest region, illustrate this. **Fossils** found in many of these layers have helped geologists date the phases of Himalayan mountain-building. The famous *shaligrams* of Muktinath in the Annapurna region contain fossilised ammonites (spiral-shaped molluscs) dating from 150–200 million years ago. Of a much more recent origin, the bones of Peking Man and primitive stone tools have been found in the Chure Hills – proving that the Himalaya are so young that early humans were present during their creation.

Nepal's **vegetation** is largely de⬛⬛⬛ altitude and can be grouped into three m⬛⬛ divisions. The lowlands include the Tarai, Chure Hills and valleys up to about 1000m; the midlands extend from 1000m to 3000m; and the Himalaya from 3000m to the upper limit of vegetation (typically about 5000m). Conditions vary tremendously within these zones, however: south-facing slopes usually receive more moisture, but also more sun at their lower reaches, while certain areas that are less protected from the summer monsoon – notably the Pokhara area – are especially wet. In general, rainfall is higher in the east, and a greater diversity of plants can be found there.

THE LOWLANDS

Most of the Tarai's remaining forest consists of *sal*, a tall, straight tree much valued for its wood – a factor which is hastening its steady removal. *Sal* prefers well-drained soils, and is most often found in pure stands along the Bhabar, the sloping alluvial plain at the base of the foothills; in the lower foothills, stunted specimens are frequently lopped for fodder. In spring, its cream-coloured flowers give off a heady jasmine scent. Other species sometimes associated with *sal* include *saj*, a large tree with crocodile-skin bark; *haldu*, a tree used for making dugout canoes; and *bauhinia*, a strangling vine that corkscrews around its victims.

The wetter **riverine forest** supports a larger number of species, but life here is more precarious, as rivers regularly flood and change their courses during the monsoon. *Sisu*, related to rosewood, and *khair*, an acacia, are the first trees to colonise newly formed sandbanks. *Simal*, towering on mangrove-like buttresses, follows close behind; it produces bulbous red flowers in February, and in May its seed pods explode with a cottony material that is used for stuffing mattresses. *Palash* – the "flame of the forest tree" – puts on an even more brilliant show of red flowers in February. All of these trees are deciduous, shedding their leaves during the dry spring. Many other species are evergreen, including *bilar*, *jamun* and *curry*, an understorey tree with thin, pointed leaves that give off a characteristic odour.

...stand
...ny way to
...nant; the most
...ragmites, *Saccharum*,
...*eda*. Most grasses reach their
...eight just after the monsoon and
flower during the dry autumn months. Locals
cut *khar*, a medium-sized variety, for thatch in
winter and early spring; the official thatch-
gathering season in the Tarai parks (two weeks
in January) is a colourful occasion, although
the activity tends to drive wildlife into hiding.
Fires are set in March and April to burn off the
old growth and encourage tender new shoots,
which provide food for game as well as
livestock.

THE MIDLANDS

The decline in precipitation from east to west
is more marked at the middle elevations – so
much so that the dry west shares few species
in common with the moist eastern hills. Central
Nepal is an overlap zone where western
species tend to be found on south-facing
slopes and eastern ones on the cooler, northern
aspects.

A common tree in dry western and central
areas is **chir pine** (needles in bunches of
three), typically found growing in park-like
stands up to about 2000m. Various **oak** species
often take over above 1500m, especially on dry
ridges, and here you'll also find *ainsilo*, a cousin
of the raspberry, which produces a sweet, if
rather dry, amber-coloured fruit in May.

Although much of the wet midland forest
has been lost to cultivation, you can see fine
remnants of it above Godavari in the
Kathmandu Valley and around the lakes in the
Pokhara Valley. Lower elevations are dominated by a zone of **chestnut** and *chilaune*,
the latter being a member of the tea family
with oblong, concave leaves and small white
flowers in May. In eastern parts, several
species of **laurel** form a third major component
to this forest, while alder, cardamom and tree
ferns grow in shady gullies.

The magical, mossy oak-rhododendron
forest is still mostly intact above about 2000m,
thanks to the prevalent fog that makes farming
unviable at this level. *Khasru*, the oak found

here, has prickly leaves and is often laden with
lichen, **orchids** and other epiphytes, which
grow on other plants and get their moisture
directly from the air; it's estimated that at least
250 orchid varieties grow in Nepal, and
although not all are showy or scented, the odds
are you'll be able to find one flowering at
almost any time of year. **Tree rhododendron**
(*lali guraas*), Nepal's national flower, grows
over 20m high and blooms with gorgeous red
flowers in March–April. Nearly 30 other
species occur in Nepal, mainly in the east – the
Milke Danda, a long ridge east of the Arun
River, is the best place to view rhododendron,
although impressive stands can also be seen
between Ghodapani and Ghandrung in the
Annapurna region. Most of Nepal's 300 species
of **fern** are found in this forest type, as is
daphne, a small bush with fragrant white
flowers in spring, whose bark is used to make
paper.

Holly, magnolia and maple may replace oak
and rhododendron in some sites. **Dwarf
bamboo**, the red panda's favourite food, grows
in particularly damp places, such as northern
Helambu and along the trail to the Annapurna
Sanctuary. Cannabis thrives in disturbed sites
throughout the midlands.

THE HIMALAYA

Conifers form the dominant tree cover in the
Himalaya. Particularly striking are the forests
around Rara Lake in western Nepal, where
Himalayan spruce and **blue pine** (needles
grouped in fives) are interspersed with damp
meadows. Elsewhere in the dry west you'll find
magnificent **Himalayan cedar** (deodar) trees,
which are protected by villagers, and a species
of cypress. Two types of **juniper** are present in
Nepal: the more common tree-sized variety
grows south of the main Himalayan crest (notably around Tengboche in the Everest region),
while a dwarf scrub juniper is confined to rain-
shadow areas. Both provide incense for
Buddhist rites. In wetter areas, hemlock, fir
(distinguished from spruce by its upward-
pointing cones) and even the deciduous larch
may be encountered.

One of the most common (and graceful)
broadleafed species is **white birch**, usually
found in thickets near treeline, especially on
shaded slopes where the snow lies late.
Poplars stick close to watercourses high up

into the inner valleys – Muktinath is full of them – while **berberis**, a shrub whose leaves turn scarlet in autumn, grows widely on exposed sites. Trekking up the Langtang or Marsyangdi valleys you pass through many of these forest types in rapid succession, but the most dramatic transition of all is found in the valley of the Thak Khola (upper Kali Gandaki): the monsoon jungle below Ghasa gives way to blue pine, hemlock, rhododendron and horse-chestnut; then to birch, fir and cypress around Tukche; then the apricot orchards of Marpha; and finally the blasted steppes of Jomosom.

Alpine vegetation predominates on the forest floor and in moist meadows above tree-line and, apart from the **dwarf rhododendron**, many **flowers** found here will be familiar to European and North American walkers. There are too many to do justice to them here, but primula, buttercup, poppy, iris, larkspur, gentian, edelweiss, buddleia, columbine and sage are all common. Most bloom during the monsoon, but rhododendrons and primulas can be seen flowering in the spring and gentians and larkspurs in the autumn.

MAMMALS

Most of Nepal's rich **animal life** inhabits the Tarai and, despite dense vegetation, is most easily observed there. In the hill regions, wild-life is much harder to spot due to population pressure – along trekking trails, at least – while very few mammals live above tree line. The following overview progresses generally from Tarai to Himalayan species.

The **Asian one-horned rhino** is one of five species found in Asia and Africa, all endangered. In Nepal, about 400 rhinos – a fifth of the species total – live in Chitwan, and about a dozen have been introduced to Bardia; they graze singly or in small groups in the marshy elephant grass, where they can be surprisingly well hidden. Although trained animals are a lingering part of Nepalese culture (see "Chitwan National Park"), **wild elephants** are seen only rarely in Nepal: as they require vast territory for their seasonal migrations, the settling of the Tarai is putting them in increasing conflict with man, and the few that survive tend to spend most of their time in India.

Koshi Tappu is the only remaining habitat in Nepal for another species better known as a domestic breed, **wild buffalo**, which graze the wet grasslands [...] poweful, the **gaur**, or [...] most of its time in the dry lower [...] descends to the Tarai in winter for water.

Perhaps the Tarai's most unlikely mammals, **gangetic dolphins** – one of four freshwater species in the world – are present in small numbers in the Karnali, Narayani and Sapt Koshi rivers. Curious and gregarious, dolphins tend to congregate in deep channels where they feed on fish and crustaceans; they may betray their presence with a puffing sound which they make through their blow-holes when surfacing. They're considered sacrosanct by Nepali Tharus, but cruelly hunted in India.

The most abundant mammals of the Tarai, *chital*, or **spotted deer**, are often seen in herds around the boundary between riverine forest and grassland. Hog deer – so called because of their porky little bodies and head-down trot – take shelter in wet grassland, while the aptly named barking deer, measuring less than two feet high at the shoulder, are found throughout lowland and midland forests. Swamp deer gather in vast herds in Sukla Phanta, and males of the species carry impressive sets of antlers (their Nepali name, *barasingha*, means "twelve points"). Sambar, heavy set animals standing five feet at the shoulder, are more widely distributed, but elusive. Two species of antelope, the graceful, corkscrew-horned **blackbuck** and the ungainly *nilgai* (blue bull), may be seen at Bardia and Koshi Tappu respectively; the latter was once assumed to be a form of cattle, and thus spared by Hindu hunters, but no more.

Areas of greatest deer and antelope concentrations are usually prime territory for **tiger**, their main predator. However, your chances of spotting the endangered Bengal tigers are slim: they're mainly nocturnal, never very numerous, and incredibly stealthy. In the deep shade and mottled sunlight of dense riverine forest, a tiger's orange and black-striped coat provides almost total camouflage. A male may weigh 250kg and measure 3m from nose to tail. Tigers are solitary hunters; some have been known to consume up to 20 percent of their body weight after a kill, but they may go several days between feeds. Males and females maintain separate but overlapping territories, regularly patrolling them, marking the boundaries with scent and driving off interlopers. Some Nepalis

...ing small ...Indian ...herds; bison, spends ...foothills, but ...Majestic and ... in ...er line. ...unt for many ... in Nepal, and are ...maller animal (males weigh ...; they prey on monkeys, dogs and livestock. **Other cats** – such as the fishing cat, leopard cat and the splendid clouded leopard – are known to exist in the more remote lowlands and midlands, but are very rarely sighted. Hyenas and wild dogs are scavengers of the Tarai, and **jackals**, though seldom seen (they're nocturnal), produce an eerie howling that is one of the most common night sounds in the Tarai and hills.

While it isn't carniverous, the dangerously unpredictable **sloth bear**, a Tarai species, is liable to round on you and should be approached with extreme caution. Its powerful front claws are designed for unearthing termite nests, and its long snout for extracting the insects. The **Himalayan black bear** roams midland forests up to tree line and is, if anything, more dangerous. **Wild boars** can be seen rooting and scurrying through forest anywhere in Nepal.

Monkeys, a common sight in the Tarai and hills, come in two varieties in Nepal. Comical **langurs** have silver fur, black faces and long, ropelike tails; you'll sometimes see them sitting on stumps like Rodin's *Thinker*. Brown **rhesus macaques** are more shy in the wild, but around temples are tame to the point of being nuisances. Many other small mammals may be spotted in the hills, among them porcupines, flying squirrels, foxes, civets, mongooses and martens. The **red panda**, with its rust coat and bushy, ringed tail, almost resembles a tree-dwelling fox; like its Chinese relative, it's partial to bamboo, and is very occasionally glimpsed in the cloud forest of northern Helambu.

Elusive animals of the rhododendron and birch forests, **musk deer** are readily identified by their tusk-like canine teeth; males are hunted for their musk pod, which can fetch $200 an ounce on the international market. Though by no means common, **Himalayan tahr** is the most frequently observed large mammal of the high country; a goat-like animal with long, wiry fur and short horns, it browses along steep cliffs below tree line. **Serow**, another goat relative, inhabits remote canyons, while **goral**, sometimes likened to chamois, lives at or above timber line.

The Himalaya's highest residents are **blue sheep**, who graze the barren grasslands above tree line year-round. Normally tan, males go a slaty colour in winter, accounting for their name. Herds have been sighted around the Thorung La in the Annapurna region, but they occur in greater numbers north of Dhorpatan and in She-Phoksundo National Park. Their chief predator is the **snow leopard**, a secretive cat whose habits are still little understood.

AMPHIBIANS AND REPTILES

Native to the Tarai's wetlands, crocodiles are most easily seen in winter, when they sun themselves on muddy banks to warm up their cold-blooded bodies. The endangered **mugger crocodile** favours marshes and oxbow lakes, where it may lie motionless for hours on end until its prey comes within snapping distance. Muggers mainly pursue fish, but will eat just about anything they can get their jaws around – including human bodies thrown into the river by relatives unable to afford wood for a cremation. The even more endangered **gharial crocodile** lives exclusively in rivers and feeds on fish; for more on its precarious state, see "Chitwan National Park" in Chapter Six.

Nepal has many kinds of **snakes**, but they are rarely encountered: most hibernate in winter, even in the Tarai, and shy away from humans at other times of year. Common cobras – snake charmers' favourites – inhabit low elevations near villages; they aren't found in the Kathmandu Valley, despite their abundance in religious imagery there. Kraits and pit vipers, both highly poisonous, have been reported, as have pythons up to twenty feet long. However, the commonest species aren't poisonous and are typically less than two feet long.

Chances are you'll run into a **gecko** or two, probably clinging to a guest-house wall. Helpful insect-eaters, these lizard-like creatures are able to climb almost any surface with the aid of amazing suction pads on their feet. About fifty species of **fish** have been recorded in Nepal, but only *mahseer*, a sporty trout that attains its greatest size in the lower Karnali River, is of much interest; most ponds are stocked with carp and catfish.

Over 800 **bird species** – one tenth of the earth's total – have been sighted in Nepal. The country receives a high number of birds migrating between India and central Asia in spring and autumn and, because it spans so many ecosystems, provides habitats for a wide range of year-round residents. The greatest diversity of species is found in the Tarai wildlife parks, but even the Kathmandu Valley is remarkably rich in birdlife. The following is only a listing of the major categories – for the complete picture, get *Birds of Nepal* (see "Books").

In **the Tarai** and lower hills, raptors (birds of prey) such as ospreys, cormorants, darters, gulls and kingfishers patrol streams and rivers for food; herons and storks can also be seen fishing, while cranes, ducks and moorhens wade in or float on the water. Many of these migratory species are particularly well represented at Koshi Tappu, which is located along the important Arun Valley corridor to Tibet. Peafowl make their meowing mating call – and peacocks occasionally deign to unfurl their plumage – while many species of woodpeckers can be heard, if not seen, high up in the *sal* canopy. Cuckoos and "brain fever" birds repeat their idiotic two- or four-note songs in an almost demented fashion. Parakeets swoop in formation; bee-eaters, swifts, drongos, swallows and rollers flit and dive for insects, while jungle fowl look like chickens as Monet might have painted them. Other oddities of the Tarai include the paradise flycatcher, with its lavish white tailfeathers and dragonfly-like flight; the lanky great adjutant stork, resembling a prehistoric reptile in flight; and the giant hornbill, whose beak supports an appendage that looks like an upturned welder's mask.

Many of the above birds are found in **the midlands** as well as the Tarai – as are mynas, egrets, crows and magpies, which tend to scavenge near areas of human habitation. Birds of prey – falcons, kestrels, harriers, eagles, kites, hawks and vultures – may also be seen at almost any elevation. Owls are common, but not much liked by Nepalis. Babblers and laughing thrushes (genus name *Garrulax*!) populate the oak-rhododendron forest and are as noisy as their names suggest. Over twenty species of flycatchers are present in the Kathmandu Valley alone.

Nepal's natio[...] coloured *danphe* (impeya[...] be spotted scuttling through the [...] in the Everest region; a range of house pa[...] has been named after it. *Kalij* and *monal*, two other native pheasants, also inhabit the higher hills and lower **Himalaya**. Migrating waterfowl often stop over at high-altitude lakes – Brahminy ducks are a trekking-season attraction at Gokyo – and snow pigeons, grebes, finches and choughs may all be seen at or above tree line. Mountaineers have reported seeing choughs on Everest at 8200m.

INVERTEBRATES AND INSECTS

No other creature in Nepal arouses such trepidation and squeamishness as the **leech**. Fortunately, these segmented, caterpillar-sized annelids remain dormant underground during the trekking seasons; during the monsoon, however, they come out in force everywhere in the Tarai and hills, making any hike a bloody business. Leeches are attracted to body heat, and will inch up legs or drop from branches to reach their victims. The bite is completely painless – the bloodsucker injects a local anaesthetic and anticoagulant – and often goes unnoticed until the leech drops off of its own accord. To dislodge one, apply salt or a cigarette; don't pull it off or the wound could get infected.

Over 600 species of **butterflies** have been recorded in Nepal, with more being discovered all the time. Although the monsoon is the best time to view butterflies, many varieties can be seen before and especially just after the rains – look for them beside moist, sandy banks or atop ridges; Phulchoki is an excellent place to start in the Kathmandu Valley. Notable hill varieties include the intriguing orange oakleaf, whose markings enable it to vanish into the forest litter, and the golden birdwing, a large, angular species with a loping wingbeat.

Termites are Nepal's most conspicuous social insects, constructing towering, fluted mounds up to eight feet tall in the western Tarai. Organised in colonies much the same as ants and bees, legions of termite workers and "reproductives" serve a single king and queen. The mounds function as cooling towers for the busy nest below; monuments to insect industry, they're made from tailings excavated from the

...eal bird, the iridescent), can often ...rounds
...ers ...gh one ...ches across ...isonous to humans).

308

Fireflies, with orange and black bodies, give off a greenish glow at dusk in the Tarai. For many travellers, however, the extent of their involvement with the insect kingdom will be in swatting **mosquitoes**: two varieties are prevalent in the lowlands, one of them *Anopheles*, the infamous vector of malaria.

BOOKS

Most of these books are easier to come by in Kathmandu, and those priced in rupees are available only in Nepal.

TRAVEL

Jeff Greenwald, *Mister Raja's Neighborhood: Letters from Nepal* (John Daniel, Santa Barbara 1986). The author went to Kathmandu to write the Great Asian Novel and ended up writing a series of letters – though perhaps contemplating his navel a bit too much in the process. Nevertheless, a vivid portrait of life in contemporary Nepal.

Harka Gurung, *Vignettes of Nepal* (Sajha Prakashan, Rs100). Probably the best book written by a Nepali in English about his country, a vivid travelogue illuminated by a native's insights.

Robert A. Hutchison, *In the Tracks of the Yeti* (Macdonald, 1989; £13.95). The official report of the Yeti '88 expedition: they didn't see one, but they remain convinced.

Pico Iyer, *Video Night in Kathmandu* (Black Swan, £4.99). A collection of essays on popular traveller hangouts in Asia that are stronger on style than substance.

Peter Matthiessen, *The Snow Leopard* (Pan, £4.95). Matthiessen joins biologist George Schaller in a pilgrimage to Dolpa to track one of the world's most elusive cats, and comes up with characteristically Zen insights. A magnificent piece of writing, filled with beautiful descriptions of the landscape – and ever-perceptive observations of how Matthiessen's quest for the Snow Lepoard became one of self-discovery.

Dervla Murphy, *The Waiting Land* (Century, £4.95). A personal account of working with Pokhara's Tibetan refugees in 1965, written in Murphy's usual entertaining and politically on-the-ball style.

COFFEE-TABLE BOOKS

Eric Valli and Diane Summers, *Honey Hunters of Nepal* (Thames & Hudson, £16.95). Amazing photos of Gurung men clinging to rope ladders while raiding beehives. The best of the photos were reprinted in the November 1988 *National Geographic*, sold in Kathmandu.

Thomas Kelly and Patricia Roberts, *Kathmandu: City on the Edge of the World* (Wiedenfield & Nicolson, £25). Stunning photography and extensive essays on culture and religion.

HISTORY

Byron Farwell, *The Gurkhas* (Allen Lane, London 1984). One of many books lionising Nepal's famous Gurkha soldiers.

Percival Landon, *Nepal* (Ratna Pustak Bhandar, Rs776). In two volumes, this was the most comprehensive study of the country at the time (1928) and is regarded as a classic – but having been commissioned by the Maharaja, it's of dubious political bias.

Padma Shrestha, *Nepal Rediscovered* (Serindia, £15). A collection of rare photographs, this presents a fascinating, if elite, view of Rana-era Nepal.

Ludwig Stiller, *The Rise of the House of Gorkha* (Ratna Pustak Bhandar, Rs65). An academic but readable account of Nepal's unification and war with Britain, written by a Jesuit priest turned Nepalese citizen.

CULTURE AND ANTHROPOLOGY

Mary M. Anderson, *The Festivals of Nepal* (Rupa, Rs196). Despite the title, this only covers the Kathmandu Valley's festivals, but it's still the the most readable and informative account.

Dor Bahadur Bista, *Peoples of Nepal* (Ratna Pustak Bhandar, Rs250). The standard overview of Nepal's ethnic groups, although much of the information has now been superceded by more recent work.

BHOTIYAS

Christoph von Fürer-Haimendorf, *Himalayan Traders* (John Murray, Rs394). An anthropological study of the impact of China's occupation of Tibet on Bhotiya and Sherpa traders.

David L. Snellgrove, *Himalayan Pilgrimage* (Shambhala, £11.95). An insightful travelogue/anthropological account of a trip through northwestern Nepal in the 1950s.

GURUNGS

Broughton Coburn, *Nepali Aama: Portrait of a Nepalese Hill Woman* (Ross-Erickson, Santa Barbara, California 1982). A delightful study of a Gurung woman in a village south of Pokhara, in her own words, with photos.

Stan Royal Mumford, *Himalayan Dialogue: Tibetan Lamas and Gurung Shamans in Nepal* (University of Wisconsin, £17.50). An account of myths and rituals practised in a village along the Annapurna Circuit – fascinating, once you get past the anthropological jargon.

MAGARS

Gary Shepherd, *Life Among the Magars* (Sahayogi,Rs100). A personal account, with plenty of pertinent insights.

SHERPAS

Hugh R. Downs, *Rhythms of a Himalayan Village* (Harper & Row, New York 1980). An extraordinarily sensitive synthesis of black-and-white photos, text and quotes, describing rituals and religion in a Solu village.

James F. Fisher, *Sherpas* (University of California, £7.95). A before-and-after account, written by a member of Edmund Hillary's 1964 school-building team, who concludes that Sherpas are more resilient than we give them credit for.

Ramesh Raj Kunwar, *Fire of Himal* (Nirala, Rs504). An excellent anthropological study of the Sherpas.

RELIGION

HINDUISM

K. M. Sen, *Hinduism* (Penguin, £4.50). An accessible survey, explanatory without being too obscure.

P. Lal (trans), *The Ramayana of Valmiki* (Tarang, £4.95). A condensed version of the classic epic.

Shri Purohit Swami (trans), *The Geeta* (Faber & Faber, £2.95). A portable and vivid translation of the *Bhagavad Gita*.

BUDDHISM

Stephen Batchelor (ed), *The Jewel in the Lotus: A Guide to the Buddhist Traditions of Tibet* (Wisdom, £9.95). An overview of the four major Lamaist sects, which may be useful to serious students.

Claude B. Levenson, *The Dalai Lama* (Unwin Hyman, £14.95). An unofficial but reasonably up-to-date (1988) biography.

Vicki Mackenzie, *Reincarnation: The Boy Lama* (Bloomsbury, £8.95). An intriguing book, recounting the lives of Lama Yeshe, the abbot of Kopan Monastery, who died in 1984, and Osel Hita Torres, who was born in 1985 and enthroned as Yeshe's reincarnation at the age of two.

ART AND ARCHITECTURE

Ydia Aran, *The Art of Nepal* (Sahayogi, Kathmandu; Rs75). Surprisingly good overview of Nepalese religion as well as stone, metal and wood sculpture and *thanka* paintings.

Yves Vequand, *The Art of Mithila: Ceremonial Paintings from an Ancient Kingdom* (Thames & Hudson, London 1977). Still the only non-scholarly book on Mithila art, with vivid illustrations.

FICTION

Diamond Shumshere Rana, *Wake of the White Tiger* (Rana, Rs60). An acclaimed novel set in the early Rana era; the poor translation and confusing geneologies, however, can be offputting.

Tara Nath Sharma, *Blackout* (Nirala, Rs168). A dark novel of life in the Nepalese hills, by an author who has served time in jail for his views.

Shailendra Kumar Singh (ed), *Contemporary Nepali Poetry* (Singh, 1989; Rs50). A slender pamphlet, but one that succeeds in capturing some of the moods that prevailed just prior to the restoration of democracy.

NATURAL HISTORY

Robert Fleming Jr., *The General Ecology, Flora and Fauna of Midland Nepal* (Tribhuwan University; Rs50). A simple ecology text drawing on examples mainly from around the Kathmandu Valley.

Robert Fleming Sr., Robert Fleming Jr. and Lain Singh Bangdel, *Birds of Nepal* (Nature Himalayas, Rs449). The authoritative field guide.

K. K. Gurung, *Heart of the Jungle* (André Deutsch, Rs300). The essential guide to Chitwan's flora and fauna, written by the former manager of Tiger Tops.

Dorothy Mierow and Tirtha Shrestha, *Himalayan Flowers and Trees* (Sahayog, Rs250). A pocket-sized guide with colour plates and some useful information at the back.

George Schaller, *Stones of Silence: Journeys in the Himalaya* (Viking, New York 1980). Written by the wildlife biologist who accompanied Peter Mattheissen on his quest for the snow leopard, this book provides a detailed view of ecosystems of the high Himalaya.

DEVELOPMENT AND POLITICS

When in Nepal, look out for *Himal*, a bi-monthly magazine devoted to development and environmental issues. It's published in Kathmandu and is available in many bookshops there.

Lynn Bennett, *Dangerous Wives and Sacred Sisters* (Columbia University Press, New York 1983). Good insight into the life and position of Hindu women in Nepal.

Indra Majpuria, *Nepalese Women* (M. Devi, Rs250). It wanders quite a bit, but forcibly gets across the hardships and problems facing women in Nepal.

Charlie Pye-Smith, *Travels in Nepal* (Aurum, £12.95). A cross between a travelogue and a progress report on aid projects, this succeeds in giving plenty of facts and analysis without getting bogged down in institutional fudge.

Leo Rose and John Scholz, *Nepal: Profile of a Himalayan Kingdom* (Westview, 1980 £23.50). A political study of Nepal concentrating on the post-1951 period.

David Seddon, *Nepal: a State of Poverty* (Vikas, 1987; £14.95). A hard look at the issues by one of the longest-serving foreign critics of Nepal's development efforts.

Ludmilla Tüting and Kunda Dixit, *Bikas-Binas, Development-Destruction* (Geobuch, Rs120). Excellent collection of articles which cover the whole gamut of dilemmas arising out of development, environmental degradation and tourism. It's supposed to speak for the entire Himalayan region, but it really focuses on Nepal.

MOUNTAINS AND MOUNTAINEERING

Mark Anderson, *On the Big Hill* (Faber & Fabe,r £12.95). Companion to the Granada TV programme of the same name following the progress of an Everest expedition.

Chris Bonington, *Everest South West Face* (Hodder & Stoughton, London 1973; o/p). An exhaustive tome covering every aspect of a major Himalayan assault – in this case, an unsuccessful one. Also look out for Bonington's *The Everest Years* (Hodder & Stoughton, £14.95) and his recently published retrospective, *Mountaineer* (Diadem, £17.95).

W. E. Bowman, *The Ascent of Rum Doodle* (Arrow, £2.99). Reprint of the classic 1956 parody of the mountaineering-account genre.

Maurice Herzog, *Annapurna* (Triad/Paladin, £3.95). Reprint of one of the first accounts of mountaineering in the Himalayas, describing the first successful ascent of an 8000-metre peak.

Reinhold Messner, *The Crystal Horizon* (Crowood, £16.95). Not very well-written (or maybe it's the translation), but a nonetheless compelling account of Messner's 1980 solo ascent of Everest.

H. W. Tilman, *Nepal Himalaya* (Cambridge University Press, 1952). A chatty account of the first mountaineering reconnaissance of Nepal in 1949–51. Though crusty, and at times racist, Tilman was one of the century's great adventurers and his writing remains fresh and witty.

Walt Unsworth, *Everest* (Oxford University Press, £19.95). Exhaustive history of mountaineering on the world's highest peak.

SPECIFIC GUIDES

John Gottberg Anderson (ed), *The Insight Guide to Nepal* (Apa, £10.95). Great pictures and occasionally readable, informative essays, but short on practical information.

John Sanday, *Illustrated Guide to the Kathmandu Valley* (Collins, £8.95). The author is the leading authority on restoration of the valley's monuments.

Trekking guides are listed in a separate "Books" section in Chapter Seven.

LANGUAGE

Nepali is surprisingly easy to learn, and local people are always thrilled when travellers make the effort to pick up a few phrases. Knowing a little bit of the language certainly comes in handy, too, since while nearly all Nepalis who deal with tourists speak English, few people do off the beaten track.

Nepali (sometimes called *Gurkhali*) is closely related to Hindi and other north-Indian languages, so Nepali-speakers and Indians can usually catch the gist of what each other are saying. However, nearly half of all Nepalis speak Tibetan, Sherpa or one of several dozen other Tibeto-Burman dialects, which are completely unrelated to Nepali – almost all speak Nepali as a second language, but sometimes with difficult regional accents. Nepali is written in a script known as **Devanagari**: there's fortunately no need for travellers to learn it since signs, bus destinations and so on are usually written in Roman script. This transliteration, though, often leads to problems of inconsistency – see the note in "Information and Maps" in *Basics* for more on this. For a **glossary of food terms**, see "Eating and Drinking" in *Basics*.

The most useful **phrasebook** on the market is Lonely Planet's *Nepal Phrasebook* (£1.95); *A Simple Nepali for Trekkers* (Rupa, Rs30), available only in Nepal, goes a little deeper into grammar, but isn't as good for quick reference. For a full-blown **teach-yourself book**, try David Matthews' *A Course in Nepali* (School of Oriental and African Studies, £18).

PRONUNCIATION

Even when Nepali is transliterated from the Devanagari script into the Roman alphabet using phonetic spellings, there are a number of peculiarities in pronunciation:

A as in *a*lone
AA as in f*a*ther
B sounds like a cross between "b" and "v"
E as in caf*é*
I as in pol*i*ce
J as in *ju*dge
O as in n*o*te
R sounds like a cross between "r" and "d"
S sounds almost like "sh"
U as in b*oo*t
W sounds like a cross between "w" and "v"
Z sounds like "dj" or "dz"

The "a" and "aa" distinction is crucial. *Maa* (in) is pronounced as it looks, with the vowel stretched out, but *ma* (I) sounds like "muh" and *mandir* (temple) like "mundeer". The accent almost always goes on the syllable with "aa" in it, or if there's no "aa", on the first syllable.

Some Nepali vowels are nasalised – to get the right effect, you have to block off your nasal passage, producing a slightly honking sound like a French "n". Nasalised vowels aren't indicated in this book, but they're something to be aware of. To hear how they should sound, listen to a Nepali say *tapaai* (you) or *yahaa* (here).

ASPIRATED CONSONANTS

The combinations "ch" and "sh" are pronounced as in English, but in all other cases where an "h" follows a consonant the sound is meant to be aspirated – in other words, give it an extra puff of air. Thus *bholi* (tomorrow) sounds like b'*ho*li and Thamel sounds like T'*ha*mel. Note these combinations:

CHH sounds like a very breathy "ch", as in pi*tch h*ere
PH makes an "f" sound, as in *ph*one
TH is pronounced as in pu*t h*ere, not as in think

RETROFLEX CONSONANTS

Finally, the sounds "d", "r" and "t" also occur in retroflex forms – ie, they're pronounced by rolling the tip of the tongue back towards the roof of the mouth. Again, it's not worth going into too much detail about this here, but it's a safe bet that whenever these letters are followed by an "h" they'll be retroflex – an obvious example is *Kathmandu*, which sounds a little like "Kartmandu". Sometimes retroflexion results in a difference in meaning: *saathi* means friend, but with a retroflex "th" it means sixty.

A BRIEF GUIDE TO SPEAKING NEPALI

GREETINGS AND BASIC PHRASES

Hello, Goodbye	*Naamaste* (said with palms together as if praying)	My name is...	*Mero naam ... ho*
		My country is...	*Mero desh ... ho*
		I don't know	*Malaai thaahaa chhaina*
Hello (more polite/formal)	*Naamaskaar*	I don't understand	*Ma bhujdaina*
Yes/No (It is/isn't)	*Ho/Hoina*	Please speak more slowly	*Bistaarai bolnuhos*
Yes/No (There is/isn't)	*Chha/Chhaina*		
Thank you	*Dhanyabaad* (only used in formal occasions)	Pardon?	*Hajur?*
		No thanks	*Nai*
How are things?	*Kasto chha?*	Begging is bad	*Magnu raamro hoina*
Okay, Fine	*Thik chha*	I'm sorry	*Maph garnuhos*
What's your name?	*Tapaaiko naam ke ho?*	Let's go	*Jaun*

FORMS OF ADDRESS

One of the many delightful aspects of Nepalese culture is the familial forms of address that Nepalis use when speaking to each other, even to strangers: use them to get anyone's attention.

Excuse me...	*O...*	Father (a man old enough to be your father)	*Baabu*
Elder brother (said to any man older than you)	*Dhaai*		
		Mother (a woman old enough to be your mother)	*Aama*
Elder sister (a woman older than you)	*Didi*		
Younger sister (a woman or girl younger than you)	*Bahini*	Shopkeeper, Innkeeper (male)	*Saahuji*
		Shopkeeper, Innkeeper (female)	*Saahuni*
Younger brother (a man or boy younger than you)	*Bhaai*		

BASIC QUESTIONS AND REQUESTS

Do you speak English?	*Tapaai Inglis bolnuhunchha?*	I'm (hungry)	*Malaai (bhog) laagyo*
		I want/don't want...	*Ma ... chaahanchhu/ chaahindaina*
I don't speak Nepali	*Ma Nepali boldaina*		
Is/Isn't there a...?	*...chha/chhaina?*	I like ... (very much) ...	*(dherai) manparchha*
Is ... possible?	*...sakchhu/sakdina?*	What's this for?	*Yo ke ko laagi?*
Is ... okay?	*...ke yo thik chha?*	What's the matter?	*Ke bhayo?*
Please help me	*Malaai maddhat garnuhos*	What's this called in Nepali?	*Eslai ke bhanchha?*
Please give me...	*...dinuhos*		

DIRECTIONS

Where is the...?	*...kahaa chha?*	Here	*Yahaa*
Where is this bus going?	*Yo bas kahaa jaanchha?*	There/Yonder	*Tyahaa/Utaa*
Which is the way to...?	*kun baato ... jaanchha?*	(To the) right	*Daayaa (tira)*
Which is the best way?	*Kun baato sabhanda raamro chaa?*	(To the) left	*Baayaa (tira)*
		Straight	*Sidhaa*
How far is it?	*Kati tadha chha?*	North	*Uttar*
Where are you going?	*Tapaai kahaa jaanuhunchha?*	South	*Dakshin*
I'm going to...	*Ma ... jaanchu*	East	*Purba*
Where are you coming from?	*Tapaai kahaa(m)baata aayeko?*	West	*Pashchim*
		Near/Far	*Najik/Taadhaa*

TIME

What time is it?	*Kati Bajyo?*	Year	*Barsaa*
What time does the bus leave?	*Yo bas kati baaje jaanchha?*	Today	*Aaja*
		Tomorrow	*Bholi*
When does it arrive?	*Kati baaje pugchha?*	Yesterday	*Hijo*
How many hours does it take?	*Kati ghanta laagchha?*	Now	*Ahile*
		Later	*Pachi*
Two o'clock	*Dui Bajyo*	Next week	*Aarko haptaa*
Nine-thirty	*Sandhe nau bajyo*	Last month	*Gayako maina*
Minute	*Minut*	Two years ago	*Dui barsaa agi*
Hour	*Ghanta*	Morning	*Bihaana*
Day	*Din*	Evening	*Belukaa*
Week	*Haptaa*	Night	*Raatri*
Month	*Maina*		

NEGOTIATIONS

How much does this cost?	*Yasko kati paaisa?*	Can I see it?	*Hernu sakchhu?*
Is there a cheaper one?	*Kunai sasto chha?*	It's too expensive	*Dherai mahango bhayo*
How much for a room?	*Rum ko kati paaisa?*		
How many people?	*Kati janaa?*	Is there anything cheaper?	*Sasto chha?*
For two people	*Dui janaa ko laagi*		
Only one person	*Ek janaa maatra*	The bill, please	*Bil dinuhos*

ADJECTIVES

A little	*Al·kati*	Easy	*Sajilo*
Alone	*Eklai*	Expensive	*Mahango*
A lot	*Dherai*	Fun	*Majaa*
Another	*Aarko*	Hot (person or weather)	*Garam*
Bad	*Kharaab, Naraamro*	Hot (liquid)	*Taato*
Beautiful, Good	*Raamro*	Hungry	*Bhog*
Big	*Thulo*	Less	*Thorai*
Cheap	*Sasto*	More	*Dherai, Jyaada*
Clean	*Safaa*	Open	*Khulaa*
Closed	*Bhanda*	Small	*Saano*
Cold (person or weather)	*Jaado*	Thirsty	*Thirkaa*
Cold (liquid)	*Chiso*	Tired	*Thaakeko*
Difficult	*Gaaro*	Very	*Dherai*

NOUNS

Bus	*Bas*	Room	*Kothaa, Rum*
Friend	*Saathi*	Shop	*Pasaal*
Food	*Khaanaa*	Teahouse	*Chiya pasaal, Hotel*
Hotel/Lodge	*Hotel/Laj*	Ticket	*Tikut*
Money	*Paisa*	Toilet	*Chaarpi*
Restaurant	*Restarant*	Trail/Main trail	*Baato/Mul Baato*
Road	*Moto baato*	Water	*Paani*

VERBS

The following verbs are given in the infinitive form. To turn a verb into a polite command (eg, "Please sit"), just add *-hos* (*Basnuhos*, which in practice sounds like *Basnos*). For an all-purpose tense, drop the *-u* ending and replace it with *-e* (eg, *Jaane* can mean go, going or went, depending on the context).

Come	*Aunu*	Give	*Dinu*	Sit	*Basnu*	Take	*Linu*
Do	*Garnu*	Go	*Jaanu*	Sleep	*Sutnu*	Walk	*Hidnu*
Eat	*Khaanu*	Return	*Pharkaunu*				

DAYS AND MONTHS

It's unlikely you'll ever have to use these. Nepali months start around the middle of our months, and vary from 27 to 32 days.

Monday	*Aditybar*	April–May	*Baisakh*
Tuesday	*Sombar*	May–June	*Jesth*
Wednesday	*Mangalbar*	June–July	*Asad*
Thursday	*Budhabar*	July–August	*Srawan*
Friday	*Brihaspatibar*	August–September	*Bhadra*
Saturday	*Shukrabar*	September–October	*Aasoj*
Sunday	*Shanibar*	October–November	*Kartik*
January–February	*Magh*	November–December	*Mangsir*
February–March	*Phalgun*	December–January	*Pous*
March–April	*Chaitra*		

NUMBERS

half	*aada*	8	*aath*	16	*serha*	50	*pachaas*
1	*ek*	9	*nau*	17	*satra*	60	*saathi*
2	*dui*	10	*das*	18	*athaara*	70	*sattari*
3	*tin*	11	*eghara*	19	*unnais*	80	*asi*
4	*chaar*	12	*baarha*	20	*bis*	90	*nabbe*
5	*paanch*	13	*terha*	25	*pachhis*	100	*sae, ek sae*
6	*chha*	14	*chaudha*	30	*tis*		
7	*saat*	15	*pandhra*	40	*chaalis*	1000	*ek hajaar*

A GLOSSARY OF RELIGIOUS TERMS

ASHTA MANGALA the eight auspicious symbols of Buddhism.

AVALOKITESHWARA the *bodhisattva* of compassion.

AVATAR bodily incarnation of a deity.

BAHUN Hindu priest.

BAJRA See "Vajra".

BETALA symbol of death, often represented by a pair of skeletons flanking a temple entrance.

BHAIRAB terrifying tantric form of Shiva.

BHIMSEN patron god of Newar merchants.

BODHISATTVA in Mahayana Buddhism, one who forgoes *nirvana* until all other beings have attained enlightenment.

BRAHMA the Hindu creator god, one of the Hindu "trinity".

BUDDHA MARGI a Buddhist Newar.

CHAITYA small Buddhist monument.

CHORTEN another name for a *chaitya* in high mountain areas.

DEVI mother goddess.

DHARMA religion; correct behaviour (applies to both Hinduism and Buddhism).

DHARMSALA rest house for pilgrims.

DORJE Tibetan word for *vajra*.

DURGA demon-slaying goddess.

GAJUR brass or gold finial at the peak of a temple.

GANESH elephant-headed god of wisdom and remover of obstacles.

GHANTA a bell, usually rung at temples as a sort of "amen".

GHAT riverside platform for worship and cremations.

GOMPA Buddhist monastery.

HANUMAN valiant monkey king in the *Ramayana*.

JHANKRI shaman, or medicine man, of the hills.

KAGYU-PA one of four main Lamaist sects.

KALI The mother goddess in her most terrifying form.

KARMA the soul's accumulated merit, determining its next rebirth.

KATA white scarf given to lamas by visitors.

KIRTIMUKHA common temple motif, a gargoyle-like face grappling with a snake.

KRISHNA one of Vishnu's *avatars*, hero of the *Mahabharata*.

KUMARI a girl worshipped by Nepalis as the living incarnation of Durga.

LAKSHMI consort of Vishnu, goddess of wealth.

LAMA Tibetan Buddhist priest: hence Lamaism.

LINGAM the phallic symbol of Shiva, commonly the centrepiece of temples and sometimes occurring in groups in the open.

MACHHENDRANATH rain-bringing deity of the Kathmandu Valley.

MAHABHARATA Hindu epic of the battle between two families, featuring Krishna and containing the *Bhagavad Gita*.

MAHAYANA non-monastic form of Buddhism followed in Nepal, Tibet and east Asia.

MANDALA mystical diagram, meditation tool.

MANDAP pavilion.

MANDIR temple.

MANTRA religious incantation.

NAGA snake or snake spirit, believed to have rain-bringing powers.

NANDI Shiva's mount, a bull.

NARAYAN common name for Vishnu.

NIRVANA in Buddhism, enlightenment and release from the cycle of rebirth.

OM MANI PADME HUM a common *mantra*, roughly translating as "Oh hail to the jewel in the lotus".

PARVATI Shiva's consort.

PATAKA (or **DHWAJA**) necktie-shaped brass ornament hanging from a temple, to be used by the deity when descending to earth.

PRASAD food consecrated after being offered to a deity.

PUJA an act of worship.

PUJARI Hindu priest.

RAMA mortal *avatar* Vishnu, hero of the *Ramayana*.

RAMAYANA popular Hindu epic in which Sita, princess of Janakpur, is abducted and eventually rescued by Rama and Hanuman.

RINPOCHE "precious jewel": title given to revered lamas.

SADHU Hindu ascetic.

SHAIVA member of the cult of Shiva.

SHAKTI in Hindu *tantra*, the female principle that empowers the male; the mother goddess in this capacity.

SHALIGRAM fossil-bearing stones found near Muktinath, revered by *Vaishnavas*.

SHIKHRA Indian-style temple, shaped like a square bullet.

SHIVA "the destroyer", one of the Hindu "trinity" – a god of many guises.

SHIVALAYA one-storey Shiva shrine containing a *lingam*.

SHIVA MARGI a Hindu Newar.

SINDUR red paste used in making *tikas* and decorating idols.

STUPA large Buddhist monument, usually said to contain holy relics.

TANTRA esoteric psycho-sexual path to enlightenment, a major influence on Nepali Hinduism and Buddhism.

TARA Buddhist goddess.

THANKA Buddhist scroll painting.

TIKA auspicious mark placed on the forehead during *puja* or festivals or before making a journey.

TULKU lama considered a reincarnation of a late great teacher.

TORANA elaborate wooden carving, or metal shield, above a temple door.

TORMA dough offerings made by Buddhist monks.

TRISUL the trident, a symbol of Shiva.

VAJRA sceptre-like symbol of tantric power.

VAJRACHARYA Buddhist Newar priest. ·

VAJRAYANA "Way of the Thunderbolt": tantric Buddhism.

VAISHNAVA follower of the cult of Vishnu.

VISHNU "the preserver", member of the Hindu "trinity", worshipped in ten main incarnations.

YONI symbol of the female genitalia, usually carved into the base of a *lingam* as a reservoir for offerings.

A GLOSSARY OF NEPALI AND TIBETAN TERMS

BAHAL buildings and quadrangle of a former Buddhist Newar monastery (a few are still active).

BAKSHISH not a bribe, but a tip in advance.

BAZAAR commercial area of a town – not necessarily a covered market.

BENI confluence of rivers.

BETEL mildly addictive mixture of areca nut and lime paste, wrapped in a leaf and chewed, producing blood-red spit.

BHAAT cooked rice; food.

BHANJYANG a pass (Nepali).

BHARAT India.

BHATTI simple hill tavern.

BHOT Tibet.

BHOTIYA highland peoples of Tibetan ancestry.

BIDESHI foreigner.

BIDI cheap rolled-leaf cigarette.

BRAHMAN member of the Hindu priestly caste; metaphysical term meaning the universal soul.

CHAARPI latrine.

CHAUTAARA resting platform beside a trail.

CHHETRI member of the ruling or warrior caste.

CHILLUM vertical clay pipe for smoking *ganja*.

CHOWK intersection, square or courtyard.

DAMARU two-sided drum.

DANDA (or **DAADA**) a ridge.

DANPHE Nepal's national bird, a pheasant with brilliant plumage.

DAPHNE shrub used in paper-making.

DAURA SURUWAL traditional dress of hill men: wrap-around shirt and jodhpur-like trousers.

DHOTI Indian-style loincloth.

DOKO conical cane basket carried by means of a headstrap.

DUN low-lying valleys just north of the Tarai (sometimes called inner Tarai).

DURBAR palace; royal court.

DZOPKIO sturdy yak-cattle crossbreed; the female is called a *dzum*.

GAINE wandering minstrel of the hills.

GAUN village.

GURKHAS Nepali soldiers who serve in special regiments in the British and Indian armies.

HIMAL massif or mountain range with permanent snow.

HITI communal water tap or tank.

HMG His Majesty's Government.

JAATRA festival.

JYAPU farmer.

KHOLA stream or river; valley.

KHUKURI curved knife carried by most Nepali hill men.

KOT fort.

KUND pond.

LA pass (Tibetan).

LALI GURAAS tree rhododendron.

LEKH mountain range without permanent snow.

MACHAAN watchtowers used by Tarai farmers to ward off wild animals.

MAHABHARAT LEKH highest range of the Himalayan foothills.

NAGAR city.

NANGLO cane tray, used for winnowing.

PANCHAAYAT council or assembly, the basis for Nepal's pre-democratic government.

PIPAL common shade tree, related to the fig.

POKHRI pond, usually man-made.

PUL bridge.

RAKSI distilled spirit.

SAHIB honorific term given to male foreigners, pronouced "sahb"; women are called *memsahib*.

SAL tall tree of the Tarai and lower hills, valued for its timber.

SARANGHI Nepali four-stringed violin.

SARDAAR Nepali trek leader.

SUDRA member of the lowest, menial caste of Hinduism.

TAL lake.

TEMPO three-wheeled scooter plying a fixed route.

THAKURI very orthodox Chhetri subcaste.

TOL neighbourhood.

TOLA unit of weight (11.5g); hashish is often sold by the *tola*.

TOPI Nepalese cap.

TUDIKHEL parade ground.

VAISYA Hindu caste of traders and farmers.

INDEX

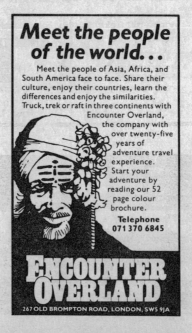